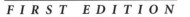

FIRST EDITION

CRITICAL ISSUES
IN CRIMINAL JUSTICE

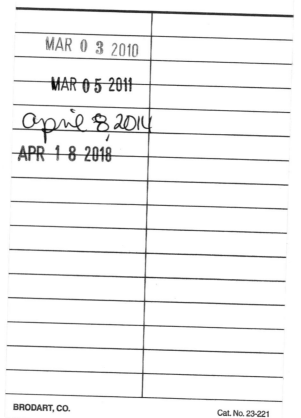

FIRST EDITION

CRITICAL ISSUES IN CRIMINAL JUSTICE

Ronald G. Burns

Texas Christian University

PEARSON

Prentice Hall

Upper Saddle River, New Jersey

Columbus, Ohio

Library of Congress Cataloging-in-Publication Data

Critical issues in criminal justice / [edited by] Ronald G. Burns.
   p. cm.
  ISBN-13: 978-0-205-55374-7
  ISBN-10: 0-205-55374-5
 1. Criminal justice, Administration of—United States. I. Burns, Ronald G.
  HV7921.C77 2009
  364.973—dc22

2008008670

Vice President and Executive Publisher: Vernon Anthony
Senior Acquisitions Editor: Tim Peyton
Editorial Assistant: Alicia Kelly
Media Project Manager: Karen Bretz
Director of Marketing: David Gesell
Marketing Manager: Adam Kloza
Marketing Coordinator: Alicia Dysert
Production Manager: Kathy Sleys
Art Director/Cover Designer: Jayne Conte
Cover Illustration/Photo: Comstock Images/Jupiter Images
Full-Service Project Management/Composition: Saraswathi Muralidhar/GGS Book Services PMG
Printer/Binder: Hamilton Printing Company
Cover Printer: Phoenix Color Corp.

Credits and acknowledgments borrowed from other sources and reproduced, with permission, in this textbook appear on appropriate page within text.

Pearson Education Ltd., London
Pearson Education Singapore, Pte. Ltd
Pearson Education Canada, Inc.
Pearson Education–Japan
Pearson Education Australia PTY, Limited
Pearson Education North Asia, Ltd., Hong Kong
Pearson Educación de Mexico, S.A. de C.V.
Pearson Education Malaysia, Pte. Ltd.
Pearson Education Upper Saddle River, New Jersey

10 9 8 7 6 5 4 3 2 1
ISBN-13: 978-0-20-555374-7
ISBN-10: 0-20-555374-5

CONTENTS

Why This Book?   *vii*

PART I Foundational Issues   1

Chapter 1   **The Case of the Unsolved Crime Decline,** *R. Rosenfeld*   3

Chapter 2   **The New Math on Crime,** *Will Sullivan*   10

Chapter 3   **Neuroscience and the Law,** *Michael Gazzaniga and Megan S. Steven*   14

Chapter 4   **Ill Winds: The Chemical Plant Next Door,** *Becky Bradway*   19

Chapter 5   **Chasing My Stolen Bicycle,** *Justin Jouvenal*   25

Chapter 6   **Virginia Tech Shooting Leaves 33 Dead,** *Christine Hauser and Anahad O'Connor*   31

Chapter 7   **Duke Lacrosse Players Relieved Case has 'Closure',** *The Associated Press*   35

Chapter 8   **O. J. Simpson's Book and TV Special Are Canceled,** *Bill Carter and Edward Wyatt*   38

PART II Policing   41

Chapter 9   **Help Wanted,** *Jack Dunphy*   43

Chapter 10   **Katrina, One Year Later . . .,** *Ann Wilder and James Arey*   46

Chapter 11   **Super Bowl XXXIX: The Successful Response of the FBI and Its Partners,** *Jeffrey Westcott*   50

Chapter 12   **Forensic Nursing: An Aid to Law Enforcement,** *Joseph R. Yost*   54

Chapter 13   **Why Racial Profiling Doesn't Work,** *Kim Zetter*   60

Chapter 14   **Mayor Meets Groom's Family in NYPD Slaying,** *The Associated Press*   65

Chapter 15   **Early Detection of the Problem Officer,** *Dino DeCrescenzo*   69

Chapter 16   **Policing the Future: Law Enforcement's New Challenges,** *Gene Stephens*   74

PART III Courts   83

Chapter 17   **A Court in a Storm,** *Aaron Kuriloff*   86

Chapter 18   **The Case Against Plea Bargaining,** *Timothy Lynch*   90

Chapter 19   **Rights of Defense,** *Andrew Rachlin*   96

Chapter 20   **How Much Should Lawyers Know When Picking a Jury?,** *M. B. E. Smith*   101

Chapter 21   **Self-Defense vs. Municipal Gun Bans,** *Robert VerBruggen*   106

Chapter 22 The Innocents: Idealistic Law Students Labor to Free the Wrongly Accused, *Michele Cohen Marill* **114**

Chapter 23 Evil Twins: And How DNA Evidence Is Useless Against Them, *John Wolfson* **124**

Chapter 24 Effects of Capital Punishment on the Justice System, *Brent E. Dickson* **127**

PART IV Corrections **133**

Chapter 25 The Carrot and the Sticks, *Jens Soering* **135**

Chapter 26 Paris Starts, Ends Week Behind Bars, *John Rogers* **140**

Chapter 27 Incarceration and Crime: A Complex Relationship, *Ryan S. King, Marc Mauer, and Malcolm C. Young* **143**

Chapter 28 Panel Suggests Using Inmates in Drug Trials, *Ian Urbina* **151**

Chapter 29 Serving Life, with No Chance of Redemption, *Adam Liptak* **155**

Chapter 30 Barred from Voting, *Katharine Mieszkowski* **160**

Chapter 31 Felon Fallout, *Alan Greenblatt* **165**

Chapter 32 Returning Home: Scholars Say More Research Is Needed on the Societal Reentry of the Formerly Incarcerated, *Ronald Roach* **171**

PART V Juvenile Justice and Emerging Issues in Criminal Justice **179**

Chapter 33 The Trouble with Troubled Teen Programs, *Maia Szalavitz* **181**

Chapter 34 Jailed for Life After Crimes as Teenagers, *Adam Liptak* **189**

Chapter 35 Young Lives For Sale, *Bay Fang* **195**

Chapter 36 Stepchildren of Justice, *Carl M. Cannon* **199**

Chapter 37 Biometrics Basics, *Law and Order Staff* **207**

Chapter 38 GPS Offender Tracking and the Police Officer, *Patrick Hyde and Nicole DeJarnatt* **214**

Chapter 39 Do Immigrants Make Us Safer?, *Eyal Press* **219**

Chapter 40 The CSI Effect, *Kit R. Roane* **225**

WHY THIS BOOK?

Criminal justice has existed in some shape or form since the origin of crime. Whether justice came in the form of retaliation (the "eye for an eye" approach) or through incarceration or some other form of punishment, those engaging in unacceptable behavior have been, and continue to be, subject to interpretations of justice. Determining if the repercussions for committing crime were and are truly just is subject to interpretation; however, we constantly seek to identify and implement appropriate responses to crime. Searching for what is fair is but one of the more exciting, intriguing, and controversial aspects of criminal justice.

Despite the long history of responding to crime with justice, the in-depth study of criminal behavior and responses to it is only about half a century old. There's much left to learn in criminology and criminal justice. Developments in society such as technological innovations continuously shape and reshape legislation, criminal justice practices, victimization, and criminal behavior. As individuals interested in criminal justice, it is our responsibility to stay abreast of such changes and consider what we can contribute to the developing study of crime and justice.

English philosopher Herbert Spencer noted: "The great aim of education is not knowledge but action." As consumers of crime- and justice-related information, criminal justice students and educators must consider how "book smarts" can be translated into practice, or action. We often hear arguments from practitioners and academics regarding the limitations of each others' camp. Practitioners argue that academics are out of touch with what happens outside the ivory towers, while academics believe practitioners operate in a nontheoretically based, bureaucratic manner. Though there is some merit to both arguments, the divide between practitioner and academic is reparable and combining book smarts with real-world events brings the two groups closer. This work helps bridge the gap by identifying and commenting on dozens of critical issues in crime and justice.

WHAT'S INSIDE?

The articles in this work enlighten readers to some of the more pressing issues within criminal justice, and the accompanying commentary frames the work with an eye toward the scholarly aspects of each topic. The articles vary in academic rigor, as some were selected from more pop-culture, mainstream outlets, while others were taken from more scholarly outlets and professional trade magazines. This text provides different perspectives on various criminal justice issues, while challenging readers to become more critical as they contemplate the issues.

The readings are organized and presented along the lines of most introductory criminal justice textbooks with an introductory section familiarizing readers with the foundational issues within criminal justice (e.g., crime statistics, laws, criminological theory), followed by parts on policing, courts, and correctional issues. The final part of the work addresses juvenile justice and several issues that will continue to significantly shape criminal justice practices in the years ahead.

Similar to introductory criminal justice textbooks, the opening section of this work both informs and prepares. Through addressing a series of topics relevant to the three main components of the criminal justice system (i.e., police, courts, and corrections), the opening section helps the novice criminal justice student get up to speed on many basic topics such as explanations for declining crime rates, the various types of crime, theoretical explanations of crime and their relation to the law (with a focus on neuroscience), victimology, and the sensationalism of crime.

The varied nature of police work made it difficult to select articles for this work. Particularly, police officers and departments face a wide array of interesting and challenging issues on a daily basis, making it difficult to select a limited number of topics. Police use of force, police discretion, police procedure . . . the list goes on. Police work intrigues many of us, as evidenced in the popularity of policing in the media. One merely needs to check the local news, TV listings, or movie theater listings to recognize society's preoccupation with police work. Consider, for instance, the premise of the highly successful TV show *COPS*. A film crew follows police officers and videotapes their practices. That's it. And many of us watch it. The popular TV show *CSI* has encouraged more than one college student to major in criminal justice, much the same way the show *Profiler* impacted criminal justice programs in the late 1990s, and the 1980s show *LA Law* directed me toward a career in justice studies.

The policing section of this work addresses several of the critical and prominent issues faced by modern police departments. These topics include the introduction and use of technology, current hiring difficulties faced by many police departments, questionably unethical police practices and responses to them, the importance of cooperative law enforcement practices, officers and departments dealing with the effects of natural disasters, and law enforcement in the future.

Society is also intrigued by our legal systems and the actors within them. If the police provide stories for action-based TV shows, the courts provide drama. My recollection is that law-based TV shows have been (and continue to be) among the most watched TV programs. Topics such as sentencing, plea bargaining, and prosecutorial and judicial discretion generate widespread societal interest in the day-to-day happenings in our courtrooms. The formality of the courtroom proceedings, including the operating procedures, the regalia, and the apparent finality of the courtroom, adds symbolic contributions to the drama that unfolds in the courtroom. Several of the key elements of the dramas occurring in and outside our courtrooms are addressed in the third section of this work.

The courts section of this book covers select critical issues that undoubtedly impact our courts and, perhaps, societal perceptions of our court system. The topics include an account of how justice was served in light of Hurricane Katrina, the controversial practice of plea bargaining, the rights of defense in the adjudication process, jury selection, self-defense as it relates to gun control, wrongful convictions, the use of DNA analyses in the courts, and the effects of capital punishment on the criminal justice system.

The fourth section of the book addresses corrections. Using the term *corrections* to encompass and describe attempts to sanction individuals seems inappropriate if for no other reason than "correcting" may not be a consideration with the penalties received by some convicted individuals. In fact, some would argue that very little "correcting" occurs in our correctional systems. The name *corrections* may seem off base, however, if nothing else it offers hope that individuals can be reformed, or make peace with their earlier misbehavior. And, similar to society's enhanced interest in policing and courts, we're enamored with prison movies and TV shows. *Prison Break, The Green Mile, The Shawshank Redemption, Oz*, etc. are popular movies and related TV shows that demonstrate that many of us wish to be in prison, yet only for voyeuristic reasons.

What are the critical issues facing today's correctional agencies and corrections in general? The list is long. This section addresses several highly significant issues, beginning with an inmate's perspective on crime and justice, followed by an account of Paris Hilton's interaction with the criminal justice system. Other issues addressed include the relationship between incarceration and the crime rate, the questionable practice of using inmates in pharmaceutical company tests involving new drugs, the unique hardships associated with serving life in prison, the removal of the voting privileges of some offenders, the impacts of increased incarceration, and the need to better understand the struggles faced by the formerly incarcerated who return to society. The significance of understanding these and related issues is even more important as society continuously relies on correctional agencies to deal with offenders and incarceration becomes increasingly institutionalized in our criminal justice system.

The final section of this work, "Juvenile Justice and Emerging Issues in Criminal Justice," includes articles and commentary regarding topics that have, and will undoubtedly continue to influence criminal justice. Four articles on dealing with juvenile offenders and justice are included. The articles cover programs targeted toward troubled teens, the impact of life sentences on juveniles, teen prostitution, and children of incarceretaed parents. The section also addresses the use of technology, particularly, biometrics and GPS tracking, as it relates to the criminal justice system. The final two selections of the book address the relationship between immigration and crime, and the impact the

TV show *CSI* has had on the criminal justice system and the study of crime and justice. Those with an interest in juvenile justice and an eye to the future should be aware of these and related issues as we progress through the twenty-first century.

ONWARD . . .

Duke lacrosse, O. J. Simpson, police brutality, prisoner reentry, etc., these topics generate images in our minds. The goal of this work is to flesh out those images with informative articles accompanied by enlightening commentary. The articles selected for this work are timely, interesting, and directly related to pressing issues within criminal justice. Articles from popular, mainstream outlets were generally chosen for this work with the belief that readers would be best able to relate to these articles. The commentary places the articles in context with regard to the academic literature. Given the vast array of topics related to criminal justice, the coverage provided in this work is not comprehensive. Readers interested in delving further into the topics covered in this work are encouraged to peruse the criminal justice and criminological research literature for elaboration.

Each article in this work examines a particular aspect of crime and/or justice. One could argue that presenting select articles as representative of crime and justice in general is to sensationalize. I agree. However, the commentary accompanying each article helps place the material in some form of academic perspective. The format of this book ensures that readers will understand how the issues fit within the context of crime and justice as they are introduced to each article.

You won't find a particular view or perspective in this collection of articles. Instead, the articles were selected based on their relationship with the topics usually addressed in an introductory criminal justice, or critical issues in crime and justice course. The commentary is offered to place the articles within some form of academic context, often through examining how the issues discussed are recognized and/or treated in the criminal justice literature. It is anticipated that readers will be thoroughly engaged in the works and enlightened by the commentary. I hope that reading this book will allow you to become better informed about criminal justice and more aware of the context and nature of crime and justice.

I

Foundational Issues

INTRODUCTION

Part I covers issues addressing various aspects of crime and justice. The topics covered in the articles included in this section prepare readers for understanding significant issues within crime and justice and help build a knowledge base for the articles addressing the core components of the criminal justice system: police, courts, and corrections. The issues covered in Part I include explanations for declining crime rates; various forms of crime (e.g., environmental crime, mass murder, bike theft); crime statistics and reporting practices; the relationship between criminological theory and the law; and sensationalism in the criminal justice system. These issues were selected based on their relevance and importance to criminal justice study.

Part I begins with a look at current crime rates including explanations for why crime is declining. Many factors influence the crime rate (e.g., economics, demographics, law enforcement practices, crime data collection, etc.). Rosenfeld, the author of the first article ("The Case of the Unsolved Crime Decline"), offers wonderful insight regarding recent declines in the crime rate. It goes without saying that understanding why crime rates decline, or increase, helps inform public policy.

Crime data influence public policy. For instance, we constantly hear and read accounts in the news that "crime is rising" or "crime is declining." Yet, how many of us actually look into the methodology of the crime data collection upon which those claims are based? Do many of us question the reliability and/or validity of the data, and are we concerned that public policy may be based on questionable data? The article "The New Math on Crime" highlights how after over a decade of decreasing crime rates it appears that crime may be on the rise. There should be no quick rush to judgment, however, as a one-year increase in crime is no reason to panic.

The first part also includes coverage of crime theory. The current work comments on how crime theory can relate to legal practices. Researchers often note how theoretical advancements are overlooked or discarded by those outside the ivory towers. While there is some merit to this argument, recent technological and scientific developments dictate that scientists and practitioners will be forced to work collectively. In the article "Neuroscience and the Law," authors Gazzaniga and Steven comment on how advancements in neurological research impact the legal arena. Needless to say, it is imperative that the criminal justice system remain abreast of developments in research regarding the brain's influence on human behavior, and more generally, the scientific advancements in all fields of study focused on human behavior.

Part I continues with a look at environmental crime in the article "Ill Winds." Environmental crime has been garnering public attention, particularly in light of concerns regarding global warming. With regard to environmental damage, the general public and law enforcement officials often face difficulty in distinguishing legitimate corporate behavior from criminal behavior. "Ill Winds" highlights the potential harms, ignorance, and deceit sometimes associated with environmental crime. This article, among other things, demonstrates the impact of environmental crime.

Has someone ever stolen your bicycle? If so, what did you do? Call the police? Get over it and buy a new bike? Did you try to track down your stolen bike? Justin Jouvenal, author of "Chasing My Stolen Bike" attempted to locate his stolen bike in the criminal underworld of San Francisco. What he found was a market for stolen goods and a general disinterest in enforcing the law surrounding petty offenses. The criminal economy as it exists in the underworld as described by Jouvenal seems as stable and comprehensive as the economy in general society. This insightful information sheds light on a world many of us have never visited, nor thoroughly considered.

Virginia Tech was the site of the deadliest shooting incident in U.S. history when a gunman opened fire on the campus, killing 32 students and eventually himself. The article "Virginia Tech Shooting Leaves 33 Dead" regenerated concerns of school shootings that occurred years ago, when great hysteria regarding murders at school led to notable changes in school safety. Among other effects, the Virginia Tech incident provided evidence of the barbaric and humanitarian sides of human nature as we read and heard accounts of the ruthless killer, the heroic victims, and the outpouring of sympathy from across the country for the victims and students.

The term "Duke University" conjures up images of top-quality students, hardcore college basketball fans, and well-to-do individuals. The term "Duke University Lacrosse," however, generates a somewhat different set of images. As evidenced in the article "Duke Lacrosse Players Relieved Case Has Closure," Duke University lacrosse players were implicated in a serious criminal incident that led to national attention. Several players were accused of raping, kidnapping, and sexually assaulting a stripper hired for a team party. This case had key ingredients for consuming public attention, and the case became even more intriguing when the District Attorney engaged in professional misconduct. The case lasted long enough to fulfill the general public's appetite for sensationalized crime before the charges against the student athletes were dropped, however.

If you're like me, you probably don't wish to hear the name "O. J. Simpson" ever again. Bear with me, however, as O. J.'s atypical criminal case can be used for educational purposes. Simpson recently reappeared in the news planning to write a book and give an interview regarding a hypothetical account of how he would have murdered his ex-wife and her friend. As you may recall, Simpson was acquitted of criminal charges in the case yet defeated in a subsequent civil trial and forced to pay monetary damages to the families of the victims. The controversial idea to publish the book and provide an interview was met with great public disapproval. The article "O. J. Simpson's Book and TV Special Are Canceled," by reporters Carter and Wyatt, addresses the circumstances surrounding the proposed book and interview and the accompanying commentary highlights the sensationalism of crime. I hope that readers will recognize this situation as atypical of most criminal events and view the case on its arguably absurd merits.

These topics provide an overview of select issues vital to understanding crime and justice. Understanding how crime is measured, various types of crime, the application of theory to practice, victimology, and crime sensationalism will provide a foundation for further study of criminal justice.

1

The Case of the Unsolved Crime Decline

By R. Rosenfeld

The United States' crime rate decreased throughout much of the 1990s and continued to decline through the early part of the twenty-first century. Decreasing crime rates changed criminological thought, in part from one largely focused on how to stop crime toward understanding why the crime rate consistently dropped. Many factors influence crime rates, not the least of which include demographics, economic factors, police practices, and the manner in which crime data are collected. Teasing out the influences of these and many other factors on crime rates provides a constant challenge for criminologists and social science researchers in general.

Crime rates are influenced by a variety of factors. Bear in mind that crime rates are collected via various means and are subject to much interpretation. For instance, the crime rate could be influenced by the reporting practices of the general public. The two main sources of crime data collected in the United States (the Uniform Crime Report and the National Crime Victimization Survey) sometimes show conflicting accounts of crime rates. However, let's assume that reporting practices are constant and have limited impact on crime rates. Why then, have the crime rates dropped for many of the past 15 years?

Among the more common explanations for the decrease in crime rates is the prosperous economy realized during much of the crime decline. Much crime is financially motivated, thus, it is expected that the crime rate will decrease when financial resources are more easily accessible. Others suggest the crime rate decline is due to the adoption of a community-oriented approach taken by many local law enforcement agencies. Focusing on building and maintaining relationships with the public is a somewhat new approach to policing that was heavily adopted in the latter part of the twentieth century. Whether or not community policing actually reduces crime remains to be seen.

Still, others suggest crime rates decreased as a result of increased incarceration rates. The United States incarcerates a larger proportion of its citizens than any other country, and prison expansion was evident prior to and during the period when crime rates notably decreased. While some question whether reliance on incarceration reduces crime or ultimately contributes to more crime, it remains that incarcerating a large number of individuals will, at least for a short time, remove a large number of offenders from the streets and impact the crime rate.

The recent drop in the crime rate, while positive news for all, provides a new set of challenges for criminologists who must figure out why the drop occurred. Similar to the difficulties associated with explaining why crime rates sometimes increase, it is difficult to definitively point out why crime rates *decrease. Understanding the latter is as important as understanding why crime increases. In the article "The Case of the Unsolved Crime Decline," Richard Rosenfeld examines these and related factors that most heavily influenced the drop in crime. Rosenfeld also offers suggestions and policies targeted to help prevent crime in the future, and aptly contextualizes the primary factors associated with the drop in crime.*

Criminologists have not yet cracked the case, but they now know more about why U.S. crime rates plummeted in the 1990s—and how to help keep them down.

For a short period during the closing decade of tile last century, U.S. crime rates dropped precipitously. Homicide, burglary and robbery rates fell more than 40 percent, to levels not seen since the 1960s. The reduction in serious felonies per capita stunned criminologists, who have struggled to provide a satisfying explanation for such an unexpected and complex phenomenon. The research community has reached a consensus on the basic contours of the 1990s crime decline the who, what, when and where—but still argues about the why.

Today, as crime rates are again creeping upward, it seems appropriate to examine the evidence associated with the 1990s drop and the theories put forth to account for it. Such an analysis could help society to better understand the causes underlying shifts in national criminal statistics and may even be used to forestall future increases in serious offenses. In this article, I will weigh the relative merits of the leading explanations and present some suggestions for policies and experiments that could help prevent the next rise in the criminal activity.

THE FACTS

To better evaluate the various theories, it helps to take a closer look at the available data. The Federal Bureau of Investigation compiles and confirms cases of serious violent and property crimes reported to local police departments and then converts the tallies into averaged rates expressed as victims per 100,000 people. Of the crime categories the FBI tracks through its Uniform Crime Reporting program, homicide statistics are the most reliable because nearly all the cases are known to the police. The graph of crime levels from 1982 through 2001 shows that the national homicide rate peaked at a high of 9.8 per 100,000 in 1991 and then fell to 5.5 by 2000—a 44 percent decline. The slump in the murder rate was accompanied by similar decreases in every major FBI crime category. The incidence of burglary (unlawful entry into a structure to commit a felony or theft) fell by 42 percent between 1991 and 2000; robbery (theft accompanied by force or the threat of force) dipped 47 percent.

The evidence depicting a drop in serious felonies in the 1990s is not limited to crimes compiled in the FBI reports, which may be affected by victims' willingness to notify police. Large contractions in burglary and robbery rates were also noted by the country's other major crime gauge, the National Crime Victimization Survey, which conducts annual polls of crime victims. This survey includes incidents that were not reported to police. Homicide victims cannot participate in polls, of course, but data collected by the National Center for Health Statistics from death certificates and coroner's reports match the homicide trends identified by the FBI.

THE PERPETRATORS

The trends are not uniform, however. According to demographic studies, the U.S. actually experienced two crime drops during the last two decades of the 20th century: one among adolescents and young adults (those under the age of 25) and the other among adults. Although the decrease in crime rates among youths has attracted more attention, the adult decline started sooner and lasted longer. Rates of homicide committed by adults have slid steadily since 1980. In contrast, youth homicide levels did not begin to fall until 1993 or 1994 and followed a dramatic increase that had originated about 10 years earlier. Robbery rates among adolescents and young adults traced the same trajectory, rising precipitously from the mid 1980s until about 1994 and descending just as sharply thereafter.

The so-called youth violence epidemic, during both its escalation in the 1980s and its subsidence during the 1990s, was itself highly concentrated in another population subset: young black men. Changes in the crime rate for young women and whites were much less pronounced. Between 1984 and 1993, homicide offenses grew nearly fivefold among black male adolescents and more than doubled among black male young adults. The rates for both categories fell rapidly afterward. Meanwhile the offense rates among black male adults dropped by more than half; those for whites of any age have shown comparatively little change over the past 20 years.

Because people of Hispanic origin may be of any race, the FBI data for Hispanics and non-Hispanic whites and blacks cannot be broken out separately. The National Center for Health Statistics series on the causes of mortality, however, has permitted such a partitioning for homicide victims (not offenders) since 1990. Those data portray roughly the same pattern among young Hispanic males—a rise in homicide incidence until the early 1990s, followed by a decline through the end of the decade; however, the Hispanic rates were lower and their increase and subsequent decrease less severe than among young black men.

The nationally aggregated crime statistics obscure important differences in the timing and location of the youth violence epidemic as it arose in various areas around the country—valuable clues regarding the dimensions of the crime drop. The rise in youth homicide and robbery rates started in the largest cities during the early 1980s and then spread to smaller ones a few years later; violent crime rates also peaked and ebbed earlier in the biggest cities.

THE WEAPONS

A final factor to note was the proliferation of firearms possession among young minority males during the past two decades, reflected in the rising proportion of violent crimes committed with guns. Most homicides and a large proportion of robberies in the U.S. are perpetrated with firearms, whereas few burglars use guns. FBI statistics indicate that nearly all the growth in youth homicide rates (the crime for which weapon use is best documented) during the 1980s and early 1990s involved firearms—usually handguns. Killings in which other or no weapons were implicated actually decreased during the escalation phase of the youth homicide epidemic and continued to drop after 1993, when firearm-related homicide rates also started to fall.

Although it is clear that guns played a prominent role in the rise in homicides beginning in the mid-1980s, this does not necessarily imply that firearms "caused" the youth violence epidemic. The relation between guns and the decline in homicide is less clear, because both firearm- and nonfirearm-related killings abated during the 1990s. Two researchers who study violent acts, Philip J. Cook of Duke University and John H. Laub of the University of Maryland, have argued that the factors associated with the "way in" to the violence epidemic differ in some respects from those contributing to the "way out." The decrease was steeper and broader than the increase' affecting crimes committed with and without guns. Keep that point in mind during the forthcoming evaluation of firearms' role in explaining the decrease in crime during the 1990s.

THE ARGUMENTS

The facts have thus led us to a set of unresolved questions that any credible explanation of the 1990s crime drop must accommodate: Why did the decline in youth violence arrive on the heels of a dramatic increase in youth violence? Why was the youth violence epidemic concentrated among young minority males? Why was the rise in youth violence—but not the fall—restricted to crimes involving firearms? Why did it start and end first in the big cities? And, not least, why has adult violence diminished over the past 20 years?

No theory accounts for all these facts, but certain hypotheses do a better job than others at explaining the many aspects of the crime decline. And some popularly held explications are plainly wrong.

DEMOGRAPHICS.   A few explanations of the crime drop can be eliminated simply because their timing is off. One such theory is based on the premise that crime rates will rise or fall in step with corresponding changes in the size of the age cohorts that are disproportionately responsible for crime. A greater proportion of adolescents and young adults take part in homicide and other crimes than adults. When the younger segment of the population shrinks, some researchers hypothesize, crime rates should as well, all else being equal. Unfortunately, all else is rarely equal. Other conditions affecting crime rates tend to change more rapidly, if less predictably, than the size of the age group mainly involved in crime. Moreover, the relative size of the demographic group at highest risk, 14- to 24-year-old black males, changed little from 1993 (the peak of the youth-violence epidemic) to 2000 (the trough)—and actually decreased during the first stages of the epidemic.

Economists John J. Donohue III of Stanford University and Steven D. Levitt of the University of Chicago offer an intriguing alternative to conventional demographic explanations of the crime drop. They attribute as much as half of the crime decline during the 1990s to the legalization of abortion in the 1970s. This change resulted in fewer births of unwanted children to low-income women, thereby, they claim, preventing the crimes those disadvantaged children would have committed some 15 to 20 years later. Though not implausible, the analysis implies that youth homicide trends should have slackened earlier than they did.

LAW ENFORCEMENT.   Policing efforts in a number of cities underwent revision during the 1990s, from the introduction of "community policing" strategies to blanket crackdowns on minor infractions. But many of these changes did not go into effect until well after the fall in crime had begun. It is true that local evidence supports the effectiveness of targeted "gun patrols" (in which police saturate areas that have a high incidence of firearm use) and of ensuring swift punishment of gang members who carry guns. Local evidence also backs computerized accountability programs, such as New York City's COMSTAT, that hold police commanders accountable for the crimes that occur in their districts. Yet sizable crime declines occurred in cities without such programs, too. No one can say whether changes in policing policies contributed to the decrease in national crime rates.

KIDS, CRACK AND GUNS.   A more promising explanation for the decrease in crime has been offered by Carnegie Mellon University criminologist Alfred Blumstein, who links the phenomenon to shrinking demand for crack cocaine in the early 1990s, which presumably resulted in less violence related to the drug's sale. Unlike other theories, this one jibes both with the timing of the crime reductions and with that of the youth violence epidemic. The popularity of cheap crack cocaine created a boom in illicit drug trade during the 1980s. To meet growing demand, dealers recruited inner-city youths to sell crack and armed them with firearms for protection against thieves, unscrupulous buyers and rival sellers. The arms race soon moved beyond the neighborhood drug markets into surrounding communities, as gun violence engendered retaliation in kind.

For reasons that remain poorly understood, crack has shown itself to be a single-generation drug. As the original addicts grew older and either stopped taking it or died, younger drug users, who preferred marijuana, did not replace them. Thus, the demand for crack began to subside. Following a lag of a year or two, rates of gun violence also began to fall off, first in the largest cities where crack took hold earlier, then afterward in smaller cities where both crack and the youth violence epidemic arrived later.

Blumstein's crack/firearms diffusion explanation squares with most of the facts of the 1990s crime drop. It accounts for why the violence epidemic was ignited by males and minority youths who sold crack and why rates of nonfirearm related violence were not affected. (In general, drug sellers do not settle disputes with fists, clubs or knives.) Blumstein's theory is consistent with survey evidence showing that inner-city youths, including gang members, acquire guns mainly for protection. Additionally, it coincides with studies of the violence common to crack markets and the comparative lack thereof in the marijuana trade.

ECONOMIC EXPANSION.   Unfortunately, the crack/firearms diffusion hypothesis does not account for the length and breadth of the decrease in youth violence, and it says nothing about the drop in property crime rates or the long-term decline in violence among adults. It is tempting to invoke the economic boom of the 1990s, especially the steep declines in unemployment rates, to explain why both adults and youth might turn away from crime and toward legal and safer sources of income. Yet property crime and adult violence rates also dipped during the less favorable economic climate of the 1980s. The relation between unemployment and crime is in fact decidedly more complex than it first appears. The so-called opportunity effects of more and bigger paychecks, which make potential crime victims more attractive targets, may cancel out the crime-cutting effects of falling unemployment levels. On the other hand, unemployed people spend more time at home, resulting in fewer home burglaries.

In addition, job and income growth may have differing consequences regarding the occurrence of crime, depending on the availability of chances for illicit income. Although dealing drugs is dangerous and uncertain work, thousands of inner-city teenagers and young adults engage in it. Legitimate employment may be more attractive when those illegal moneymaking opportunities disappear, such as during the crash in the crack markets in the early 1990s. This situation implies that the growth of legal job availability has a greater effect on crime rates when and where drug markets have dried up because of lower demand or effective law enforcement efforts. To date, no published studies have examined this hypothesis.

PRISON EXPANSION.   If the long-term decline in adult crime cannot be explained by improved economic conditions, perhaps it is associated with the corresponding escalation in incarceration rates during the past two decades. The U.S. incarcerates a larger proportion of its citizens than any other nation, and the size of the American prison population quadrupled between 1980 and 2000. It would be surprising if mass incarceration had no impact on crime, but like economic conditions, the ramifications of imprisonment are complex. Growth in imprisonment undoubtedly cuts crime in the short run; one study estimates that roughly a quarter of the drop in crime during the 1990s can be attributed to the sharp escalation in incarceration rates. Large-scale confinement, however, may boost crime rates in the long term by breaking up families, driving up unemployment rates, and otherwise depleting the social capital of those communities hardest hit by both crime and imprisonment.

The incarceration boom also may have contributed, albeit indirectly, to the youth homicide epidemic. As the demand for crack climbed during the 1980s and adult vendors increasingly sat behind bars, drug dealers turned to younger sellers. If such a labor shortage was created and all else held constant, sharper rises in youth homicide should have been observed in those areas with the greatest increases in adult imprisonment for drug crimes. This hypothesis merits further research.

DOMESTIC VIOLENCE AND FIREARMS POLICIES.   Two additional arguments have been offered for the decline in adult crime. The first links the drop in domestic homicide to the expansion of hotlines, shelters, judicial protection orders, and other domestic violence resources during the 1980s and 1990s. The second attributes lower incidence of adult victimization to the expansion of "concealed carry" laws, which permit adults to bear concealed weapons. Laura Dugan of the University of Maryland, Daniel Nagin of Carnegie Mellon and I conducted research that showed that domestic homicide rates fell more rapidly in cities with the greatest growth in legal advocacy and other services for victims of domestic abuse. We found, though, that other responses to domestic violence, such as a policy of mandatory arrest for offenders, may actually increase the likelihood of homicide under some conditions, presumably because offenders are angered by the legal intervention or because the resulting sanctions are not sufficient to protect victims from further violence.

Economist John R. Lott, Jr., of the American Enterprise Institute has proposed that laws permitting the carrying of concealed weapons have reduced violent crime rates by making would-be offenders aware that potential victims could be armed. His research indicates that the rates of serious crime are lower in places with concealed-carry laws than elsewhere, controlling for other conditions affecting crime. Other scholars using similar data and methods, however, have not been able to reproduce Lott's results. For now, the case for "more guns, less crime" remains unproved.

Clearly, a single theory encompassing all the facts of the crime drop does not exist. The closest approximation of such an explanation is the link between the rise and fall in youth violence and corresponding shifts in the crack cocaine trade. The longer declines in adult violence and property crime are probably associated with the explosive growth in imprisonment, the adoption of domestic violence policies and programs, and the economic boom of the 1990s—but mass incarceration, tougher arrest policies, more jobs and larger incomes may increase as well as reduce the occurrence of crime.

THE VERDICT

Considering the complexities of crime, what lessons can society draw to help anticipate and even head off another rise in criminal activity? Three guidelines seem appropriate.

TAKE APART THE TRENDS.   As we have seen, the crime drop seems to have resulted from the confluence of two separate crime trends: one for adults and one for youths. Distinct explanations and policies apply to each of them. Adults are subject to incarceration in state and federal prisons, are legally entitled to possess firearms and are directly affected by efforts to stem domestic violence. Youths have a low risk of imprisonment and cannot legally possess a handgun if they are younger than 21 (or own a long gun until they are 18). Domestic and family violence policies do affect children and adolescents, but only indirectly, through their parents—and the consequences of such policies for youth crime may not show up for a number of years.

Young people did not participate equally in the violence epidemic of the late 1980s and early 1990s, which was concentrated primarily among inner-city black and Hispanic males. Small-town and suburban white youths were involved in several highly publicized school shootings, but fortunately these events were not numerous enough to reverse the decline in youth firearm-related homicide. Policies and programs to prevent school shootings or reduce the already comparatively low level of violent crime among more affluent youths are likely to differ from those intended to suppress an arms race among inner-city youths. A wise strategy would be to tailor crime control policies to the particular circumstances of different groups of victims and offenders.

WATCH FOR ACCIDENTAL POLICY EFFECTS.   Stiffer sentences for adult drug offenders may facilitate the criminal careers and shorten the lives of the youthful drug sellers who take their place. Mass incarceration reduces crime in the short run—but at great monetary and social costs—and may contribute to the chronically high levels of crime in those distressed communities from which prisoners are disproportionately drawn and to which they return. Some domestic violence policies may result in more, not less, violence and abuse. That is not to say society should close prisons or stop arrests. Instead communities should stay alert for the unexpected aftereffects that large-scale social interventions inevitably produce. Policymakers must understand the trade-offs between intended and unintended consequences and change policies if they are doing more harm than good. This lesson should be applied first to sentencing policies such as "three strikes and you're out" and mandatory minimum sentences, which have made the U.S. the world leader in incarceration.

CONDUCT EXPERIMENTS IN CRIME-CONTROL POLICY.   Public safety would benefit from a reversal of the standard sequence of implementing a crime-control policy or program first and then determining if it works. The National Institute of Justice, the research arm of the U.S. Department of Justice, has funded many field studies of domestic violence interventions, innovative policing practices, alternatives to prison for drug offenders, and greater penalties for gang members and other youths who carry guns. The term "experiment" must be used advisedly when referring to such research: for example, batterers cannot be assigned randomly to households, and legal barriers prevent the alteration of sentences for the most serious law violators. But threats to the validity of crime-control research can be lessened through the careful selection of comparison groups and the introduction of rigorous statistical controls. The point is to perform policy experimentation before implementing policies. Research findings alone will not prevent future increases in crime, but control policies that have been pretested stand a much better chance of succeeding.

OVERVIEW/THE 1990S CRIME DROP

- Serious violent and property crime rates—for homicide, burglary and robbery—in the U.S. decreased substantially during the 1990s. The rates for these serious offenses tumbled by more than 40 percent.
- Analysts have attributed the 1990s crime drop to various causes. These include changes in demographics, law-enforcement practices, economic conditions, incarceration rates, domestic violence and firearm policies, and the use of guns by young crack cocaine dealers.
- Society can draw three lessons from research on the crime decline that may help anticipate and even head off the next rise: divide crime trends into their components parts, look for unintended policy effects and engage in research-based policy experiments before new programs are implemented.

Discussion Questions

1. Discuss recent trends in the crime rate. Do you anticipate further changes? Why or why not?
2. Identify and discuss the factors proposed to influence the crime rate.

3. Considering the complexities of crime, what lessons can society learn to help anticipate and even head off another rise in criminal activity?

The New Math on Crime

By Will Sullivan

Following over a decade of declining crime rates, it appears that crime rates may be rising once again. Crime rates generally fluctuate depending on a number of variables. Recently however, researchers have identified two distinct patterns in the crime rate: a notable increase from the mid-1980s to the early 1990s, when crime rates began to decline. The decrease has been constant until recently, when it appears the crime rate is once again on the rise. Should we be alarmed? Is it time to rethink our crime policies? Probably not, but the latest trend certainly warrants attention.

Actual criminal behavior certainly influences the crime rate; however, the crime rate is not an exact tally of crime in society. For instance, the manner in which crime is reported, counted, and compiled influences the crime rate. Crime reporting practices have a distinct impact on crime as reported in the Uniform Crime Report (UCR), compiled by the Federal Bureau of Investigation (FBI). The UCR consists of crimes known to police, which means it doesn't include crimes not known to police. While more serious crimes such as murder are most often reported, many smaller crimes go unreported. The Bureau of Justice Statistics attempts to measure the crimes that go unreported in its National Crime Victimization Survey (NCVS); however, it too is limited in several ways.

If indeed crime is increasing, the question then becomes, why? The answer is not simple, as evident in the extensive criminological literature. Historically, several factors are identified as influencing the crime rate, including economics, demographics, the rise of gang activity, and drug-related crime. Furthermore, fluctuations in the crime rate could be attributed to law enforcement practices. The crime rate is influenced by several factors related to law enforcement, not the least of which involve the aggressiveness with which officers enforce the law, the relationship between the police and the community, and the number of law enforcement agents patrolling the streets. Many other factors also influence the crime rate. The dubious challenge is to identify all of the factors influencing crime rate and assess the impact and extent of each.

How, then, do we know how much crime exists? We don't know exactly how much crime there is, although we can speculate based on our measurements. We certainly make efforts to understand how much crime exists, however measuring crime is very difficult, for instance, due to the failure to report crime and the limitations of survey research as evidenced in the NCVS. Even more challenging is comparing crime rates internationally. Consider, for instance, the difficulties in comparing crime rates in the United States and Iraq. The two countries differ in many notable ways, not the least of which involves the respective laws and how they are applied, and the ability to measure crime rates in both countries.

Crime prevention and crime control policies are often based on crime statistics. We've progressed regarding our data collection procedures, however, much work remains. Accordingly, crime-related policies *should be established only after policy makers are confident that the data used to make policy are valid and reliable. To rush to judgment and critically react, for instance by building more prisons, to the suggestion that crime is increasing seems premature. Time, advanced statistical analyses, due consideration of qualitative data, and the continued advancement in crime data collection will provide more effective guidance for crime-related policy.*

Even before the fireworks launched from the French Quarter's Jackson Square, 2006 went out with a bang in New Orleans—a handful of them, actually. At 7 P.M. on December 31, several of those bangs felled a 42-year-old man, who was found inside his FEMA trailer with multiple gunshot wounds to the back of his head. At 8:45 P.M., another man was shot several times and left dead on the sidewalk. At 10:12 P.M., a third was killed inside his home.

The three men were some of the last murder victims in an unusually bloody 2006. The year is expected to snap a long stretch of relatively good news on the homicide front nationwide, moving questions about the causes of crime increases off the back burner they have occupied for more than a decade. Those questions have so far eluded satisfying answers, and many experts contend that fears of a sustained rise in murders have little foundation. But the numbers are causing more than a little alarm and getting more than a little attention—from the nation's police chiefs, from Congress, from the Justice Department, perhaps even from the president in his State of the Union speech later this month. Slowly but surely, violent crime is returning to the national agenda.

Nationwide murder totals for 2006 will not be available until the fall, when the FBI releases its annual Uniform Crime Report. But an analysis by *U.S. News* shows a substantive, if uneven, increase in homicide in the nation's 20 largest cities. The 19 cities for which data were available had 4,152 homicides in 2006, compared with 3,919 the previous year—a 6 percent increase. Phoenix, which could not provide a year-end number, had neared its 2005 total of 238 by the end of November.

Murder is considered the most reliable crime statistic because such a high percentage of killings are reported. So the numbers are always watched closely as an indicator of crime trends. The beginning of the crack epidemic brought soaring murder numbers—a 31 percent increase between 1984 and its peak in 1993. But as the drug's popularity waned, so did murder, falling to around 16,000 a year and staying there for the early years after the millennium. More recently, the plateau has ended. Homicide showed an uptick in 2005, and the FBI's preliminary numbers from the first six months of 2006, along with the yearlong data collected by *U.S. News,* suggest the increase continued last year.

Some cities were hit especially hard. Philadelphia's 406 homicides were the most in the City of Brotherly Love since 1997. Oakland, Calif., topped its 2005 homicide tally by more than 50, and Cincinnati's 85 homicides were literally unprecedented.

As the year's crime numbers come in, the Police Executive Research Forum has sounded the alarm. An October report from the police advocacy group, titled "A Gathering Storm," expresses concern that the increases signal the beginning of "an epidemic of violence not seen for years." Though not all cities have suffered a crime spike, PERF pushes for more federal cooperation with local law enforcement and more federal funding. "If the pandemic flu were to hit 20 cities in the United States, I don't think the Centers for Disease Control would say, 'Well, let's see how many other cities it hits,'" says Chuck Wexler, the group's director.

ANOMALIES. But there are plenty of caveats to the new numbers. New York City's nearly 10 percent rise in murders—to 590—doesn't look as bad after taking account of the city's unusually high number of "reclassified deaths," those resulting from injuries in prior years. And the city's number of homicides is still historically low; more than 2,000 people were killed in New York in 1990 alone. Houston neared its highest number of murders in a decade, but the increase largely matches the city's surge in population from Hurricane Katrina evacuees.

Several big cities, including Dallas and San Francisco, bucked the murder trend completely. Washington, D.C., ended the year 27 murders shy of its 2005 total. Los Angeles's historically under-manned police force saw its fifth straight year with a reduction of violent crime.

In fact, the 6 percent increase in murders in the country's 20 largest cities is lower than the 9 percent rise the FBI charted in the first six months of the year. And once smaller cities are included, the FBI recorded only a 1.4 percent increase in that time. On average, smaller cities actually showed dramatic declines in their number of homicides.

That is more variability than was seen in the '80s and '90s, when murders spiked and then plummeted almost everywhere. The inconsistency leads some experts to contend that this year's in-crease is more an idiosyncratic phenomenon than a national crisis. Even among criminologists, there's not a lot of agreement over what's happening—or why.

In his new book, *The Great American Crime Decline,* Franklin Zimring, a professor at the University of California–Berkeley law school and an expert on crime statistics, tackles the prevailing explanations for what causes changes in crime numbers and finds them wanting. "Any blip in homi-cide statistics is unnerving because we don't know why we've had this epidemic of good news," he says. "There are a hundred theories and no confirmations."

Yet even some experts who remain agnostic on the significance of the more recent rise in homicides point to factors that could have contributed. Alfred Blumstein, a criminology professor at Carnegie Mellon University, highlights a diversion of resources from traditional crime fighting to preventing terrorism and a reduction in social services to the poorest neighborhoods. He also notes the phasing out of federal money for the Clinton-era COPS program, which gives grants to put more police officers on the street. The PERF report, "A Gathering Storm," partially blames the loss of funds for shrinking police forces in many cities. "I must confess, I expected [murder] to go up two or three years ago," Blumstein says.

With the Dow reaching new records last year and relatively low unemployment, an eco-nomic explanation for the rise in violence would seem unlikely. But Richard Rosenfeld, a crimi-nology professor at the University of Missouri–St. Louis, says the economy's strong finish in 2006 belied a volatile year, with concerns about fuel costs and the end of the housing boom. The lack of economic stability especially impacts the urban poor, who are most likely to turn to crime, he says.

That explanation doesn't convince Philip Cook, an economist and professor at Duke University who has written on crime numbers. He disputes the grim portrayal of the 2006 economy and also argues that the link between the economy and murder levels is unproven. Recall the '60s, Cook says, when the economy and murder numbers grew hand in hand.

Police departments have widely cited armed young people as the cause of their recent violence woes, and some speculate that the rise in murders is simply the result of a larger segment of the pop-ulation entering the prime years for committing crime—generally thought to be ages 15 to 24. The claim is bolstered by FBI statistics showing that the number of murder offenders under the age of 18 and 22 both jumped dramatically in 2005. But the number of young people has risen for some years, with no discernible impact on crime before now.

Some experts suggest the country is suffering the fallout of its own "get tough" crime policies in the 1980s and '90s. The problem was explored in a 2003 Urban Institute study of Maryland, which suggested that the state will face increasing challenges in dealing with a growing population strug-gling to re-enter society after being incarcerated.

G-MEN.   The uncertainty has not deterred federal eyes from turning back to the problem of urban crime. Under pressure from police groups, Attorney General Alberto Gonzales announced the Initiative for Safer Communities in October, a study of 18 areas with both rising and falling crime to analyze the most effective law enforcement methods. Last month, California Sen. Dianne Feinstein sent a letter to FBI Director Robert Mueller, urging the agency to "re-evaluate its priorities" and place a higher emphasis on investigating violent crime. And Bush administration officials say the president could make an anticrime effort part of his State of the Union address January 23 or put a new initiative in his proposed budget for fiscal year 2008.

Local officials are also rethinking their efforts. In Indianapolis, which saw homicides climb from 110 in 2005 to 137 last year, police have installed their own version of the increasingly popular Compstat system, which combines computerized crime mapping with management brainstorming sessions on how best to combat the latest local crime trends. Recommendations from a mayor's task force are also expected shortly. "We're very optimistic that we'll see a decrease in those numbers in 2007," says Police Chief Michael Spears.

But the year didn't start well. About four hours into 2007, 27-year-old Eric Munoz was found dead in the clubhouse of Indianapolis's Naptown Riders motorcycle club. For Spears, the homicide was humbling, a reminder of a police department's limitations. "If we had 10 officers on patrol outside that location, it wouldn't have prevented it," he says.

The news is worse in New Orleans, where at least seven people have been murdered since the New Year—six within 24 hours. One was 36-year-old Helen Hill, who was shot in the neck inside her home. When police arrived, they found her husband bleeding from gunshot wounds to his hand, arm, and cheek. He was holding the couple's 2-year-old son. The statistics may be ambiguous, but in many cities, the bangs are real.

Discussion Questions

1. Discuss recent trends in the criminal homicide rate.
2. Discuss the recent steps law enforcement agencies have taken to address homicide.
3. How has the federal government helped local law enforcement agencies decrease the number of murder cases? What else could the federal government do to help?

3

Neuroscience and the Law

By Michael Gazzaniga and Megan S. Steven

Why do people commit crime? This question has challenged researchers for centuries. The three main bodies of criminological thought suggest that sociological, psychological, and/or biological factors are to blame. Within each of these three vast fields, however, reside numerous theoretical explanations for criminal behavior. More interdisciplinary approaches to criminological thought suggest that the study of motives for criminal behavior involve input from multiple schools of thought.

Sociological explanations involve societal factors as the cause of crime. The impacts of poverty, peer pressure, social structure, power differentials, and other social impacts are proposed to influence the likelihood that one will engage in crime. Changing criminal behavior requires changing the society in which an individual lives. Psychological explanations look more toward the inner mental processes of the individual who commits crime. One's development, from infancy throughout life, is proposed to influence one's likelihood of engaging in crime.

Earlier biological explanations of crime were primitive by today's standards. For instance, early researchers examined body types to assess propensity for criminal behavior. The insufficiency of early biological explanations and lack of scientific knowledge of biological issues led researchers to largely abandon the study of biological explanations of crime for some time. Recently, however, as medical science has progressed, researchers are revisiting the impact of biological factors on criminal behavior. With the technology to closely examine and take measurements of a living brain over time, researchers are again focusing on the relationship between biology and crime, particularly on brain activities and body chemistry.

The concept of "free will" is of great significance to criminal justice. Our society holds individuals accountable for a crime if prosecutors prove that they knowingly engaged in illegal activity. However, the term "knowingly" has been the subject of much debate. Sometimes one's intent to commit a crime is difficult to prove, because intentions are not always blatantly obvious. Legal scholars and others often speculate about intent, leading to much controversy in the courts. As discussed in the article "Neuroscience and the Law," the implications of studying the brain can help alleviate some of this controversy, yet simultaneously generate new concerns.

The ethical and legal implications of understanding the relationship between the brain and human behavior are notable. For instance, understanding how deficiencies in the brain impact violent tendencies will assist the courts as they attempt to define terms such as "knowingly" and "intent," yet from a crime prevention perspective, would it be ethical to closely monitor those with similar deficiencies even though they haven't broken the law? In other words, if we know, based on the examination of one's brain, that an individual is predisposed to violence, should we cautiously monitor his or her behavior? Strong arguments could be made that violent tendencies do not necessarily result in criminal behavior.

Many boxers and football players have made a living from violence. Furthermore, identifying and labeling individuals as "likely to engage in violence" may perpetuate their violent tendencies. On the other hand, wouldn't such information provide a viable crime prevention tool? This article generates many insightful questions, not the least of which is "what do we do with the information we obtain via neuroscience?"

Imagine you are a juror for a horrific murder case. Harry is the defendant. You sit down with 11 of your peers—people who may not be up on the latest scientific understanding about human behavior. Most of the jurors have never heard the word "neuroscience" nor given a moment's thought to the concept of "free will." And you know that most jurors have little patience for criminal-defense arguments based on such notions as "temporary insanity." The jurors are there to determine whether Harry committed the crime, and if they decide he did, they will deliver their verdict without regret. But have they considered whether Harry acted freely or as an inevitable consequence of his brain and his past experiences?

Although advances in neuroscience continue at a rapid pace, their ethical and legal implications are only beginning to be taken into account. The link between the brain and behavior is much closer than the link between genes and behavior, yet the public debate about the legal implications of genetic findings far outweighs that given to brain research.

Progress in neuroscience and technology raises numerous issues with respect to the core constructs of law, such as competency to stand trial, the genesis of violent behavior and the determination of whether witnesses are lying. For example, knowing that a brain deficiency predisposes certain people to violence would present a host of controversial questions, including whether we might "mark" these people for surveillance by authorities; whether preemptive treatment of these people is desirable; whether juries are likely to discriminate against them; and whether society might change how it punishes and rehabilitates such people who are convicted of crimes. How far along are we, today, in being able to make such determinations?

FREE WILL VS. FREE WON'T

Perhaps the most fundamental implication of 21st-century brain science is that a way may exist to evaluate free will. The logic goes like this: The brain determines the mind, and the brain is subject to all the rules of the physical world. The physical world is determined, so our brains must also be determined. If so, then we must ask: Are the thoughts that arise from the brain also determined? Is the free will we seem to experience just an illusion? And if free will is an illusion, must we revise our conception of what it means to be personally responsible for our actions?

This conjecture has haunted philosophers for decades. But with new imaging tools that show the human brain in action, these questions are being reexamined by neuroscientists and, increasingly, the legal world. Defense lawyers are looking for that one pixel in their client's brain scan that shows an abnormality—some sort of malfunction that would allow them to argue: "Harry didn't do it. His brain did it. Harry is not responsible for his actions."

At the same time, we must realize that even if the causation of an act (criminal or otherwise) is explainable in terms of brain function, that does not mean that the person who carries out the act is exculpable. Although brains can be viewed as more or less automatic devices, like clocks, we as people seem free to choose our own destiny. Is there a way to settle this dilemma?

A first step was taken in the 1980s by Benjamin Libet, now emeritus professor of physiology at the University of California at San Francisco. If the brain carries out its work before one becomes consciously aware of a thought, as most neuroscientists now accept as true, it would appear that the brain enables the mind. This idea underlies the neuroscience of determinism. Libet measured brain

---

"Neuroscience and the Law" by Michael S. Gazzaniga and Megan S. Steven, *Scientific American Mind*, Volume 16, Number 1, 2005. Reprinted with permission. Copyright © 2005 by Scientific American, Inc. All rights reserved.

activity during voluntary hand movements. He found that between 500 and 1,000 milliseconds before we actually move our hand there is a wave of brain activity, called the readiness potential. Libet set out to determine the moment, somewhere in that 500 to 1,000 milliseconds, when we make the actual conscious decision to move our hand.

Libet found that the time between the onset of the readiness potential and the moment of conscious decision making was about 300 milliseconds. If the readiness potential of the brain is initiated before we are aware of making the decision to move our hand, then it would appear that our brains know our decisions before we become conscious of them.

This kind of evidence seems to indicate that free will is an illusion. But Libet argued that because the time from the onset of the readiness potential to the actual hand movement is about 500 milliseconds, and it takes 50 to 100 milliseconds for the neural signal to travel from the brain to the hand to actually make it move, then there are 100 milliseconds left for the conscious self to either act on the unconscious decision or veto it. That, he said, is where free will arises—in the vetoing power. Neuroscientist Vilayanur S. Ramachandran of the University of California at San Diego, in an argument similar to 17th-century English philosopher John Locke's theory of free will, suggests that our conscious minds may not have free will but do have "free won't."

RESISTING VIOLENT TENDENCIES

Many other experiments show that our brain gets things done before we know about them. But what does this mean for real-life problems of free will, such as violent behavior? Is there a way to use current scientific knowledge to argue for reduced culpability under the law?

Evidence from patients with brain lesions confirms that the prefrontal cortex plays a critical role in social behavior. And psychological exams indicate that people who repeatedly commit violent crimes often have antisocial personality disorder (APD). It would therefore be interesting to know if criminals with APD, who demonstrate abnormal social behavior similar to that of patients with prefrontal lobe damage, also have abnormalities in the prefrontal areas of the brain. To address this question, Adrian Raine, a psychology professor at the University of Southern California, and his colleagues imaged the brains of 21 people with APD and compared them with the brains of healthy subjects and other controls. They found that people with APD had a reduced volume of gray matter and a reduced amount of neural activity in the prefrontal areas as compared with the controls. This finding indicates that there is a structural difference between the brains of criminals with APD and the brains of the normal population. The outcome also suggests that a volume difference in gray matter in that area of the brain may lead to a functional difference in social behavior.

In 2002 Antonia S. New, associate professor of psychiatry at the Mount Sinai School of Medicine, looked at a specific characteristic of APD—impulsive aggression. Using positron emission tomography, her team monitored the metabolic activity of the brain in response to an excitatory chemical called m-CPP in people with impulsive aggression and in healthy, nonaggressive controls. M-CPP normally activates the anterior cingulate (a frontal area of the brain known to be involved in inhibition) and deactivates the posterior cingulate. The opposite was found to be true for people with impulsive aggression: the anterior cingulate was deactivated, and the posterior cingulate was activated. The investigators concluded that people with impulsive aggression have less activation of inhibitory regions and that this may contribute to their difficulty in modulating aggression.

If findings such as these are true, it is still possible that certain violent people do not inhibit their impulses even though they could inhibit them—and therefore should be held responsible for their actions. Future research will be needed to determine how much prefrontal damage is necessary, or to what degree the gray matter is reduced, for the cessation of inhibitory function and thus perhaps for the mitigation of responsibility.

Neuroscientists must realize, however, that for any given brain state, the correlation of nonviolent behavior could be just as high as the correlation of violent behavior. For example, most patients who suffer from lesions involving the inferior orbital frontal lobe (in the prefrontal cortex) do not exhibit antisocial behavior of the sort that would be noticed by the law. Even though a patient's wife, say, might sense changes in her husband's behavior, the man is still constrained by all the other forces in society, and the frequency of his abnormal behavior is no different than would be seen in the normal population.

The same view is true for people with schizophrenia, a disease marked by disassociation between intellect and emotions and by difficulty controlling moods and actions. The rate of aggressive criminal behavior is not greater among schizophrenics than it is among the normal population. Because people with lesions in the inferior orbital frontal lobe or with schizophrenia are no more likely to commit violent crimes than unaffected people, it seems that merely having one of these brain disorders is not enough to remove responsibility.

AUTOMATIC BRAINS, INTERPRETIVE MINDS

Although mechanistic descriptions of how the physical brain carries out behavior have added fuel to the general idea of determinism, experts have argued that the concept of free will can coexist with determinism.

In 1954 noted English scientist and philosopher Alfred J. Ayer put forth a theory of "soft determinism." He argued, as Scottish moral philosopher David Hume had two centuries earlier, that even in a deterministic world, a person can still act freely. Ayer distinguished between free actions and constrained actions. Free actions are those that are caused by internal sources—by one's own will (unless one is suffering from a disorder). Constrained actions are those that are caused by external sources—for example, by someone or something forcing you physically or mentally to perform an action, as in hypnosis or in disorders such as kleptomania. When someone performs a free action to do A, he or she could have done B. When someone makes a constrained action to do A, he or she could have done only A.

Ayer argued that actions are free as long as they are not constrained. Free actions are not dependent on the existence of a cause but on the source of the cause. Although Ayer did not explicitly discuss the brain's role, one could make the analogy that those actions—and indeed those wills—that are caused by a disease-free brain are not constrained, even though they may be determined. In this way, the brain is determined, but the person is free.

With each passing decade, the world knows more about the mechanistic action of the nervous system and how it produces perceptual, attentional, and mnemonic functions and decisions. Yet there is still much to learn about how the brain enables the mind.

We recently attended a conference at which more than 80 leading scientists presented their findings on this very subject. It became obvious that the central question remains not only unanswered but unexamined. The brain scientists who are addressing issues of human cognition are illuminating which brain systems correlate with particular measurable human behaviors. For example, a series of studies might investigate which areas of the visual system become activated when a person attends to a particular visual stimulus. Although these correlations are of interest, the question of how the brain knows whether, when and how to increase the activity of a particular neuronal system remains unknown. Overall, modern studies always seem to leave room for the metaphorical homunculus, the little ghost in the machine that directs all brain traffic. It is common in neurology circles to hear the phrase "top-down versus bottom-up processes"—processes driven by feedback from "higher" areas of the brain rather than direct input from the sensory stimuli—but the fact is that no one knows anything about the "top" in "top-down." This is a major problem of cognitive neuroscience today, and we hope that it will soon become the subject of research.

CHANGING THE LAW

For now, we must operate with what we do know about the brain—and how that can influence the law. To address this, we must consider the current legal system's view of human decision making.

Under our legal system, a crime has two defining elements: the actus reus, or proscribed act, and the mens rea, or guilty mind. In order for Harry to go to prison for murder, both elements have to be proven beyond a reasonable doubt. The courts and the legal system typically work hard to determine the agency of the crime. Where they want help from neuroscience is on whether or not Harry should be held "personally responsible." Did Harry do it, or did his brain? This is where the slippery slope begins. Our argument is that neuroscience can offer very little to the understanding of responsibility. Responsibility is a human construct, and no pixel on a brain scan will ever be able to show culpability or not.

In practice, legal authorities have had great difficulty crafting standards to divide the responsible from the not responsible. For example, the rules for a finding of legal insanity that have existed in various forms for more than 150 years are all lacking. Experts for the defense and prosecution argue different points from the same data. What they would like, instead, is for neuroscience to come to the rescue.

But the crux of the problem is the legal system's view of human behavior. It assumes Harry is a "practical reasoner," a person who acts because he has freely chosen to act. This simple but powerful assumption drives the entire legal system. Even though we might all conceive of reasons to contravene the law, we can decide not to act on such thoughts because we have free will. If a defense lawyer can provide evidence that a defendant had a "defect in reasoning" that led to his inability to stop from committing the crime, then Harry can be deemed exculpable. The legal authorities want a brain image, a neurotransmitter assay or something to show beyond a reasonable doubt that Harry was not thinking clearly, indeed could not think clearly, and therefore could not stop his behavior.

The view of human behavior offered by neuroscience is at odds with this perspective. In some ways, it is a tougher view, in other ways more lenient. Fundamentally, however, it is different. Neuroscience is the business of describing the mechanistic actions of the nervous system. The brain is an evolved system, a decision-making device that interacts with its environment in a way that allows it to learn rules to govern how it responds. It is a rule-based device that, fortunately, works automatically.

Critics might raise the objection: "Aren't you saying that people are basically robots? That the brain is a clock, and you can't hold people responsible for criminal behavior any more than you can blame a clock for not working?" That is not the case. The comparison is inappropriate because the notion of responsibility has not emerged. It has not been denied; it is simply absent from the neuroscientific description of human behavior, as a direct result of treating the brain as an automatic machine. But just because responsibility cannot be assigned to clocks does not mean it cannot be ascribed to people. In this sense, human beings are special and different from robots.

This is a fundamental point. Neuroscience will never find the brain correlate of responsibility, because that is something we ascribe to people, not to brains. It is a moral value we demand of our fellow rule-following human beings. Brain scientists might be able to tell us what someone's mental state or brain condition is but cannot tell us when someone has too little control to be held responsible. The issue of responsibility is a social choice. According to neuroscience, no one person is more or less responsible than any other person for actions carried out. Responsibility is a social construct and exists in the rules of the society. It does not exist in the neuronal structures of the brain.

For now, that is all we can say. It would be rash to conclude on any other note than one of modesty about our current understanding of the brain and mind. Much more work is needed to clarify the complex issues raised by neuroscience and the law.

Still, we would like to offer the following axiom: brains are automatic, rule-governed, determined devices, whereas people are personally responsible agents free to make their own decisions. Just as traffic is what happens when physically determined cars interact, responsibility is what happens when people interact. Brains are determined; people are free.

Discussion Questions

1. What are some of the ethical issues associated with using neuroscience in criminal justice?
2. Discuss the relationship between neuroscience and free will. Specifically, identify whether free will actually exists in light of what is known about human brain behavior.
3. Do you believe neuroscience will or will not have a significant impact on our court systems in the near future? Why or why not?

4

Ill Winds: The Chemical Plant Next Door

By Becky Bradway

Environmental hazards abound in society. We don't often recognize harms to the environment in the same manner as we view harms against one another; however, it would be foolish to believe that environmental harms do not pose serious threats. Global warming is no longer a buzzword used by environmentalists as a scare tactic. Instead, global warming and other environmental hazards are now seriously considered by many countries, individuals, and companies that previously gave the environment little thought. Much has changed since the 1970s when the roots of environmental regulation were established. Fortunately, committing environmental crime is not as easy as it once was.

Despite the optimism, much work remains before environmental harms subside. Consider the environmental harms associated with the life of one motorcycle: the production, use, and disposal of one motorcycle may seem insignificant to most, yet consider the need for various factories to make the parts for the motorcycle. Then consider the environmental harms stemming from the company that assembles and tests the motorcycle. Next, there's the transnational or interstate transport for sale of the motorcycle. There are also harms associated with riding the motorcycle, including pollution, and finally, consider what's to be done with the motorcycle and its many parts once the motorcycle is no longer usable.

I'm not anti-motorcycle by any means. The life cycle of one motorcycle demonstrates how many intangible environmental impacts are associated with the production and use of any material good. Now consider a Cadillac Escalade or some other large SUV— there are more parts to this vehicle, and it's much larger and it gets far worse gas mileage than a motorcycle. The examples provided thus far consider just one vehicle, when indeed, there are several hundred thousand vehicles on our roads. Environmental crime, much like other forms of white-collar crime, is often overlooked by the general public and criminal justice authorities, as evidenced in this article that emphasizes the views taken by affected and interested parties in a town being harmed by a chemical plant.

The historical failure to prosecute environmental crime is attributable to, among other things, the harms associated with industrialism often being viewed as the cost of doing business. There's often no obvious intent on behalf of environmental offenders, making the enforcement of environmental crimes challenging. Furthermore, the corporations committing violations are sometimes powerful enough to locate or generate successful responses to any accusations of wrongdoing; both within and outside the courtroom.

Legislators and environmental regulators must balance the need for corporations to remain competitive while protecting the environment. Over-regulating industry may be harmful to economic security, though under-regulating industry is harmful to the well-being of the planet. The effects of under-regulation are evident in Bradway's article.

From the time I was eight until I was 10, I lived in a pea-sized town down the road from the chemical plant and the munitions factory. Buffalo, Illinois had a bank, a grocery store, a post office and a park. And enough houses to hold three hundred people. This was where we moved, a few miles from my grandparents, after we left Phoenix. My mother never wanted to come back to Illinois. Once she was there, she only spoke to the relatives, and when they were with us they seemed to mask the hole in her life.

I loved that town nearly as much as my mother hated it. She hated it so much that she never went outside except to get in her car and drive away. She sent me to the post office and the grocery store, had my dad do the yard work. She sat in the dark living room watching soap operas and folding clothes. The kitchen was for packing my father's suppers. He worked swing shift—3 to 11 P.M.—or graveyard, the night shift. When he was gone, we would eat Kraft Macaroni and Cheese and carrot sticks. When he was home, we would have pork chops or the end of a roast. We tried not to spill the milk or sing at the table.

Anyway, it was the town that mattered. A town, or what it should be, is a community of hope. It's bustle and defiance out here in nowhere. Buffalo was my sanctuary, my circle. Friends, school, church, street, sidewalk, lawn, bells. They were not artificial constructions. They were not just institutional and conformity-approving props. We need these places. I needed them.

Concerned grown-ups asked questions that I would dodge. I took their offerings of Bible verse and story and hid them beneath my bed, to be brought out at quiet times. I kept the letters from pen pals and the stamps from foreign countries and I told the man and woman at the post office some jokes. I ambled the sidewalks, looked up at the leaves, listened to mourning doves, chatted with pals on the steps of the church, rode my bike anywhere I wanted to go, even past the edges of the town. I never passed the tavern, and I avoided the stares from that weird (some said retarded) man who lived alone and spent his days on his porch. I played jacks, petted dogs, swapped notes. I learned to say dirty words, even though I had no idea what they meant. My boyfriend, Toby, gave me a gumball machine ring, a rectangular green stone set in bendable gold.

The town was heaven. Not that it was really that way. All is comparison and perspective—what I chose to see, what I didn't have to know. I didn't know about unemployment and pollution and the other weights that pushed under the people. I didn't care about commodity prices and the sale of beans and hogs. The world was sun and dark, and I would choose my own gradations and ignore the rest.

Buffalo, this town where we lived, was right down the road from Borden Chemical.

BORDEN AND BUFFALO

When Mom got sick, I decided to dredge up the dirt about Borden. She didn't link the floating fish to herself, but as her thoughts grew foggy, and she grew thinner, she kept coming back to the fish kill. She was sure Borden was the murderer. Was her body telling her something? I owed her some cause-and-effect explanation. I read books, tapped into environmental and scientific list serves, and watched documentaries. Whatever I could dig up about the chemical industry, I dug. Pesticides, herbicides, industrial chemicals, even cow shit: I know it all. Factories, coal tar, farms, sewage: put them all together, and beings die.

But Mom wanted to know about Borden Chemical. That bulbous monstrosity on Route 36. In looking there, I came across Buffalo again. I came across people. Those who I knew, whose fates were tied to the wind that blew vinyl chloride across their town. Why do we bring disaster upon ourselves?

"Ill Winds: The Chemical Plant Next Door" by Becky Bradway, first published in *E/The Environmental Magazine*. Reprinted by permission of Featurewell.com.

Embrace it, fund it, serve it? Facts don't mean that much. It's feeling that matters. It's earth, the ground where we plant our feet. It's what we do to compromise, what we ignore in order to stay in one place. To understand Borden, I'd have to understand the town that allowed the factory to stay: Illiopolis. And to understand Illiopolis, I'd have to go back to the town where I lived for two years: Buffalo. These were the towns nearest to Borden. I lived there. I drank that water and breathed the air. I had cancer, my mother and uncle died of cancer. Is this what fed the cells? Made us dizzy, made our joints creak, created multiplication inside that we couldn't even feel until it was late and it had compromised our systems? In comprehending these places, I hoped to get a grip on death and rage and the dark side and sex and all that stuff that comes up in nightmares, as if by grasping it all with logic I could keep from being consumed. Maybe someone would stop it.

Nobody cares about rural people, though. Let's be real about that. They're the butt of jokes; they have no power. A friend who teaches in Illiopolis joked that everyone in the town is inbred. They all have the same last names. Uh-huh, I said. Tell me about it. Feuding strands of my cousins' family, the Pattons, wind all over Central Illinois. The inbreeding isn't a matter of genetics, but of attitudes and ideas and career options and life choices that limit them to a 10-mile radius. Kids look to the chemical plant, figuring they can get a job there after they get married. They marry soon after they graduate high school, or even before. Some want to leave but lack opportunity or nerve, so they stay stoned, vandalize, fight, or maybe kill themselves driving too fast on the curving country roads.

All small towns are turned inward upon themselves: behind the times, idyllic, poor, happy, and at the mercy of whatever industry runs the place. Right at the literal center of Illinois, Illiopolis cropped up in 1833, when pioneers cleared the prairie grass and planted cabins. A fire wiped them out, leaving the land to weeds, until the railroad line from Springfield to Decatur made the town a loading point. The prairie was drained and there it appeared: farmland. Fed by decomposing roots, rich because for centuries it had been let be. Illiopolis grew along the tracks; by 1900 it had a railroad depot, grain elevators, a post office, a grocery store, a hardware store-mortuary combination (making it easy to hammer down the coffins), a lumber yard, blacksmith shops, two hotels, three churches, livery stables, a school, and, of course, a bar. Not a whole lot is different today, except that the shops that once serviced horses now service cars.

A white church with an elegant steeple looms over frame houses with added-on bedrooms. A ranch house huddles next to a rehabbed mansion, a trailer rests perpendicular to a beauty shop, a junkyard lurks up the hill from thin-walled family homes. Its bar proclaims Habits and Vices, a cavalier admission, a plainspoken truth. Johnson's Grocery sits beside the Citgo gas station with its all-night stock of liquor, chips and cigarettes. In the Business District—you know it's the business district because that's what the signs tell you—is the bank and an antiques store crammed floor to ceiling with ceramic figurines and Depression glass. That's it. Kids still drive around and around this "square" at night, swigging from beer cans in cup coolers. They honk at each other, swap joints, and screw in back seats. Then they settle down and get to the grinding work of factory shifts and child rearing. And when their children grow up, those kids drive around the square.

RELICS REMAIN

After my parents died, I drove a couple times a week down Route 36, straight through Buffalo. It became familiar, like a rusted Chevy with bad sparkplugs. The change came not in design, but in wear. Like my parents, the town had gotten old, and it seemed to be on the verge of dying, too.

The gray one-story befits my father's grimy years of commuting to Decatur's Firestone plant. I want to hate my former home. I want to understand my mother's furious depression. But although I can see that the house is ugly, it doesn't seem ugly to me. Lilies of the valley once drooped in the shade at the side of the house, peony bushes and rhubarb grew beside the storm cellar, the laundry line ran from the house to the shed, and an alleyway provided a path where my friends and I walked barefoot. I imagine that these relics still remain. The old neighbor's tended lawn, the tree that I climbed in the front yard, the holes that my brother and I dug with Tonka trucks. What kids remember.

Route 36 used to be the only road that linked the cities of Springfield and Decatur. This pitted two-lane takes you through or near a string of towns: Illiopolis, Lanesville, Mechanicsburg, Dawson, Buffalo, Riverton. As a child, I knew the road mostly as one that shouldn't be crossed. The countryside around it is littered with faded cafes and junked VW vans, silos and leaning barns. Cattails and coreopsis droop in ditches, while stands of trees clump amidst nothing. Make-out roads stop at a field's edge or a washed-away bridge. Folks live in the middle of nowhere because it's cheap and they're comfortable; as my mom said, "We don't have to put on airs. I can go out without a bra on and I'm invisible," or, according to Grandpa, "I can scratch my ass and nobody's going to take a picture." Along the road you'll see a house grown over with vines and weeds, whatever's visible needing a paint job, greeting visitors with a No Trespassing sign and a pit bull/hound. People keep a good distance.

Near the chemical plant, the view evolves from corn to boxcar. Abandoned train cars line the right side of the road, though the active tracks are on the left. On one car, someone has spray-painted this profound truth: Decatur Sucks. Spew can be seen in the sky miles before I see the factory. Bunkers and dilapidated buildings left from the munitions grounds announce the "industrial complex." Fencing higher than my head surrounds an array of pipes and wire and bulbous tanks and fences and stacks. KEEP OUT! PRIVATE! DANGER! warn the signs. As if anyone enters by choice. These jobs are necessities.

Borden's specialties were resins and formaldehyde. The Illiopolis plant once produced my childhood friend, Elmer's Glue, and a competitor to Saran Wrap called Resinite. Borden didn't start out being one of the largest producers of plastics in the world. If you're old enough, you may remember Elsie the Cow, the smiling mascot of Borden's Dairy. When I was a six year old, living in the desert, Elsie represented everything good about the Midwest: a place of endless green, plentiful food, and kind relatives. I even had an aunt named Elsie. So imagine my sense of betrayal when I realized that Borden had gone from producing milk to producing chemicals. While it's hard to imagine doing without plastic wrap, the fact is that it leaches into foods when microwaved. The white glue that we used in school is made with non-toxic levels of the same chemicals. The big product in Illiopolis now is polyvinyl chloride (PVC), used in tile, plastic water pipes, siding and wire insulation. What goes into PVC? Vinyl chloride, a flammable gas, and vinyl acetate, a toxic gas. When they shoot into the air or get into the water, they cause everything from a bad cough to paralysis. Workers in plants that make the stuff have high rates of liver and breast cancer. Vinyl chloride stays in water for decades, where it is absorbed into fish flesh. The fish we ate on those glorious summer cookouts.

Borden Chemical has undergone some particularly colorful corporate transformations. In 1987, according to a spokesperson, it came under the ownership of Borden Chemicals and Plastics Limited Partnership (BCP), which is now twisting in the wind of Chapter 11 bankruptcy. In April of this year, the Illiopolis plant was sold to Taiwan-based PVC-maker Formosa Plastics, which not only has a record of environmental violations in several states but was also tied to campaign finance scandals in the Clinton White House.

Chemicals were and still are dumped in rivers and wells and underground tanks and landfills, floating and settling all across the Sangamon Valley. Companies dodge environmental protection laws by getting waivers and exemptions. Since we need our conveniences, the wastes have to go somewhere—why not some hick's backyard?

When the fish turned up dead, my relatives blamed Borden. But with so many companies and farms polluting the Sangamon River, we can never be sure. But Borden has an unenviable environmental record. It was even caught shipping 2,500 drums of highly toxic mercury waste to South Africa. The stockpiled drums leaked contaminants—a disaster that led to both criminal and civil investigations in South Africa.

At one of Borden's biggest plants, in Geismar, Louisiana (home of BCP), according to *Time* magazine, a "witches' brew of toxic chemicals" descended not once, but several times. The chemicals that Borden reportedly released into the air were ethylene dichloride, vinyl-chloride monomer, hydrogen chloride, hydrochloric acid and ammonia. In 1994, three years before Geismar's first toxic spew, the U.S. Justice Department filed a lawsuit accusing the company of illegal hazardous waste storage, contaminating groundwater, burning waste without a permit and neglecting to report chemical releases into the air. In 1998, without admitting wrongdoing, Borden settled for $3.6 million and agreed to spend $3 million to clean up the Louisiana water.

The Illinois Pollution Control Board exempted Illiopolis' Borden plant from many Environmental Protection Agency (EPA) regulations. Borden's wastewater is still high in "total dissolved solids, or TDS"—all of the solid contaminants put together, like calcium, magnesium, iron, lead, nitrates, chloride and sulfate. This is twice as high as the average, and the Illinois Department of Energy and Natural Resources says that these flows are carried downstream to the Sangamon River. The plant can legally dump 800,000 gallons of wastewater into the stream every day. In two miles, this water reaches the Sangamon. Because the area around the stream is wooded, locals hunt and fish there. EPA studies show the river from Decatur to Springfield to be especially toxic: the river where we caught fish, used water for crops, and walked when the currents were low. The river that one naturalist calls "a drainage ditch." Because the water runs low and bends, poisons gather, plants die, and invasive species bloom. Little is washed away.

In May of 1999, Borden Chemicals and Plastics did to Illiopolis what it did to Geismar, Louisiana: It released 500 pounds of vinyl chloride gas. An "accidental" release, they said. Ten years before this, in 1989, the Illinois Attorney General's Office sued the plant for releasing the same gas 14 times over a four-year period. In response to the 1999 incident, Borden was forced to hold public hearings detailing an emergency evacuation plan. Not counting accidents, the plant routinely releases 65,000 pounds of vinyl chloride and 40,000 pounds of vinyl acetate into the Central Illinois air every year. Along with causing cancer, vinyl chloride is suspected of disrupting our hormones, which makes us—especially women and girls—vulnerable to all kinds of illnesses. I was not reassured by what I found out about Borden Chemical and its history of environmental abuses, but I can't assume the same about the residents of Illiopolis.

Why did the thousand people in this town welcome Borden Chemical, working there, sending their children to work there? Because they need to eat. And because they can't do anything about it, and around here, people don't worry about what they can't fix. What are they going to do, drive to Decatur to work at Archer Daniels Midland, where four employees died in an assortment of industrial accidents? Or to A.E. Staley, with its 12-hour shifts? At least it's a job.

BLUE-COLLAR RISKS

When I visited the family over Easter, Uncle Wade talked about men who worked in a Taylorville factory. Each had died or was dying from a rare cancer. They'd been forced to climb into tanks to clean out mystery chemical crap. Anyone who said no was fired. "They swelled up big as blimps before they kicked off," Wade said. "Pathetic bastards."

Since he owned his own construction business, my uncle never had to worry about being in any employer's pocket. They took on other blue-collar risks: My uncle can barely move from motion injuries. But they chose the work, and that makes all the difference. My cousin Mike, who took over the business from his father, says if you don't become "a boss" by 40, you'll turn into a cripple. "Your joints stop working," he said. He told stories of danger and carelessness: men with hands stapled to walls, men with nails driven into legs. Which tools cause arthritis in the long run. "You got to know what you're doing." But, he said, it's better than being a factory cog.

We had thought our choices made us safe. We lived in the country by the river, away from the city and its violence. We never traveled, never took a plane or train or bus, never drove farther than "town." My family never went to college, where they might meet scary people. But for all that, my mother spent the Christmas of 2000 stuck in a chair because of the swelling in her legs. The tumor caused the swelling, she claimed. It was only later, by stealing a look into her medical chart that I found out her new diagnosis: lymphoma.

"So, did you ever find out anything about that fish kill?" I asked Mom, as we nibbled Teresa's peanut butter fudge and watched through the windows at the kids sledding down the long, steep riverbank. Mom didn't look sick—more lined, puffier, but normal enough. I bet then that she might have a few years left. She never mentioned time, never talked about her illness, and if pressed, she lied. I considered calling her doctor for the truth, but what would be the point? We knew it was beyond surgery, and that chemo wasn't going to do it. Mom was still convinced that the treatments would work, though, and blamed everything on her doctor. "She's given up on me," was her line. "She thinks I should go into a hospice. She wants to shove me into a corner so she doesn't have to deal with me." Chemo splints and radiation blasts were getting it, Mom insisted, even though the doctor said otherwise. Though Mom grew more bloated and forgetful, though she rarely ate. It was easy to take her word for it, as if what I saw was just a delusion, and the will truly was greater than the body. Families can convince themselves that what we choose to believe is what is true.

"Borden might've done it," I said. "But other factories were doing the same thing."

"It was Borden," she insisted. "That's what your grandpa said."

"How did he know?"

"It was in the paper." But I looked for proof in the newspapers, and never found it. There had been other fish kills that year. The signs pointed more to the Decatur Sanitary District than Borden. "It could have been anyone," I told her.

"Everyone knows it was Borden. You'd think they would've had more respect for the fish."

"What about respect for the people?"

"Well, nobody ate the fish after that. Nobody died," she said, lighting up a cigarette.

Discussion Questions

1. Identify and discuss the harms associated with the environmental degradation discussed in the article.

2. What steps could have been taken to prevent the damages stemming from the Borden Chemical plant in Buffalo?

3. Discuss the penalties associated with the environmental harms noted in the article. Do you believe stricter punishments would be more effective? Why or why not?

5

Chasing My Stolen Bicycle

By Justin Jouvenal

Have you ever had something stolen? Chance are, you have. What did you do? Call the police? Nothing? Try to track down your goods? In "Chasing My Stolen Bicycle," Justin Jouvenal attempts to track down his stolen bicycle and takes us to an interesting side of town, the underworld of crime. He exposes the criminal justice system's lack of concern for, and inability to fight petty crime. Among other things, this insightful account sheds light on a world unknown to many of us.

Crime clearance rates are based on the number of crimes cleared by an arrest. Clearance rates are much higher for serious crimes such as murder, rape, and robbery than they are for petty crimes, such as bike theft. Societal concern regarding violent crimes dictates that law enforcement agencies devote substantial efforts toward clearing such crimes while creating subunits such as homicide task forces. Nevertheless, we're more likely to be the victim of a petty crime than a more serious crime. So why shouldn't we have bike-theft task forces? The answer is simple: Violent crime is more harmful and instills substantial fear—bikes can be replaced. But can't we adequately address both?

Given limited resources and pressure to solve high-profile crimes such as murders, law enforcement agencies prioritize. This approach seems rational, unless it is your property that is stolen. How would you feel if your bike was stolen and the police did very little to help? Would it make things worse if you went searching for your bicycle, only to find out there's a well-established underworld that steals, sells, and buys stolen goods? Jouvenal visited the criminal underworld and spoke with involved individuals.

The criminal underworld is not unlike the outside, or "noncriminal" world. There are relations, exchanges, interactions, and expectations. The illegal nature of the economy gives it its distinct flavor. It is particularly important that the criminal underworld impacts our everyday lives. That stolen car stereo of yours? The CDs taken from your car? They have likely been indoctrinated into the other world's viable market for stolen goods. And police and prosecutors know about it.

Aside from the police and prosecutors who ignore the goings-on of the criminal underworld, others are responsible for its existence: the thieves who steal the goods, the stores that sell the goods, and consumers who knowingly purchase stolen goods. The recent popularity of e-commerce facilitates the exchange of stolen goods. A recent story in my local newspaper involved a group of citizens who contacted the police after thieves stole video equipment from cars parked in their neighborhood. After a lackadaisical or nonexistent response, the citizens searched eBay for the goods. Sure enough, someone in proximity was selling the items. The citizens arranged to meet the seller at a local shopping center where the thief showed up with the goods. Such citizen participation in crime control can be dangerous, yet victims may feel the need to take the law into their own hands when they believe law enforcement won't respond.

I stalked across the parking lot of the Mission District's Best Buy. Like the hordes of people that streamed into the store, I was there to do a little shopping, but it wasn't for a flat-screen TV or an iPod. I was in the market for a stolen bike.

I bypassed the aisles of buzzing electronics and headed around the back of the store to a trash-strewn alley. It was empty except for a beat-up white van with its side door ajar. I took a nervous breath and knocked on the side.

A blond man in a sweat-stained undershirt threw open the door to reveal what looked like an upended Tour de France chase car: piles of tire rims, gears, and bike frames were scattered everywhere. The powerful stink of unwashed bodies stung my nostrils. A man in a tracksuit slumbered on a seat. The blond man looked sleepy and annoyed but waited for me to speak.

My $600 bike was stolen—the third in five years—from my Mission garage the night before, and it's here I was told by a bike messenger that I might find it. These guys were rumored to be bike thieves operating in the Mission.

"Hey man, have you *seen* a black and gray Fuji Touring?" I asked, employing a euphemism.

"No, we don't steal bikes," the man said, catching my drift. "We collect bikes off the street, repair them, and then sell them. We're like independent businessmen."

Interesting way of putting it, I thought, as I glanced at the "businessman" slumbering on a van seat. I glanced around the van half expecting to see my Fuji, but it wasn't there, so I left.

As I trudged home I stewed. I had lost more than $1,000 worth of bikes in San Francisco. Bike theft is a virtual right of passage for most cyclists in the city, and the city's thieves seem to operate with ninjalike stealth and efficiency. One cyclist told me how a thief stole his locked ride while he picked up a burrito from a taquería. He wasn't away from the bike for more than five minutes.

The city's thieves have even won a silver medal for their efforts: in 2006 the lockmaker Kryptonite ranked San Francisco as the nation's second worst city for bike theft, behind New York.

Gradually, my anger hardened into resolve, or more precisely, a mission. It would be virtually impossible, but I would set out to find my bike. The thought that my life would mirror the plot of a Pee-wee Herman movie was more than a little amusing, but I had a job to do.

In my months-long quest I crisscrossed the city, chasing down Dickensian thieves, exploring the city's largest open-air market for stolen goods, and finally landing in the surprising place where hundreds of stolen bikes—perhaps yours—end up. Unwittingly, I pedaled right into San Francisco's underworld.

THE GURUS OF GREASE

Bike theft may seem like petty street crime, but it's actually a humming illegal industry. Consider this: thieves steal nearly $50 million worth of bikes each year in the United States, far outstripping the take of bank robbers, according to the FBI. And in San Francisco's rich bicycling culture, thieves have found a gold mine. About 1,000 bikes are reported stolen in the city each year, but the police say the actual number is probably closer to 2,000 or 3,000, since most people don't file reports.

"It's rampant," Sgt. Joe McCloskey of the San Francisco Police Department told the *Guardian.*

I sought out McCloskey, the SFPD's resident expert on bike theft, and another man, Victor Veysey, to give me a wider view of San Francisco's world of bike thieves and possibly a lead on where I might find my bike. Several cyclists had recommended Veysey, saying he could provide a "street level" view of bike theft.

Veysey is the Yoda of San Francisco's bike world. For more than a decade, the 39-year-old has worked on and off as a bike messenger, mechanic, and member of the city's Bike Advisory Committee. He also ran the Bike Hut, which teaches at-risk youth how to repair bikes. And he's in a band that plays a tune called "Schwinn Cruiser."

"Chasing my Stolen Bicycle" by Justin Jouvenal, San Francisco Bay Guardian online. Reprinted by permission of Justin Jouvenal.

Despite their different perspectives (the city's police and biking communities are not the best of friends), McCloskey and Veysey painted remarkably similar pictures of San Francisco's black market for bikes.

In the wide world of illegal activity, bike thievery seems to occupy a criminal sweet spot. It is a relatively painless crime to commit, and city officials do little to stop it. As McCloskey readily admitted, bike theft is not a priority for law enforcement, which he said has its hands full with more serious crimes.

"We make it easy for them," McCloskey said of bike thieves. "The DA doesn't do tough prosecutions. All the thieves we've busted have got probation. They treat it like a petty crime."

Debbie Mesloh, a spokesperson for District Attorney Kamala Harris, said most bike thieves are not prosecuted, but that's because they are juveniles or they qualify for the city's pretrial diversion program. The diversion program offers counseling in lieu of prosecution for first-time nonviolent offenders. Bike thieves qualify for it if they steal a bike worth $400 or less. Mesloh said the District Attorney's Office prosecutes felony bike thefts, but it doesn't get very many of those cases.

"The DA takes all cases of theft seriously," Mesloh wrote in an e-mail.

As for the police, McCloskey was equally blunt. "You can't take six people off a murder to investigate a bike theft. [Bike theft investigations] are not an everyday thing. No one is full-time on bike theft. As far as going out on stings and operations, I haven't heard of one in the last year. Bike theft has gone to the bottom of the list."

McCloskey's comments were particularly interesting in light of the conversation I had with Veysey, whom I met at the Bike Hut, an off-kilter wood shack near AT&T Park that appears as if it might collapse under the weight of the bicycle parts hanging on its walls. Veysey has a loose blond ponytail and greasy hands. He wields a wrench and apocalyptic environmental rhetoric equally well.

"Bikes are one of the four commodities of the street—cash, drugs, sex, and bikes," Veysey told me. "You can virtually exchange one for another."

Veysey believes bike thefts are helping prop up the local drug market. It sounds far-fetched, but it's a notion McCloskey and other bike theft experts echoed. The National Bike Registry, a company that runs the nation's largest database for stolen bikes, says on its Web site, "Within the drug trade, stolen bicycles are so common they can almost be used as currency." Veysey believes the police could actually take a bite out of crime in general by making bike theft a bigger priority in the city.

Perhaps bikes are so ubiquitous in the drug trade because they are so easy to steal. McCloskey and Veysey said thieves often employ bolt cutters to snap cable locks or a certain brand of foreign car jack to defeat some U-locks. The jack slips between the arms of the U-lock and, as it is cranked open, pushes the arms apart until the lock breaks. A bike-lock maker later showed me a video demonstrating the technique. It took a man posing as a thief less than six seconds to do in the U-lock.

As with any other trade, McCloskey and Veysey said there is a hierarchy in the world of San Francisco bike thieves. At the bottom, drug addicts (like the one Veysey believes stole my bike) engage in crimes of opportunity: snatching single bikes. At a more sophisticated level, McCloskey said, a small number of thieves target high-end bikes, which can top $5,000 apiece. In 2005 police busted a bike thief who was specifically targeting Pacific Heights because of its expensive bikes. The thief said he wore natty golf shirts and khaki pants to blend into the neighborhood.

The Internet has revolutionized bike theft, just as it has done for dating, porn, and cat videos. McCloskey said thieves regularly fence bikes on eBay and Craigslist. In August 2004 police busted a thief after a Richmond District man discovered his bike for sale on eBay. Police discovered more than 20 auctions for stolen bikes in the man's eBay account and an additional 20 stolen bikes in a storage space and at his residence.

When bikes aren't sold outright, they are stripped, or in street vernacular, chopped, and sold piece by piece or combined with the parts of other bikes, Veysey said. He said people occasionally showed up at the Bike Hut trying to sell him these Frankenstein bikes. But by and large, McCloskey and Veysey said, bike stores are not involved in fencing stolen bikes. However, McCloskey said bikes stolen in the city often are recovered at flea markets around the Bay Area. He believes thieves ship them out of the city to decrease the chance of being caught. The National Bike Registry reports bikes are often moved to other cities or even other states for sale.

The idea of Frankenstein bikes was intriguing, so I told Veysey I was going to look into it. He suggested I make a stop first: Carl's Jr. near the Civic Center. I was slightly perplexed by his suggestion, but I agreed to check it out.

FAST FOOD, HOT BIKES

"Welcome to the San Francisco Zoo—the human version," said Dalibor Lawrence, a homeless man whose last two teeth acted as goalposts for his flitting tongue. His description of the place was brutally apt: a homeless man banged on one of those green public toilets, shouting obscenities; a woman washed her clothes in a fountain; and several crackheads lounged on a wall with vacant stares.

I was at the corner of Seventh and Market streets. City Hall's stately gold dome rose a short distance away, but here a whole different San Francisco thrived. Men slowly circulated around the stretch of concrete that abuts UN Plaza. Every so often one would furtively pull out a laptop, a brand new pair of sneakers, or even—improbably enough—bagged collard greens to try to sell to someone hustling by.

Seventh and Market is where the city's underground economy bubbles to the surface. It's a Wal-Mart of stolen goods—nearly anything can be bought or, as I would soon find out, stolen to order. McCloskey estimated as many as three in seven bikes stolen in San Francisco end up here. The police periodically conduct stings in the area, but the scene seemed to continue unabated.

I made my way to the front of the Carl's Jr. that overlooks an entrance to the Civic Center BART station. I didn't know what to expect or do, so I apprehensively approached three men who were lounging against the side of the restaurant—they clearly weren't there for lunch. I asked them if they knew where I could get a bike. To my surprise, the man in the center rattled off a menu.

"I've got a really nice $5,300 road bike I will sell you for $1,000. I've got another for $500 and two Bianchis for $150 each," he said.

I told him the prices he listed seemed too good to be true and asked him if the bikes were stolen. People gave them to him, he explained dubiously, because they owed him money. I asked him about my Fuji, but he said he didn't have it.

I walked around until I bumped into a woman who called herself Marina. She had a hollow look in her eyes, but I told her my story, and she seemed sympathetic. She sealed a hand-rolled cigarette with a lick, lit it, and made the following proposition: "I have a couple of friends that will steal to order—bicycles, cosmetics, whatever—give me a couple of days, and I will set something up."

I politely declined. McCloskey said steal-to-order rings are a common criminal racket in the city. Police have busted thieves with shopping lists for everything from Victoria's Secret underwear to the antiallergy drug Claritin. In one case, McCloskey said, police traced a ring smuggling goods to Mexico.

A short time later a man rode through the plaza on a beat-up yellow Schwinn. He tried to sell the 12-speed to another man, so I approached him and asked how much he wanted for it. He told me $20. With a modest amount of bargaining, I got him down to $5 before telling him I wasn't interested.

Just before I left, two police officers on a beat patrol walked through the plaza. Sales stopped briefly. As soon as the officers passed out of earshot, a man came up to me. "Flashlights," he said, "real cheap."

INSIDE A CHOP SHOP

After striking out at Seventh and Market, I figured it was time to investigate the chop shops Veysey mentioned. The San Francisco Bicycle Coalition (SFBC) reports bicycle chop shops operate all over the city. Thieves strip bikes because the parts (unlike the frames) don't have serial numbers and can't be traced as stolen once they are removed from a bike. The parts can be sold individually or put on another stolen bike to disguise it, hence the Frankenstein bikes that show up at the Bike Hut.

When Veysey told me about bicycle chop shops, I pictured something from a '70s cop movie—a warehouse in an industrial district populated with burly men wielding blowtorches. But the trail led me somewhere else entirely: Golden Gate Park.

SFBC officials said they had received reports from a gardener about chop shops in the park. When I called Maggie Cleveland, a Recreation and Park Department employee responsible for cleaning up the park, she said they do exist and would show me what she thought was one if I threw on a pair of gloves, grabbed a trash bag, and joined one of her cleanup crews. I agreed.

Shortly before 8 A.M. on a foggy, chilly morning, the crew and I picked up mechanical grabbers and industrial-size trash bags and then climbed a steep hill near 25th Avenue and Fulton Street on the Richmond District side of the park. We plunged into a large camp in the middle of a hollowed-out grove of acacia bushes.

The camp looked like a sidewalk after an eviction. Books and papers vomited from the mouth of a tent. Rain-soaked junk littered the camp, including a golf bag filled with oars, an algebra textbook, a telescope, and a portable toilet. A hypodermic needle stuck in a stump like a dart and a gaudy brass chandelier swung from a branch. Amid the clutter was one constant: bicycles and their parts.

A half dozen bikes leaned against bushes in various states of repair. There were piles of tires and gears scattered around. The noise of the crew had awoken the residents of the camp. A man and two women sprung up and immediately tried to grab things as the crew stuffed the contents of the camp into trash bags. They grew more and more agitated as two dozen bags were filled.

Cleveland said the group may have been operating a chop shop, but she didn't have definitive proof, so they were let go with camping citations. I asked one of the campers if their bikes were stolen.

"We find this stuff in the trash. There's an economy here. We exchange stuff for other stuff," he said.

Cleveland said the camp was typical of what the crews find around the park. One of the most notorious campers goes by the name Bicycle Robert. Cleveland said park officials have found a handful of his camps over the past couple years. One contained more than two dozen bikes, but Robert himself has never turned up.

Occasionally, cyclists will get lucky and find their bikes at a chop shop. Max Chen was eating dinner in North Beach one night when his Xtracycle, a bicycle with an elongated back for supporting saddlebags, was stolen. Chen didn't hold out much hope of getting it back, but he put up flyers around the neighborhood anyway.

The next day Chen got a call from a friend who said he saw a portion of the distinctive bike behind the Safeway at Potrero and 16th streets. Chen went down to the spot and found a group of guys with an RV, a handful of bicycles, and a pile of bike parts. His bike was there—sort of.

"The frame was in one place, and the pedals were on another bike. Other parts were on other bikes. I pointed to all the stuff that was mine and had them strip it. My frame had already been painted silver," Chen told me.

Not surprisingly, one of the men said he had bought Chen's bike from someone in the Civic Center. Chen just wanted his bike back, so he forked over $60. The guys handed him a pile of parts in return.

WHERE BIKES GO TO DIE

A few days after the trip to Golden Gate Park, I finally got around to doing what I should have done when my bike was stolen: file a police report. Frankly, I waited because I held out little hope the police would be of any help.

It's true few people get their bikes back through the police, but that's in part because most people don't try. In fact, the police are sitting on a cache of stolen bikes so big that it dwarfs the stock of any bike store in the city.

SFPD Lt. Tom Feney agreed to show it to me, so I trekked out to Hunters Point. The police stolen property room is located in an anonymous-looking warehouse in the Naval Shipyard. Feney ushered me through a metal door to the warehouse and then swept his hand through the air as if pointing out a beautiful panorama.

"There it is," he said.

Behind a 10-foot chain-link fence topped with razor wire, row upon row of bikes stretched along the floor of the warehouse. There were children's bikes with hot pink paint, $2,000 road bikes, and everything in between. In all, the police had about 500 stolen bikes in the warehouse. The bikes are found abandoned on the street, recovered from stings on drug houses, and removed from bike thieves when they are busted. Many of the bikes aren't stolen—they've been confiscated during arrests or are evidence in various cases. The department can't return the stolen bikes because the owners haven't reported them stolen. After holding them for 18 months, the police donate the bikes to charity.

I intently scanned up and down the rows looking for my bike. I didn't see it. My last, best chance for finding it had disappeared. My heart dropped knowing my Fuji Touring was gone. Feney ushered me out the door, and I began the long, slow walk back to the bus stop.

The most frustrating part is that it doesn't have to be this way. Police and bicycle groups said there are some simple steps city officials could take to cut down on bike theft, but the issue has long slipped through the cracks.

Officer Romeo de la Vega, who works the SFPD's Fencing Unit, said he proposed a bike registration system a few months ago, but it was shot down by the police brass. De la Vega said he was told there simply weren't enough officers available to staff the system. Under his plan cyclists would register their bike serial numbers with police. In return the cyclists would get a permanent decal to place on their bikes. De la Vega said this would discourage thieves from stealing bikes since it would be clear they were registered, and it would speed bike returns.

With police officials claiming there are few resources to combat bike theft, it seems logical they might reach out to the community for help. But officials with the SFBC report just the opposite.

"In the past we've tried to connect with the police to jointly tackle the problem, but we haven't had much luck. We don't even know who is handling bike thefts," Andy Thornley, the SFBC program director, said.

Thornley said the coalition is willing to use its membership to help police identify chop shops and fencing rings around the city. He said the police need to do a better job of going after the larger players in the bike theft world and the District Attorney's Office needs to take a tougher stance on prosecution.

Ultimately, Thornley said, enforcement is not the key to reducing bike theft. He said the city must make it easier for cyclists to park their bikes safely. The coalition is crafting legislation that would require all commercial buildings to allow cyclists to bring their bikes inside—something many currently prohibit. The coalition would also like to see bike parking lots spring up around the city, with attendants to monitor them.

Supervisor Chris Daly, who is an avid cyclist and has had six bikes stolen, said he is willing to help.

"It's clear we are not doing very much," Daly said. "I think if there were a push from bicyclists to do a better job, I would certainly work toward making theft more of a priority."

Discussion Questions

1. Describe the criminal underworld the author of this article visited.

2. How does law enforcement, including prosecutors, respond to petty crimes such as bike theft?

3. What is the author referring to in the section "Fast Food, Hot Bikes?"

6

Virginia Tech Shooting Leaves 33 Dead

By Christine Hauser and Anahad O'Connor

Incidents such as the shooting on the Virginia Tech campus in April 2007 demonstrate the power of human nature. Many asked how and why the shooter, student Seung-Hui Cho, could commit such an act. Conversely, the positive side of human nature became evident as stories of heroism emerged and nationwide support for the victims followed. We may never know exactly why the shooter acted as he did; however, we can take solace in the ability of the victims, and society in general to persevere and not let such violence have a continuous negative impact on our lives.

As a society, we'd like to think that all crimes can be prevented through effective policy. For instance, a policy to assess mental stability or gun control may prevent some dangerous individuals from threatening society. We like to believe that limiting access to guns will eliminate gun crime. Neither policy, used in this discussion because they pertain to the incident at Virginia Tech, can truly prevent all crime. Some say that Cho, who was declared mentally ill, shouldn't have been in society, and certainly shouldn't have had access to firearms. In reality, it is difficult to completely enforce all policies in a country known for its liberties and freedoms.

School shootings were prominent in the news in the late 1990s through the early part of the twenty-first century. For instance the Columbine (CO) school shootings led us to question whether or not our schools are safe. In response, there was an intense crackdown on student safety and, in the end, schools are safe. In fact, schools are very safe. To consider how safe schools really are, put aside the incident in Virginia and consider the last time you heard of a student being shot at school. These few incidents must be considered in light of the millions of students in schools every day.

The killing of students conjures up particular emotions not aroused by shootings that occur in a dark alley during a drug deal. Student-victims have not had a chance to fully begin their adult lives or careers simply because of the actions of troubled individuals. Schools are supposed to be places to better one's self; not a place to kill or be killed. For the large majority, schools are safe. Unfortunately, incidents such as Virginia Tech generate responses, and for better or for worse, we set stricter policies and reduced freedoms as we try to find the proper balance between crime control and individual rights. Such is the nature of crime and criminal justice.

Thirty-three people were killed today on the campus of Virginia Tech in what appears to be the deadliest shooting rampage in American history, according to federal law-enforcement officials. Many of the victims were students shot in a dorm and a classroom building.

"Today, the university was struck with a tragedy that we consider of monumental proportions," said the university's president, Charles Steger. The campus police chief said this evening that 15 people were wounded by the gunman, although there were other reports of higher numbers of injuries.

Witnesses described scenes of mass chaos and unimaginable horror as some students were lined up against a wall and shot. Others jumped out of windows to escape, or crouched on floors to take cover.

The killings occurred in two separate attacks on the campus in Blacksburg, Va. The first at around 7:15 A.M., when two people were shot and killed at a dormitory. More than two and a half hours later, 31 others, including the gunman, were shot and killed across campus in a classroom building, where some of the doors had been chained. Victims were found in different locations around the building.

The first attack started as students were getting ready for classes or were on their way there. The university did not evacuate the campus or notify students of that attack until several hours later.

As the rampage unfolded, details emerged from witnesses describing a gunman going room to room in a dormitory, Ambler Johnston Hall, and of gunfire later at Norris Hall, a science and engineering classroom building. When it was over, even sidewalks were stained with blood. Among those dead was the gunman, whose body was found along with victims in Norris Hall.

"Norris Hall is a tragic and sorrowful crime scene," said the campus police chief at Virginia Tech, Wendell Flinchum.

Chief Flinchum said the gunman took his own life. He said at a televised news briefing this evening that the police had a preliminary identification of the suspected gunman but they were not yet ready to release it. He said the gunman was not a student.

According to a federal law enforcement official, the gunman did not have identification and could not be easily identified visually because of the severity of an apparently self-inflicted wound to the head. He said investigators were trying to trace purchase records for two handguns found near the body.

At televised news conferences this afternoon and this evening, Chief Flinchum and Mr. Steger tried to explain why authorities did not act to secure the rest of the campus immediately after the first shooting.

Chief Flinchum said that initially officials thought that the shooting was "domestic," suggesting that it was between individuals who knew each other, and isolated to the dormitory. He said the campus was not shut down after the first shooting because authorities thought that the attacker may have left the campus, or even the state.

"We knew we had two people shot," he said. "We secured the building. We secured the crime scene." He later added: "We acted on the best information we had at the time."

Chief Flinchum said officers initially began investigating a "person of interest," as a result of the dormitory shootings. The person, a male, was described as a friend of one of the dorm victims, but Chief Flinchum said the police had not detained him.

At 9:45, police got another 911 call about shootings at Norris Hall, just as university officials were meeting to discuss the first shootings. "We were actually having a meeting about the earlier shootings when we learned that another shooting was underway," Mr. Steger told reporters Monday night. By the time officers arrived the shooting had stopped and the gunman had killed himself, the Chief said.

Police appeared to believe that the two shootings were related, but said they could not confirm that until they had the results of a ballistics analysis.

A parent of one student, Elaine Goss, said her son, Alec Calhoun, a junior engineering major, jumped out a second-story window in Norris Hall when the gunman entered his classroom.

She said that she first spoke to her son, "I couldn't understand him; it was like gibberish."

"It took a while to figure out shootings, lots of shootings, and that his whole class had jumped out the window," she said.

Ms. Goss said that her son hurt his back in the jump and went to the hospital.

Another student, Jessica Paulson, said she was on the fourth floor at Ambler Johnston Hall when the shootings occurred on the opposite side of the floor.

"You could hear two shots," one followed shortly by a second," recounted Ms. Paulson, who was preparing to go to an early class. Neither she nor most of the other students nearby understood what had happened until several hours later.

At least 17 Virginia Tech students were being treated for gunshot wounds and other injuries at Montgomery Regional Hospital, and four of them were in surgery, according to a hospital spokesperson. At Lewis-Gale Medical Center, in Salem, Va., four students and a staff member were treated for injuries. Two were in stable condition, and the conditions of the other three were described as "undetermined."

Officials said there may have been more injured and taken to other medical facilities.

The university has more than 25,000 full-time students on a campus that is spread over 2,600 acres.

The atmosphere on the Virginia Tech campus was desolate and preternaturally quiet by this afternoon. Students gathered in small groups, some crying, some talking quietly and others consoling each other.

Some students complained that they had not been notified of the first shooting on campus for more than two hours.

Kirsten Bernhards, 18, said she and many other students had no idea that a shooting had occurred when she left her dorm room in O'Shaughnessy Hall shortly before 10 A.M., more than two hours after the first shootings.

"I was leaving for my 10:10 film class," she said. "I had just locked the door and my neighbor said, 'did you check your email?'"

The university had, a few minutes earlier, sent out a bulletin warning students about an apparent shooter. But few students seemed to have any sense of urgency.

Ms. Bernhards said she walked toward her class, preoccupied with an upcoming exam and listening to music on her iPod. On the way, she said, she heard some loud cracks, and only later concluded they had been gunshots from the second round of shootings.

But even at that point, many students were walking around the campus with little if any sense of alarm.

It was only when Ms. Bernhards got close to Norris Hall, the second of two buildings where the shootings took place, that she realized something had gone wrong.

"I looked up and I saw at least 10 guards with assault rifles aiming at the main entrance of Norris," she recalled.

Up until today, the deadliest campus shooting in United States history was in 1966 at the University of Texas, where Charles Whitman climbed to the 28th-floor observation deck of a clock tower and opened fire, killing 16 people before he was gunned down by police. In the Columbine High attack in 1999, two teenagers killed 12 fellow students and a teacher before killing themselves.

While few confirmed details about the gunman and the motive were clear, students told reporters at WTKR, a local television station, that the gunman had been looking for his girlfriend, and at one of the locations he lined up some students and shot them all, according to Mike Mather, a reporter for the station.

President Bush offered condolences this afternoon to relatives of the victims, and said federal investigators would help the Virginia authorities in any way possible. "We hold the victims in our hearts; we lift them up in our prayers," Mr. Bush said at the White House.

President Bush was "horrified" at the news of the shooting, said Dana Perino, a White House spokeswoman, earlier in the day.

One student captured partial images, broadcast on CNN, using his cellphone video camera showing grainy dark-clad figures on the street outside of campus buildings. Popping sounds from the gunfire were audible.

"This place is in a state of panic," said a student who was interviewed on CNN, Shaver Deyerle. "Nobody knew what was going on at first."

He said that the shooting reminded him of the Columbine High School killings.

Today's shooting at Virginia Tech comes in the same week, eight years ago, as the shooting at Columbine on April 20, 1999.

The police were slowly evacuating students from campus buildings and all classes have been canceled.

Families were told to reunite with students at the Inn at Virginia Tech, a facility of conference space and hotel rooms. The university community was told to assemble on Tuesday at the Cassell Coliseum to start to deal with the tragedy, a campus statement said.

Images on CNN showed the police with assault rifles swarming several buildings, sirens blaring in the background and a voice over a loudspeaker warning people across the campus to take cover in buildings and stay away from windows. Many students could be seen crouching on floors in classrooms and dormitories.

The police evacuated students and faculty, many of them to local hotels, and witnesses said that some students were seen scrambling out of windows to get to safety. A Montgomery County school official said that all schools throughout the county were being shut down.

The shooting was the second in the past year that forced officials to lock down the campus. In August of 2006, an escaped jail inmate shot and killed a deputy sheriff and an unarmed security guard at a nearby hospital before the police caught him in the woods near the university.

The capture ended a manhunt that led to the cancellation of the first day of classes at Virginia Tech and shut down most businesses and municipal buildings in Blacksburg. The accused gunman, William Morva, is facing capital murder charges.

Discussion Questions

1. How does the Virginia Tech shooting incident rank among the deadliest school shootings? Describe other tragic school shootings.
2. After reading the account of the Virginia Tech shootings, do you see any precautionary steps that could have been taken by law enforcement and the university to minimize the harms?
3. What steps can be taken to prevent school shootings in the future?

7

Duke Lacrosse Players Relieved Case has 'Closure'

By The Associated Press

Sensationalized criminal events occur on a regular basis in society. The nature of the incident and/or the individuals involved separate sensationalized cases from ordinary cases. Examples of sensationalized incidents include Scott Peterson killing his pregnant wife Lacey Peterson, the infamous case involving professional football star O. J. Simpson, and the conviction and incarceration of media mogul Martha Stewart. More recently, rape, kidnapping, and sexual assault charges were filed against Duke University lacrosse players following a complaint by a stripper hired to perform at one of the team's parties. The case contained the ingredients necessary to become sensational, and needless to say, it captured public attention. Charges against the student athletes were ultimately dropped following the disclosure of DNA evidence that exonerated the students. Adding intrigue to the case were charges of prosecutorial misconduct.

Unfortunately, the offenses involved in sensationalized crimes occur relatively often, yet they go largely unnoticed by the public. Something about particular events captures the public's attention, and leads to them becoming sensationalized. The variables that attracted public attention to the case involving the Duke lacrosse players involved race, gender, and class. The students, who attended prestigious Duke University, were different from the alleged victim in many facets. Particularly, the alleged victim in this case was an African American female stripper. Add to this case an unethical district attorney and extensive media coverage, and you have a sensationalized incident.

Why don't all crimes receive as much attention? Why are murders typically the top story on the local news? The research literature on media depiction of crime is filled with evidence that crime is presented in a distorted manner which in turn shapes the public's perception of crime. The public's fear of crime is impacted by what's on the news. One must keep in mind that the media have no obligation to present crime as it typically occurs, however. Would you stay tuned to the news if the teaser prior to commercial involved a news story about a stolen car radio? Probably not, though, you may be interested to hear about the serial killer who struck again. The media are interested in appeasing viewer desires. We who watch or read the news contribute to the problem through our interest in the atypical.

Like all other sensationalized crimes, the Duke lacrosse story had many interesting angles that separated it from the many other crimes that occurred that day, including the corrupt actions of the district attorney Mike Nifong. Among other things, Nifong failed to disclose the DNA test results that showed no involvement by the lacrosse players. Had the results not been disclosed, the players may well have spent much time in prison. In this regard, this case highlights the power maintained by prosecutors and the need to keep prosecutorial discretion in check.

While capturing our attention for some time, the Duke lacrosse incident highlighted the power of prosecutorial discretion; the influence of false accusations; the significance of the emerging use of DNA analyses in criminal justice; and issues pertaining to race, class, and gender. It also fed society's need for sensationalized crime stories.

R ALEIGH, N.C.—Nearly a year after calling the rape accusations he and two Duke lacrosse teammates faced nothing but "fantastic lies," David Evans again stood before the cameras and proclaimed his innocence.

This time, there was no room for doubt.

North Carolina Attorney General Roy Cooper didn't just dismiss all the remaining criminal charges against Evans, Reade Seligmann and Collin Finnerty. He took the extra step of declaring the players innocent—the victims of a "tragic rush to accuse" by a rogue prosecutor who could be disbarred for his actions.

"This case shows the enormous consequences of overreaching by a prosecutor," Cooper said.

The attorney general took over the case in January [2007] from Durham County District Attorney Mike Nifong after the state bar charged Nifong with ethics violations over his handling of the case. On Wednesday, Cooper said the state's investigation into a stripper's claim that she was sexually assaulted at a team party last spring found nothing to corroborate her story.

The investigation, he said, "led us to the conclusion that no attack occurred."

The dismissal brought an abrupt end to a yearlong case that heightened long-standing racial tensions in Durham and ignited a debate of race, sex and class at the private, elite university. The woman is black and attended nearby North Carolina Central University, a historically black school; all three Duke players are white.

In the uproar over the allegations, Duke canceled the rest of the team's 2006 season, the lacrosse coach resigned under fire and a schism opened between faculty who supported the athletes and those who accused them of getting away with loutish frat-boy behavior for too long.

"It's been 395 days since this nightmare began. And finally today it's coming to a closure," said Evans, his voice breaking at one point. "We're just as innocent today as we were back then. Nothing has changed. The facts don't change."

The notice of dismissal prepared by the attorney general's office for each player declared "this individual is innocent."

Joseph Cheshire, who represented Evans, said defense attorneys will soon begin work to have their clients' arrest record expunged. He called Nifong "a man who had not a care in the world about justice, but only about his personal agenda."

Finnerty's parents, speaking in an interview aired Thursday on CBS's "The Early Show," said the room broke into cheers when they heard the attorney general declare the three innocent.

"He was crying. We were crying, hugging," father Kevin Finnerty said. "I think it was just such a sensitive moment, it just blew us away."

The past year had been a nightmare for the families as well as the three men and their former teammates, Finnerty's mother, Mary Ellen Finnerty, said.

"Many times, I'd say to the lawyers, 'I feel like there's a mad man chasing my son down the street and there's nothing I can do to stop him,'" she said. "He was willing to use these boys for his own gain."

Nifong was out of town and could not immediately be reached for comment. But his lawyer, David Freedman, said: "If further investigation showed the boys were innocent, he would be in agreement with what the attorney general's office decided to do."

Evans, Seligmann and Finnerty were indicted last spring on charges of rape, kidnapping and sexual offense after the woman told police she was assaulted in the bathroom at an off-campus house during a March 2006 team party where she had been hired to perform. Nifong dropped the rape charges in December after the accuser said she was no longer certain she had been penetrated.

Cooper offered no explanation for why the woman told such a story and would not discuss her mental health. However, he said no charges will be brought against her, saying she "may actually believe" the many different stories she told.

"We believe it is in the best interest of justice not to bring charges," he said.

The accuser's whereabouts were not immediately known. The Associated Press generally does not identify accusers in sex-crime cases.

Seligmann thanked his lawyers for sparing him from 30 years in prison for a "hoax" and complained that society has lost sight of the presumption of innocence.

"This entire experience has opened my eyes up to a tragic world of injustice," he said.

Finnerty's attorney, Wade Smith, told CBS Thursday that television reporter Ed Bradley's interview with the players on "60 Minutes" had helped the world see the three as human beings. Others criticized the media for not pressing Nifong for evidence.

Nifong withdrew from the case in January after the North Carolina bar charged him with making misleading and inflammatory comments to the media about the athletes under suspicion. The bar later added more serious charges of withholding evidence from defense attorneys and lying to the court.

Among other things, Nifong called the athletes "a bunch of hooligans" and declared DNA evidence would identify the guilty. He was also accused of withholding the results of lab tests that found DNA from several men—none of them lacrosse team members—on the accuser's underwear and body.

Portraying Nifong as a "rogue prosecutor," Cooper called for the passage of a law that would allow the North Carolina Supreme Court to remove a district attorney where justice demands it. He declined to say whether he believes Nifong should be disbarred.

When asked about the prospect of filing some sort of civil suit against Nifong, defense attorneys didn't rule it out.

"There's almost always been almost absolute immunity for anything a prosecutor says in court," said Stan Goldman, a professor at Loyola Law School in Los Angeles. "Those rules are usually off the table when we're talking about faking evidence or conspiring to hide evidence."

Duke suspended Seligmann, 21, of Essex Fells, N.J., and Finnerty, 20, of Garden City, N.Y., after their arrest. Both were invited to return to campus this year, but neither accepted. Evans, 24, of Bethesda, Md., graduated the day before he was indicted in May.

Former Duke lacrosse coach Mike Pressler, who resigned under fire and is now lacrosse coach at Bryant University in Smithfield, R.I., said he was convinced early on that his former players were innocent.

"Two days after this happened, I knew what the truth was," he said. "When you say you believe in somebody, when you say you believe the truth, you stand by them."

Discussion Questions

1. What factors contributed to the high-profile nature of the Duke lacrosse incident?

2. How was prosecutorial discretion misused in this case?

3. Do you believe the outcome of this case would have been different if the defendants were poor, inner-city young adults who were unable to hire private attorneys? Why or why not?

8

O. J. Simpson's Book and TV Special Are Canceled

By Bill Carter and Edward Wyatt

Just when you thought you'd heard the end of O. J. Simpson, he once again appeared in the news and of course generated controversy. Simpson agreed with the News Company, which owns the Fox television network and the book publisher HarperCollins, to write a book and sit for a broadcast interview detailing a hypothetical account of how he might have murdered his ex-wife and her friend years ago. Word of the projects generated much public outrage, leading to the cancellation of both projects.

After revisiting its decision to go forward with the projects, the News Corporation apologized to the families of the victims and ordered the recall and destruction of books that had been sent to book stores. They also agreed to not release the video. The initial decision to proceed with the projects did not come as a surprise to many, as the Fox network has a reputation for pushing the limits of broadcasting and sensationalism, particularly regarding crime. The network is responsible for bringing COPS, the show that lets viewers basically ride along with police officers for a look at "real" policing, into living rooms each night. Many viewers, however, may fail to realize that a great deal of editing goes on behind the scenes, and be left with a distorted view of crime and police practices. Fox has also broadcast shows on amazing police chases, deaths, and the like.

Simpson, who is often the target of public disdain, earlier moved from California to Florida to protect his assets from a civil judgment that required him to pay $33.5 million to the families of the murdered victims. It is likely that Simpson still earned money from the book and interview deal, because it was the decision of the News Corporation to cancel the projects. This leads to the controversy regarding profiting off of crime. It is illegal in some states for convicted criminals to profit from their crimes through writing books, granting interviews, and the like. However, Simpson was acquitted of criminal charges, and thus was free to offer his input on the unfortunate situation.

The Simpson case fits the mold of sensationalized crimes, because the individual charged with the crime had much fame and notoriety. Like other sensationalized criminal events, this one keeps reappearing. Eleven years after the event, there was still enough discussion and interest that both a book and interview were scheduled by a leading media company. This begs the question, why are we so intrigued by sensationalized events? Perhaps we like to humanize others who have been put on a glamorized pedestal. Simpson was a Heisman trophy winner, all-star professional football player, and actor. Seeing him and other celebrities caught up in the law strangely makes life seem better for some individuals. In this situation, however, it appears that the public has had enough. We've heard too much about O. J., and providing him the opportunity to cash in didn't appeal to us. In fact, public disgust generated the pressure necessary to prevent us from hearing from him, which is atypical of sensationalized events.

Simpson resurfaced in the news when, in September 2007, he was arrested for a series of felonies including robbery with a deadly weapon, assault with a deadly weapon, and other serious charges following an "incident" in Las Vegas. Given recent developments, it is unlikely, although not out of the question, that O. J. will be granted a book contract and an interview to share this story.

Bowing to intense pressure both outside and inside the company, the News Corporation today canceled its plans to publish a book and broadcast an interview with O. J. Simpson in which he was to give a hypothetical account of how he might have murdered his ex-wife, Nicole Brown Simpson, and her friend Ronald Goldman.

The company was responding to a week's worth of ferocious criticism that included threats of boycotts of advertisers who might sponsor the television broadcast on the Fox network, refusals by stations to carry the program, open opposition from television hosts like Bill O'Reilly, on the Fox News Channel—which, like Fox, is owned by the News Corporation—and statements by stores that they might not stock the book, which was titled "If I Did It." The book was to be published by HarperCollins, also owned by News Corporation.

Rupert Murdoch, the chairman of News Corporation, issued a statement today announcing that the television show would not be broadcast and the book would not be published.

"I and senior management agree with the American public that this was an ill-considered project," Mr. Murdoch said. "We are sorry for any pain this has caused the families of Ron Goldman and Nicole Brown-Simpson."

Any projects involving Mr. Simpson have met with public outrage in the 11 years since he was acquitted of the murders in one of the most covered criminal trials in American history. He was later found responsible for the deaths in a civil trial and ordered to pay $33.5 million in restitution to the families of the victims.

Mr. Simpson, a former football star and actor, moved from his home in Los Angeles to Florida partly to protect his assets from that civil judgment. He has only occasionally appeared in public in recent years and had never stopped declaring himself innocent of the murder charges.

Today's decision to cancel the twin Simpson projects was greeted with widespread expressions of relief. Mike Angelos, a vice president of Pappas Telecasting Companies, the owner of four Fox-affiliated stations, which had informed the network Friday that its stations did not intend to broadcast the interview, released a statement today calling the network's decision "a victory for the people who spoke out." The statement concluded: "This special would have benefited only O. J. Simpson, who deserves nothing but contempt, and certainly no benefit."

Numerous staff members at News Corporation, and the Fox network, all of whom spoke on the condition of anonymity because they had been ordered not to comment about the Simpson deal, said they were thankful the company had abandoned the project. A News Corporation executive said that internally the project had been considered a disaster for the company.

Another executive said that the company had badly miscalculated the public's tolerance for anything having to do with Mr. Simpson, thinking enough time had passed for Mr. Simpson to be considered less a pariah by the public.

Neither of the two top News Corporation executives would comment beyond the statement today. Mr. Murdoch was said to be in Australia on business and not available. A News Corporation spokesman said that Peter Chernin, the president of News Corporation and the executive with direct authority over the Fox network, would have no comment.

No one at the company would discuss on the record the exact details about how the project had been accepted in the first place. But one News Corporation executive who was involved in the

"O.J. Simpson's Book and TV Special Are Cancelled" by Bill Carter and Edward Wyatt, *The New York Times*, November 20, 2006. Copyright © 2006 by The New York Times Co. Reprinted with permission.

negotiations about the book and the television special said that Mr. Murdoch had been aware of both deals before they were announced publicly last week.

The executive said in a telephone interview that payments to representatives for Mr. Simpson would probably still have to be made for his participation in the book and the television interviews.

Standard publishing contracts call for a percentage of an author's advance, usually up to 50 percent, to be paid when a contract is signed, and for the remainder to be paid when the finished book is accepted by the publisher. The executive said that Mr. Simpson's book is covered by a standard publishing contract.

In an interview last week, Judith Regan, the publisher, said her imprint, ReganBooks, which is owned by HarperCollins, had signed a contract with "a manager who represents a third party" who owned the rights to Mr. Simpson's account.

Because News Corporation and ReganBooks decided on their own to cancel the book and the television special, that money is likely to still have to be paid.

A spokesman said Ms. Regan declined to comment today on the book's withdrawal.

Erin Crum, a spokeswoman for HarperCollins, said today that some copies of the books have already been shipped to stores. Those books will be recalled and destroyed, she said.

Last Friday, Borders announced that it would donate the net proceeds from sales of Mr. Simpson's book to a nonprofit organization for victims of domestic violence.

Ann Binkley, a spokeswoman for Borders, said she received a call from HarperCollins this afternoon notifying her that the book would be recalled. No explanation was offered for the decision. "I think everybody knows why," Ms. Binkley said.

Many bookstores, including Book Soup in West Hollywood, which had ordered eight copies, had placed orders for the book but had not yet received copies by this afternoon.

Still, the rights to the book could be sold to another publisher, said the News Corporation executive involved in the book negotiations.

There is precedent for a recalled book to be sold to another publisher and then to the public. In 1990, Vintage Books, a division of Random House, bought the rights to "American Psycho," a novel by Bret Easton Ellis, after the original publisher, Simon & Schuster, withdrew from publishing it because of the novel's graphically violent content.

As for the television interview, it could also be offered to other television outlets, although at least two other networks. ABC and NBC, have reported that they turned it down before it was accepted by Fox. Still, Ms. Regan—who conducted the on-camera interview with Mr. Simpson and is presumed to own the rights to it—could still seek a sale either to a cable channel or even a pay-per-view company.

The fact that the interview already exists on tape, executives at Fox and News Corporation said, means that it is likely to turn up somewhere, perhaps on the Internet.

But it will not show up on the Fox network. That pleased many of those who had opposed the broadcast.

Scott Blumenthal, an executive vice president of Lin Television Corporation, which had already announced it would not broadcast the Simpson interview on its five Fox affiliates, said in a telephone interview from the company's headquarters in Providence, R.I., "Our actions spoke for themselves. At this point, the discussion is moot. We just felt the program was inappropriate for our markets."

Asked if he supported the cancellation of the interview by Fox, Mr. Blumenthal said: "Only Fox knows whether or not they did the right thing."

Discussion Questions

1. Do you believe the News Corporation should have published O. J.'s book and aired the interview regardless of public backlash? Why or why not?

2. What factors did the News Corporation consider in deciding to cancel plans for airing the interview with O. J. and distributing his book?

3. Some states prevent convicted criminals from profiting from their crimes. O. J., however, was acquitted in criminal court, though he was successfully sued by the victims' families. Regardless of legal requirements, should O. J. surrender his earnings from the projects to the families?

II

Policing

INTRODUCTION

The police are charged with serving and protecting the public. It says so on the doors of most police cruisers. Such vague tasks can be broken down into three primary duties: law enforcement, service, and order maintenance. Finding the proper balance between these tasks and performing them according to accepted standards is sometimes easier said than done. Nevertheless, the police provide an invaluable service to society.

The public is intrigued with police work. Televisions shows such as *COPS* and *CSI*, and various big-screen movies have captured the public's imagination. These and other depictions of police provide the public access to the issues faced and generated by the police. We hear much about the controversy surrounding the police, yet little about the benefits police offer our everyday lives.

Part II covers eight distinct topics pertaining to the police. The opening selection, "Help Wanted," highlights the difficulties associated with hiring police personnel. Departments across the country are scrambling to find suitable candidates to fill job openings. The need to identify, recruit, and select appropriate personnel is significantly important to police work, as the consequences involved in policing can be a matter of life or death.

The article "Katrina, One Year Later" demonstrates the difficulties faced by the New Orleans Police Department following the devastation caused by Hurricane Katrina. We take for granted that the police will assist us, even during natural disasters. However, we must remember that police officers have personal lives and maintain a concern for safety much like we do. How does a department pick up the pieces and serve and protect the public in the wake of devastation? A look back at the events following the hurricane sheds light on the many challenges associated with police work.

Police departments and law enforcement agencies in general have often been criticized for a lack of interagency coordination: crime fighting and prevention efforts would be more effective if there was greater cooperation and coordination among police departments. The article "Super Bowl XXXIX" highlights the type of cooperation needed in law enforcement. Hosting a major event such as a Super Bowl requires years of preparation. From a security and law enforcement perspective there is a demonstrated need to ensure the safety of all; accordingly, it takes the efforts and assistance of many public service providers. The article provides a refreshing look at cooperation in law enforcement as it documents the security and law enforcement preparation associated with Super Bowl XXXIX.

Police officers are expected to perform many duties in addition to law enforcement. For instance, as first responders to crime scenes, they need to be trained in emergency response. The recent adoption by many police departments of a community-oriented approach has required the police to wear numerous hats, and has demonstrated the benefits of police departments incorporating the assistance from others in their work. The article "Forensic Nursing" highlights how different groups can provide great assistance to policing and the criminal justice system in general.

Racial profiling is one of the more controversial police tactics. For better or for worse, extra-legal variables such as race, class, age, and gender are considered by practitioners in each component of the criminal justice system. For instance, age is considered regarding one's ability to determine right from wrong. Race, however, has been a more controversial variable. Recently the practice of racial profiling has been called into question as unethical because individuals are being identified as potential threats based solely on race. Some police officers argue that consideration of race can assist crime control efforts; however, others suggest racial profiling is unethical and leads to the perpetuation of injustices against minorities.

Police officers have a great deal of discretion in their duties. Decisions regarding whether to stop, detain, or arrest an individual are common in policing. However, the stakes are raised when the decision involves whether or not to shoot someone. The article "Mayor Meets Groom's Family in NYPD Slaying" addresses the controversy that surrounds officers' use of discretion. Officers in New York were charged with serious crimes following what they argue was a justified use of deadly force. Others, however, view the officers' use of discretion differently. The article highlights race relations as they pertain to police behaviors and controversial police practices in addition to officers' use of discretion.

Would you agree it's worse for a police officer to break the law than it is for a citizen? Why? A strong argument could be made that criminal cops are hypocrites in addition to law violators. Addressing police corruption has long challenged police administrators. Much of the problem stems from the reactive approach often taken by police departments: waiting until something bad happens and then reacting. The article "Early Detection of the Problem Officer" comments on a more proactive approach to identifying potentially corrupt officers. Early detection could have many benefits, not the least of which are enhanced public safety, fiscal prudence for the city avoiding civil litigation, and improved public perception of the police.

The final selection of Part II looks to the future of policing. The article "Policing the Future" provides insights from respected leaders on the future direction of policing. Understanding what the future holds allows law enforcement agents to avoid potential pitfalls and direct resources toward a more promising tomorrow. The challenge, however, is to best forecast the future and react accordingly. The article provides guidance to police departments shaping their goals and practices while anticipating the future.

The articles chosen for Part II are timely and comment on the state of modern policing. Through understanding current, critical issues, readers will have a better idea of what policing entails. Historically, our perceptions of the police were largely based on our interactions with officers and media accounts of officer practices. Unfortunately, many of our encounters with the police come under discouraging situations, for instance, after you've been victimized or perhaps because you're a suspect in a crime. The selections in Part II attempt to better shape our perceptions of the police, particularly in light of the many challenges they face on a daily basis, and the continued evolution of policing.

9

Help Wanted

By Jack Dunphy

People become police officers for a variety of reasons. Some enjoy the variety and/or spontaneity associ-ated with the job; others like the salary and benefits, helping people, changing society, and the level of job security that comes with the position. Currently, however, police departments nationwide are strug-gling to fill vacancies, as noted in this article. In response, police recruiters are reaching far and wide to attract suitable candidates.

The attractiveness of a position in policing varies based on several factors, not the least of which is the opportunity for employment in other areas. When employment opportunities are more abundant in society, police departments face difficulty in finding candidates. In times of high unemployment, policing often becomes an attractive option. Currently the war in Iraq has depleted the number of avail-able officers. Furthermore, the number of federal law enforcement positions has increased as federal law enforcement agencies expand their workforce with concern for homeland security. Fortunately, there is hope in sight, as veterans with law enforcement experience return from the war and assume positions in policing.

The need for qualified officers comes at an interesting time in policing. The educational require-ments of police departments are increasing as more agencies that have adopted the community-oriented approach seek college graduates. Unfortunately, this requirement limits the applicant pool. Questions currently challenging police departments around the Unites States include: Should departments forgo the requirement of a college education for police officers? Should they require a set number of college hours instead? Lowering the hiring standards is seen by some as a defeatist and dangerous approach, yet it may be the most practical option for some departments in need of personnel. Requirements con-cerning prior criminal record, history of drug use, and educational levels are all subject to change in response to the need for candidates. Departments are hesitant to lower their hiring standards for many reasons, not the least of which includes the increasing number of lawsuits filed in response to alleged officer misconduct.

Some departments offer incentives for employment instead of lowering standards. Signing bonuses and higher salaries are popular with some police departments seeking to fill vacancies. Financial incentives, however, pose several problems, including experienced officers becoming envious and departments not maintaining the resources to raise salaries. Raising salaries can come at the expense of public protection, given that paying officers more results in cutbacks in other areas (e.g., technology and training).

The onus is on police recruiters to identify qualified candidates and entice them to assume a career in policing with their department. Many big-city departments must compete with suburban departments with greater funding and less crime. Recruiters must more proactively seek candidates by attending college recruitment fairs, advertising in nontraditional outlets, and adopting a more sales-like attitude. Although departments are now struggling to fill positions, history suggests policing will again become a popular career choice for many.

Are you looking for a job with low pay? Does the idea of working miserable working hours appeal to you? How about working weekends and holidays? Is the daily risk to life and limb on your checklist of must-haves for your next job? If so, the New York Police Department has a job for you.

Last month Mayor Michael Bloomberg and Police Commissioner Ray Kelly announced an expansion plan that will put 1,200 more officers on the streets of New York. The plan calls for the hiring of 800 cops and an additional 400 civilian employees who would take over desk jobs currently held by police officers. The proposed expansion comes after a five-year decline in the number of officers on the NYPD, from 40,700 in 2001 to about 37,000 today. Bloomberg and Kelly hope the added officers will keep the city's crime on the downward trend seen over the past several years. The overall crime rate for the city is down about two percent this year and 24 percent from five years ago. There were 540 murders committed in New York in 2005, a disturbing number, certainly, but take a moment to consider that this is less than half the number seen in 1995 and about one quarter of the figure seen in the early 90s during the dystopian days of the Dinkins administration.

These are impressive accomplishments, to be sure, but there are signs that New York's crime may be on the rise. Thirty-four of the city's 76 police precincts have seen an increase in crime since the beginning of this year, with one precinct in Queens up almost 20 percent. Perhaps it has finally occurred to Bloomberg and Kelly that they can't expect crime to continue dropping while thousands of cops leave the job and go unreplaced.

There's just one flaw in their planned expansion: there aren't enough people who want the job. The *New York Daily News* reported that the number of applicants for the NYPD's February 2006 test was down 31 percent from the year before, making it difficult for the department even to keep pace with normal attrition, let alone expand the ranks. The Daily News story also caught Bloomberg fudging with the numbers when it came to police compensation. The mayor's press release dangled a nice, fat carrot in front of prospective police recruits: "The 800 new recruits, over the course of their police academy training (6 months) and their first six months on the force, will receive an average total cash compensation of $35,000, plus an additional $1,000 uniform allowance. By their sixth year on the force, the average total cash compensation will rise to $72,000, plus an additional $1,000 uniform allowance."

Not so fast, Mr. Mayor. "The actual salary after one year of employment is $28,900," says the Daily News. "To reach the higher number, the administration added in holiday pay, overtime, shift differential and uniform allowance." Only officers who work between 4 P.M. and 8 A.M. receive the shift differential, and overtime is not always available in some precincts. Indeed, according to Policepay.net, the NYPD ranks 44th on its index of the country's 200 largest police departments. When adjusted for cost of living it drops to 157th place. The departments in Yonkers, Syracuse, Rochester, and Buffalo all rank far higher when cost of living is factored in.

"I'm told by our personnel bureau that it will be a challenge [to hire the 800 officers]," Commissioner Kelly told the Daily News. "They believe that they can hire these classes of 2,000 both in July and next January. I can tell you one thing: We're not lowering our standards in any way, shape or form to reach those numbers."

And if that's true, more power to him. But other police departments are finding that lowering their standards is exactly what's required to fill their vacancies. *The Washington Post* reported Monday that police departments across the country are having trouble attracting applicants. According to the Post, more than 80 percent of the nation's 17,000 law enforcement agencies are

"Help Wanted" by Jack Denphy, *National Review*, April 4, 2006. © 2006 by National Review Online, www.nationalreview.com. Reprinted by permission.

finding it difficult to keep their police officer positions filled. My own Los Angeles Police Department, for example, has more than 700 vacancies, and even at full strength, it has about half as many officers per capita as New York City.

"I was just at a conference of police chiefs," LAPD Chief William Bratton told the Post. "It was all everybody was talking about."

The Post cited economic factors, changing demographics, and societal changes as reasons that police jobs are going begging. "The wars in Iraq and Afghanistan have siphoned off public-service-minded people to the military," the story says. "Hundreds of law enforcement officers have handed in their badges to take higher-paying positions in the booming homeland security industry."

And maybe all of that is true, but neither the Post story nor any other commentary I've seen on the subject has explored a big reason why cops are walking away from their jobs and potential applicants are looking elsewhere: politics.

Most people who enter police work do so, at least in part, out of an obligation to serve their communities. I, for example, might have taken my college degree and gone into some line of work that would have provided greater financial rewards, but I grew up here in Los Angeles and dreamed of joining the LAPD as early as grade school. Many of my colleagues grew up with the same dream. But my colleagues and I know, just as cops in New York and elsewhere know, that if we go out on the streets tomorrow and get into a scrape that brings down media attention on our heads, the city we serve will turn its back on us before we can drive back to the police station. This is particularly true if the incident carries even a hint of racial overtones.

Witness the ordeal endured here in Los Angeles by John Hatfield, the LAPD officer fired after being shown on television hitting a fleeing car thief with a flashlight. Though the car thief was injured only slightly, the LAPD treated Hatfield like a leper for over a year before finally firing him. And now Officer Steve Garcia, who shot and killed a 13-year-old who tried to run him down with a stolen car, faces the prospect of being fired despite being cleared in the shooting by the district attorney, an internal LAPD inquiry, and Chief Bratton himself. And yet they wonder why the LAPD can't fill its vacancies.

There are similarly dispiriting stories all across the country. No one comes into police work for the money. All we ask for is a decent living and to be treated fairly when things get dicey. Sadly, cops and potential cops are discovering this is too much to ask. Can higher crime be far behind?

Discussion Questions

1. Discuss why police departments are struggling to fill job vacancies.
2. What can be done to address the shortage of qualified police officers?
3. In light of recent decreasing crime rates, do we need more police officers? Discuss why or why not.

10

Katrina, One Year Later . . .

By Ann Wilder and James Arey

Police work does not exist in a vacuum. Officers and departments are constantly faced with changes and unexpected events. Such instability and uncertainty attracts some individuals to the field. It also tests the departments' and officers' ability to adequately respond to challenges. As noted in this selection, Hurricane Katrina provided a true test of the New Orleans Police Department's ability to respond to a traumatic incident.

Emile Durkheim earlier used the term "anomie" to describe a state of normlessness. The city of New Orleans was in a true state of anomie following Hurricane Katrina. Many people lost their lives, homes, and possessions, and life was turned upside down for many. In times of trouble, we often turn to the police for assistance, the period following the natural disaster in New Orleans was no different. As public servants, the police were called upon to address a wide array of issues.

In such an uncertain time, police officers assume the identity of those who can "fix things," or "have the answers." In reality, police officers are human beings just like you and me. They have the title of "police officer" and "public servant;" however, they are simply doing a job, and their home life is just as important as the next person's. In times of natural disasters, they need to consider their own personal safety, their family's security, and our well-being, and these considerations may sometimes conflict with one another.

Police leadership becomes notably important in times of crises. There is a close-knit society within policing, and leadership guides, directs, and dictates officer performance. It is often said that "the apple doesn't fall far from the tree," and leadership within policing is significantly influential. Officers look for guidance from other officers, and arguably even more so from their leaders. Fortunately, the leadership that remained in place during Hurricane Katrina provided a great sense of stability for the New Orleans Police Department.

It is difficult to train police officers to respond to natural disasters. For instance, not many people anticipated the chaos and disaster in New Orleans following the hurricane. Though officers can be taught in a classroom, nobody really knows what challenges will accompany a natural disaster. It is particularly difficult to anticipate how the public will respond to the situation. Unfortunately, a few individuals found the chaos following Katrina an ample opportunity to commit crime, which, needless to say, made a troubling situation worse.

The New Orleans police officers should be commended for their ability to function following Hurricane Katrina. Their response demonstrated once again the ability of police officers to respond to traumatic incidents. The officers who put their lives on the line to help others should be recognized, much like the public support for the New York City police officers in the wake of the terrorist attacks in

New York in 2001. Furthermore, the department's response to the situation also provides information for other departments to consider as part of their emergency response training.

The New Orleans Police Department continues to fight its way back from the devastation of Hurricane Katrina. Now, in the midst of the 2006 hurricane season, officers still are displaced, the police headquarters is located in trailers, and only a few sections of the city are fully functioning. In spite of the incredible odds against them, officers in the department remain on the job and plan to be better prepared for the storms to come.

The rising waters set the priorities for us last time. We had no time to give any thought to anything but saving people before they were swept away. The men and women of the department on the job on Aug. 29, 2005, instinctively knew that the decisions they made that day would stay with them forever. Responses were immediate. There was no thought to personal safety or outcome. The only reason none of us died was because of teamwork. During the aftermath of Katrina, most officers pushed emotions down, aside, or away.

About three months after Katrina, officers were asked to complete a survey from the Centers for Disease Control and Prevention. Out of the 912 officers who completed the survey, 55% said their homes were not inhabitable, 69% were currently separated from their immediate families, 67% had upper respiratory problems, cough, or sinus congestion, 54% had skin rashes, and 45% were experiencing some form of post traumatic stress or depression.

Captain John Bryson, commander of the Public Information Office, said, "We are getting back to police work. The department suffered such a heavy loss of our facilities that it set back our operations considerably. Individual commanders are being called upon to motivate and keep their people focused in a positive direction—despite all of the distractions from the destruction."

Bryson continues, "It is difficult for an officer to come out of their FEMA trailer, go to work and act like nothing is happening in their personal life, but a professional attitude impacts performance—and we have to maintain our professional attitude."

In the post-Katrina environment, the job of each officer is more difficult because officers have to manage customer contact in a professional way while having to deal with their own families being separated, houses and personal belongings being destroyed, opportunities to earn extra income through details no longer exists, and the entire future of their hometown hangs in the balance between insurance companies and government agencies.

Bryson explains, "No one calls the police when good things are happening. Customers are angry and upset when they have a need for the police. These emotions are running higher in the midst of all of the destruction and uncertainty." Bryson discusses the bad press that the department received in the wake of some officers leaving their post and others being accused of looting. "More importantly than what people say about us is what we say about ourselves."

Captain Harry Mendoza, commander of the Traffic Division, said a city with no traffic lights due to lack of power posed major problems. "Our safety signals were completely knocked out for months after the storm. We were very pleased with the response of our community. People became more cautious and adjusted their driving to four-way stops. People actually raised their awareness and increased their ability to manage their own personal safety."

Mendoza said his officers quickly adapted. "We practiced adaptation, not change. Successful commanders standardized the daily routines, provided structure and certainty in a chaotic environment." Mendoza continues to work with traffic officers to be patient with drivers who are totally stressed and exhausted. "A normal traffic stop should take about 10 minutes, but citizens are upset about everything and vent to our traffic guys. There is a lot of depression and suffering. It affects everyone."

"Katrina, One Year Later . . ." by Ann Wilder and James Arey, *Law and Order*, April 2007. Reprinted with permission of Reprint Management Services.

Captain Jeff Winn, commander of Special Operations Division, explained the importance of having a plan and having command in place. "The only people who survived this thing are people who had a plan and leaders who were not afraid to lead. Our officers are men and women who count on their rank to take charge and make quick, solid decisions. The plan we had for Katrina worked. SOD was able to save every vehicle in our particular fleet."

Winn continues to look ahead and has requested Katrina equipment, i.e., swim fins, masks or goggles, boats, underwater lights and other gear that works in and around water. Though few of these items appeared on the department's equipment list before Katrina, Winn believes it should be standard equipment now. Winn also believes that his tactical team should do water-borne training.

"Leadership made the difference," he said. "The difference between a great job and an adequate job is leadership. This is even more important in a crisis like this. It was not an option to let people down."

Because of the complete loss of communication systems, access to equipment and the general chaos that ruled in the aftermath of Katrina, NOPD is compiling its own disaster response plan. These plans coordinate with the overall emergency response plan devised by the city, but officers insist that Katrina "taught us that we better be able to take care of ourselves."

The federal response took six days. Bryson said, "I have met with business managers and hotels. I have chosen alternate locations and made arrangements for enough supplies to sustain life for seven to 10 days." Because Bryson (who was captain in the Fifth District at the time of Katrina) lost his entire fleet, he had to rely on 25 years of training to improvise and adapt.

Not only does Bryson maintain a response plan for his officers, he has an evacuation plan for his family. "It is harder to focus on my job if I have no idea where my family is or if they are safe. The officers that didn't prepare . . . their lives fell apart."

A general consensus throughout the department is that the job has returned to normal police work, but the officers have fewer tools with which to work. Conditions are worse for the most part. They don't have normal equipment and supplies. Many have had to find new homes and replace all of their personal belongings.

Some positive changes have come out of Katrina. Superintendent Warren Riley has created an anti-looting squad that is focusing on the unoccupied residential areas. "Due to the devastation following the storm, our mode switched from policing to rescue. We made efforts to stop the looting, but when the water attacked our city, we had to switch to rescue mode. That took every bit of manpower we could manage."

Riley continued, "There is a lot to learn from a disaster of this magnitude. We have changed our Hurricane Preparedness Plan to include lessons learned and eliminate the mistakes we made."

In an effort to keep dialogue open and to stay in touch with the needs of the residents, he created a Police Community Relations Board. "I've included a representative of every ethnic background in our city." The board was created in December 2005 and meets monthly. Members discuss various incidents that were problematic and give an objective opinion. "This helps us train our officers better," Riley said. "We want to understand the needs of our citizens, but we also need them to understand the needs of the department."

As the criminal element began to repopulate the city, Riley created a Criminal Intelligence Bureau (CIB). "As the citizens began to return home, we found we had to refocus our energies on gathering intelligence about people involved in violence and drug trafficking. We have already apprehended 11 of our top 100. We feel very good about that."

New uniforms are among the changes the department has had to make. So many of the old uniforms were lost or stolen that Riley changed the entire look of NOPD switching from the long standing traditional blue to black. "It was jeopardizing the safety of our citizens. They must be able to recognize a police officer without fear that it might be an imposter."

Riley is also updating the fleet of department vehicles. "The new cars have a new look," he said. "We have added the fleur de lis to our markings. We have a pride in our city, our survival—we want our cars to reflect how serious we are about our commitment to rebuilding and keeping the city safe."

Riley's team-building efforts have expanded beyond the confines of NOPD. "We are working on a regional approach. We want to be able to share resources, improve communications between all of the agencies—local, state and federal." Riley continued, "We are looking at a regional training academy, a combined crime lab, and sharing information to assist with all investigations."

The NOPD Police Academy has graduated two classes since Katrina. Funding for equipment, vehicles, overtime, uniforms, etc., all continue to be a problem. "We work closely with the New Orleans Police Foundation to find funding opportunities for the things we still need."

Remembering that about 80% of the officers lost everything to the flood waters, "We need to try to help them get back on their feet and bring their families home—so we are always trying to find funding for that too," Riley said. "Many of our officers are now taking care of two households because their families have been displaced, their details are no longer available—these officers are still going through a lot."

The major issues to be better prepared for a disaster include, 1) supplies enough to sustain life for seven to 10 days, 2) fuel, 3) immediately available support from National Guard units, 4) vehicles appropriate for the situation, i.e., high-water vehicles and boats, 5) medical supplies, 6) communication system shared by state, local and federal agencies, 7) training, 8) plan with primary and secondary staging areas identified and 9) recruiting new officers to expand the size of the department.

Captain Winn understands the pressures on the officers in post-Katrina New Orleans and vows to keep the officers in a state of readiness. Winn said, "It is a different world now. I work to keep my team as busy as possible—having stuff to do will keep their minds working."

Winn also insists on physical fitness. "I make sure that they maintain their workout routine."

He also addressed the emotional health of his SWAT officers. "We have a lot of mental health issues. I still have men whose families are living out of state. Life is not anywhere near being back to normal.

"If ever there was a need to remember to life live one day at a time … it is now." Winn said, "There is no reason to worry about the next step until you finish the step you are on. We are here to protect this city and the citizens. We did it during Katrina, and we will keep on doing it."

Discussion Questions

1. How did Hurricane Katrina affect the personal lives of New Orleans police officers?
2. From a law enforcement standpoint, what did we learn from Hurricane Katrina? What major issues need to be addressed so we can be better prepared for a natural disaster?
3. What immediate changes did the New Orleans Police Department make following Hurricane Katrina?

11

Super Bowl XXXIX:
The Successful Response
of the FBI and Its Partners

By Jeffrey Westcott

The decentralized approach to law enforcement practiced in the United States both helps and hinders law enforcement. U.S. law enforcement agencies exist at local, county, state, and federal levels, which, among other things, provides greater autonomy in decision making, enhanced opportunities to address particular jurisdictional concerns, and greater accountability. On the other hand, a decentralized approach results in, among other things, fragmentation, or different law enforcement agencies not cooperating as effectively as possible. The lack of a centralized national law enforcement agency discourages cooperation among law enforcement agents, although, as this article notes, coordinated efforts are necessary and do exist in current law enforcement practices.

A high-profile event such as a Super Bowl, which attracts the attention of much of the country, requires perfection regarding security concerns. Law enforcement agents charged with ensuring that all goes well must coordinate and cooperate with various groups, including other law enforcement agencies. Such cooperation could be considered a nontraditional representation of community-policing efforts in that traditional community-policing efforts request input from citizens (e.g., in reporting crime, being the eyes and ears of the police, etc.). This article depicts a non-traditional view of community policing and a glimpse of how cooperation among law enforcement agencies can truly benefit law enforcement practices.

Requesting and receiving assistance from various law enforcement groups seems simple; however, the decentralized approach to law enforcement in the United States has hampered interagency coopera-tion. If nothing else positive emerged from September 11, 2001, at the very least the terrorist attacks led to significant restructuring of federal law enforcement. The restructuring is largely recognized in the creation of the Department of Homeland Security (DHS)—which was part of the largest government reorganization in 50 years. In 2003, the Homeland Security Act (the legislation responsible for creating DHS) transferred all or part of 22 existing federal agencies to DHS. Thus DHS surpassed the Department of Justice as the federal department employing the greatest percentage of federal officers with arrest and firearm authority.

Should the United States adopt a centralized organizational design regarding policing—the "United States Police Department" with officers having jurisdiction to enforce laws throughout the country? To do so would require significant changes, not the least of which would include the elimination of all current distinctions among law enforcement agencies.

After several gray, damp days that had city officials and host committee members wringing their hands, Sunday, February 6, 2005, dawned clear and bright in Jacksonville. As the sun rose over northeast Florida, the curtain soon would come up on the city's performance in the world's biggest show—Super Bowl XXXIX. In a few short hours, attention would shift from the parties and celebrity sightings, away from the lingering questions about whether Jacksonville had what it needed to host the event, and onto the game itself.

But, while the world waited for the kickoff of Super Bowl XXXIX, another equally important performance unfolded backstage. The players in this drama did not wear cleats and helmets; in fact, many of them had no unique uniforms. They included the hundreds of professionals from the FBI and more than 40 other law enforcement and public safety agencies charged with safeguarding the security of the game and the surrounding events. And, by the time the smoke from the final fireworks cleared and the last of the weary fans caught their flights out of town, the efforts of these behind-the-scenes heroes would prove a resounding success.

TEAMWORK

Building a Partnership

Representing the smallest FBI field office ever to face the responsibility for coordinating counterterrorism efforts related to such an event, agency personnel in Jacksonville knew a big job lay ahead. Fortunately, some personnel had gained pertinent knowledge. Having visited San Diego during the 2003 Super Bowl, agents from Jacksonville learned even more during their trip for the 2004 game in Houston; they went to the FBI's field office and the city's central command post, observing the joint law enforcement effort and learning from everyone they could. They left with some important ideas and also a grasp of the considerations presented by the different circumstances in Jacksonville. Clearly, they faced a challenge and knew they had to do more with less; the FBI office in Houston devoted about 40 special agents to prepare for Super Bowl XXXVIII, more than the entire agent complement in Jacksonville.

Personnel began contacting counterparts at various FBI offices and other agencies to ensure coverage of all pertinent areas. For instance, they coordinated maritime and airspace security with the appropriate organizations, helped establish the intelligence and information teams that would be on the ground at the various Super Bowl-related venues, and worked with personnel at outside agencies and FBI Headquarters to handle other security issues. Of course, finding lodging for over 200 FBI personnel proved challenging as well.

Many agencies would become partners, including, of course, the Jacksonville Sheriff's Office (JSO). As the lead agency with the primary responsibility for overall event security, JSO was on task from the start. And, in the months leading up to the game, more than 150 attendees from dozens of agencies would crowd into the planning sessions at the Fraternal Order of Police's banquet hall to strategize, compare notes, and work out details.

Working Together

Because the FBI's mission would overlap those of numerous other organizations, establishing liaison with key players proved critical. As the special agent in charge (SAC) of the FBI's Jacksonville office stated, "Our mission was twofold. First and foremost, we had the responsibility to plan for—and prevent—potential acts of terrorism. Second, we had to take the lead in collecting, analyzing, and disseminating any intelligence involving potential threats to the security of the Super Bowl and the city of Jacksonville." These responsibilities would cut across FBI programs and functions and would involve SWAT teams, bomb technicians, maritime and aviation operations, and WMD specialists. To some extent, other agencies shared each of these functions and had concurrent jurisdiction. This presented no difficulties—the FBI and its partners worked together effectively.

One instance involved the cruise ships that the Super Bowl host committee had contracted to provide the minimum number of hotel rooms required by the NFL. These ships presented security challenges, including the need to conduct underwater hull searches for bombs and other hazards. Working together, the FBI and the U.S. Coast Guard got divers from the Environmental Protection Agency in Miami—which routinely handles inspections of cruise ships and other international vessels—to handle the job with some help from JSO.

Aviation security represented another area highlighting interagency cooperation. A committee chaired by FBI and U.S. Customs and Border Protection (CBP) personnel decided to request a temporary flight restriction zone with an unprecedented 10-mile radius around the stadium (zones in previous Super Bowl cities extended only 7 miles). Better yet, after conferring with Transportation Security Administration officials in Washington, D.C., the FBI obtained a 20-mile-radius "positive control airspace" designation, which required pilots entering that zone to contact air traffic control and identify themselves. The responsibility for implementing these restricted zones fell to the Federal Aviation Administration, and CBP handled the coordination of all federal law enforcement air assets.

Another key partner, the Florida Department of Law Enforcement (FDLE)—the state's primary investigative agency—already had a close working relationship with the Jacksonville FBI office through their combined efforts in counterterrorism. When it became clear that neither the city of Jacksonville nor the FBI had adequate space to house a multiagency command post, FDLE offered its downtown training center as a site. By the time Super Bowl week arrived, representatives from more than 30 agencies—everyone from surrounding sheriff's offices to firemen and Federal Emergency Management Agency (FEMA) personnel—had set up in the joint operations center (JOC) that FBI technicians had wired, secured, and equipped with high-tech telecommunications and computer gear.

Using lessons learned from past Super Bowls and working within the constraints imposed by both space and budget concerns, law enforcement personnel in Jacksonville developed a unique command structure. The city's downtown operations facility, renamed the event operations center (EOC) for the week, housed the heads of the primary public safety agencies—Jacksonville Fire and Rescue, JSO, the U.S. Coast Guard, and the FBI—and key operations personnel from a number of other city and state organizations. The lower level of the facility contained the joint information center, where public information officers and media representatives from JSO, the FBI, and several other agencies fielded calls from the media, ensuring a unified, consistent message.

A mile to the north, at the FDLE site, the JOC served as the nerve center of the FBI's intelligence and counterterrorism mission. Out front sat "Big Blue," manned by a team from the FBI's Technical Response Unit. Big Blue served as a mobile facility affording the requisite security for the physical handling of classified documents, and it also provided a backup platform for satellite uplinks and secure communications in the event the systems in place suffered a massive failure.

Inside the JOC, agents, analysts, and supervisors from all major FBI components—intelligence, investigations, legal, information technology, tactical, evidence, technical, administrative, and media—compared notes, staffed telephones, and worked closely with representatives from the more than 30 other agencies sharing the space. In one corner, a team from the National Geospatial-Intelligence Agency busied itself by generating and printing poster-sized photos and graphics of the various Super Bowl venues. The JOC had more than 150 telephone extensions, a multitude of computer workstations, and an electronic projection screen that showed an event board listing the status of any security-related incidents. Several wide-screen plasma televisions displayed local and national news channels and—on Sunday night—the game itself.

Next door to the JOC was the Intelligence Operations Center (IOC). Inside, analysts from joint terrorism task force agencies continued their work from the past months: collecting and analyzing intelligence and making appropriate dissemination decisions. By the time game day arrived, analysts had performed more than 30,000 background checks—including some 9,500 requested by the Super Bowl host committee—on volunteers, cruise ship crews, port workers, and taxi and limousine drivers. The IOC analysts also processed dozens of real-time checks on data coming in from intelligence and information teams on the street, which comprised 120 officers from eight different agencies.

SUCCESS

The partnership's efforts proved a resounding success. As Jacksonville's SAC said, "The level of cooperation was incredible. Fortunately, we had no major incidents, but even if there had been, I am confident we had the proper infrastructure and lines of communication in place to address them."

Throughout the week, agency heads held daily meetings at the downtown EOC followed by press-availability sessions. Stories that received the most attention included a nearly tragic boating accident in which two JSO marine officers sustained serious injuries and the police pursuit of a stolen limousine that ended in a fiery crash.

Police easily handled the expected increase of incidents of disorderly conduct, pick-pocketing, and prostitution, and JSO detectives and U.S. Immigration and Customs Enforcement agents teamed up to make several arrests of individuals selling counterfeit tickets and souvenirs. The Florida Highway Patrol played a crucial role in assuring safe passage on area highways and over the many bridges of this "river city."

Bomb technicians from the FBI, ATF, and several other agencies responded to calls concerning suspicious packages, and when a student pilot strayed into restricted airspace on Sunday morning, CBP pilots quickly escorted him out of the area and forced the student to land before questioning and releasing him. SWAT, HAZMAT, and evidence response teams were able to focus the bulk of their time on training opportunities, and crisis negotiators had little to discuss except the relative strengths of the Eagles and Patriots.

The more than 3,000 members of the media did not have much to report pertaining to security and public safety, despite the thorough coverage. Crews from the national networks fanned out across the city, capturing images of everything from U.S. Coast Guard patrol boats to bomb-sniffing dogs. Reporters from the national media shot footage at the EOC during halftime of the game and interviewed law enforcement personnel as part of a tour of the JOC.

The reports were almost uniformly positive, and they served to showcase the combined efforts of all agencies involved. As Jacksonville's sheriff told reporters, "This was the Pro Bowl of law enforcement."

CONCLUSION

Overall, law enforcement's coordinated response to this event showed what such a cooperative effort can accomplish. Fortunately, not many people—except a few cynical sportswriters—had much to comment on but the area's hospitality, golf courses, beaches, and natural beauty.

And, the combined response to the few minor incidents that did surface further proved the success of the plan. As is always the case in the behind-the-scenes world of intelligence and counterterrorism, the success of Super Bowl XXXIX can be measured as much by what did not happen as by what did.

Discussion Questions

1. Discuss how law enforcement agencies cooperated for safety and security reasons in preparation for Super Bowl XXXIX.

2. What important actions did law enforcement agencies take in preparation for Super Bowl XXXIX?

3. What were the results of the cooperative actions of law enforcement agencies regarding Super Bowl XXXIX?

12

Forensic Nursing: An Aid to Law Enforcement

By Joseph R. Yost

I often encourage students interested in earning a criminal justice degree to specialize in a particular area and/or do things to separate themselves from other qualified individuals with whom they will be competing for jobs. For instance, as a faculty advisor I constantly pester my advisees to set themselves apart from other students through learning a second language, gaining advanced computer skills, traveling abroad, and/or minoring in a particular area. Students often ask, "What should I minor in?" My reply is often along the lines of "Pretty much whatever interests you." My response seems unimaginative and soulless; however, there are two primary reasons why I encourage students as I do: (1) the minor may ultimately impact or open up career choices and (2) most disciplines are related to criminal justice in some manner.

It is easy to see the relationship between criminal justice and other disciplines such as sociology, political science, and foreign languages. However, the relationship between criminal justice and nursing is not well established. Nurses know much about crime and its repercussions; however, nursing students rarely minor in criminal justice and vice versa. The fit just doesn't seem to be there. However, this article demonstrates the significance of nursing to criminal justice and suggests changes may be in order.

Forensic nurses play the vital role of supporting law enforcement agents by examining sexual assault victims, working in correctional and geriatric facilities, providing a bridge between legal matters and medicine, investigating crime scenes, and dealing with various pediatric and psychiatric issues. While these activities have been conducted by various individuals with different backgrounds, the relatively new field of forensic nursing helps provide consistency regarding many law enforcement support services.

Some students are hesitant to declare criminal justice as their major because they feel the degree limits career opportunities to a select, few areas. For instance, many students believe majoring in criminal justice means one will become a cop, a judge, an attorney, or a prison officer. These are all respectable and possible career options for those studying criminal justice, but there are many more career options that go unnoticed. Forensic nursing is an example.

Current community-policing efforts require crime control and crime prevention efforts from the public and the police. These efforts also require greater interagency and intergroup exchange. Recognizing and incorporating the services of forensic nurses will undoubtedly enhance police services.

The need for and use of forensic nurses demonstrates the interdisciplinary nature of criminal justice. Perhaps most importantly, the use of forensic nurses enhances victims' services, an area that has only recently drawn attention from the criminal justice system and society in general.

The unidentified male is rushed to the hospital via ambulance. He is unconscious, with a gunshot wound to his chest. The trauma team has been alerted prior to his arrival. While each team member has a role in the immediate care of the victim, the forensic nurse cuts off his clothes, careful to avoid the bloody hole where the bullet pierced his shirt. The nurse puts each article of clothing in a separate container, places brown bags over the patient's hands, and searches his pockets for anything that could identify the young man.[1]

Gunshot wounds, drug overdoses, sexual assaults, and stabbings constitute just a few cases that involve forensic nurses who administer medical attention to individuals with traumatic injuries and those involved in catastrophic accidents, as well as provide assessment and care to both victims and perpetrators of crime and to their families.[2] A relatively new field in the criminal justice arena, forensic nursing originated in the early 1990s. While not lawyers or police officers, forensic nurses provide a needed link between medicine and the law. In 1992, 70 nurses gathered in Minneapolis, Minnesota, for the first national convention of sexual assault nurses, which led to the formation of the International Association of Forensic Nurses (IAFN).[3] Three years later, the American Nurses Association officially recognized forensic nursing.[4] As of 2004, the IAFN has over 2,400 members.[5] As a result, forensic nursing has become one of the fastest growing specialties in the field of nursing.

Forensic nurses must be a registered nurse (RN),[6] a trained medical professional licensed by a state authority.[7] Once they have earned an RN license, nurses who desire to specialize can take selected courses in the field of forensic science that would cover such topics as collection and preservation of physical evidence, wound identification, law enforcement investigation, documentation procedures and chain of custody, and preparation for court testimony.[8] Various universities across the nation provide education and training for those seeking a career as a forensic nurse, presenting them with classroom lectures and discussions, laboratory experience, and internships at local hospitals. One forensic nurse indicated that she first became an RN and later decided to become a forensic nurse. She successfully completed the required courses, including evidence preservation and collection, photography, and wound identification. She also observed the functions of law enforcement by riding with a police officer for a specified number of hours and learned about the courtroom process by witnessing trial procedures.[9]

THE LAW ENFORCEMENT ASSOCIATION

The general term forensic nurse encompasses several areas of expertise that RNs can specialize in to aid law enforcement officers in many ways. These include sexual assault nurse examiners, forensic correctional nurses, forensic geriatric nurses, forensic legal nurse consultants, forensic nurse investigators, forensic pediatric nurses, and forensic psychiatric nurses.

Sexual Assault Nurse Examiners

The sexual assault nurse examiner (SANE)[10] specializes in providing care and treatment to sexual assault victims.[11] The duties of the SANE include assessing injury, objectively documenting the health history of the victim, recording information about the crime, screening for sexually transmitted diseases, collecting and preserving forensic evidence, and aiding the victim.[12]

Because SANEs frequently work closely with assault victims, most possess some education and knowledge in the field of victimology, the study of victims and crime.[13] Most SANEs follow the victim through the entire criminal justice system, often offering a sympathetic ear. SANEs operate on the belief that victims should receive thorough medical evaluations, treatment by skilled professionals, and knowledgeable support.[14]

"Forensic Nursing: An Aid to Law Enforcement" by Joseph R. Yost, *FBI Law Enforcement Bulletin*, 2006. Reprinted with permission of the author.

All SANEs have to be certified through a comprehensive, usually 40-hour, training program that includes gathering medical histories from victims, conducting physical exams, identifying wounds and patterned injuries, and collecting evidence, as well as learning some interview techniques and basic forensic photography. This training also may prove valuable to law enforcement officers investigating cases of assault.[15]

Forensic Correctional Nurses

Forensic correctional nurses provide medical attention to individuals charged and convicted of a crime. They often are employed in prisons, jails, and juvenile detention centers.[16] Their responsibilities include giving prescribed medications to inmates, running the correctional facility's hospital, and treating the victims of inmate fights. Forensic correctional nurses also serve as potential negotiators. For example, an inmate barricaded himself in his room and, using a mop ringer as a weapon, threatened to kill the first person who attempted to intervene. Officials called in a forensic correctional nurse who told the prisoner that police officers were en route, and, if he did not immediately calm down, they would take corrective action. The inmate, known to tear through restraints, broke down and submitted without incident.[17]

Forensic Geriatric Nurses

Forensic geriatric nurses care for aging individuals and often handle the human rights issues of abuse, neglect, or exploitation.[18] Nursing home facilities or retirement communities usually employ these nurses who also can have their own independent practices.[19] They use their knowledge and skills most often in cases of elder abuse or neglect. In one incident, an elderly woman arrived in the emergency room of a hospital with a swollen right eye, bruises on her arms, and severe dehydration. The forensic geriatric nurse on staff took pictures of the injuries as they appeared to be possible signs of elder abuse. When the elderly woman became coherent 2 days later, she explained that her son had become frustrated with her declining health. She stated that he would tell her that she needed to try harder. If she failed to do so, he would strike her. The intervention of the forensic geriatric nurse prevented the woman from being released her back to her son. Instead, she was immediately assigned to an assisted living center where she would have minimal contact with her son.[20]

Forensic Legal Nurse Consultants

Forensic legal nurse consultants use their clinical knowledge to assist attorneys in cases where law and medicine overlap.[21] They often use their knowledge in civil, rather than criminal, cases.[22] These nurses typically have their own practices or work for major law or insurance firms. Their duties can include verifying malpractice and negligence claims, preparing and analyzing records, providing legal assistance, and serving as expert witnesses.[23] While law enforcement officers focus on criminal law, they also may have to testify in civil litigations (tort actions), such as automobile accidents and assaults. The forensic legal nurse consultant could aid officers in understanding the components of civil actions. For example, in a malpractice case where a man died as a result of a farming accident, a forensic legal nurse consultant reviewed the file information and testified that the doctor was negligent when allowing the patient to be air transported to the hospital before he was stable.[24] If police officers had arrived on the scene to assist the victim or to investigate the incident, they most likely would have been named in the lawsuit.

Forensic Nurse Investigators

Employed by medical examiners, forensic nurse investigators conduct scientific investigations of the crime scene and the circumstances surrounding the victim's death.[25] For instance, a 6-month-old baby was found dead in his crib, and the forensic nurse investigator was called to investigate the death. Upon arrival at the scene, she was told that there was no history of disease or abuse. When the nurse entered the child's room, she noticed a distinct odor of vomit. She asked the mother if the baby had been sick. The forensic nurse investigator learned that while the baby had shown no signs of previous illness, his older brother had complained of stomach problems for several days. The nurse observed green paint peeling off the steam radiator pipe that snaked across the apartment. She lifted the dead infant's lip and observed a thin, bluish lead line on the baby's gums. She then instructed the mother to have herself and her children tested for lead poisoning. The test verified the nurse's suspicions. The entire family had contracted lead poisoning from the paint flaking off the pipe.[26]

Forensic Pediatric Nurses

Forensic pediatric nurses care for children and often encounter the human rights issues of abuse, neglect, or exploitation.[27] These nurses often are in independent practices or work in the pediatric department of hospitals.[28] In one case, an 8-year-old girl was brought into the hospital one night complaining of pain in her pelvic region. The forensic pediatric nurse on staff performed a pelvic exam on the youngster and discovered several abrasions and bruises. Further investigation revealed that the father had sexually abused her. As a result of the forensic pediatric nurse's examination, the physical evidence collected, and the testimony of the child, authorities arrested the father and charged him with molestation.

Forensic Psychiatric Nurses

Forensic psychiatric nurses handle offenders who are mentally ill. They often work in forensic psychiatric practices, state hospitals, and psychiatric facilities within correctional institutions.[29] One of their major roles involves determining the competency of offenders. These nurses must have a thorough understanding of the criminal justice system, as well as the necessary elements for competency.[30] Forensic psychiatric nurses often testify in court regarding competency issues. In one instance, a judge asked a forensic psychiatric nurse to determine the competency of a subject who had brutally murdered his mother. After conducting an extensive interview with the son, the forensic psychiatric nurse determined that he exhibited signs of mental illness and required hospitalization and, therefore, was not competent to stand trial.[31]

THE EVIDENCE CONNECTION

Documentation of evidence proves critical to any investigation, including ones where forensic nurses have become part of the effort. These nurses should adhere to all evidence collection and preservation techniques without exception and maintain the chain of custody to ensure that no evidence is ruled inadmissible in a court of law.

Collecting Evidence

Forensic nurses may prove invaluable to investigators, particularly when a victim is transported to an emergency room. In that setting, forensic nurses on staff should document all proceedings pertaining to the victim, including a complete medical report that covers all treatment administered and the location of any bruises, cuts, scrapes, or lacerations.[32] Photographs of all of the victim's injuries also are essential for proper documentation and should include close-up, mid-range, and full-body images.[33] When practical, they should contain a photographic scale or ruler for comparison.[34]

When collecting physical evidence, forensic nurses should wear gloves to minimize contamination and follow basic techniques and procedures. Law enforcement investigators attempting to collect evidence from victims may seek assistance from forensic nurses who could swab for saliva or semen, collect bullets and gunshot residue from the body, and bag the victim's clothing for future analysis.[35]

Handling Evidence

Once they have collected the evidence, forensic nurses should place each sample in a separate container and seal it to prevent contamination. The victim's name, date, time, and case number should appear on the label accompanying the evidence, along with the forensic nurse's name, identification number (if any), and location where the evidence was recovered. It would prove helpful to law enforcement officers to assist in training forensic nurses, particularly when requesting forensic evidence and adhering to the proper chain of custody. Failure to maintain proper evidence and chain of custody may jeopardize a case. In a hypothetical situation, a forensic nurse collected evidence, but, in a rush to treat another victim arriving in the emergency room, failed to include the date and time. This type of action would break the chain of custody and cause the court to rule the evidence inadmissible.

In addition to maintaining a proper chain of custody, forensic nurses must be careful in handling evidence. For example, a victim with a single gunshot to the head arrived at a hospital. In the emergency room, the forensic nurse removed the bandages from the victim's head that the emergency medical technicians had applied at the scene of the shooting. Unknown to the forensic nurse, the bullet had dislodged into the bandages. While the projectile was later discovered in the trash, the evidence was inadmissible because it could not be traced to the victim.[36]

Testifying in Court

Forensic nurses also may serve as expert witnesses in court. Sometimes, this poses problems. When a doctor and forensic nurse provide contradicting information, attorneys can use this to their advantage. If a nurse and doctor provide conflicting information, the testimony of the doctor most likely will be believed over that of the nurse. For example, a SANE had performed an examination on a sexual assault victim. The doctor on call deemed it necessary that he be there to sign off on the case, even though he did not conduct the examination. As both the doctor and the forensic nurse were present during the examination, both were subpoenaed to court. When providing their testimony, both the doctor and the SANE identified the same injuries but in different locations on the body. The judge considered the doctor's testimony, which later proved incorrect, as more accurate. The defense counsel noticed the discrepancy in the two testimonies and used it to win the case.[37]

CONCLUSION

While a relatively new profession, forensic nursing already has successfully helped bridge the gap between the two fields of law and medicine. The high demand for forensic nurses will likely continue as doctors and law enforcement officials recognize the need for their valuable expertise. Those not currently employing forensic nurses can contact their local hospital or the nearest forensic nurse program by accessing the International Association of Forensic Nurses' Web site at http://www.iafn.org/. Bringing the two worlds of medicine and law enforcement together can help both fulfill their different, yet complementary, missions.

Endnotes

1. Karla A. Knight, "The Real CSI: Forensic Nursing in the ED," *Nursing Spectrum*, September 20, 2004; retrieved on May 11, 2005, from http://include.nurse.com/apps/pbcs.dll/article?AID=/CM/20070101/MS/70101019&SearchID=73309472369806.

2. "Forensic Specialties"; retrieved on September 27, 2005, from http://www.forensiceducation.com/forensic_files/specialties.htm.

3. Valerie Nelson, "Shattering the Myths About Forensic Nursing," *Nurseweek/Healthweek*; retrieved on March 2,

2005, from http://www.nurseweek.com/features/98-7/forensic. html.

4. Javacia N. Harris, "Forensic Nursing: Fast-Growing Field," *Seattle Times,* 4th ed., July 5, 2004; retrieved on March 22, 2005, from http://seattletimes.nwsource.com/ html/localnews/2001972154_nurse05m.html.

5. Ibid.

6. "Forensic Files: FAQs"; retrieved on April 17, 2005, from http://www.forensiceducation.com/forensic_files/faq.htm.

7. *New Standard Encyclopedia,* 1963 ed., s.v. "nursing."

8. American Forensic Nurses; retrieved on April 17, 2005, from http://www.amrn.com.

9. Interview by author, April 13, 2005.

10. Serita Stevens, *Forensic Nurse: The New Role of the Nurse in Law Enforcement* (New York, NY: St. Martin's Press, 2004), 44.

11. Supra note 2.

12. Supra note 10, 45.

13. Supra note 10, 48.

14. Supra note 10, 48.

15. Supra note 10, 48.

16. Supra note 6.

17. Supra note 10, 206.

18. Supra note 2.

19. Supra note 6.

20. Supra note 10, 183–184.

21. Supra note 2.

22. Sue E. Meiner, "The Legal Nurse Consultant," *Geriatric Nursing* 26, no. 1 (January/February 2005): 34–36.

23. Ibid.

24. Supra note 10, 148–149.

25. Supra note 2.

26. Supra note 10, 157–158.

27. Supra note 2.

28. Supra note 6.

29. Supra note 2.

30. Supra note 10, 212.

31. Supra note 10, 210–211.

32. Serita Stevens, "Cracking the Case: Your Role in Nursing," *Nursing* 2005 34, no. 11 (November 2004): 54–56.

33. Ibid.

34. Ibid.

35. Ibid.

36. Supra note 10, 22–23.

37. Supra note 10, 130–131.

Discussion Questions

1. Discuss the origins of forensic nursing.
2. How do forensic nurses assist policing and the criminal justice system in general?
3. Could police cooperation with forensic nursing be considered part of a community-oriented approach to policing? Why or why not?

13

Why Racial Profiling Doesn't Work

By Kim Zetter

Assume you're a police officer on patrol. You see an expensive new car in a poverty-ridden neighborhood. What are your initial thoughts? Is someone lost? Did somebody win the lottery? Are drug dealers visiting? Perhaps nothing comes to mind. Many of us would consider the car to be out of place. Suppose an African American man enters the car. Is he out of place? As a police officer, what would you do, if anything?

Racial profiling is a term used to describe the practice of determining a person's likelihood to commit crime based on racial characteristics. Racial profiling has existed in law enforcement arguably since the origins of policing, yet only recently has it received notable attention, for instance, as the legality of using race as a basis to justify a traffic stop has been challenged in court.

Profiling can involve factors other than race or ethnicity. For instance, the opening example initially says nothing about race; instead, the profiling is based on socioeconomic factors. Profiling doesn't have to be controversial. For example, in high-profile cases in which a suspect has not been identified, law enforcement officials often assemble a profile of an individual they believe may have committed the crime. That profile may be based on a host of psychological variables, a fascination with weapons, anger issues, or other factors that law enforcement officials believe may have contributed to the commission of a crime. Part of the controversy with profiling is that it is an inexact science based on probabilities and grounded assumptions.

Criminal justice officials are continuously trying to balance respect for individual rights with a concern for crime control. They must perform their job of promoting justice for those who break the law; however, they must be continuously cognizant of due process and individual rights. Some police officers suggest that racial profiling doesn't work. Others argue that racial profiling is effective, albeit illegal. Does racial profiling work all of the time? No. Therein lies the problem. Individual rights are violated when someone is stopped for no other reason than their race. However, those engaging in racial profiling argue that the inconvenience of being wrongfully stopped is small compared to the crime protection benefits of using race as a means to confront crime.

Police officers often engage in a professional version of the children's game "Which one doesn't belong here?" Particularly, officers look for cues suggesting that something isn't right. Is it an expensive car in a poverty-ridden neighborhood? A Caucasian male in a predominantly minority neighborhood? A homeless man in a wealthy neighborhood? Officers become familiar with the norms of the neighborhoods they patrol and often gain an understanding of how things are and how they should be. Something out of the ordinary may be cause for investigation. For better or for worse, racial differences may be the variable officers use to decide whether or not to act.

Criminal profiling is not restricted to street cops. One merely needs to observe historical and current security practices at our major airports to see profiling in action. In this article, author Kim Zetter argues that racial profiling doesn't work. Zetter examines the evidence collected post-September 11, 2001, and suggests that current efforts to identify terrorists at airports and elsewhere are doomed to fail. She also argues that behavior profiling is more effective than racial profiling.

A ugust 22, 2005—By anyone's standard, Anne-Marie Murphy didn't look like a terrorist threat. In 1986, Murphy was a 32-year-old hotel chambermaid from Dublin, Ireland, who was six months pregnant and on her way to marry her fiancé in Israel. Authorities discovered a bomb in her carry-on bag as she boarded a plane in London on her way to Tel Aviv.

Kozo Okamoto didn't fit the profile of a terrorist, either. In 1972, he and two other Japanese passengers had just arrived in Tel Aviv on a flight from Puerto Rico when they retrieved guns from their checked bags and opened fire in the arrival terminal at Ben Gurion International Airport, killing more than two dozen people and injuring nearly 80.

Nor did Patrick Arguello seem like a state enemy in 1970 before he tried to hijack an Israeli El Al plane flying from Amsterdam, Netherlands, to New York. Arguello, who was killed by Israeli sky marshals as he tried to carry out his attempt, was a Nicaraguan who had attended high school in Los Angeles.

Enemies, Israel has learned, don't always look like the known enemy. Terrorists, both willing and unwilling (such as Murphy, who was unwittingly used by her Palestinian fiancé as a carrier for his bomb), come in many guises, including color, ethnicity, and gender.

Which is why racial profiling (in which authorities target people of certain races or ethnicities) has never worked very well in any environment, including Israel.

That racial profiling can be a tricky tactic is something Americans should understand by observing the diversity of some of the terrorists who have operated on domestic soil or against Americans— Timothy McVeigh (the Oklahoma City bomber), Eric Rudolph (the abortion clinic bomber), Richard Reid (the ponytailed British-Jamaican who tried to bring down an American Airlines jet with his shoe), and the Arab hijackers who crashed into the World Trade Center's twin towers.

Yet last month, when Mayor Michael Bloomberg announced a program to randomly search New York subway passengers after the London tube bombings, two city politicians called for racial profiling instead. They insisted that the enemy's face is an easy one to spot and that authorities shouldn't waste time randomly searching, say, Norwegian grandmothers when the real threat comes from Middle Eastern and Asian men.

New York Assemblyman Dov Hikind, a Democrat, plans to introduce a bill that would roll back anti-racial-profiling legislation and allow police to stop whomever they want to stop in their efforts to prevent terrorism. Councilman James Oddo, a Staten Island Republican, promises to introduce a similar resolution in the City Council.

"I thought [Hikind] was courageous to say publicly what many New Yorkers felt privately," Oddo tells Salon.

Although Bloomberg denounced the proposals immediately, Oddo says he got e-mails from more than 80 people outside New York who expressed overwhelming support for his proposal. They included a military major serving in Iraq and the relative of a victim killed in the Oklahoma City bombing. But many Manhattanites called him un-American and racist. And Oddo's fellow council members vowed to introduce their own resolution to express support for current laws that prohibit profiling based on race, ethnicity, or religion.

Oddo, who voted for the anti-racial-profiling laws, says that he and Hikind aren't calling for racial profiling, a loaded term that conjures up disturbing images. They simply don't want police to

"Why Racial Profiling Doesn't Work" by Kim Zetter, Salon.com, August 22, 2005. This article first appeared in Salon.com, at www.Salon.com. An online version remains in the Salon archives. Reprinted with permission.

fear that if they stop "an inordinate number of people who look a particular way," someone will accuse them of violating the individuals' rights.

"Racial profiling is when you stop people because they look a certain way, without cause, and you're trolling to find trouble," Oddo says. "We never said, 'Stop only Arab [or] Muslim men, and don't stop whites.' We just said, 'If you're going to engage in these searches, do it in a manner that's more efficient and more effective.'"

Being more effective, he explains, means recognizing that the bombings of the Marine barracks in Lebanon, the USS Cole in Yemen, and the World Trade Center in New York all had something in common. "The common denominator is that every jihadi who is engaged in international terrorism has been a young fundamentalist," Oddo says. "We shouldn't try to couch that reality in some politically correct terms."

Some people do consider racial profiling unethical, but there are plenty of other reasons to reject racial profiling, even aside from its violation of equal protection rights.

David Harris, professor of law and values at the University of Toledo College of Law in Ohio, says that focusing on specific ethnic groups alienates the very people authorities need to help them catch terrorists. "By the time the threat is at the subway or airport, we're down to the last line of defense," Harris says. "You really want to catch these people before they go to the subway."

That can be accomplished only by gathering information from people who live in the communities where sleeper cells reside and can tell authorities who's new in a neighborhood and who seems to have income without holding a job.

But the most important reason to oppose racial profiling, says Harris, the author of *Profiles in Injustice: Why Racial Profiling Cannot Work,* is that, as the title of his book suggests, it simply doesn't work.

Harris says that when police use race or ethnic appearance as a factor in law enforcement, their accuracy in catching criminals decreases. Even worse, it can lead to accidental deaths, such as the fatal shooting by London police of an innocent Brazilian man after the bombings there.

Harris points to a study of New York's "stop and frisk" campaign in the late 1990s, when police were stopping people in the streets on a regular basis in an effort to confiscate illegal weapons and reduce crime. The campaign created tension between the police and minority communities, who thought they were being unfairly targeted for frisks. It turned out they were right.

After Amadou Diallo, an unarmed West African immigrant, was killed during a stop, New York attorney general Eliot Spitzer ordered a study of 175,000 "stop and frisk" records and found that although African-Americans composed only 25 percent of New York City's population at the time, they made up 50 percent of the people who were stopped. Latinos were roughly 23 percent of the population and 33 percent of those stopped, while whites were 43 percent of the population and 13 percent of those stopped.

Those findings interested Harris less than what the statistics indicated about the results: Police were going to a lot of trouble for little reward, especially when the people they stopped were African-Americans.

Harris looked at what he called "hit rates"—the percentage of stops in which the police found drugs, a gun, or something else that led to an arrest—and noted that the number of hits in general was very low for the number of stops that police made. But more interesting was that the rate for African-Americans was much lower than the rate for Caucasians. Police had a hit rate of 12.6 percent when they stopped Caucasians and only 10.5 percent when they stopped African-Americans. The hit rate for Latinos was 11.5 percent.

"You might say that we have a difference of 2.1 percent between blacks and whites. But it's actually a difference of 20 percent when you do the math right," Harris says. And "the difference between whites and Latinos is about 10 percent."

Essentially, police were stopping more African-Americans than Caucasians but finding fewer criminals among the former. Why? Not because blacks commit proportionately fewer crimes than whites do (the data vary according to the type of crime and other factors) but because police were looking at the wrong factors when they stopped people, Harris says.

"They're focusing on appearance when they should be focusing on behavior," he says. "When they're not distracted by race, they're actually doing a more accurate job" of picking out the right people.

Focusing on appearance produces a lot of false positives. And "every time you introduce a false positive, you take resources away from your ability to focus on people who are really of interest—those who are behaving suspiciously," Harris says. "If it's a question of finding a needle in a haystack . . . don't put more hay on the top."

What does work in preventing terrorism, Harris says, is behavior profiling. "If you're going to catch people who mean to put bombs on your subway trains or in airplanes, you don't actually care [if they're] young Muslim men . . . You care about [keeping] anyone from boarding the airplane who is going to behave like a terrorist."

Yuval Bezherano agrees. Bezherano is the executive vice president of New Age Security Solutions, a company that teaches people how to identify behaviors that indicate a person is concealing something and could be a security risk. The technique is called behavior pattern recognition and is modeled after methods used in Israel. NASS's president, Rafi Ron, is a former security chief at Ben Gurion Airport. The company has trained authorities at Boston's Logan International Airport as well as personnel at the Statue of Liberty. Recently the company trained about 100 employees of New York's subway and bus system.

The signs to watch for can be as obvious as someone acting nervous and sweating profusely on a cold day or as subtle as someone walking awkwardly in a way that indicates the person could be wearing a belt of explosives.

"It's always the unusual, the thing that doesn't fit," Bezherano says. "If you know your environment and what is usual for the environment, you know what to look for."

Depending on the situation, the next step might be to engage the person in a targeted conversation to determine whether he or she should be elevated to a higher level of risk or cleared from consideration.

It was this kind of screening that caught Anne-Marie Murphy, who initially raised interest among El Al's security staff because she was a pregnant woman traveling a long distance alone, something that Bezherano says is unusual behavior. She'd already cleared three security checkpoints at London's Heathrow Airport before an El Al "profiler" asked her where she'd be staying in Israel. Murphy's fiancé had warned her not to tell authorities about him because they would interrogate her if they knew she had an Arab boyfriend, so she told the profiler she'd be staying at the Hilton Hotel in Bethlehem. The profiler knew there were only two Hiltons and that neither was in Bethlehem. When authorities searched Murphy's bag, they discovered several pounds of plastic explosives concealed in a false bottom and a microchip detonator hidden in a pocket calculator.

Behavior profiling is much more effective than racial profiling, Bezherano says, because it's not unusual for terrorist groups to outsource their operations to individuals or groups who don't fit the expected racial or ethnic profile.

Patrick Arguello was a member of the Sandinista National Liberation Front when he posed as the husband of a woman who was an operative for the Popular Front for the Liberation of Palestine to help her hijack the El Al plane.

Kozo Okamoto was a member of the Japanese Red Army, which attacked Ben Gurion Airport; the group shared the Marxist ideologies of the PFLP.

Bezherano says there's no reason to believe that al-Qaida won't, or doesn't, farm out some of its tasks to other groups. "The philosophy of terrorist organizations is that the enemy of your enemy is your friend," Bezherano says. "Even though al-Qaida is very extreme, [its members] will collaborate with others as long it as it serves their cause."

If those working to prevent terrorist attacks on U.S. soil engage in racial or ethnic profiling, they're merely playing into terrorists' hands—and are likely to miss some of the enemies right in front of their eyes.

Discussion Questions

1. Discuss the pros and cons of racial profiling.
2. What evidence suggest racial profiling is an ineffective law enforcement tool?
3. Discuss how the following groups likely feel about racial profiling:
   - law enforcement
   - minority groups
   - conservatives
   - liberals

14

Mayor Meets Groom's Family in NYPD Slaying

By The Associated Press

Police officers are given special powers to enforce the law. With these powers, they must abide by procedural law, which involves the manner in which laws are enforced. Substantive law pertains to the laws by which we all must abide. Procedural law, much like substantive law, is subject to interpretation. In other words, police practices are sometimes called into question regarding whether they fall within the law.

As evidenced in this selection, the actions of four detectives and one police officer in New York City were called into question after the officers fired nearly 50 shots at three unarmed young men. One of the men, who was to be married later in the day, died as a result of the shooting. Three of the officers were charged with crimes: Two of the officers faced first-degree and second-degree manslaughter charges, while the third faced a misdemeanor endangerment charge. The other two officers were placed on desk duty during the investigation of the incident. Three of the five police officers involved in the shooting were indicted by a grand jury.

This incident spurred accusations of racist police officers, and the threat of public unrest became real. The incident also brought back images of the 1999 incident involving controversial conduct when New York Police Department officers fired 41 shots at an unarmed man named Amadou Diallo, and the 1997 sexual assault by police officers of Abner Louima while he was in police custody. These and related incidents have fueled tensions between New York's minority community and police department.

At the backbone of policing and prominent among police practices is the use of officer discretion, which involves calculated decision-making. Unfortunately, the nature of policing is such that officers sometimes misuse their discretion, either intentionally or unintentionally. The intentional misuse of discretion, which provides particular challenges for policing, displays policing at its worst. Again, we give the police special powers to enforce the law and expect them to abide by the law. For instance, officers are sometimes required to make life or death, split-second decisions. Failure to make the correct decision could result in deaths. It is sometimes difficult to precisely identify, from an outsider's view, whether discretion was used properly. Officers may believe that a substantial threat requires immediate attention. In hindsight, however, the situation may not have been so serious. Nevertheless, officers don't always have the luxury of looking back, and sometimes must react quickly.

When discretion is unintentionally misused, police departments may be cited and held accountable for failing to properly train officers. Accordingly, the onus is on police departments to properly train police officers, which has become more important in our highly litigious society.

I cannot tell you if the officers reacted properly to the situation involving the groom. I can tell you, however, that several variables in this incident strongly attract public attention. To begin, minority groups accusations of unethical police conduct will attract public attention, as will the killing of an unarmed man on his wedding day (particularly in light of the large number of shots fired) and the apparent misuse of discretion by officers from a department with poor community relations. Here's hoping the courts sort it all out and find justice.

NEW YORK—Mayor Michael Bloomberg met with the family of a black man who was killed on his wedding day in a barrage of police gunfire as he and two of his friends left his bachelor party. All three men were unarmed.

Three days after the fatal encounter, it remained unclear Tuesday why four detectives and one police officer opened fire while conducting an undercover operation at a strip club.

Police also questioned an unidentified witness who was on a darkened block in Queens when five police officers killed 23-year-old Sean Bell and injured two friends as the three sat inside a car, officials said.

There are two other civilian witnesses: One woman on the street who says she saw officers firing their weapons, and a second woman who from her window spotted a man running away from the area around the time of the shooting. Investigators tried to determine if that man had been with the three who were shot.

On Tuesday, Bloomberg went to the Bell family's Queens church, where he met for about an hour with the parents and fiancée of the victim, along with the Rev. Al Sharpton. The mayor then met at a restaurant with about 50 community leaders.

The mayor held a similar meeting Monday at City Hall in which he declared that officers appeared to use "excessive force" when Bell was killed hours before his wedding. He stood by his comments Tuesday.

"I am a civilian. I am not a professional law enforcement officer," he said. "I used the word excessive, and that's fine. That was my personal opinion. It may turn out to be that it was not excessive."

Some have questioned whether the shooting was racially motivated because the victims were all black men. The five officers who fired their guns included two blacks, two whites and one Hispanic.

OFFICIAL WARNS OF POSSIBLE UNREST

Councilman James Sanders Jr. of Queens said he warned Bloomberg about possible unrest.

"I alerted the mayor that the temperature on the streets has increased to a large degree," he said. "While we are sitting in these meetings, a lot of people are out on the streets."

Police Commissioner Raymond Kelly said some tension was inevitable because of "the nature of what police departments do—we arrest people, we give them summonses, we're the bearers of bad news, we use force and sometimes we use deadly force."

Police investigators have not interviewed the officers because of a district attorney probe that could result in criminal charges, nor have the officers spoken publicly. An attorney for the detectives' union, Philip Karasyk, has called the incident "a tragedy, but not a crime."

Union officials familiar with the officers' account say at least one undercover detective was convinced there was a gun in the car. They also allege that Bell defied orders to stop and used the vehicle as a weapon, bumping the undercover detective and ramming an unmarked police van.

"They are genuinely concerned and very sympathetic toward the three men who were shot," said Michael Palladino, president of the Detectives' Endowment Association. "However, they are anxious to speak to the district attorney in Queens and tell their side of the story."

"NO RUSH TO JUDGMENT"

Queens District Attorney Richard A. Brown said Monday that his office was investigating the Saturday morning shootings and that the results would be presented to a grand jury.

"I will be guided only by the law and the facts," Brown said in a statement. "I will reach no conclusions until the investigation is complete. There will be no rush to judgment."

Bell, 23, was killed and two of his friends wounded after a bachelor party at the strip club the night before his wedding. The men were unarmed.

The undercover operation that began 1 A.M. Saturday at the strip club Kalua Cabaret was part of a city wide crackdown sparked by the case of a New Jersey teenager who was abducted, raped, and killed following a night of partying earlier this year at a Manhattan nightclub.

OFFICERS AUTHORIZED "TO HAVE TWO DRINKS"

Police said they had received several complaints about prostitution and drug dealing at Kalua Cabaret before sending in two undercover detectives who left their guns behind because of searches at the door.

The detectives apparently spent the next few hours nursing drinks and mingling with the crowd. Critics have questioned why the officers were allowed to consume alcohol, but police officials said the officers weren't impaired.

"We authorize them to have two drinks, and not more," said Kelly.

The situation began to unravel when one of the officers alerted the backup team outside that a man inside was possibly armed. During a later altercation among patrons, police claim they heard a member of Bell's bachelor party, say, "Yo, get my gun."

One of the undercover detectives responded by retrieving his weapon and confronting Bell and his friends after they entered their car. Kelly suggested that it was unorthodox for the officer to blow his cover rather than rely on other officers to make the arrest.

"He was still acting in an undercover capacity when he followed the group down the street and apparently took some enforcement action, and that was unusual," Kelly said.

Union officials insist the detective took out his badge, identified himself, and ordered the men to stop before the car, driven by Bell, lurched forward and bumped him. The vehicle then smashed into an unmarked police van, backed up, and smashed the van again before the shooting began.

DEADLY ESCALATION

The crashes—along with the fear that one of the men had a gun—seem to be what escalated the situation to a hail of gunfire by five officers.

It is not immediately clear if the men in the car knew they were dealing with a police officer. Friends and family have speculated Bell was frightened by having a gun pointed at his vehicle, possibly crashing the car in a panic.

The NYPD discourages officers from firing on a moving vehicle. But Michael Palladino, president of the Detectives Endowment Association, argued that the officers had a right to fire if the car posed a lethal threat.

"The driver of that vehicle—his actions were a contributing factor," Palladino said. "The amount of shots fired does not spell out excessive to me."

"NO ONE GIVES ANYONE THE RIGHT TO KILL SOMEBODY"

In her first public comments on the shooting, Bell's fiancée, Nicole Paultre, told a radio station Monday that the people who shot her husband shouldn't be called officers.

"They were murderers, murderers," she told hip-hop station Power 105.1. "They were not officers. No one gives anyone the right to kill somebody."

None of the five unidentified officers had ever fired their 16-shot semiautomatic pistols on patrol before that morning, officials said. The undercover officer fired first, squeezing off 11 rounds; another, a 12-year-veteran, fired 31 times, meaning he paused to reload.

Officials said all the officers would have received training to combat against "contagious or sympathetic fire"—when police become disoriented by the sound of friendly fire and blast away at a phantom threat.

The survivors were Joseph Guzman, 31, who was shot at least 11 times, and Trent Benefield, 23, who was hit three times. Guzman was in critical condition, and Benefield in stable condition Monday.

Discussion Questions

1. Describe the incident that prompted the New York City Mayor to meet with the groom's family. Do you believe the officers acted professionally?

2. Identify three examples of police use of discretion in this incident. Which do you believe was most influential in the harms that occurred?

3. Discuss the concerns associated with using undercover police agents. Identify how undercover work influenced the events described in this article.

15

Early Detection of the Problem Officer

By Dino DeCrescenzo

Deviant police officers pose trouble for many groups. Among other things, the problem police officer stains the reputation of police officers in general. They give their department a bad reputation. And, problem officers fail to provide fair protection for the citizens they're supposed to serve. Yet, the autonomy given to police officers and the hidden nature of much police work make it difficult to detect the problem officer.

This article examines a process by which unethical policing can be addressed early on, which is significant, given the messages sent by a department's failure to address unethical police behavior in a timely manner. Permitting corrupt officers to continue their unethical ways without detection sends a message to the officer and other officers that corruption goes without recognition and punishment. It also suggests to the public that the police department has limited means to monitor its officers, or it simply doesn't care. Permitting police corruption may also lead to corrupt officers becoming bolder, and perhaps engaging in higher levels of corruption.

Police accountability comes primarily in two forms, external and internal. Internal forms include the presence of an effective internal affairs division; proper recruitment, selection, and training of officers; peer or coworker pressure; and legislation and department policy that dictates officer behavior. Externally, civilian review boards and citizens reporting deviant police behavior are prominent among the means of police accountability. Despite the various avenues through which police practices are monitored, there are occasions when officers step outside the law.

Early warning systems provide police administrators the ability to assess officer behavior over a period of time. The additional record-keeping and analyses involved with the data consume precious police resources; however, there are benefits to removing unethical officers as early as possible. In a litigious society such as ours, where filing lawsuits has become increasingly common and easy, early detection helps police departments proactively identify officers who pose risks to the community.

Most officers abide by the laws they enforce. There are a few, however, who sometimes give policing a bad name. Police administrators often face difficulty in determining the legitimacy of questionable police practices. The nature of police work is such that questionable police practices, at their most basic level, often involve the officer's word against the complainant's. Occasionally, there is concrete, visible evidence (or a lack thereof), so decision making on behalf of police administrators is simplified. The discretion inherent in policing, in which officers constantly use their decision-making skills, and the volatile and dangerous nature of police work dictate that problem officers be identified and reprimanded, trained, or released quickly.

Though today's police officers are more professional, better trained, and better educated than at any other period in history, accounts of police misconduct will likely continue but undoubtedly at a much reduced rate. Continued developments in the field of policing, such as early warning systems, will certainly reduce the likelihood of corrupt policing.

Sadly, a disturbing trend has begun to emerge concerning the law enforcement profession. That is, allegations against those officers facing suspension or termination rarely seem to surprise members of their departments and, at times, many residents of their communities. Over the past several decades, investigative journalists have found that in some agencies, as few as 2 percent of officers held responsibility for 50 percent of citizen complaints.[1] In addition, numerous police chiefs reported that 10 percent of their sworn personnel caused 90 percent of the problems.[2] Also, studies on the issue repeatedly indicated that an extremely small and disproportionate number of officers incurred most of the accusations.[3]

In reality, the majority of law enforcement officers are supremely dedicated individuals severely offended by the behavior and acts committed by those few who have tarnished the image of their profession.[4] These officers and the citizens they serve have begun to demand reasons for why such employees have remained on the job, even though they have violated departmental and societal rules. The awareness of these problem officers has existed for some time. In 1981, the U.S. Commission on Civil Rights recommended that all police departments create an early warning system to identify problem employees who often receive the highest number of complaints or display patterns of inappropriate behavior.[5] In today's world of terrorists and increasingly violent criminals, such efforts may prove more important than ever before.

INTERVENTION APPROACH

According to the U.S. Department of Justice, early warning systems take the form of databases that contain personnel information designed to identify problem behavior and allow early intervention to correct the misconduct. Generally nonpunitive, the systems include peer review, additional training, and counseling. They can provide supervisors and managers with information relating to potential patterns of at-risk conduct. Most systems require intervention after recording a certain number of complaints of a particular type within a specified time frame.[6] Although a few departments use only citizen complaints to select officers for intervention, most rely on a combination of behavior indicators.[7] Early warning systems should consider the totality of officer work histories, including accidents, pursuits, transfers, training, grievances, education, drug usage, civil suits, truthfulness, property damage, discourtesy, false arrest claims, and insubordination.[8] They should track all complaints, sick time used, resisting arrest incidents, assaults on officers, obstruction of officer arrests, and disorderly conduct arrests made by officers.[9] These last four behavior indicators appear to be significant measuring devices of potential problem employees. A higher number of these types of arrests when compared with those of other officers may reveal personnel acting beyond their scope of authority.

The theory behind an early warning system is that such incidents individually may mean nothing, but the combined totality of behaviors may signal a developing problem that needs attention.[10] These indicators, compiled into a single place, can flag a potential pattern of problematic behavior and identify an officer at risk of engaging in misconduct.

The phenomenon of early detection or early warning systems within law enforcement agencies is a fairly new concept that has begun to spread more rapidly since Congress passed the Violent Crime Control and Law Enforcement Act, which empowered the federal government to investigate and bring suit against those officers who routinely abused their authority.[11] For the most part, when

---

"Early Detection of the Problem Officer" by Dino DeCrescenzo, Detective Lieutenant, Barrington, Rhode Island, Police Department, as appeared in *FBI Law Enforcement Bulletin*, 2006. Reprinted with permission of the author.

departments have suits brought against them, they enter into a consent decree with the government agency agreeing on the changes required and to being monitored until the judge lifts the decree.[12] More often than not, the recommendations stemming from such investigations include implementation of an early warning or detection system as a first step in the process of abolishing the pattern and practice of conduct by the officers.

RESEARCH FINDINGS

The first in-depth study of early warning systems found that 27 percent of the agencies surveyed in 1999 had such a mechanism in place while another 12 percent planned on implementing one.[13] The participating agencies were police departments employing a minimum of 80 officers and serving populations of at least 50,000. However, 87 percent of police departments in the United States have fewer than 25 sworn officers.[14] So, while less than 40 percent of the large agencies surveyed either had or planned to have an early warning system in 1999, the majority of police departments in the country most likely did not have nor plan on implementing such a system at the time.

If administered properly, an early warning and detection system should allow the department to quickly intervene and help modify the behavior of the officers identified. Moreover, a successful early detection system not only can identify negative behavior but also can recognize conduct worthy of commendation.[15] The study further indicated that early warning systems substantially reduced citizen complaints and other problematic behavior. For example, three large police departments with early warning systems in effect for at least 4 years had substantially fewer citizen complaints and use-of-force incidents after the intervention. A successful system can benefit the entire agency, the community, and the troubled or problem officer with prompt intervention administered properly. Experts stress that using an early warning system to punish officers will undermine its effectiveness, but applying the information learned from the data to counsel and train them will expand its value.[16]

Some departments have successfully employed early warning systems for over a decade with beneficial results.[17] However, these programs still may not accurately identify every specific pattern of behavior that may ultimately lead to misconduct. In addition, the study found that no standards had been established for identifying officers in the early warning systems examined. Instead, only a general agreement existed on some of the criteria that should influence their selection.[18] These issues demonstrate that agencies must carefully analyze the information compiled on their personnel and establish strict selection guidelines to ensure that they correctly determine those officers in need of intervention.

Finally, the study noted that the implementation of an early warning system can prove compatible with both problem-oriented and community policing. The law enforcement administrator can incorporate the warning system into the department's overall philosophy and goals, recognizing that the new system must involve counseling and training as the main objective in modifying the behaviors of the officers selected and flagged for intervention. The administrator, however, must remember that the police union and the officers may suspect a new warning system and possibly resist its implementation. One early warning discipline system stressed the police union's involvement in the process prior to implementation of a program that provided predictable sanctions agreed upon by management and the union.[19] Because most complaints by unions involve the unequal treatment of personnel and ambiguous, unknown, or unpredictable punishments, this system established a disciplinary matrix with minimum and maximum penalties and ensured that the administration and the collective bargaining unit agreed upon predictable, reliable, equitable, and valid sanctions. Such involvement by the union or collective bargaining unit can greatly increase the success of an early warning system.

POSITIVE CHANGE

Law enforcement agencies throughout this country generally have pursued a traditional approach when dealing with officer misconduct.[20] Most have dealt with this issue through reactive as opposed to proactive efforts, primarily using citizen and internal complaints to identify such behavior. In addition, most departments impose corrective action only after the misconduct has occurred.

To effect positive change in the behavior of the few officers that create the majority of problems, departments must begin to take sufficient action against those repeatedly accused of excessive force and continually look for patterns in officer conduct.[21] They also must seriously discipline such personnel, not merely reassign them to other duties. Finally, agencies must provide troubled officers with counseling and other services. As one official said, "We have a tendency to go from zero to 60, by focusing only on the egregious, but not having a system to correct or discipline the behavior that is nonegregious."[22]

Officers who have exhibited less than stellar behavior need help to return to their former standards of professionalism. Departments should endeavor to find out what these officers need to overcome their problems and, once again, become valuable, contributing members of their profession. To this end, an early warning system can offer an effective approach for agencies to use.

CONCLUSION

Today's law enforcement administrators must identify problem officers and intervene appropriately with counseling, training, and other methods in an attempt to modify and change their behavior. Managers will benefit their departments, communities, and problem officers with the implementation of a properly administered early warning system. Such an approach can help agencies combat the disturbing trend that seems to indicate that they disregard officer misconduct.

Early warning systems demonstrate that departments and administrators have developed a clear policy regarding misconduct, have put a program in place to correct negative behavior, and have made a good-faith effort to identify employees whose performance is less than satisfactory.[23] The majority of their officers who valiantly place themselves in harm's way every day to protect the citizens of their communities deserve no less.

Endnotes

1. C.R. Swanson, L. Territo, and R.W. Taylor, Police Administration: Structures, Processes, and Behavior, 6th ed. (Upper Saddle River, NJ: Prentice Hall, 2004).

2. S. Walker, G.P. Alpert, and D.J. Kenney, "Early Warning Systems: Responding to the Problem Police Officer," National Institute of Justice Journal (July 2001); retrieved on January 28, 2005, from http://www.ncjrs.org/pdffiles1/nij/188565.pdf.

3. S. Slahor, "Earlier Is Better When Solving Problems," Law and Order, June 2004, 6.

4. J. Arnold, "Special Report II: Ethics—Early Misconduct Detection," Law and Order, August 2001, 8.

5. Supra note 2.

6. Supra note 4.

7. Supra note 2.

8. Supra note 3.

9. T.F. Kennedy, Preventing, Detecting, and Investigating Employee Misconduct, paper presented at a Roger Williams University Conference, Bristol, RI, October 2003.

10. R.G. Dunlop and J. Adams, "System to Spot Troubled Officers Not Fully Used: Goal Is to Detect Small Problems, Prevent Big Ones," Louisville Courier Journal, April 2, 2000.

11. "Pittsburgh's Experience with Police Monitoring," Vera Institute of Justice, June 17, 2004; retrieved on January 28, 2005, from http://www.vera.org/project/project1_1.asp?section_id=7&project_id=13.

12. Ibid.

13. Supra note 2.

14. S.F. Kelly, "Internal Affairs: Issues for Small Police Departments," FBI Law Enforcement Bulletin, July 2003, 1-6.

15. Supra note 3.

16. "Best Early Warning Tool Is Informative," Organized Crime Digest 22, no. 13 (August 10, 2001).

17. Supra note 4.

18. Supra note 2.

19. R.W. Serpas, J.W. Olson, and B.D. Jones, "An Employee Disciplinary System That Makes Sense," The Police Chief, September 2003.

20. Supra note 4.

21. D. Washburn, D. Hasemyer, and M. Arner, "A Question of Force: Dealing with Multiple Shooters Has Been a 'Huge' Issue," The San Diego Union-Tribune, January 19, 2003; retrieved from http://www.signonsandiego.comnews/reports/shootings/20030122-9999_mz1n19questn.htm.

22. Supra note 3.

23. Supra note 2.

Discussion Questions

1. What methods are used to detect police misbehavior prior to notable problems emerging?

2. Have early warning systems been effective in identifying potentially problematic officers?

3. Describe how traditional methods of police accountability were reactive in nature, and how early warning systems provide a more proactive approach.

16

Policing the Future: Law Enforcement's New Challenges

By Gene Stephens

What does the future hold for policing? There is no simple answer to the question. Forecasting the future largely involves observing qualitative and quantitative trends and making educated projections as to what we can expect. With regard to policing, recent qualitative trends in society suggest we can expect greater concern for homeland security and continued development of community-policing programs. Such projections, however, involve the short-term future of policing. What should we expect from policing 50 years from now? What about in 100 years?

Projecting far into the future is difficult for many reasons. Unexpected events and/or developments can change the course of an entire country. Consider policing as it existed on September 10, 2001, and how it changed the very next day. Consider policing 20 years ago, when technology had not made much of an impact in the day-to-day functioning of law enforcement. A primary challenge in forecasting the future is that the future is not predetermined. Unexpected events can and do shape our future.

Prominent among the factors that influence changes in society and, more specifically, changes in policing are demographics, technology, the economy, and crime-related issues. Demographics shape policing, for instance, as juveniles and young adults commit a disproportionate amount of crime. Increases in the number of juveniles and young adults in society would assumedly result in increases in crime. Demographic changes in society could also influence the hiring practices of police departments. For instance, fewer young adults in society suggest a forthcoming shortage of viable candidates who ultimately become officers. Other factors, such as the economy are closely related to the crime rate and therefore influence police practices. Given that most crime is financially motivated, a slow in the economy would assumedly result in an increase in crime rate. The relationship can be depicted in mathematical equations: fewer jobs = more need to steal . . . more jobs = less need to steal. Economics could also influence the ability of a police department to remain financially stable. Should the community's tax base disappear, along with it may go many police officer positions.

Technology has shaped policing in many ways. Consider the police officers of the 1950s. Jump ahead 50 years and consider the changes in policing. Today's officers have computers in their cars; access to databases containing information on many people, places, and things; and communication and technical support never before seen in policing. Technology, however, has also brought about many new types of crimes that traditional police departments are ill-equipped to fight. Internet crime has provided new challenges to modern policing, and traditional methods of fighting crime do not necessarily apply. In the future policing must take a more proactive approach to addressing the threats associated with Internet crime.

Concerns for terrorism and homeland security have changed the nature of policing and have encouraged police departments to stretch their budgets, for instance, as they hire and train new officers. Furthermore, crime is becoming increasingly international, thus requiring greater international cooperation.

The future of policing looks promising if the past 15 years provide an indicator of things to come. Crime rates have declined, police–community relations are much better than in the past, and police officers are more educated and better trained than at any other point in history. Nevertheless, one must keep in mind the uncertainty of the future.

What role will the police play in the future: keepers of the peace, antiterrorism specialists, or community outreach agents? A noted criminal-justice futurist surveyed police experts to find out. They concluded that better-educated police officers with improved people skills and a stronger grasp on emerging technologies will be crucial to successful policing in the future.

When public policing was first formally instituted in London in 1829, the emphasis was on preventing crime: The public and officers themselves regarded successful policing as the "absence of crime." The first U.S. police were also "peace officers"; however, a distinctly American style of policing began to emerge in the United States following the end of the Civil War. As settlers populated the West, they found there was no safety unless they provided it. This led to vigilante committees that would pass a set of town laws and often hire a "gunfighter" as town sheriff in hope of a modicum of protection. In time, the American system replaced preventing crime by keeping the peace with catching and punishing law violators, a "law enforcement" model that prevails and is emulated in many other countries to this day.

Many credit the return to community-oriented policing for the downward trend in street crime that began in 1994. This approach has worked well where it has been implemented, especially when combined with modern research techniques, such as psychological profiling, and technologies, such as high-tech surveillance, to help anticipate and prevent crime.

The twenty-first century has put policing into a whole new milieu—one in which the causes of crime and disorder often lie outside the immediate community, demanding new and innovative approaches from police. Most ordinary street crime involves perpetrators and victims from the same or nearby communities; thus, prevention involves closely watching and analyzing activity in the immediate area and taking action to head off problems (leading to what some call "problem-solving policing"). As street crime has diminished, new and more insidious types of offenses, especially terrorism and Internet-assisted crimes, have replaced it. Here, offenders are often thousands of miles away while planning and even while committing these crimes. With a rudimentary mastery of modern technology, terrorists from anywhere in the world can bring chemical and biological mayhem to any place on earth. Hackers and crackers halfway around the globe can shut down a chosen community's Internet-dependent monetary or energy systems. Already, identity theft, often assisted by Internet scams, has become the most prevalent crime in the United States and other developed societies.

Future policing in large part will depend on the type of society being policed—the social, economic, and political realities and, in more-developed countries, the technological sophistication of the populace. In countries such as Iraq, police are much like soldiers and will continue to use "combat policing" methods in some areas, while seeking to gain support and help from the public in more secured communities. In theocracies and dictatorships, policing likely will remain dedicated to protecting and serving the needs of those in power.

"Policing the Future: Law Enforcement's New Challenges" by Gene Stephens, *The Futurist*, March/April 2005. Used with permission from the World Future Society, 7910 Woodmont Avenue, Suite 450, Bethesda, Maryland 20814, Telephone: 301/656-8274; Fax: 301/951-0394; www.wfs.org.

THE POLICE FUTURISTS INTERNATIONAL

If anyone in the policing profession has a handle on what lies ahead and how to cope, it is the members of the Society of Police Futurists International (PFI). Based on more than 30 years of experience researching, teaching, and training police, I believe that these indeed are the individuals on the cutting edge in policing.

"PFI brings together the finest minds in policing—practitioners and scholars—to focus on researching ways to better anticipate future issues through the use of scientific methods and application of high technology," says PFI founder William Tafoya. These are the men and women most likely to understand the road ahead and to be able to predict the threats and promises to expect in the next few years. The police futurists contributing to this article focus on policing in at least partially democratic societies, especially those increasingly dependent on high-tech communication and service delivery—a situation that likely will eventually include most of the world. To glean their insights on the future of policing, I queried PFI members via interviews, a structured questionnaire, and the PFI Listserv.

Policing has traditionally been a closed, slow-to-change subculture. Even the most optimistic future-oriented thinkers in the field find it difficult to imagine how police will be able to cope with the emerging complexity of combating terrorism and Internet crime while simultaneously keeping a lid on conventional street crime and creating cohesive neighborhoods. Yet no one on the panel was willing to say that doing both just couldn't be done. Most agreed that success is possible if new personnel come from better-educated applicants who are then better trained and mentored to fit into a reorganized structure designed to meet the new roles and demands of policing. That is a tall order, as today more than 90% of police agencies in the United States require only a high-school diploma or equivalent to qualify for employment; increasingly, however, applicants have done at least some college work.

Current police training in the United States (usually three or four months plus a probationary period on the job) remains committed to the basics of combat policing—self-defense, firing range, field tactics—with little time left for the skills needed for preventing crime and improving community services and relationships. Most PFI respondents agreed more education and more and refocused training will be necessary to cope with emerging international and high-tech crime and disorder. Here's what they had to say.

Panelists

- **Alan Beckley,** chief inspector (retired), West Mercia Constabulary, United Kingdom; past president, PFI.
- **Maj. Tyree Blocker,** Pennsylvania State Police; past president, PFI.
- **Capt. Gordon Bowers,** Burbank, California, Police Department.
- **Jim Conser,** criminal justice professor, Youngstown State University; secretary, PFI.
- **Tom Cowper,** state police inspector; treasurer, PFI.
- **Joe Grebmeier,** chief, Greenfield, California, Police Department.
- **Kenneth Hailey,** manager of planning and research, St. Louis Metropolitan Police Department.
- **Steve Hennessy,** associate professor, St. Cloud State University; president, PFI; former police-training administrator, Phoenix.
- **Eugene Hernandez,** chief, Chino, California, Police Department; past president, PFI.
- **Bernard "Bud" Levin,** director, Waynesboro, Virginia, Police Research and Development Division; head, Social Sciences Department, Blue Ridge Community College; research director, PFI.
- **Judith Lewis,** captain (retired), Los Angeles County Sheriff's Department; past president, PFI.
- **Gary Sykes,** director, Institute for Law Enforcement Administration, Piano, Texas.
- **William Tafoya,** criminologist, retired FBI agent, and founder, PFI.

RECENT CHANGES IN POLICING

The participating Police Futurists generally agreed that local law enforcement is taking a back seat to pressures from homeland security and similar non-neighborhood or off-site threats.

Judith Lewis: The expectations of law enforcement as first responder for homeland security have put an almost unachievable burden on local law enforcement, as has the explosion of crimes like identity theft. Local law enforcement is not designed organizationally to support the cooperation needed, and its officers don't have the training and technology to do the job. So my view is that, currently, traditional law enforcement is being left behind.

William Tafoya: With the exception of better-educated personnel and the use of technology, little has changed in the past 50 years with regard to the role of policing.

Jim Conser: Societal expectations are changing, and policing has some difficulties keeping up with the services that society requires. In some communities, the disconnect is quite serious; in others, the police are very professional and serve their communities well. But policing is still a local community activity, and there are great discrepancies in levels of service across the United States.

CHANGES IN THE NEXT FIVE YEARS

The biggest issues affecting most aspects of both near-term and long-term policing trends involve technology and funding. Many of the PFI respondents agree that technologies will revolutionize the use of force and tactics, but how those technologies will be paid for remains to be seen. When asked about the next five years, the panel had this to say about what to expect.

Tom Cowper: Exponential technological advancements will continue to increase social vulnerability and fear, give terrorists and criminals new methods and opportunities, and give police new tools to stop them. Privacy issues will constrain the ability of police to employ many new technologies to control crime and terrorism, forcing police to deal with even more complex issues and situations with outmoded tools and processes.

Kenneth Hailey: We can expect smaller budgets and higher expectations. We will get communities to take charge of their own destinies; however, the labor-intensive, small, personal beats required to maintain neighborhoods will be expensive. Police departments will be run on more of a business, problem-solving model than a paramilitary model.

Tyree Blocker: Public policing will be customized to the individual in the near future. Policing style may differ from neighborhood to neighborhood, depending on the threats to and needs of different citizens.

Bud Levin: I see a need for linkages with military and the international scene—boundaryless policing. Cooperation of police at all levels along with coordination with other agencies will be necessary to cope with crime that is increasingly cross-jurisdictional—Internet offenses and terrorism, for example.

Joe Grebmeier: People will want more answers and results from us while budgets and resources will remain scarce. Organized street gangs will grow and become more dangerous.

POLICE AND THE WAR ON TERRORISM

A Canadian police administrator (who preferred to remain anonymous) summarized the consensus of the group regarding the role of police and the war on terrorism as "protecting the community, emergency response as may be required, effective intelligence gathering and sharing." Most respondents, however, were concerned that funding for meeting this mission might not be forthcoming.

Lewis: Local police are the first responders and the best hope of prevention. They need to be reorganized, trained, and funded to meet this need.

Conser: Local police need to learn who is in their community and what goes on there. They need to be the neighborhood constable whom everyone respects and shares information with. Local police need to work with their state and federal counterparts, but make sure that local citizens' concerns are treated fairly.

Steve Hennessy: Patrol officers should be trained in noticing minor anomalies in behavior of people they come in contact with during their primary role of monitoring public safety and keeping the peace.

NEW TECHNOLOGIES

Several respondents noted technology is like a double-edged sword—it will continue to create new crimes even as it assists crime fighters. Among the technologies mentioned were biometrics to assist in positive identification; nonlethal weapons to provide an option to deadly force; digital documentation of everything officers see, say, and do; a virtual cashless society to reduce robbery rates; intelligent vehicles to reduce accidents; and networked clothing and equipment for easier, speedier locating.

Lewis: If someone figures out that we need to invest in homeland security, and if financial institutions figure out that they can't afford the losses to identity theft and other sophisticated crimes and need the help of law enforcement, then with funding they can get the technology needed.

Conser: Local economies cannot support the new technologies over the long term; there will have to be additional federal and state funding. However, local communities will discover that some personnel are not capable of using modern technology and that an investment in training and education will be required.

Cowper: Technology will create a rapidly changing social environment to which police will have to adapt. At the same time, technology will permit radical new policing methods, systems, and processes that police will have to envision, create, incorporate, and learn. Technology will also create new opportunities for criminals and terrorists to prey on the innocent and exploit society's vulnerabilities. Technology will also allow fewer people to do much greater damage, driving an increased public demand for security; this will in turn impact privacy and civil liberties, exacerbating tensions between the police and the community.

Hailey: Tactically, many items of equipment being tested on the military battlefield today will find their way into American policing in the near future (e.g., surveillance via global positioning satellites and unmanned aerial drones). There appear to be technologies that will improve officer safety, such as better and faster communication in the field and improved identification and tracking procedures so the officer knows who he really has in custody and the location of the person or vehicles he's seeking. The less-than-lethal-force initiatives will get much more attention.

SAFETY VS. CIVIL LIBERTIES

A majority of respondents believe it is possible to increase surveillance and add high-tech spyware to better protect homeland security without interfering greatly with personal liberty. However, a significant minority wasn't so sure. All agreed, however, that vigilance on the part of both police and citizenry will be necessary to protect safety and rights absolutely. Said one Canadian respondent, "Accountability, professionalism, and ethics within an organization go a long way to help achieve this."

Alan Beckley: Citizens must accept that higher levels of security must result in reduced civil liberties.

Gary Sykes: There will have to be extensive accountability from police management and the courts if rights are to be protected.

Hailey: New technologies should add to public safety, but we may have to let go of a few civil liberties to get the maximum effect. It is all going to depend on the priorities of the people. What do they want, and how far do they want to go to get it?

Grebmeier: It will be a struggle. We must remain dedicated to protecting the Constitution.

Groups Dedicated to the Future of Policing

The Society of Police Futurists International (PFI) was officially constituted in August 1991. Its mission is "to foster excellence in policing by promoting and applying the discipline of Futures Research." Among its goals are:

- Establishing partnerships among law enforcement, the academic community, and the private sector.
- Sharing knowledge, information, and data among those partners.
- Developing long-range forecasts for trends affecting law enforcement and for law enforcement impacts on society.
- Serving as a clearinghouse for communicating creative, innovative, and proactive policing strategies.

PFI holds its annual meeting jointly with the World Future Society, where PFI offers several panels on law enforcement/criminal justice topics on the WFS program. PFI also provides an online newsletter and a Listserv for members. Asked what the role of PFI should be in the future, PFI founder William Tafoya said, "To serve as a clearinghouse for research and as a vanguard to inform the public about innovations in policing."

For more information, visit the PFI Web site, *www.policefuturists.org.*

The **FBI National Academy,** founded in 1935, provides leadership and specialized training. The Academy uses a stringent selection process to choose top and mid-level agency managers from departments across the United States and, since 1962, from more than 150 other countries.

In 1999, FBI Supervisory Agent Carl Jensen reintroduced the futuristics course at the National Academy and, in 2000, coordinated a conference on futuristics and law enforcement. As a result of this conference and the tragedy of September 11, 2001, the FBI collaborated with PFI to create a joint **Futures Working Group** (FWG) to help law enforcement deal with issues that will confront them in the near future.

The FWG, created in 2002, strives to "identify and promote innovation for the future of policing" by developing and promoting the use of forecasts and strategies to "ethically maximize the effectiveness of local, state, federal, and international law enforcement bodies as they strive to maintain peace."

Among FWG's early projects was a study of police and augmented-reality technology by PFI members Thomas Cowper (a state police inspector) and Michael Buerger of Bowling Green State University. The two dozen members of the group are also working on a national intelligence model, strategic-thinking training for the FBI's College of Analytical Studies, futures research training for the FBI Virtual Academy, a project on policing's vanishing boundaries, and a "best practices" in policing project, among others. Details: *www.fbi.gov/hq/td/fwg/workhome.htm.—Gene Stephens*

Conser: Where civil liberties seem to be an issue, it is often because the police are not trusted or have a less-than-stellar track record in upholding the trust of the people when it comes to protecting constitutional rights.

Eugene Hernandez: To balance safety and liberty, the citizenry will need to show greater flexibility and patience than has ever been exhibited in the past.

Cowper: One key is to dramatically improve the way police do business. Networked organizational models that radically improve information flow, reduce centralized decision making, and increase the speed and efficiency of police operations are essential to providing both safety and liberty.

Hailey: Police might follow the lead of the courts, which continue to shift from the "individual rights" era to the "greater good" era and look at what is beneficial for the greater good and sustenance of America.

THE PROMISES OF THE FUTURE

Better technology, better educated and trained officers and leaders, and better community ties were seen by most as the significant promises in the future of policing. One respondent added increased diversity, awareness, and knowledge, as well as increased information and knowledge sharing and communication, to the list.

Conser: I see positive and true leaders in the field who practice and demand professionalism, who challenge their officers to be the best, and who have an open, honest dialogue with their communities as being among the most significant highlights for the future of policing.

Cowper: I see an increased willingness of police agencies to work together, communicate, and share information across jurisdictions and levels of government.

Hernandez: Greater partnerships with the community, enhanced technology, and ethical, educated employees hold the most significant promise for policing's future.

Levin: Someday, we may learn to give up power in order to build relationships in our community, to see ourselves as professional service providers—and hire low-paid line workers to carry out the garbage (i.e., to conduct "combat policing").

THREATS IN POLICING'S FUTURE

The possibility that police will not be able to keep up with rapid change—terrorism, cybercrime, technology—was seen as the most serious threat, followed by the fear that higher priority for homeland security will result in the police becoming a serious threat to civil liberties. Another potential danger: misuse of power and abuse of authority by the men and women in charge. Policing, furthermore, has long been a "closed society" to outsiders, the so-called "blue brotherhood." Many of the threats mentioned by the respondents stem from the long-standing ability of police to operate independently and without close public scrutiny, a situation that is rapidly changing in this transparent information age.

Tafoya: Unqualified leadership—lacking vision or a sense of public service—poses the greatest threat to police. The greatest threat to the public is police enforcing the law and providing service that is directed by unqualified or underqualified leaders.

Bowers: Misuse of power and feelings of entitlement are likely to accompany any increases in authority.

Sykes: Aggressive policing and racial profiling could undermine the public's trust more than at present.

Hernandez: I see increased community pressure to return to a warrior officer who suppresses, through legal mandate, more civil liberties in response to homeland security.

Conser: There are not enough positive and true leaders to make sweeping changes to the field. Some other threats include:

- Terrorist tactics being used by domestic criminals (e.g., sophisticated gangs and/or drug operations) to divert police resources and keep populations insecure. The result could be vigilantism.
- Federalization of policing efforts in terms of policy, funding, direction, and control.
- Entangling alliances with private-sector corporations wherein there is no accountability for abuses that occur.
- Not looking to policing models and standards in other countries for innovations and possible alternatives (e.g., nations that have been dealing with terrorism for a long time, such as England, Ireland, France, and Israel, and countries whose police forces have higher entrance and training standards).

FINAL WORDS FROM THE PANELISTS

Lewis: Police must gain a grasp on emerging high-tech crime if they are to fulfill their sworn duty of protecting and serving the public. I once overheard a work-release prisoner discussing with a park worker at the beach how one went about stealing a person's identity. This is a new cottage industry that police don't investigate.

Cowper: Twentieth-century solutions executed with twentieth-century speed will not solve twenty-first-century problems.

Grebmeier: Every U.S. law enforcement officer takes an oath to defend and protect the Constitution. We cannot allow public fear or political pressure to sway us from our original oath. We exist to protect the rights of the public. We are the first line of defense in protection of the Constitution and the Bill of Rights. Our role is to provide leadership, direction, and set the standard, both professionally and ethically.

FROM WARRIOR COPS TO COMMUNITY BUILDERS

PFI members expressed cautious optimism about the potential for defining and fulfilling an effective mission for policing in the future.

The paramilitary, combat model dominating policing around the world for more than a century will likely continue to prevail in nations ruled by dictators or military force. In democratic countries, however, a consensus model based at the community level will slowly replace this approach to "fighting" crime, and this is the model that will prevail in policing within the next few years. Combat will still be necessary occasionally to root out terrorists and violent gang activity, but even here police-community partnerships to proactively prevent such activity have begun to replace military tactics.

One major change will be refinement of the new model, already begun with the New York City Police Department's COMSTAT (computer comparison statistics) program. COMSTAT has been so successful in reducing street crime and violence that it is being adopted by police agencies across the United States and beyond. St. Louis police researcher and PFI member Kenneth Hailey described the process as "communicate, cooperate, gather information, share information, investigate relentlessly, and follow up." The four major goals established for COMSTAT are accurate and timely intelligence, effective tactics, rapid deployment of personnel and resources, and relentless follow-up and assessment.

The top cops admit that even this will not be enough to cope with the complex, high-tech information age. Bioterrorism, identity theft, cyber-stalking, and crimes not yet defined will require more intelligent, better educated and trained, and more tech-savvy officers and leaders than are now available in policing. Today a large majority of agencies require only a high-school diploma or equivalency to begin a career in policing. Training usually consists of 12 to 16 weeks of academy work and a six-month probationary period, during which superiors evaluate the new officer. A few departments have specialists coping with Internet crime, but most do not. Leadership and management courses are offered for some, but coping with emerging technology and transnational crime and disorder has just begun to be part of the training.

Police need a new structure that fosters teamwork and cooperation with other agencies and community groups—where police in some cases must give up some of their power and become subsidiaries in a larger operation. The "cowboy" officers drawn to policing to shoot guns, bark orders, and "kick butt" are unlikely to accept the new role or be competent to fill it.

The twenty-first-century police candidate, thus, must be carefully chosen and then trained and mentored to fill the role of modern policing. Only then will policing become a true profession; and only then will police be able to deliver on their mission to protect and serve the citizenry.

Discussion Questions

1. What changes can we anticipate regarding the future of policing?
2. Discuss the particular threats posed to the future of policing, and identify means by which these threats can be addressed.

3. Describe policing in the year 2070. Will there be a need for traditional policing? What role will technology play?

III

Courts

INTRODUCTiON

The American court system provides perhaps the most symbolic image of justice. The symbolism associated with the courts, including the judge's robe and gavel, the courtroom design, and the formality expected in the courtroom, suggests that justice will be served. Society has an expectation that courtroom professionals, such as judges, prosecutors, and defense attorneys, will convene in the courtroom and the truth and justice will emerge. Though we'd like to believe that truth and justice always emerge from the courtroom, this is not the case. Determining just how often justice is served has challenged researchers for quite some time.

Courts serve the vital function of adjudication. Accordingly, defendants enter court for several reasons, including an initial appearance, an arraignment, and a trial. In the United States, there are different levels of courts that have specific jurisdictions and serve different functions. For instance, there are trial and appellate courts, courts of limited jurisdiction and general jurisdiction, and state and federal courts. Furthermore, there are drug courts, teen courts, and various other specialized courts.

Part III highlights critical issues facing our courts. Among the issues are the challenges of dispensing justice immediately following a natural disaster, plea bargaining, the rights of defense attorneys, jury selection, self-defense, wrongful convictions, the use of DNA in the criminal justice system, and capital punishment. Part III begins with an examination of how justice was to be served in light of a natural disaster. The article "A Court in a Storm" addresses the challenges faced by courtroom personnel following Hurricane Katrina. Though the devastating effects of Katrina were well documented in the media, we heard little about how the natural disaster impacted the courts. Crime continued in the wake of the hurricane, and dispensing justice was troublesome to say the least.

Plea bargaining has become the backbone of the U.S. court system. Roughly nine out of ten cases entering the courts are settled via plea negotiations. Despite the benefits of plea bargaining, some question whether negotiated justice is true justice. In other words, our system wasn't designed to rely primarily on negotiations in efforts to find justice. However, our system wasn't designed to accommodate the large numbers of individuals entering our courts. Plea bargaining prevents our court systems from becoming ever more overburdened, although some question whether we're sacrificing due process rights for the sake of public order when the court system encourages individuals to plead guilty through offering incentives.

". . . You have the right to consult an attorney. If you cannot afford an attorney, one will be appointed for you before any questioning." These words, as found within the Miranda warning issued to all arrestees prior to questioning, inform defendants of their Sixth Amendment right to representation. Providing representation to all attempts to ensure that justice, not necessarily victory, is attained. The article "Rights of Defense" highlights specific challenges faced by defense attorneys, who are hired to represent individuals who are technically "innocent until proven guilty," but who are sometimes informally viewed as "guilty until proven innocent."

Effective jury selection requires a great deal of skill on behalf of attorneys. Deciding who should or should not be included in a jury is a challenge for all criminal attorneys. Jury selection not only involves evaluating members of a jury pool to determine their suitability to serve on a jury, but also structuring a jury that may view issues in a particular manner. The article "How Much Should Lawyers Know When Picking a Jury?" addresses one of the more controversial aspects of jury selection. Should attorneys know as much as possible about potential jury members, or should their decision to accept or reject individuals be based on the impression potential jurors make during voir dire?

Part III continues with examination of the controversy surrounding the use of claims regarding self-defense. The article "Self-Defense vs. Municipal Gun Bans" documents a situation in which an individual believed that he was protecting himself and his family, yet found himself in violation of the law. Gun control is always a controversial subject, as society remains divided regarding the situations under which we should have the right to bear arms, and whether the right to bear arms applies to all individuals and all types of arms. The article demonstrates how policies designed to protect individuals in society may sometimes come back to haunt them.

You're sitting in your home watching television. The police knock on the door and barge into your house. They have an arrest warrant for you; however, you've done nothing wrong. You're placed under arrest in front of your family and are removed from your home. You're eventually convicted of a crime you didn't commit and serve five years in prison. Could a situation like this actually occur, and if so, how? Put simply, yes, a similar situation could occur and misinformation could be one of the many reasons. Wrongful convictions damage the reputation of the criminal justice system by highlighting the weaknesses in the system. The article "The Innocents" addresses the plights of several wrongfully convicted individuals, providing readers insight to lives turned upside down.

Each human being consists of DNA, which has recently become a tool used in the courts to convict and acquit with greater certainty. DNA analyses are notably convincing, and the use of DNA has arguably lowered the error rate in our courts. The selection "Evil Twins" highlights a limitation to DNA analysis: Identical twins share the same DNA, making it difficult to directly implicate an individual who shares the same DNA with another person.

The final selection in Part III concerns the impact of capital punishment on the criminal justice system. Many aspects of capital punishment are controversial. For instance, some claim the punishment is in violation of the Eighth Amendment protection from cruel and unusual punishment. The effects of capital punishment are felt by many: victims, offenders, the victims' families, and the justice system. The impact of capital punishment on courtroom personnel is discussed in the article "Effects of Capital Punishment on the Justice System." We often assume that the courtroom personnel are distanced from the impact of courtroom actions and results. However, these employees sometimes find it difficult to distance themselves from the human tragedy that often exists in our courts.

The courts can provide great drama, as it is during the adjudication process that "the story is told." In other words, the case is discussed in court and details are shared. The police make arrests and corrections officers enforce penalties; however, the courts are where information is provided for public consumption.

Our courts are far from perfect. However, adjudication practices have progressed since the days when guilt or innocence was determined via trial by ordeal and other primitive means. For instance, defendants in earlier times were expected to stick their hand into a pot of boiling water for a period of time. They were deemed guilty if they died, and innocent if they lived. (I personally believe such tests of justice had much to do with the temperature of the water and how long one's hand was in the water.) Fortunately, today's quest for justice is far more civilized.

17

A Court in a Storm

By Aaron Kuriloff

What do you do if you're a judge and a catastrophic hurricane devastates your community? Carry on business as usual, of course. Such was the case in St. Bernard Parish following Hurricane Katrina. Though New Orleans was in a state of emergency following the natural disaster, crime did not stop. Nor did the need for justice. The individuals who carried on the courtroom proceedings did so without the modern conveniences they enjoyed prior to the hurricane. However, the Louisiana rules of criminal procedure require all defendants to appear before a magistrate within 72 hours. The rules say nothing about exceptions made for devastation following a hurricane. There is a clause, however, permitting the governor to suspend filing deadlines and statutes of limitations, and the governor utilized the clause. Eventually, all legal proceedings in the greater New Orleans area would be halted by the state Supreme Court.

As evidenced in this selection, judges, defense attorneys, prosecutors, and all others involved in courtroom proceedings felt the impact of Hurricane Katrina both personally and professionally. Similar to the New Orleans police officers who had to ensure the well-being of themselves, their families, and others, the New Orleans courtroom personnel had to ensure their safety, and then recognize their professional obligation to ensure that justice was served.

Crime problems compounded the chaos in New Orleans following Hurricane Katrina. The norm-lessness in the community, the pressing need for emergency response, the devastation of courthouses, and the lack of communications for law enforcement provided ample opportunities for criminals to commit crime. Those who were caught, however, initially had to face makeshift courtrooms where a sense of frontier justice existed. After a period of time, defendants were sent to a safer, more functional juris-diction for processing. While sending the defendants to another jurisdiction may seem to have limited repercussions, consider that many courtrooms across the country are already overcrowded. Consider the docket of the courtrooms that had to deal with the burden of cases from New Orleans in addition to their regular caseloads. The impact of Hurricane Katrina was certainly felt inside and outside of New Orleans.

Place yourself in the role of a defense attorney preparing for a capital murder case. You're expected at court the morning after Hurricane Katrina hits. However, the phone lines are down, you cannot drive on the city streets, you're unsure if your friends and family members are safe, you cannot locate your key witnesses, and the evidence you collected to help win the case was washed away after your office was flooded. You also have a series of other cases and are unsure whether you'll be prepared for them until you return to your flooded office, which may be in a few weeks. Now consider that you're but one of many defense attorneys impacted by the hurricane, and there are likely an equal number of prosecutors facing the same challenges. Judges had the unenviable task of reassembling courtrooms and adjudicating a backlog of cases upon return to New Orleans. Locating witnesses, prosecutors, defense attorneys, police officers, and related individuals were among the many challenges judges faced.

The professional considerations in this account pale in comparison to the tragic personal stories we heard from New Orleans following the hurricane. Nevertheless, Hurricane Katrina undoubtedly impacted all components of the criminal justice system, which in turn impacted many lives, and liberties.

Hurricane victims find protection and prosecution behind the walls of a Louisiana courthouse.

ST. Bernard Parish lies in the coastal marshes of Louisiana, just east of New Orleans. It is a blue-collar suburb of more than 65,000 people, many of them fishermen and oil-refinery workers. On its Plain of Chalmette, Andrew Jackson fought the Battle of New Orleans 191 years ago, defeating the British and ending the War of 1812. Today, Chalmette is the parish seat. Near its center, just opposite the levee holding back the Mississippi River, stands the parish courthouse, an Art Deco edifice built in 1939 of gray stone, concrete, and rebar. In 1965, it was one of the few structures to survive Hurricane Betsy unscathed, which is why, as Hurricane Katrina barreled toward St. Bernard Parish 40 years later, Judge Kirk Vaughn concluded that his tiny courtroom on the building's second floor was the safest place to be.

St. Bernard's voters have kept Vaughn on the state District Court bench for 15 years—longer than any other judge in the parish. It is a distinction that no doubt derives from the laconic 55-year-old's talent for resolving disputes at a brisk, inexorable pace. He prepared for Katrina by clearing the docket, working into the night on Sunday, August 28, until the local jail was empty and the prisoners were on their way to safety. He had finished by the time the hurricane made landfall early Monday morning. Vaughn's wife, son, and daughter, as well as his son's girlfriend, joined him in his office next to the courtroom, and the three-story building's thick walls and roof muffled the wind and rain. Around 8 A.M., a levee broke on the Industrial Canal to the west, and, as water surged over the adjacent neighborhoods, residents fled to the courthouse for shelter. They came by the dozens in trucks and on foot, telling of torrents and walls of water and of buildings collapsing beneath them. They bedded down on floors, in jury boxes, anywhere they could find space. And as water streamed under the building's heavy front doors, it became clear that the business of the courthouse was no longer justice.

St. Bernard Parish may have suffered from Katrina as much as any region in greater New Orleans. At least 123 people died there, and while the courthouse stood up to the elements, almost all of the other 27,000 or so stores, houses, and public buildings were destroyed. Waterways border all four sides of St. Bernard, and levees broke on three. Floods inundated the parish to a depth of 20 feet, submerging single-story structures and overwhelming rescue workers. The notion of maintaining any semblance of law and order seemed absurd at the time, and yet, to a remarkable degree, Vaughn and the people who worked by his side kept the legal system intact.

The levee breach along the Industrial Canal was an early sign of disaster. The water rose so fast that it trapped 11 St. Bernard sheriff's detectives on the second floor of their office near the railroad tracks bordering New Orleans. The unnerved detectives radioed the courthouse for Sheriff Jack Stephens, a 6 foot 4 inch former high school lineman who approaches problems the way he once approached opposing running backs. Stephens grabbed an assistant and navigated a small boat through the flooded streets, reaching the trapped detectives within minutes. He pulled them through a second-story window and whisked them to the courthouse.

Minutes before the courthouse also started to flood, Vaughn left to move his car from a nearby parking lot to a spot above the rising water. As he opened the car door, puddles splashed around his ankles. "Next thing I knew, water was coming into the car," he said, describing the short drive to higher ground. "And by the time I got out, it was coming over the wheels." Back at the courthouse, black, muddy pools spread under the building's front doors, across the marble floors, and down three steps to the clerk of courts' office and record room. Thousands of documents were saturated. By nightfall, the water stood three feet deep on the first floor and continued to rise. The courthouse had no lights or electricity and scant supplies of canned food and drink. The taps stopped running when the water mains broke. Toilets overflowed, sending sewage into the stagnant floodwater. Dozens of dogs and cats roamed the hallways, and smoke from cigarettes hung thick in the air. An elderly woman died—of exposure, stress, or a pre-existing medical condition; nobody knew for sure—leaving behind her weeping husband. She was laid to rest temporarily in the back corner of the state's largest courtroom, in the wan light from decorative-glass windows.

Still, the business of criminal justice carried on. Sheriff's deputies conducting rescue operations in small boats arrested one man who had apparently looted global positioning systems and other navigational gear from flooded retailers and wrecked work boats that had washed into town. The deputies also brought in several men and women who had gotten drunk and started fights at rescue shelters. The Louisiana rules of criminal procedure require that all suspects face charges before a magistrate judge within 72 hours or be set free. So Vaughn, working off a yellow legal pad and dressed in the jeans he had worn since Katrina hit land two days before, sat in his clothes-strewn office and held hearings to approve or dismiss the charges against the suspects.

It was little more than "frontier justice," Vaughn explained later. The suspects did not have legal representation, because no defense attorneys were at the courthouse or reachable in the outside world. Criminal records were soaked, so the judge pieced together the suspects' arrest histories by relying on his memory and the files of District Attorney Jack Rowley, who had been with Vaughn since Sunday. Nobody discussed whether the hearings were constitutional. "I wish we could say we did that," said Vaughn, "but we had no time." In any event, the jail had become an emergency medical facility, so all the cases ended the same way: suspects released on bail or their own recognizance, then turned over to deputies for evacuation.

After several days of the makeshift hearings, Vaughn received notice of a state Supreme Court order halting all legal proceedings in the greater New Orleans area. The damage that the hurricane and floods had inflicted on the legal system was just too great, the court concluded. Besides, an emergency order from the governor's office soon suspended filing deadlines and statutes of limitation, so "there was no pressing need to meet deadlines," Vaughn said. The judge finished his last hearing on September 1, four days after his vigil at the courthouse began, and set about the business of pressing federal officials for the people and equipment necessary to make the courthouse run again.

Crime, of course, did not stop. Residents were ordered to leave St. Bernard a few days later, and sheriff's deputies guarded the bridges to the parish against the residents' return. In mid-September, a truck slipped into a convoy of pickups carrying contractors. When the truck tried to leave the parish a few hours later, it was stopped, and the three people inside were searched. Sheriff's deputies found muddy tools, three ounces of cocaine, and other items apparently looted from the deserted houses and stores. With legal proceedings suspended and the parish jails sheltering the injured, the deputies were forced to improvise. They ferried the suspects to a jail in neighboring Plaquemines Parish, and then had them moved upriver to St. Gabriel Parish for a magistrate hearing. When the suspects couldn't come up with bail, they were transferred to the Louisiana State Penitentiary at Angola. The prison houses some of the state's most dangerous criminals, including those on death row, making the incarceration of mere suspects there "not really a good thing," explained Col. Richard Baumy of the sheriff's office.

In late September, Vaughn stopped spending nights on an air mattress in his office and, his house destroyed, moved to the Scotia Prince, a retired ferry docked nearby on the Mississippi River. His family had left the courthouse earlier in the month to stay temporarily at a home north of Lake Pontchartrain, but Vaughn stayed to help rebuild the judicial system, living on chicken and jugs of water supplied by the National Guard.

By mid-October, the water had drained from the courthouse, electrical power had been restored, and the clerk's office had opened again. Clerk of Courts Lena Torres sent sodden case records to an ice cream company for preservation in a freezer. They were later taken to be freeze-dried in Texas and, if they are not much the worse for wear, will return to Torres when business approaches normal in St. Bernard.

Discussion Questions

1. Discuss how court personnel in New Orleans initially responded to Hurricane Katrina.
2. What is the author implying with the term "frontier justice" as it applied to the courts of New Orleans following Hurricane Katrina?

3. What impact did the Louisiana governor have on the adjudication of suspects following Hurricane Katrina? Discuss how this action could have violated the individual rights of those caught up in the system.

18

The Case Against Plea Bargaining

By Timothy Lynch

Plea bargaining is vital to criminal justice practices. Over 90 percent of criminal cases are settled via a plea bargain, despite the fact that plea bargaining isn't a formal step in the criminal justice system. Defendants do not have a right to plea bargain—it's an informal exchange between the prosecution and the defense that comes to fruition only upon approval of a judge. Cases go to trial if one of the parties involved in plea negotiations or the judge declines the offer.

So, what exactly is plea bargaining? It involves defendants admitting guilt in exchange for some reward. The reward could involve (1) being charged with a lesser offense, which in turn brings about a reduced sentence; (2) a reduction in counts in cases in which a defendant is charged with multiple counts of a crime; (3) a promise by the prosecutor to recommend to the judge that a lenient sentence be imposed; or (4) an alteration in the charges filed against a defendant to something more socially acceptable (e.g., changing the charge from sexual assault to assault). The benefits associated with plea bargaining contribute to its widespread use; however, there are some serious concerns regarding the heavy reliance on plea bargaining, as noted in this selection.

The high percentage of cases settled via plea bargaining is largely attributable to the associated benefits. For instance, judges benefit from plea bargaining through the expedition of cases in their typically busy courtrooms. Prosecutors and victims enjoy the security of a conviction after successfully engaging in plea bargaining, whereas defendants and their attorneys receive whatever rewards the prosecution offered during plea negotiations. Why, then, is there concern regarding the practice?

Critics of plea bargaining contend that true justice is not served when a defendant is enticed or persuaded into admitting guilt in exchange for a reward. They argue that a disturbing number of individuals will admit guilt in cases when they are indeed innocent simply to avoid serious punishment. Plea bargaining, they argue, damages the integrity of our courts and justice system. Our system was not built on the idea that justice would be determined through negotiation. Instead, it was proposed that justice would be determined via a sharing of evidence and informed discussion.

Imagine that you've been arrested for an armed robbery you didn't commit. You face 10 years in prison. Let's assume the evidence is such that you face a 50 percent chance of being acquitted. This also means, however, you face a 50 percent chance of being convicted. The prosecutor approaches your attorney with a deal. If you plead guilty, the prosecutor will see to it that you receive a sentence of only five years. Would you do it? What if the deal was that you admit guilt and serve three years? One year? Now would you do it? How about probation in return for you admitting guilt? By now, most people will agree to admit guilt to something they didn't do, simply because the deal was enticing. Given that there is a point at which most people will admit guilt to something they didn't do, consider how many innocent people enter our correctional system.

Will plea bargaining remain the primary means through which we seek justice in our courts? Only time will tell. However, clogged courtroom dockets and a large number of defendants entering our courts require expediency. For better or for worse, informal negotiations in the form of plea agreements provide a resource-saving alternative to jury trials and keep our courts on track. The biggest challenge is to ensure that we're not sacrificing justice for the sake of efficiency.

Plea bargaining has come to dominate the administration of justice in America. According to one legal scholar, "Every two seconds during a typical workday, a criminal case is disposed of in an American courtroom by way of a guilty plea or nolo contendere plea." Even though plea bargaining pervades the justice system, I argue that the practice should be abolished because it is unconstitutional.

THE RISE AND FALL OF ADVERSARIAL TRIALS

Because any person who is accused of violating the criminal law can lose his liberty, and perhaps even his life depending on the offense and prescribed penalty, the Framers of the Constitution took pains to put explicit limits on the awesome powers of government. The Bill of Rights explicitly guarantees several safeguards to the accused, including the right to be informed of the charges, the right not to be compelled to incriminate oneself, the right to a speedy and public trial, the right to an impartial jury trial in the state and district where the offense allegedly took place, the right to cross-examine the state's witnesses, the right to call witnesses on one's own behalf, and the right to the assistance of counsel.

Justice Hugo Black once noted that, in America, the defendant "has an absolute, unqualified right to compel the State to investigate its own case, find its own witnesses, prove its own facts, and convince the jury through its own resources. Throughout the process, the defendant has a fundamental right to remain silent, in effect challenging the State at every point to 'Prove it!' " By limiting the powers of the police and prosecutors, the Bill of Rights safeguards freedom.

Given the Fifth Amendment's prohibition of compelled self-incrimination and the Sixth Amendment's guarantee of impartial juries, one would think that the administration of criminal justice in America would be marked by adversarial trials—and yet, the opposite is true. Fewer than 10 percent of the criminal cases brought by the federal government each year are actually tried before juries with all of the accompanying procedural safeguards noted above. More than 90 percent of the criminal cases in America are never tried, much less proven, to juries. The overwhelming majority of individuals who are accused of crime forgo their constitutional rights and plead guilty.

The rarity of jury trials is not the result of criminals who come into court to relieve a guilty conscience or save taxpayers the costs of a trial. The truth is that government officials have deliberately engineered the system to assure that the jury trial system established by the Constitution is seldom used. And plea bargaining is the primary technique used by the government to bypass the institutional safeguards in trials.

Plea bargaining consists of an agreement (formal or informal) between the defendant and the prosecutor. The prosecutor typically agrees to a reduced prison sentence in return for the defendant's waiver of his constitutional right against self-incrimination and his right to trial. As one critic has written, "The leniency is payment to a defendant to induce him or her not to go to trial. The guilty plea or no contest plea is the quid pro quo for the concession; there is no other reason."

Plea bargaining unquestionably alleviates the workload of judges, prosecutors, and defense lawyers. But is it proper for a government that is constitutionally required to respect the right to trial

"The Case Against Plea Bargaining" by Timothy Lynch, *Regulation*, Fall 2003, pp. 24–27. Reprinted by permission of Regulation Magazine.

by jury to use its charging and sentencing powers to pressure an individual to waive that right? There is no doubt that government officials deliberately use their power to pressure people who have been accused of crime, and who are presumed innocent, to confess their guilt and waive their right to a formal trial. We know this to be true because prosecutors freely admit that this is what they do.

Watershed precedent

Paul Lewis Hayes, for example, was indicted for attempting to pass a forged check in the amount of $88.30, an offense that was punishable by a prison term of two to 10 years. The prosecutor offered to recommend a sentence of five years if Hayes would waive his right to trial and plead guilty to the charge. The prosecutor also made it clear to Hayes that if he did not plead guilty and "save the court the inconvenience and necessity of a trial," the state would seek a new indictment from a grand jury under Kentucky's "Habitual Criminal Act." Under the provisions of that statute, Hayes would face a mandatory sentence of life imprisonment because of his prior criminal record. Despite the enormous pressure exerted upon him by the state, Hayes insisted on his right to jury trial. He was subsequently convicted and then sentenced to life imprisonment.

On appeal, Hayes argued that the prosecutor violated the Constitution by threatening to punish him for simply invoking his right to a trial. In response, the government freely admitted that the only reason a new indictment was filed against Hayes was to deter him from exercising that right. Because the indictment was supported by the evidence, the government maintained that the prosecutor had done nothing improper. The case ultimately reached the U.S. Supreme Court for a resolution. In a landmark 5–4 ruling, *Bordenkircher v. Hayes,* the Court approved the prosecutor's handling of the case and upheld the draconian sentence of life imprisonment. Because the 1978 case is considered to be the watershed precedent for plea bargaining, it deserves careful attention.

The *Hayes* ruling acknowledged that it would be "patently unconstitutional" for any agent of the government "to pursue a course of action whose objective is to penalize a person's reliance on his legal rights." The Court, however, declined to overturn Hayes's sentence because he could have completely avoided the risk of life imprisonment by admitting his guilt and accepting a prison term of five years. The constitutional rationale for plea bargaining is that there is "no element of punishment or retaliation so long as the accused is free to accept or reject the prosecution's offer."

WHY THE SUPREME COURT WAS WRONG

Initially, the Court's proposition in *Hayes* seems plausible because criminal defendants have always been allowed to waive their right to a trial, and the executive and legislative branches have always had discretion with respect to their charging and sentencing policies. But a closer inspection will show that the constitutional rationale underlying plea bargaining cannot withstand scrutiny.

First, it is important to note that the existence of some element of choice has never been thought to justify otherwise wrongful conduct. As the Supreme Court itself observed in another context, "It always is for the interest of a party under duress to choose the lesser of two evils. But the fact that a choice was made according to interest does not exclude duress. It is the characteristic of duress properly so called."

The courts have employed similar reasoning in tort disputes between private parties. For example, a woman brought a false imprisonment action against a male acquaintance after he allegedly forced her to travel with him in his automobile when it was her desire to travel by train. According to the complaint, the man boarded the train, seized the woman's purse, and then disembarked and proceeded to his car. The woman then left the train to retrieve her purse. While arguing with the man in the parking lot, the train left the station. Reluctantly, the woman got into the vehicle to travel to her destination. The man maintained that the false imprisonment claim lacked merit because he exercised no physical force against the woman and because she was at liberty to remain on the train or to go her own way. The court rejected that defense and ruled that the false imprisonment theory had merit because the woman did not wish to leave the train and she did not wish to depart without her purse. The man unlawfully interfered with the woman's liberty to be where she wished to be. The fact that the man had given the woman some choices that she could "accept or reject" did not alter the fact that the man was a tortfeasor.

Second, the Supreme Court has repeatedly invalidated certain governmental actions that were purposely designed to coerce individuals and organizations into surrendering their constitutional rights. In the 1978 case *Marshall v. Barlow's Inc.,* the Court ruled that a businessman was within his rights when he refused to allow an Occupational Safety and Health Administration inspector into his establishment without a search warrant. The secretary of labor filed a legal brief arguing that when people make the decision to go into business, they essentially "consent" to governmental inspections of their property. Even though the owner of the premises could have avoided such inspections by shutting down his business, the Court recognized that the OSHA regulations penalized commercial property owners for exercising their right under the Fourth Amendment to insist that government inspectors obtain search warrants before demanding access to the premises.

In the 1978 case *Nollan v. California Coastal Commission,* the Court ruled that the state of California could not grant a development permit subject to the condition that the landowners allow the public an easement across a portion of their property. Even though the landowners had the option of "accepting or rejecting" the Coastal Commission's deal, the Court recognized that the permit condition, in the circumstances of that case, amounted to an "out-and-out plan of extortion."

Similarly, in the 1974 case *Miami Herald Publishing Co. v. Tornillo,* the Supreme Court invalidated a so-called "right of reply" statute. The Florida legislature made it a crime for a newspaper to criticize a politician and then to deny that politician a "right to equal space" in the paper to defend himself against such criticism. Even though Florida newspapers remained free to say whatever they wished, the Court recognized that the statute exacted a "penalty" for the simple exercise of free speech about political affairs.

Finally, the ad hoc nature of the *Hayes* precedent becomes apparent when one extends its logic to other rights involving criminal procedure. The Court has never proffered a satisfactory explanation with respect to why the government should not be able to use its sentencing powers to leverage the waiver of constitutional rights pertaining to the trial itself. Can federal prosecutors enter into "negotiations" with criminal defendants with respect to the exercise of their trial rights? For example, when a person is accused of a crime, he has the option of hiring an experienced attorney to prepare a legal defense on his behalf or representing himself without the aid of counsel.

Can a prosecutor induce a defendant into waiving his right to the assistance of counsel with a recommendation for leniency in the event of a conviction? Such prosecutorial tactics are presently unheard of. And yet, under the rationale of the *Hayes* case, it is not obvious why such tactics should be constitutionally barred. After all, under *Hayes* there is no element of punishment or retaliation so long as the accused is free to accept or reject the prosecutor's offer.

Sophistry to pretend otherwise

Plea bargaining rests on the constitutional fiction that our government does not retaliate against individuals who wish to exercise their right to trial by jury. Although the fictional nature of that proposition has been apparent to many for some time now, what is new is that more and more people are reaching the conclusion that it is intolerable. Chief Judge William G. Young of the Federal District Court in Massachusetts, for example, recently filed an opinion that was refreshingly candid about what is happening in the modern criminal justice system:

> Evidence of sentencing disparity visited on those who exercise their Sixth Amendment right to trial by jury is today stark, brutal, and incontrovertible. . . . Today, under the Sentencing Guidelines regime with its vast shift of power to the Executive, that disparity has widened to an incredible 500 percent. As a practical matter this means, as between two similarly situated defendants, that if the one who pleads and cooperates gets a four-year sentence, then the guideline sentence for the one who exercises his right to trial by

jury and is convicted will be 20 years. Not surprisingly, such a disparity imposes an extraordinary burden on the free exercise of the right to an adjudication of guilt by one's peers. Criminal trial rates in the United States and in this District are plummeting due to the simple fact that today we punish people—punish them severely—simply for going to trial. It is the sheerest sophistry to pretend otherwise.

SANDEFUR'S CHALLENGE

Attorney Timothy Sandefur . . . concedes that plea bargaining is "rife with unfair prosecutorial tactics" and needs "reform." But he rejects the proposition that plea bargaining is unconstitutional. Let us examine Sandefur's defense of plea bargaining.

First, everyone acknowledges that the state may not punish or penalize a person for simply invoking a right that is supposed to be guaranteed under the Constitution. And yet, this is precisely what the government does with plea bargaining. For example, every month police officers in Washington, D.C. encounter tourists who are carrying handguns. The tourists are unaware of the District's strict laws against handgun possession. They regularly surrender handguns to police officers who are supervising metal detectors at museums around the capital. When the tourists openly surrender their firearms, they mistakenly believe that they are doing nothing illegal. The gun is then confiscated and the tourist is arrested. If a tourist agrees to forgo a trial and plead guilty, prosecutors do not request jail time. However, if a tourist were to seek a jury trial, prosecutors would respond with additional charges, such as possession of illegal ammunition (conceivably, a count for each bullet in the pistol chamber). Not surprisingly, 99.9 percent of the tourists decide to plead guilty.

Sandefur argues that, in such cases criminal defendants are not being punished for a refusal to bargain; they are instead being punished for "violating the law." According to Sandefur, the tourists have no right to complain because they have no "right to leniency." That line of argument has surface appeal, but it is defective. The logical fallacy of division says that what may be true for the whole is not necessarily true for the parts. Thus, a prosecutor can indeed "throw the book" at any given tourist. However, if it came to light that the prosecutor was targeting, say, Hispanics for harsher treatment, we would know that something was very wrong. The retort that Hispanic arrestees do not have a "right to leniency" would be an unsatisfying defense of the prosecutor's handling of such cases. Plea bargaining tactics fail for similar, though perhaps more subtle, reasons. Just because the state can throw the book at someone does not mean that it can use its power to retaliate against a person who wishes to exercise his right to a trial.

Sandefur's defense of plea bargaining repeatedly returns to the idea that criminal defendants have the "right to make a contract," as in other free-trade situations. But plea bargaining is not free trade. It is a forced association. Once a person has been charged with a crime, he does not have the option of walking away from the state.

Sandefur argues that because individuals can waive many of their constitutional rights, they can also "sell" their rights. Even if that argument had merit, it is not the law. But, more importantly, one suspects that it is not the law because the argument lacks merit. Imagine four people who are charged with auto theft. One defendant pleads guilty to the offense and receives three years of jail time. The second defendant insists upon a trial, but sells his right to call his own witnesses. After conviction, he receives four years. The third defendant insists on a trial, but sells his right to be represented by his famous attorney-uncle, F. Lee Bailey. Instead, he hires a local attorney and, in addition, sells his right to a speedy trial. After conviction, he receives five years. The fourth insists upon a trial, presents a rigorous but unsuccessful defense and, after conviction, receives a prison sentence of 10 years. Are the disparate punishments for the same offense sensible? The courtroom just does not seem to be the proper place for an auction and haggling.

The constitutional defect with plea bargaining is systemic, not episodic. The rarity of jury trials is not the result of some spontaneous order spawned by contract negotiations between individuals.

CONCLUSION

Thomas Jefferson famously observed that "the natural progress of things is for liberty to yield and government to gain ground." The American experience with plea bargaining is yet another confirmation of that truth. The Supreme Court unleashed a runaway train when it sanctioned plea bargaining in *Bordenkircher v. Hayes*. Despite a steady media diet of titillating criminal trials in recent years, there is an increasing recognition that jury trials are now a rarity in America—and that something, somewhere, is seriously amiss. That "something" is plea bargaining.

As with so many other areas of constitutional law, the Court must stop tinkering around the edges of the issue and return to first principles. It is true that plea bargaining speeds caseload disposition, but it does so in an unconstitutional manner. The Framers of the Constitution were aware of less time-consuming trial procedures when they wrote the Bill of Rights, but chose not to adopt them. The Framers believed the Bill of Rights, and the freedom it secured, was well worth any costs that resulted. If that vision is to endure, the Supreme Court must come to its defense.

Discussion Questions

1. Discuss the primary arguments against plea bargaining. What are the benefits of plea bargaining?
2. Discuss the significance of plea bargaining regarding the court case *Bordenkircher v. Hayes*.
3. What do you believe could be done to address the limitations of plea bargaining? Keep in mind that our courts are currently overcrowded and plea bargaining expedites the adjudication process.

19

Rights of Defense

By Andrew Rachlin

In 1963, the U.S. Supreme Court ruled that states were constitutionally required to provide representation to everyone, including those who cannot afford it. This decision, as stated in the case Gideon v. Wainwright, largely impacted the criminal justice system. Consider our criminal justice system if only those with means maintained representation in criminal case processing. One can only imagine the level of injustice that would exist if the poor, who are disproportionately represented in our courts, were not provided representation. While the Court ruled that indigent defendants are to be provided representation, it said little about the quality of the representation.

Representation for the indigent (i.e., those who cannot afford representation) comes in various forms. Public defender's offices are created solely to provide representation for the poor. Their offices are primarily in large cities where most crime occurs. Some jurisdictions use the assigned counsel system in which attorneys practicing in a particular jurisdiction are encouraged or required to provide indigent representation. Other areas use contract systems in which a law firm will contract with the court to provide representation to the indigent for a set period of time for an established cost.

Indigent defense is not a high priority for many jurisdictions. To begin, those who enter courts are technically "innocent until proven guilty." In reality, they may appear "guilty until proven innocent." The challenge for indigent defendants is to find adequate representation. The level of resources devoted to indigent representation is nowhere near the level of resources provided to district attorneys. In turn, attorneys representing the indigent are faced with large caseloads and limited resources—two significant challenges to say the least.

Let's assume you're a taxpaying citizen. You're provided a breakdown of where your tax money goes. Would you rather your money go toward the defense attorney (who indeed represents mostly, although not all, guilty individuals) or toward the district attorney's office, where the prosecution of criminals is a priority? Chances are, you'd like to have the bad guys put away, thus you'd prefer your resources go toward crime control and the district attorney's office. However, consider the plight of the poor in our criminal justice system. They are constitutionally guaranteed representation. Where, do you suggest, funding for their representation comes from? Would you like to devote a small portion of your taxes toward representing them? Does your response seem fair? Defendants are innocent until proven guilty. Wouldn't it make more sense, given their status prior to conviction, to devote more resources to indigent representation?

Let's be real. Most defendants who enter courts are guilty. The challenge is to provide adequate representation for all. Some cases are clear-cut and defense attorneys know they are dealing with a no-win situation. Should they pretend that their client is innocent and continue to waste government resources? No—but their job is to secure the best outcome for their clients. Again, all defendants are innocent until proven guilty. Thus the job of the defense attorney is to protect defendants' rights.

Indigent representation is a difficult subject for the general public. In one sense, the public generally prefers that everyone receive a fair day in court. On the other hand, some believe that some defendants try to beat the system and waste government resources. In the end, it's a classic battle of respecting individual rights while maintaining concern for crime control.

Jeremy Gersovitz is a lawyer in Helena, Montana. Lately he has been having a pretty good run. In the past few months, his office has added several new attorneys, beefed up its support staff, and completely renovated its technology, putting in a first-class computer system that links him to lawyers all around the state. He and his assistants have gotten salary bumps and a new car to ferry them around.

None of this would sound unusual if *Gersovitz* were a partner at *a high-priced* corporate law firm. But he's a defense attorney for the indigent—the head of the regional public defender's office in Helena. He has a job notorious for crushing its practitioners under mountains of stress and disillusionment. Not too long ago, Gersovitz was feeling a little disillusioned himself, overwhelmed by a sense that he was frantically "treading water." That has changed.

It has changed because of a single lawsuit—one that didn't even come to trial. Four years ago, the American Civil Liberties Union took the state of Montana to court, charging that its indigent-defense system was so feeble as to violate the constitutional rights of the clients. The ACLU convinced the state that the consequences of losing the case would be cataclysmic. Thousands of old cases might have been reopened on the grounds that the convicts had not received proper representation. Faced with the terrifying prospect of a justice system thrown into chaos, the Montana attorney general agreed to go to the legislature as an advocate of reform—and won a major expansion of the indigent program, big enough to pay for more lawyers, better computers and even more comfortable offices.

Montana isn't the only state that has undertaken wholesale renovation of its indigent-defense procedures in recent years. Motivated by a wave of successful lawsuits and a sympathetic political climate, legislatures are enacting reforms that even the most skeptical observers admit have the potential to bring important changes to the process of criminal justice in America.

The changes have been a longtime coming. It was back in 1963 that the U.S. Supreme Court ruled, in *Gideon v. Wainwright,* that states were constitutionally required to provide publicly funded counsel to criminal defendants who could not afford a lawyer. After the ruling, many activists rejoiced; the poor were finally going to get a fair chance to win when their cases came to trial.

But anybody who expected a revolution out of the *Gideon* case was soon disappointed. The Supreme Court left the implementation of indigent-defense systems to the individual states, and in most places, the indigent were not a high-priority constituency for lawmakers. The result, according to a recent article in the *Capital University Law Review,* was "a vicious cycle of politically unpopular subject matter leading to a lack of funding and, consequently, exhausting caseloads."

A 2004 report by the American Bar Association reached a similar conclusion. It found horrific caseloads: In Pennsylvania, for instance, an office that had been handling 4,172 cases in 1980 was handling 8,000 cases 20 years later with the same number of attorneys. The ABA also declared that "inadequate compensation for indigent-defense attorneys is a national problem." In Massachusetts, public defenders were starting at salaries of $35,000 a year, and even after 10 years of service were earning just $50,000. Indigent-defense programs were finding it impossible to compete not only with private-sector firms but with public prosecutors' offices. Nationwide, the ABA found, states and counties were spending almost twice as much on prosecution—$5 billion—as on defense—$2.8 billion.

Funding was seen as inadequate for expert witnesses, investigators and other support services, as well as for the defense lawyers themselves.

Given those statistics, it's no surprise that the quality of defense most indigent persons receive has been compromised. In Riverside County, California, in 2003, more than 12,000 people pleaded guilty to misdemeanor charges without benefit of counsel because there were no resources to provide attorneys for municipal court arraignments.

By almost any standard, indigent defendants do not fare as well in court as defendants who provide their own lawyers. A U.S. Department of Justice report found that while indigent defendants and defendants who can afford counsel are found guilty at roughly comparable rates indigents are incarcerated at significantly higher rates—88 percent versus 77 percent in federal courts and 71 percent versus 54 percent in large counties.

VICTIMS OF INCOMPETENCE

Indeed, indigent-defense horror stories have become commonplace. Of these, Calvin Burdine's is perhaps the most famous and the most appalling. Burdine was charged with the 1983 murder or W. T. Wise. During the trial, Burdine's lawyer, Joe Cannon, fell asleep 10 times, sometimes for as long as 10 minutes at a stretch. According to some accounts, Cannon never once intervened during the prosecution's lengthy examination of his client, and joined with the prosecutor in mocking his gay client as a "queer" and a "fairy." Burdine was found guilty and served 15 years in prison before a federal court overturned the conviction and granted him a new trial.

Cases such as this turn up every few years or so, and sometimes generate a minor media frenzy. But the furor tends to die down without generating any serious changes in the system. Most of the time, something more than scandal or media attention is needed to create the momentum for serious reform of the system. Increasingly often, the momentum is coming from lawsuits.

A lawsuit can scare a state into reforming, as in Montana, or, if that fails, courts can order a state to change its practices. Still, without some direction as to what an adequate system should look like, it's difficult for lawmakers to set priorities and targets. There have been blue-ribbon commissions and advisory panels, but in the absence of clear rules, few states have been able to address the problems that indigent-defense attorneys say keep them from doing their jobs well.

After years of largely futile effort, the American Bar Association began moving several years ago to establish clearer guidelines for states to follow. In 2002, the ABA pared its gargantuan rulebook on indigent defense, which totaled nearly a thousand pages, down to 10 simple recommendations.

It was the first of the ABA recommendations, requiring an indigent-defense system independent of political influence and overseen by a nonpartisan body, that convinced Montana legislators there was no way to shoehorn reform into the state's old structure, in which each county set up, managed and funded its own indigent-defense system. "They realized that they had to centralize," says David Carroll, of the National Legal Aid and Defender Association. "They had to provide funding and administration at the state level."

Montana's legislature established the position of chief state public defender, with responsibility for staffing, training and overseeing 11 regional offices. The state pays the bill for all the offices. Public defenders are free from the vagaries of county budgets, and from the control of local governments in which their natural adversaries—police departments and prosecutors—often have heavy influence.

Centralization also adds to the level of available expertise in areas where it is badly needed. When Montana's system was county-based, rural public defenders faced with the most complex cases, such as capital murder trials, were in trouble. Many had never seen a capital case and had limited resources to devote to a lengthy and intricate trial. Now the central office can dispatch a specialist in capital cases and shift resources to support a rigorous defense.

LEGAL HURRICANE

In Louisiana, the event that triggered reform wasn't a lawsuit but Hurricane Katrina. In the view of Walter Sanchez, a member of the state's Indigent Defense Board, Katrina "really exposed the holes in the system; people could see how bad things had gotten."

Katrina strained Louisiana's already fragile indigent-defense system past its breaking point. Understaffed offices lost precious members, and precarious local funding sources dried up. Judges eventually had to halt prosecutions of the poor in some areas, insisting that they could not receive even the semblance of decent representation under the existing system. In that context, lawmakers had little choice but to sit up, take notice and make changes.

In the wake of these problems, Louisiana's Indigent Defense Task Force suddenly acquired the clout it needed to change the process. Long a toothless tiger, subservient to district attorneys and unable to compel individual offices to submit the most basic caseload data, the Indigent Defense Board is now empowered to collect a wide array of performance data and to enforce minimum caseload requirements, in accordance with the ABA's 10th principle, which calls for defenders to be "systematically reviewed for quality and efficiency according to nationally and locally adopted standards."

In those states where legal pressure, administrative process and political fortune have come together to drive efforts at systemic reform, the results sometimes have been dramatic. Paul DeWolfe, the public defender in Montgomery County. Maryland, boasts of a series of impressive victories under a new, centralized state public defender system. There was the pregnant 16-year-old who was about to be sentenced to a year in residential treatment and the loss of her child when the indigent-defense office intervened. Taking advantage of social workers assigned as part of the Maryland public defender system's new "comprehensive service" model, DeWolfe's team put together an alternative plan to keep the girl out of incarceration and together with her child. The plan provided for counseling and supervision, monitored by the public defender's office itself. The judge accepted the plan, and both mother and child have stayed out of trouble.

Then there was the case of a man accused of the misdemeanor theft of $50. Because of a long list of prior offenses, the state's best plea-bargain offer was seven years in jail. Rather than take the plea, DeWolfe's office took the case to trial. They produced evidence that he had been the victim of a robbery and shooting several years before and had become addicted to prescription painkillers during his recovery. All of his crimes had occurred after the trauma of the shooting. The public defenders proposed treatment instead of jail time, and the judge agreed.

In addition to Maryland, Montana, and Louisiana, several other states have begun reforming their indigent-defense programs, most notably North Dakota, Georgia, and Virginia. But it's far too early to say whether these reforms will have the impact their backers hope for. Most of the revamped programs are in their infancy—Montana's came into effect on July 1 of this year—and so it will be a while before any hard data emerges to suggest what they are accomplishing. Stories of young mothers saved and accidental junkies brought back from the brink by dedicated, well-trained, well-supported public defenders are hopeful signs, but for now, the bulk of the evidence is still anecdotal.

And cost remains a powerful obstacle. As compelling as the moral and legal arguments in its behalf may be, indigent defense is expensive, and while some claim that it can at least partially pay for itself by shortening the amount of time people are incarcerated before sentencing and keeping innocent people out of jail, those complex calculations will take time to confirm.

Meanwhile, even the most robust reform programs frequently falter at budget time Mississippi passed sweeping reforms in 1998 only to repeal them a few years later when funding had still not materialized. Montana's 2007 allocation for indigent defense, while it has brought striking improvements to offices such as the one Jeremy Gersovitz runs in Helena, falls short of the state's original funding targets by more than $3 million. Money, says Ronald Waterman of the ACLU," is what keeps me up at night now. If the state doesn't fully fund this program, it won't work."

Discussion Questions

1. Discuss how the indigent-defense system in Montana was overhauled.
2. What are the primary limitations of many indigent-defense systems? What can be done to address these limitations?

3. Discuss the significance of the U.S. Supreme Court case *Gideon v. Wainwright*.

20

How Much Should Lawyers Know When Picking a Jury?

By M. B. E. Smith

In his commentary, "How Much Should Lawyers Know When Picking a Jury?" Professor Smith addresses one of the more controversial aspects of criminal justice: jury selection. Many attorneys and legal scholars admit that criminal trials are sometimes won or lost during jury selection. Accordingly, it is important that we maintain strong concerns for equity, justice, and fairness during the identification, questioning, and selection of jurors.

The Sixth Amendment provides defendants the right to a trial. Defendants are also granted the right to a public trial, a trial by peers, and a speedy trial. The terms "public," "peers," and "speedy" are subjective in nature, leading to varied interpretations of each. For instance, who exactly constitutes a defendant's peers? What is speedy? While the courts have interpreted these and related subjective terms in order to ensure justice, equity, and fairness, grey areas have become the topics of criminal case appeals.

Let's examine, for instance, jury selection. Jurisdictions use several means to construct a jury pool from which prospective jurors are selected and questioned. Voter registration lists (the most commonly used) are often supplemented with driver's license lists, automobile registration lists, and property tax rolls. The Federal Jury Selection and Services Act of 1968 prohibits the exclusion of individuals based on religion, race, gender, nationality, or economic status, yet there remains uncertainty regarding whether currently used lists adequately provide a cross-section of society. Minorities and low-income individuals are less likely than their counterparts to own property and cars, be registered voters, or have a driver's license, and thus are less likely to be identified for jury selection. Some jurisdictions use multiple lists of potential jurors to widen the pool and help ensure that the jury will represent the defendant's peers.

Potential jurors receive a summons in the mail directing them to report to a particular location on a specified date for jury duty. However, not all who are required to report to jury duty will be selected for participation on a jury. Some potential jurors will be excused prior to voir dire (the process in which prospective jurors are questioned by a judge and/or attorneys to determine their suitability for serving on a jury) and some will be excused following voir dire.

Voir dire, the final step in jury selection, is used to assess whether jurors are familiar with the primary actor(s) in the case, the potential juror's beliefs or attitudes concerning specific issues that may arise in the trial, and other matters that may impact a prospective juror's ability to offer a fair decision in the case. Assessment also involves attorneys and judges asking potential jurors a series of questions and evaluating the responses. Jurors deemed unsuitable are dismissed by the court during voir dire in one of two manners: challenges for cause and peremptory challenges.

Jurors displaying an identifiable bias or another sign suggesting their inability to serve as a juror may result in attorneys filing a challenge for cause motion. Jurors are also dismissed when attorneys use peremptory challenges, which permit attorneys to eliminate unfit potential jurors without the need for justification. Attorneys are provided only a select number of peremptory challenges.

Some commentators suggest the use of professional juries to replace the current practice of requiring laypersons to serve. Professional jurors are full-time, paid professionals whose understanding of the law and courtroom procedure would provide them an advantage over everyday citizens serving as jurors.

In the end, assembling a jury requires crafty consideration of human nature on behalf of the attorneys. Attempting to understand individuals based on their responses to a series of questions is an inexact science that makes jury selection quite unpredictable.

Jury selection is an arcane topic that occasionally captures public attention during some celebrated criminal trial, like those of O. J. Simpson or Michael Jackson in California. It took two months to pick O. J.'s jury—a bit *over* a month for Michael Jackson's. Such cases are far from the norm. But they have taught the public: that selection of a criminal jury can be protracted and expensive—at least when the defendant is well heeled. What has perhaps escaped notice is that other states—for example, my own Massachusetts—streamline jury selection, so that if rarely takes more than a day and never more than a week. The fact deserves attention. Court hearings consume much high-priced labor—at least two lawyers, one judge, a clerk, a stenographer, and as many court officers as the county can afford. A trial-day is an expensive commodity. And in most cases all the expense of a criminal trial is borne by the state, since, most defendants are indigent. So, should other states pick juries Massachusetts's way?

The primary business of jury selection is to hear challenges by the prosecution and the defense—that is, requests made of the judge to eliminate particular prospective jurors. (There are also what might be called "self-challenges," as when a juror persuades the judge that he would suffer some special hardship or when he announces that he cannot decide fairly because of his hatred for the crime at issue.) Each party is allowed any number of challenges for cause, when one persuades the Court there is a substantial risk that a juror is unfit. Parties are also allowed peremptory challenges, which is the right to dismiss prospective jurors for any reason at all (save race or gender). California gives each side twenty peremptory challenges in capital felony cases, and otherwise ten. Massachusetts allows twelve peremptory challenges in the trial of life felonies—where conviction can result in a life sentence to state prison—and otherwise four. If the judge decides to sit alternate jurors, both parties receive an additional peremptory challenge for each alternate.

Two factors seem to account for the difference in time the two states expend in selecting juries. Firstly, California but not Massachusetts allows the parties to make a searching inquiry into the prospective jurors' particular circumstances. In O. J.'s case, when the 250 prospective jurors first assembled, they were ordered to complete a 79-page questionnaire comprising 294 separate entries, suggested by the parties and approved by the Court.[1] Many were dubiously relevant:

- **39.** While in school, what was your favorite subject?
- **212.** Do you believe it is immoral or wrong to do an amniocentesis to determine whether a fetus had a genetic defect? Yes? No? Don't have an opinion?
- **252.** What are your leisure time interests, hobbies and activities?

Other questions were intimate and personal—and also dubiously relevant:

- **72.** Do you think using physical force on a family member is sometimes justified?
- **186.** Have you ever dated, a person of a different race? Yes? No? If yes, how did you feel about it?

M.B.E. Smith, "How Much Should Lawyers Know When Picking a Jury?" as appeared in *Criminal Justice Ethics*, Volume 24, Issue 2, (Summer/Fall 2005), pp. 2, 53–54. Reprinted by permission of The Institute for Criminal Justice Ethics, 555 West 57th Street, Suite 607, New York, NY 10019-1029.

201. Do you have a religious affiliation or preference? Yes? No? If yes, please describe. How important would you say religion is in your life? Would anything about your religious beliefs make it difficult to sit in judgment of another person? Yes? No? Possibly? How often do you attend religious services?

205. Do you consider yourself politically: Active? Moderately active? Inactive?

211. Have you ever provided a urine sample to be analyzed for any purpose? Yes? No? If yes, did you feel comfortable with the accuracy of the results? Yes? No?

Secondly, California but not Massachusetts routinely permits individual *voir dire* by the prosecution and defense counsel: that is, each prospective juror is summonsed alone to a witness box, placed under oath, and is then questioned by the lawyers and perhaps by the judge about anything that might conceivably betray a predisposition to favor *one side* over the other. The inquiry is searching. Practice books counsel lawyers to question prospective jurors at length to smoke out evidence of bias. In high-profile cases jury consultants on both sides analyze each questionnaire and suggest particular lines of inquiry to the attorneys. The process is slow. Had the examination of O. J.'s jury pool averaged twenty minutes each, *voir dire* alone would have consumed eighty-three hours—or about fourteen trial-days. Juries in ordinary California cases are selected much more quickly than was O. J.'s or Michael Jackson's. Still, the availability of individual *voir dire* by counsel must inevitably prolong the process.

In Massachusetts a fresh jury pool is randomly selected in each county every court-day. A questionnaire is sent out with the jury summons, but the information requested is meager. Each is asked to give her name, sex, zip code, age, and marital status; the number and age of her children; her occupation, employer and its type of business; her spouse's occupation, employer, and type of business; her previous service as a juror; whether she or a family member is or has been a party or a victim in a civil or criminal case; whether she is related to a law enforcement officer; and anything else she thinks relevant to her ability to be impartial. In high profile cases lawyers sometimes request that an expanded questionnaire be sent out, but almost always to no avail. A *Judicial Comment* in a recent practice manual observes, "Most Superior Court judges find the use of an expanded questionnaire to be a cumbersome and time-consuming procedure and consider it to be an overly intrusive inquisition into the personal lives of jurors."[2]

The jury pool reports to the Courthouse at 8:00 A.M., about an hour before Superior Court convenes. The potential jurors assemble in a large room, where their attendance is noted by court officers, they are assigned a number, their questionnaires are collected and copied, and they are shown a video explaining basic legal concepts. Court officers then bring the jury pool into the Courtroom, where they are at first seated toward the rear in the spectator area. At this point—or perhaps a few minutes before—copies of the questionnaires are given to the prosecution and defense, who immediately and frantically search through them for reasons to make challenges for cause and for clues as to whom to challenge peremptorily. Defendants usually review them too, jury selection being one of their few chances to take an active part in their defense.

The jury pool is first sworn in—whereupon the judge introduces the lawyers to the venire, tells them the nature of the case to be tried and offers her best guess as to how long the trial will last. She also tells them the names of the expected witnesses and the towns in which they reside. She then asks them collectively a series of questions: whether any of the jurors is related to any of the parties or has an interest in the case; whether any juror has expressed or formed an opinion about the case; and whether any juror is aware of any bias or prejudice that might affect his impartiality. She explains briefly the governing principles of law, and asks whether any juror has difficulty in understanding or applying them. Typically, the judge also, asks whether any juror would suffer a special hardship were he selected. Attorneys frequently request that additional questions be asked, and judges sometimes comply. For example, in a drunk driving case most judges upon request will ask whether any of the venire belongs to Mothers Against Drunk Driving. (But a refusal to ask a question only rarely will be a ground for appeal.) During the judge's questioning, the attorneys are usually still hard at work mining the questionnaires for hints as to whom to challenge.

Jurors flag affirmative responses to the judge's questions by raising their hands. Court officers bring the respondents one by one to the bench, where the judge questions them as to their ability to decide fairly. These colloquies rarely take more than a minute or two. If a challenge for cause is apparent—the juror is related to the alleged victim—he will be excused forthwith. Otherwise, if after a few brief questions the juror expresses confidence that she can decide the case fairly, she will be pronounced "indifferent," and returned to the pool. In a few kinds of cases—for example, those involving sexual abuse of a child—the judge must question the venire individually about whether any event in their past would prevent their deciding fairly. Individual voir dire prolongs the jury selection process—although usually not for very long, since the judge alone conducts the questioning, which is tightly focused upon the issue that prompts individual examination.

After the jury pool has been questioned and the judge has found that those remaining are indifferent, the clerk randomly selects twelve jurors and up to four alternates, who are seated in the jury box. At this point, the prosecutor exercises his peremptory challenges. Randomly selected members of the remaining pool replace the excused jurors; until the prosecutor announces, "The Commonwealth is satisfied." The defendant then makes his peremptory challenges until his counsel announces that he is satisfied. If the prosecutor has challenges remaining, he may use them only upon jurors seated after the defendant's challenges. Then, if the defendant has challenges remaining, he may use them upon jurors chosen after the prosecutor's last round. The process continuous until each side is satisfied or has run out of challenges. If the pool is exhausted before the jury is complete, the remaining jurors will be taken the next day from a fresh venire.

Massachusetts lawyers have limited information on which to base challenges for cause and virtually none upon which to base peremptory challenges. But one must decide, so one resorts to stereotypes and hunches. For example, as a defense attorney in a drunk driving case, I would never advise my client to challenge an overweight, divorced, middle-aged salesman with a ruddy complexion—even though for all I know he is a teetotaler with a punitive attitude towards those who drink alcohol. I probably would advise him to challenge a social worker, as it's my impression that their constant exposure to human frailty often gives them jaundiced expectations of human behavior. Prosecutors too rely upon stereotypes. Hampshire County contains a large university and four mid-sized colleges, so jury pools here often have a sprinkling of faculty. I've noticed that prosecutors almost always challenge academics, although I don't quite understand why.

Does the quality of Massachusetts's justice suffer as a result of attorneys' lack of information about the particularities of individual jurors? It is difficult to say. Many juries are selected every court day. No records are kept that could allow anyone to tell how many or which juries were biased toward one party or the other. Nonetheless, I think there are several reasons to the sanguine.

Perhaps the strongest is that Massachusetts's lawyers seem satisfied with the juries they find. They are aware of other systems: our federal courts use one much like California's. But there is no expressed dissatisfaction, no movement for change—which there certainly would be were either the defense bar or prosecutors persuaded that their clients' interests were impaired by the present system.

Secondly, although I have had no experience with an information-rich system, I wonder whether it results in fairer juries. It certainly wouldn't help me to make more intelligent peremptory challenges. Even if I knew a jury pool's answers to a questionnaire akin to O. J.'s, I should still have to rely in the end upon stereotypes and hunches. Perhaps jury consultants' stereotypes and hunches are more reliable than my own—although I find myself skeptical about this too. But suppose that experts can reliably discern how prospective jurors will lean. How will their work be used? Trial attorneys don't hope for impartial juries but rather for those that will decide favorably to their clients. Hence, a probable result of enabling lawyers to choose more intelligently among prospective jurors is that more biased ones are selected to serve.

Thirdly, to the extent that jury consultants are effective in choosing jurors biased in their client's favor, they exacerbate the advantage that the rich have over the poor when charged with a crime. Most criminal defendants have court-appointed, state-compensated counsel. No state will also provide jury consultants to indigents as a matter of right—not even to those accused of murder.

However, the Massachusetts system of jury selection precludes effective use of jury consultants by any defendant, because it gives them neither the time nor the information that they need to work their magic. An attractive principle of criminal justice is that we should reduce indigents' relative disadvantage whenever possible, so long as we are not thereby unfair to rich defendants. By this test Massachusetts's system seems markedly superior to California's.

Finally, Massachusetts better respects the privacy of jurors—at least in cases with rich defendants willing to pay for elaborate jury questionnaires and searching individual *voir dire* by attorneys. I know that I should have been uncomfortable answering the O. J. questionnaire, and I wouldn't want to have been questioned closely in open court about the issues it raises. Since the justice system depends upon a ready supply of citizens willing to perform their civic duty, it seems unwise to make their experience more onerous than it need be.

Some may conclude from these arguments that states ought to abolish peremptory challenges altogether in criminal trials, allowing only challenges for cause. As a defense attorney I wouldn't favor this change. (I shouldn't mind were prosecutors denied peremptory challenges.) My reason isn't that they help me select juries disposed favorably to my clients, but rather that they are a mark of respect for defendants' moral personalities. Particularly for the intelligent and active, much of the peculiar terror that afflicts criminal defendants stems from the utter passivity of their role—unless they are so foolish as to defend themselves. They have a constitutional right to testify but are nearly always unwise to exercise it. Apart from putting on a good appearance and maintaining their composure they can do nothing to affect their fate. However, they can help pick those who will decide it. In my experience almost all defendants want the final say about whom to challenge. My impression is this helps reassure them about the fairness of the ordeal they are soon to experience. If true, this surely justifies some small inefficiency in the trial process.

Endnotes

1. All my information about the O. J. Trial is gleaned from Prof. Douglas O. Lander's website. See http://www.law.umkc.edu/faculty/projects/ftrials/Simpson/simpson.htm.

2. R. H. Balm, Jr (ed), *Massachusetts Superior Court Criminal Practice Manual* (Mass. Continuing Legal Education, 2003), 11–13.

Discussion Questions

1. Discuss the steps involved in selecting a jury. What limitations do you see regarding selecting a fair, unbiased jury?
2. How does the lack of information provided to attorneys impact their ability to effectively engage in jury selection?
3. How would you overhaul jury selection practices? What changes would you make to current jury selection practices?

Self-Defense vs. Municipal Gun Bans

By Robert VerBruggen

Consider the following scenario. You're in bed sleeping. You hear someone enter your house. You grab your handgun and head downstairs to investigate. You find someone rummaging through your valuables. It's dark. Your children are asleep upstairs. The individual makes a move that you find threatening and, in response, you fire the gun. The victim is wounded and running away. You fire again, several times. The victim escapes. The police respond and you're charged with violating a municipal handgun ban because someone broke into your house and you tried to protect yourself and your family. This scenario is based on the account described in the article "Self-Defense vs. Municipal Gun Bans" in which author Robert VerBruggen documents the case of a man living in the Chicago suburbs who is accused of wrongdoing following an incident that many might consider self-defense.

Gun control is one of the most debated topics in criminal justice and society in general. Should individuals be permitted to own weapons and under what circumstances can they use them? These loaded questions generate numerous passionate responses. It seems almost every gun-related incident conjures up questions of whether gun control legislation is too strict or not.

Among other factors, proponents of gun control cite the constitutional right to bear arms, the recreational purposes associated with guns, and the need for self-defense as reasons why we should be permitted to own guns. Particularly, they argue that individuals using guns harm others—that guns are simply a tool used by people to sometimes harm one another. In contrast, critics point to the lethality of gun-related crime, the number of gun-related crimes, and the ease with which gun-related crime is committed as reasons why guns should be banned. Critics agree that guns don't necessarily kill people; however, they argue that killings are much easier when guns are freely available.

Gun control policies such as waiting periods to purchase weapons and prohibiting particular individuals from purchasing guns are controversial. Typically, Democrats and liberals are less likely to support an extended right to bear arms. Republicans and conservatives, on the other hand, are more likely to support the personal use of guns. Society is divided, as some individuals believe we've gone too far with gun control, while others believe we have much work left.

Will society ever come to agreement regarding how far we should go with gun control? It is doubtful. Similar to the division in society regarding the appropriateness of capital punishment, gun control is a polarizing issue and is the topic of many radio talk shows, television news shows, and student discussions. The issue won't go away, as debates will rage any time a heinous crime is committed with a gun. It is hard to imagine society suddenly coming to agreement regarding the issue.

The powerful lobbyists in support of gun control and the influential groups and individuals argu-ing in support of gun control have battled, and will continue to do so, for some time. As policy makers change, so does gun control legislation. History suggests that the restrictions placed on guns fluctuate according to public opinion, the orientation of legislators, and the frequency of high-profile gun crimes.

When Hale DeMar shot an intruder in his house, he may well have saved his children's lives. So why was he charged with a crime?

On the night of December 29, 2003, Morio L. Billings was AWOL from the Army, in violation of his probation, and driving a BMW X5 sport utility vehicle he'd stolen less than a day earlier. The 31-year-old was staying with his mother in Chicago, but he wanted "blow and crack" badly enough to risk yet another jail stay. He had been taken into custody at least six times in 2003, with police alleging residential burglary, receiving stolen property (twice), driving while suspended (twice), auto theft (three times), and possession of a controlled substance.

Driving to Wilmette, a Chicago suburb, Billings parked the SUV on Laurel Avenue, a short walk from his target house on Linden Avenue, the same place he'd hit the night before. Last time he'd gone through the dog door, but he'd taken the keys (along with a Sony PlayStation 2, a TV set, and the SUV) before leaving. He "didn't care if anyone was home," he'd later tell police.

Entering the house through the kitchen door, Billings heard an alarm go off but proceeded to explore the home anyway. He saw a computer monitor and tugged on it.

Hale DeMar, a 54-year-old restaurateur who had recently separated from his wife but was watching their two children that night, was asleep upstairs when Billings entered his kitchen. DeMar had been unable to get his locks changed on short notice after the previous night's burglary (he would later be accused of not trying hard enough), but he had activated the security system. He had also put six hollow-point rounds into his Smith & Wesson .38 Special and placed it under his bed. It was one of two handguns he'd owned for more than 20 years without loading them; until the bur-glary he'd kept them locked in a safe, still in their original packaging.

Around 10:30 P.M. DeMar was awakened by the security system, which indicated a kitchen-door entry. Relying on the system to contact police, he grabbed the .38 and went downstairs. Months later, *Chicago Tribune* columnist Eric Zorn would call DeMar—who is five feet, nine inches tall and weighs 140 pounds—a "suburban cowboy." Wilmette Chief of Police George E. Carpenter would say he put himself at risk "unnecessarily, on multiple levels."

SHOTS IN THE DARK

DeMar faced more than second-guessing after the break-in. He was charged with violating Wilmette's handgun ban, an offense that carries a $750 fine. His attempt to challenge the fine in court shows how difficult it can be to assert a right to armed self-defense in the United States, despite an explicit constitu-tional guarantee that would seem to preclude gun laws like Wilmette's. Illinois courts have been so hos-tile to this right that DeMar's lawyer never cited the Second Amendment in his arguments, relying in-stead on other, tangentially related constitutional provisions. Ultimately it was the state legislature rather than the courts that prevented DeMar from being punished for daring to protect himself and his family.

When he got downstairs, DeMar saw a man in his dark family room. Since he "didn't see any flesh," he thought the intruder was masked. He was right. From the kitchen, DeMar fired two shots. One struck Billings in the upper left arm.

Now both men wanted the same thing: Billings out of DeMar's house. Billings ran, heading through the family room, dining room, and living room. He passed a door leading outside but

"Self-Defense vs. Municipal Gun Bans" by Robert VerBruggen, *Reason*, June, 2005, Vol. 37, (2), pp. 40–47. Reprinted by permission of the Reason Foundation.

didn't go through it. "I don't know," he'd later say. "I guess I should've. I just wanted to get the fuck out."

Billings came to a hallway connecting the kitchen, front door, living room, and stairs. DeMar fired two more shots, one of which dug into Billings' left leg. Billings broke a living room window, climbed through, and ran westward through the dark. DeMar went back to his bedroom. Trembling, he called the police.

At some point the phone rang, and DeMar's 10-year-old son, Jack, picked it up. It was the alarm company. Jack explained the situation.

As the police responded, a neighbor called in a suspected burglary. Billings, once again in DeMar's SUV, had cut through a yard on Laurel Avenue, breaking a fence on his way to Evanston's St. Francis Hospital. It was further than Evanston Hospital, but he wanted to get as far away as possible, and he was more familiar with St. Francis, which is the hospital where he was born.

Arriving at DeMar's house to find him on the phone with their department, the police took both of his guns. They came across several bullet holes, a black and tan baseball cap, a "skull cap/dew [sic] rag," and blood. At the property on Laurel Avenue through which Billings had driven they found broken pieces of plastic from the SUV's passenger-side mirror housing. At St. Francis Hospital were the rest of the vehicle and the offender. Billings had parked the SUV across a sidewalk near the hospital, gotten out, and collapsed; staff had taken him inside. In August 2004 he'd receive a seven-year prison sentence.

Two days after the break-in, the Cook County state's attorney's office released a statement declaring DeMar's actions self-defense. But Illinois requires gun owners to keep a firearm owners' identification card, and DeMar's had expired in 2000. On January 8, 2004, he was charged with that violation, which carries a maximum penalty of a $2,500 fine and a year in jail. Prosecutors dropped the charges about a month later, saying they did not want to "revictimize" DeMar for a "lapse."

But the Village of Wilmette fined DeMar $750 for disobeying its handgun ban. "Our function is not to make ordinances but to enforce them," says Brian King, deputy chief of operations at the Wilmette Police Department. "The individual told us he was knowingly in violation of the ordinance for a long time. If you don't enforce it in that case, it makes it impossible to enforce it for anybody else." Chief Carpenter acknowledges that the department could have made an exception in light of the circumstances. "There is discretion involved," he says, "but we felt it was appropriate in this case."

Carpenter argues that DeMar should have stayed upstairs with his son and his 8-year-old daughter, Madeline, instead of seeking a confrontation. "Our culture seems to define the family protector's role as seeking out the enemy, or the intruder," he says. "What we tell people is: You're the last line of defense. Don't leave your family."

DeMar explains his actions this way: "I suppose some would have grabbed their children and cowered in their bedroom . . . praying that the police would get there in time to stop the criminal from climbing the stairs and confronting the family in a bedroom, trembling, dreading the sound of the door being kicked in. That's not the fear I wanted my children to experience, and it is not the cowardly act that I want my children to remember me by."

Another issue was a missing bullet, as police reports accounted for only three of the four rounds. Investigators found two holes in window panes, the third in a wall. Bernard Michna, a Wilmette trustee (the town's equivalent of a city councilman), cites the bullet holes and the stray round to bolster his support for the handgun ban and the fine imposed on DeMar. "We need to set the example that we're trying to protect our citizens," he says. "He's endangering innocent civilians."

LOCAL GUN BANS

It's a matter of contention whether there are more defensive gun uses or criminal misuses in the United States, but it's clear that armed self-defense occurs on a regular basis. Florida State University criminologist Gary Kleck has concluded, based on national telephone surveys, that up to 2.5 million defensive incidents occur each year. This figure compares favorably to the roughly 350,000 firearm-related murders, robberies, and aggravated assaults the FBI reports yearly. In the vast majority of defensive uses, the victim simply brandishes the gun and the offender leaves—which is why one rarely hears about such incidents, Kleck argues.

Using different methods, other scholars have come up with much lower numbers. In *Gun Violence: The Real Costs* (2000), Philip J. Cook of Duke University and Jens Ludwig of Georgetown University report, based on data from the National Crime Victimization Survey (NCVS), that only 100,000 defensive gun uses occur each year. (The NCVS, which is sponsored by the Bureau of Justice Statistics, uses interviewers who visit people's homes and ask them to describe their personal experiences with crime.) In *Evaluating Gun Policy: Effects on Crime and Violence* (2003), Cook and Ludwig consider in-home incidents of armed self-defense, suggesting a range of 32,000 (based on an NCVS analysis by Cook) to 503,000 (based on a DataStat telephone survey commissioned by the federal government).

The NCVS consistently elicits fewer claims of defensive gun use than do telephone surveys. Critics have questioned the accuracy of telephone interviews, noting that gun owners may perceive threats that aren't real. But the results of victimization surveys are debatable as well: They don't always ask directly about defensive gun use, and people who scare off would-be assailants might not consider themselves crime victims.

It is rare for an American to get into legal trouble after using a gun defensively, but it has happened before. In 1986 prosecutors charged Oak Park, Illinois, gas station owner Donald Bennett with violating the village's handgun ban after he shot at armed robbers. A jury acquitted him later that year despite his obvious guilt. In 2003 Brooklyn computer engineer Ronald Dixon spent three days in jail after shooting a home invader. Dixon's handgun permit had not yet been approved.

Strict gun laws got a boost after the Chicago suburb of Morton Grove successfully defended its handgun ban, which was passed in 1981 and immediately challenged in state and federal court. The lawyers who filed the suits tried a variety of arguments, citing privacy, the Second Amendment, and a similar provision in the Illinois Constitution's Bill of Rights ("Subject only to the police power, the right of the individual citizen to keep and bear arms shall not be infringed").

In the 1982 decision *Quilici v. Village of Morton Grove*, a panel of the U.S. Court of Appeals for the 7th Circuit rejected these arguments by a 2-to-1 vote. The Illinois Supreme Court followed suit, by a 4-to-3 margin, in the 1984 ruling *Kalodimos v. Village of Morton Grove*. The U.S. Supreme Court declined to hear an appeal of *Quilici*.

To gun control advocates, the Morton Grove decisions proved there was nothing unconstitutional about banning specific categories of weapons. Several municipalities followed in Morton Grove's footsteps, including Chicago; its suburbs Evanston, Oak Park, Winnetka, and Wilmette; and Washington, D.C. But the decisions also provoked a backlash in state legislatures. By 1991, according to the pro-gun control Violence Policy Center, 38 states had passed laws pre-empting local handgun bans, in addition to three that had done so before Morton Grove passed its prohibition.

DEFENSE OF SELF-DEFENSE

The Wilmette Board of Trustees got a taste of the backlash against gun bans after Hale DeMar was fined. "None of the trustees had asked that the ordinance be changed," says Trustee George M. Pearce. Gun rights supporters nevertheless crowded the board's January 13, 2004, meeting to discuss the case. "Probably half of them were from outside of Wilmette," says Pearce.

To this day no trustee has proposed amending the handgun ban. Both Pearce and Bernard Michna, another trustee, say most Wilmette residents support it. Opponents are "a small but vocal minority," Michna says.

State Sen. Edward Petka (R-Plainfield) and state Rep. John Bradley (D-Marion) decided to take action. Within two days of the Wilmette trustees' meeting, both had filed bills creating a defense for people in DeMar's situation. "A village can still file a charge, but the person who is charged can assert an affirmative defense and state that he violated the ordinance in defending himself," Petka explains. "If it's believed by judge or jury, it would constitute a defense to the charge." The legislation applies only on a person's land or in his or her "abode" or "fixed place of business."

Concerning the bill, Michna says "the downstate mentality is that guns are there for your protection and so forth, and no downstate legislator is going to come out and vote against something like that. If you say what really is true about handguns, people are going to twist it and turn it and turn you into some kind of abolitionist."

The bill's opponents raised two issues: local control and the possibility that the law might encourage people to own handguns. "Local control has nothing to do with denying what I consider a basic right under the state and federal constitutions," Petka says. "A village can no more deny self-defense than they can pass an ordinance that you can't publish articles in their territory." Petka does not deny the law might encourage handgun ownership, but he suggests handguns pose less of a danger to neighbors than the more-powerful shotguns and rifles that Wilmette's ordinance permits.

The Illinois General Assembly sided with Petka. In May 2004 the House passed the bill by a vote of 90 to 25, the Senate by a vote of 41 to 16. Both votes surpassed the three-fifths majority necessary for a veto override, and on August 20 Gov. Rod Blagojevich (a Democrat) made one necessary. In November the Senate and the House overrode his veto by votes of 40 to 18 and 85 to 30, respectively.

CONDOMS, PORN, AND WEAPONRY

In early February 2004 the *Chicago Tribune* announced that Hale DeMar was challenging Wilmette's handgun ban in Cook County Circuit Court. DeMar invoked the Second Amendment in an interview with the *Tribune*, but it was the last time anyone mentioned the right to keep and bear arms in connection with the case. DeMar's attorney, Robert Orman, instead argued that the ban violated the right to privacy; was "arbitrary and capricious," in violation of the 14th Amendment's Due Process Clause; and conflicted with another local ordinance that allows residents to discharge firearms in self-defense.

Only the privacy claim received media attention. The Constitution does not mention a right to privacy but does imply one (in the Fourth Amendment's prohibition of "unreasonable searches and seizures," for example), and privacy is a part of America's common law heritage. The Supreme Court has cited privacy in decisions protecting abortion rights, access to birth control information, possession of pornography in the home, and sodomy between consenting adults. One of Orman's briefs cited *Paris Adult Theatre I v. Slaton*, a 1973 case that held pornography in theaters open to the public is not protected by the right to privacy. The ruling stated, "This privacy right encompasses and protects the personal intimacies of the home, the family, marriage, motherhood, procreation, and child rearing." The handgun ban, Orman claimed, violated this right.

In her reply brief, Mary Beth Cyze, assistant corporation counsel for Wilmette, argued that constitutional privacy protection applies only to "fundamental" rights, and that the courts have never put owning a handgun in that category. "It is difficult to imagine a scenario under which a ban on one category of weapons, i.e., handguns, impinges on a 'personal' or 'intimate' matter even vaguely resembling abortion, contraception or procreation," she wrote.

Cyze pointed out that Orman's reasoning was similar to that of 7th Circuit Judge John Coffey, who wrote a privacy-based dissent in *Quilici v. Morton Grove*. "Surely nothing could be more fundamental to the 'concept of ordered liberty' than the basic right of an individual, within the confines of the criminal law, to protect his home and family from unlawful and dangerous intrusions," Coffey wrote. That argument, Cyze said, had been considered and rejected by the 7th Circuit.

Orman also argued that the ordinance was "arbitrary and capricious as applied to [DeMar] under the facts and circumstances of this case" and therefore a violation of his right to due process. Courts can strike down decisions or laws as "arbitrary and capricious" if they are unreasonable or do not logically relate to a legitimate function of government. Orman offered six points to back this assertion, most of them relating to DeMar's right to protect himself, his family, and his home. "The sole and only realistic protection for most real and decent people in their homes is the handgun," he contended. As Richard Pearson, director of the Illinois State Rifle Association, put it, a .38-caliber revolver is "not too powerful, and it's not too big."

But Cyze argued that DeMar was free to shoot Billings with a rifle or shotgun, adding that it was legally irrelevant whether a handgun is the safest weapon for in-home use. She offered a similar reply to Orman's claim that Wilmette's gun ban contradicted its ordinance allowing citizens to fire weapons in self-defense.

Orman's briefs did not mention the Second Amendment: "A well regulated Militia, being necessary to the security of a free State, the right of the people to keep and bear Arms, shall not be infringed." Given the failure of the challenges to Morton Grove's ban, the omission was not surprising.

PLEADING THE SECOND

The U.S. Supreme Court has never struck down a gun control measure on Second Amendment grounds. In the last Second Amendment case it heard, *United States v. Miller* (1939), the Court ruled that a ban on sawed-off shotguns did not violate the Constitution because "it is not within judicial notice that [such weapons are] any part of the ordinary military equipment or that [their] use could contribute to the common defense." This ruling certainly suggested that some categories of weapons are legitimate targets of legislation. Orman called the Second Amendment issue "a matter of settled law." Cyze went so far as to say "nobody would suggest that the Second Amendment applies to an individual."

Stephen Halbrook would. A Virginia-based attorney who has taken part in numerous high-profile gun cases (he helped fight the Morton Grove ban), Halbrook is co-author of *Supreme Court Gun Cases*, which argues that the high court has repeatedly acknowledged, in cases not directly involving guns, that the Second Amendment protects an individual right. In the 1990 case *United States v. Verdugo-Urquidez*, for example, Chief Justice William Rehnquist's majority opinion concluded that the phrase "the people"—which, Rehnquist noted, appears in the Second Amendment as well as the First, Fourth, Ninth, and 10th amendments—is "a term of art" that "refers to a class of persons who are part of a national community." Halbrook is also the author of *That Every Man Be Armed: The Evolution of a Constitutional Right*, which makes the case that the Framers understood the Second Amendment as guaranteeing an individual right to arms—a view that has attracted growing support among legal scholars in the last two decades.

But even Halbrook agrees that citing the Second Amendment in the 7th Circuit, which includes Illinois, would have been a mistake. "Picture the Bill of Rights with 'void where prohibited by law' stamped over the Second Amendment," he says. According to the view that still holds sway in most circuits, he says, "It's a weird, collective right, not a right 'of the people' like the amendment says." Only the U.S. Court of Appeals for the 5th Circuit, in the 1998 case *U.S. v. Emerson*, has explicitly rejected the collective-right interpretation of the Second Amendment and endorsed the individual-right view.

With most circuits seeing the Second Amendment as no obstacle to gun control, advocates of gun rights have turned to other constitutional provisions. As Cyze, Wilmette's lawyer, noted in one of her briefs, their record is not a strong one. Appeals courts have rejected challenges to gun control based on the Fifth, Eighth, Ninth, 10th, and 14th amendments. No more effective have been challenges based on the 13th Amendment's prohibition of slavery or attempts to define gun laws as bills of attainder, ex post facto laws, or violations of the Commerce Clause.

That's not to say all non-Second Amendment claims are without merit. "One constitutional claim is the Ninth Amendment," which protects unenumerated rights, notes Cato Institute legal scholar Robert A. Levy. "Whether the Second Amendment pertains to a state or an individual is irrelevant if each of us has a Ninth Amendment right to defend ourselves." He concedes, however, that the Ninth Amendment has "never been given a whole lot of weight by the courts."

The Ninth Amendment case cited by Cyze is *United States v. Broussard*, a 1996 5th Circuit decision in a drug trafficking case. The court's Ninth Amendment finding was based on lack of argument, not a thorough analysis of the claim. The co-defendant Claude Merritt "does not point to any authority in support of his argument," the court said. "Nor does he advance any rationale to support his assertion that the right to possess weapons is among the rights reserved to citizens under the Ninth Amendment. Merritt relies solely on a law review article to support his contention."

Whatever possibilities these constitutional arguments hold, the best chance for a win may ultimately lie in the Second Amendment, says Arizona attorney David T. Hardy, a gun rights advocate. "Anything could be successful," he says, "but if you can't win on the Second Amendment with [a right to weapons] spelled out, you probably wouldn't win without it. I don't see where the Ninth Amendment or privacy would give you a tactical advantage."

THE NEXT BATTLES

DeMar was not present on October 29, when Cook County Circuit Judge Thaddeus Machnik called Orman and Cyze to the front of his Skokie courtroom and handed each a copy of his 16-page decision dismissing DeMar's challenge to Wilmette's gun ban. Parts of Machnik's opinion seemed taken straight from Cyze's briefs: The right to privacy did not apply to handguns in the home. The ordinance was not arbitrary or capricious. And because DeMar could have used a long gun instead, the handgun ban was consistent with the ordinance allowing citizens to discharge firearms in self-defense. The opinion dismissed DeMar's counterclaim, but it did not rule on the initial charge.

That ruling never came. On December 22 both parties agreed to dismiss the case. With the new state law protecting defensive gun use on the books, the village recognized it couldn't win.

The outcome disappointed Orman. "I don't think our position was successful," he says. "Even though we won and effectively got everything we wanted, we didn't get it the right way." Although "the legislature took the first positive step," Orman wanted the courts to "recognize a constitutional right to protect the home." Wilmette's handgun ban remains in effect.

There are two other high-profile gun ban challenges still pending, both involving Washington, D.C., which has a law even stricter than Wilmette's. In addition to effectively banning handguns, the city requires that all long guns be kept unloaded and locked.

Parker v. District of Columbia, in which Cato's Robert Levy serves as co-counsel, seeks a ruling based solely on the Second Amendment. *Seegars v. Ashcroft*, backed by Stephen Halbrook and the National Rifle Association, names the U.S. Department of Justice as a defendant, since the DOJ prosecutes handgun possession cases in D.C., and complements (or complicates) the Second Amendment argument with claims based on the Fifth Amendment's guarantees of property and equal protection, the Civil Rights Act of 1866, and a D.C. law requiring that ordinances be "usual and reasonable."

Both cases lost in U.S. district court. U.S. District Judge Emmet G. Sullivan "indicated that he found our arguments credible, but he thought *U.S. v. Miller* bound him" Levy says of his case. U.S. District Judge Reggie B. Walton dismissed Halbrook's case for lack of standing: None of the plaintiffs had tried to register a handgun, been denied, and exhausted the appeals process. In February the U.S. Court of Appeals for the D.C. Circuit agreed with Walton, but as of this writing the *Parker* attorneys have yet to argue their appeal; at the city's request, the court delayed consideration of *Parker* until the resolution of *Seegars*.

As happened in the DeMar case, legislative action could make these challenges moot. The D.C. Personal Protection Act, which would allow handgun ownership, eliminate registration, and repeal storage laws in the nation's capital, passed the House of Representatives in late September and is awaiting action in the Senate. It is likely to be a close vote.

Levy doesn't support the bill. He says it "could be repealed by the next liberal Congress; it doesn't provide the kinds of permanent protection a court ruling can." In any case, he adds, "I don't think the D.C. Council would be stymied. There are all sorts of bureaucratic and administrative things that can be used to deny people the right to have a handgun." Regardless of how the bill fares, Levy hopes to push a viable case to the forefront as soon as possible. "You don't want a bank robber or a crackhead up there as a poster boy for the Second Amendment," he says.

David Hardy favors waiting, predicting a 10-year battle. He hopes the Bush administration, which has endorsed the individual-right interpretation of the Second Amendment, will appoint gun-friendly justices to the Supreme Court. "Now we've got three votes for sure, and the rest are in the other camp," he says. "I'd like to see four or five in our back pocket, with a really good test case. Once you have a ruling you're only halfway through, because the lower courts will resist. It will be a battle to get the lower courts in line, and I doubt it would be a quick fight."

Discussion Questions

1. Do you believe Hale DeMar, who was protecting his children and home, should have been charged with violating the city's gun ban? Why or why not?
2. Discuss the Supreme Court's practice regarding gun control measures in light of the Second Amendment.
3. Compare the statistics regarding defensive gun use and the use of guns to commit crime. Do these statistics suggest we should impose tougher or more lenient gun control laws? Or, are current gun control laws seemingly adequate?

22

The Innocents: Idealistic Law Students Labor to Free the Wrongly Accused

By Michele Cohen Marill

The criminal justice system is in a state of transition. Specifically, the increasing use of DNA analyses is improving, yet damaging the system. The use of DNA analysis certainly gives jurors and courtroom personnel greater confidence in their decisions to convict or acquit defendants. In contrast, however, the increasing use of DNA analysis highlights the historical inaccuracies of the system. For instance, analysts, detectives, prosecutors, and others are revisiting questionable convictions from earlier cases and are realizing that some mistakes have been made and some individuals have been wrongfully punished. The selection "The Innocents" highlights the situation.

DNA analysis is changing the criminal justice system for the better. At the very least, the introduction of hard science into the courts provides more credibility to the judicial system. In criminal cases DNA analysis enables prosecutors, judges, and jurors to make more confident decisions regarding criminal case processing. Unfortunately, DNA analyses were not used until recently. As a result, we're transitioning to using DNA analysis to a much greater extent than ever before, which should increase the accuracy of courtroom decisions from here forward. The future should hold fewer wrongful convictions. The transition, however, involves revisiting cases in which DNA analysis was not used, and we're finding an uncomfortable error rate of convictions, resulting in a disturbing number of individuals are being freed from prison. While it is comforting that the wrongfully accused are being released, it is disturbing to believe that so many were wrongfully incarcerated.

The use of DNA analysis undoubtedly helps the courts. However, it is not always 100 percent accurate. The evidence containing DNA must be properly gathered and secured, because tampering with the evidence can lead to errors. The courts put much trust in the accuracy of DNA evidence, however, we must consider how the DNA evidence was collected, handled, and stored.

The current criminal justice system is the target of criticism for many reasons. Prominent among them is the rate of wrongful convictions. The use of DNA analysis in the courts helps us estimate the percentage of wrongfully accused, as we can revisit earlier cases to confirm or refute the courtroom decision. However, we'll never know the true rate of wrongful convictions as it is difficult to determine who has been wrongfully convicted and the evidence is not always available.

Law enforcement officials are faced with numerous duties and challenges. Therefore, revisiting evidence from closed cases often takes a backseat to current top priorities. Furthermore, is it in the best interest of the criminal justice system to search for and highlight inaccuracies? From a moral stand-point, it is. With regard to public relations, revisiting earlier cases means bad publicity. For the sake of justice, criminal justice officials must continue to review cases and forgo concerns of bad publicity. Who will assume the duty of revisiting earlier cases? The Innocence Project is groups of students who wish to make an impact. Also some law students put their studies to good use through correcting inaccuracies of the criminal justice system. It's hoped that the need for their efforts is only temporary as the effectiveness of our court system increases through advancements such as DNA analyses.

The letters are desperate. They are filled with obvious lies, or sorrowful grievances, or unrestrained outrage, or childlike hope. They are peppered with grammatical errors of the uneducated and the legalese of the jailhouse lawyer.

I have been in prison for more than 15 years . . . I need help Desperatly. The DA is stopping me at every turn . . .

More than 2,200—some scrawled, some in careful script—have been meticulously logged. They're stacked beside the fax machine and on the hand-me-down desks and filing cabinets of the Georgia Innocence Project. This is a threadbare operation that relies on the idealism of unpaid law students who take up residence at the mismatched desks or cluster around a small table in front of the executive director's desk; one favors a private spot in a utility closet. They pore over the tales of rapists and murderers, giving each claim of innocence a fair shot even if it seems preposterous.

Somewhere in these piles is another person sitting in a cold cell, breathing stale, cigarette-stained air, doing time for a crime he didn't commit. The interns long to find him. The innocent. The one they can exonerate.

FIRST LESSON: THE SEARCH FOR JUSTICE IS PAINFUL

If you want to believe that most everyone is innocent, you'll discover that most prison inmates really are guilty. If you think most of them really are criminals, you'll find cases that haunt you with lack of proof. If you believe in the system, you'll realize that it's sloppy and uncaring. If you believe in the quest for truth, you'll learn that truth is almost impossible to find.

In the cluttered, windowless Midtown office of the Georgia Innocence Project, executive director Aimee Maxwell tries to tell the interns what to expect. But she knows that, in the end, they will have to learn this lesson on their own.

Nationwide, 164 people have been exonerated by innocence projects. The original was founded by lawyers Barry Scheck and Peter Neufeld in 1992 and based in New York City. In 1999, the New York group's work led to the exoneration of Calvin Johnson, who had spent 16 years in a Georgia prison for a rape he didn't commit. In late 2005, their efforts helped free Georgian Robert Clark, falsely imprisoned for 24 years.

In 2002, two Georgia State University law students approached the Georgia Association of Criminal Defense Lawyers and asked simply: Why can't we do this here? The question ultimately came to Maxwell, 44, who ran a criminal defense training program for lawyers. Self-effacing and soft-spoken, she's a natural champion of the underdog. Within four months, she raised $100,000, gathered a board of directors (which now includes Calvin Johnson), found office space donated by ChoicePoint (an information broker that has a DNA testing subsidiary) and formed the Georgia Innocence Project.

"The Innocents: Idealistic Law Students Labor to Free the Wrongly Accused" by Michele Cohen Marill, *Atlanta*, February 2006, 45(10). Reprinted by permission of the author.

At the time, Maxwell had a job offer from a blue-chip law firm. She turned it down and now lives and breathes the Innocence Project, acting as a surrogate mother to the interns and a personification of the Lady of Justice to convicted inmates.

I'm writing to ask you for help again and to make you aware that I understand you droping [sic] my case because they say there's no DNA to prove me innocent. But if there is a State law to force me to take a DNA test to prove me guilty of a charge I haven't been arrested for then the State should have to give me a DNA test to prove me innocent of a crime that I was convicted of!

But if there's no DNA from the crime scene, we can't help you! Sometimes the interns wish they could dash back letters filled with as many exclamation points and as much frustration as the ones they receive. Instead, they vent to each other and then practice their best lawyerly skills, drafting coolly polite responses.

So when someone has a particularly weak claim or a case without a shred of evidence that can be tested, the interns dismiss it as cleanly as they can. Periodically, they gather in a borrowed conference room with Maxwell to review the cases.

Lindsay Reese, 22, a slender, married student who lives in Alpharetta, readjusts her wire-rimmed glasses nervously as she opens her files. She tucks a blond strand behind her ear and begins in a methodical tone: "File 86 is getting a 'no' letter. There's no DNA. File 398 is getting a 'no' letter. There was no rape kit done. File 1246 thinks you are a man. *Dear sir, Mr. Aimee Maxwell.* He's going to get a 'no' letter. It was child molestation, and there's no DNA."

She has one case she has been running over and over in her mind. His name is Ira Glenn White. He was convicted of breaking into a woman's apartment, hiding in the dark and smoking a cigarette until she got home, then raping and sodomizing her. He is serving two life sentences plus 60 years.

"[The victim] said he was 5'5" to 5'7". This guy is 5'11". She said that she didn't have to look up at him, but she was only 5'1". My husband is 10 inches taller than me. So I asked him to stand kind of close to me. I never really noticed it before, but I do have to look up to him," says Reese. "And then he sent us a copy of the photos she was shown in the lineup. She described her attacker as light-skinned. This guy was the only light-skinned person. The one guy. I looked at the pictures, and five of them were dark-skinned. You know, it's kind of suspicious."

Maxwell directs Reese, a second-year law student at Georgia State, to file an open records request to review the district attorney's file.

Melissa Arcila, a native of Colombia, is a disarmingly blunt 22-year-old law student from the University of Georgia. She formed Students for Latino Empowerment at UGA. Her top case involves an inmate convicted of raping a woman at gunpoint in the back seat of her car while her 9-year-old son crouched under the dashboard. The inmate was sunk when his own fingerprint analyst linked him to a partial thumbprint on the doorknob. He insists on his innocence though, and Arcila wonders just how much you can tell from a partial thumbprint.

Marcus Sellars, a second-year student from Mercer University Law School in Macon, who sits across from Reese, hasn't had much to work with. He brings up one complicated case involving rape, sodomy and kidnapping for ransom. Three life sentences plus 20 years.

Sellars launches into an explanation of the two types of sperm found in the rape investigation, motile and nonmotile, including some abnormal sperm that had two tails. It's clear the inmate has been wondering for 25 years whether someone could prove those weren't his sperm.

"He doesn't have abnormal sperm?" asks Maxwell.

"Yeah [he does], but the fact of the matter is, the sperm were never tested to determine who they belonged to."

At 36, Sellars is the oldest intern. He has an entire career behind him, having burned out as a history teacher in inner-city middle and high schools. He's also the only African-American. He grew up in Rochester, New York, in rough, crime-ridden neighborhoods. He says of about 20 childhood buddies, he's the only one who went to college. Five are dead. Ten are in prison—or have been.

For Sellars, law is not just a career. It's a quest to exonerate. He has two brothers, an uncle and a cousin in federal prisons, and he believes them when they say they are not guilty. He's quiet when the other interns banter and prod each other as they sit shoulder to shoulder in the cramped office. He hasn't even told them the story of his background and relatives. He doesn't want to impose his experience on their idealism.

Sellars leans across the table with a question for Maxwell: "Does this carry any weight with you that this was 25 years ago and he still says "I'm not guilty'?"

"No," she retorts. The interns laugh at the crispness of her response, particularly since she's known for her soft-heartedness. "There are things that make me think they're not guilty, but that's not one of them."

SECOND LESSON: BELIEVING IN INNOCENCE IS ONE THING. PROVING IT IS ANOTHER

There's no better mark of proof than DNA, the tiniest shards of identity. When you walk into a room, you leave not just fingerprints but a few random skin cells. A hair. Perhaps a trace of saliva on a water glass. If someone could gather those infinitesimal pieces of you, they could trace your presence on the scene. They could prove that this genetic detritus belonged to you and not to someone else. Or that it could not possibly have belonged to you, that someone else had been there.

Fifteen or 20 years ago, when most of the inmates now appealing to the Project were convicted, the best anyone could do was match blood types or compare hairs microscopically. For example, in Calvin Johnson's case, an analyst testified that he had type O blood and that he was a "secretor"—his blood type could be found in saliva and semen—the same as the rapist. Yet those facts would be true for about 40 percent of African-Americans, explains Greg Hampikian, an Innocence Project board member and forensics expert. The hair evidence, in fact, did not match Johnson's.

To understand DNA testing, think back to high school biology, DNA is made up of patterns of nucleotides known as A, G, C and T. DNA tests look for "short tandem repeats" (STRs)—sequences of A, G, C and T that repeat at a given location. For example, four repetitions on the chromosome from your mother and seven on the chromosome from your father would make you a "4-7" at that location.

In the early days, analysts needed a large quantity of DNA and only tested one or two locations. Today's labs can replicate DNA to create larger samples and compare STRs in 13 locations. When Calvin Johnson finally had his DNA tested—16 years after he entered prison—it showed he couldn't have been the rapist. The actual criminal is still at large.

Science is a savior for the wrongly convicted—but only if there's evidence to test. These inmates wore out their legal appeals long ago. Georgia law now requires evidence to be preserved for at least 10 years after a conviction, but in older cases, the evidence is elusive.

It could be in the court reporter's house, the district attorney's file, a police department storage shed—or destroyed. The interns file open records requests and bounce from one bureaucratic department to another. No one is too fired up about trying to help unearth a long-lost rape kit or pair of panties. Yet the interns know that without the semen or blood stains, they will never uncover an innocent person and set him free.

THIRD LESSON: INNOCENCE ENDURES THE TEST OF TIME

Clarence Harrison knocks lightly on the door before entering the office. He's a shock of athletic red, with shorts and sleeveless tee and logo-less baseball cap. It's all so coordinated, except for the enormous silver cross hanging around his neck, but it looks incongruous on this paunchy man with a trim, graying beard.

It's been more than a year and a half since Harrison was released from prison after serving 17 years for a rape he did not commit, and he still has the air of a modern-day Rip Van Winkle. Harrison stands in the doorway hesitantly until Maxwell spies him from her office. "What's that outfit?" she prods teasingly.

"Just tryin' to be comfortable."

Harrison looks around at the interns, who have swiveled in their chairs to smile at him. "What y'all comin' up with? Anything good?"

"We're going to have to visit some courthouses to look at some cases," responds Arcila. "Look at some shady DA work."

He laughs. "That's pretty much it."

"I just want to see what evidence they've got. It doesn't seem like there will be any. But I think everybody's shady. I'm just into conspiracy theories." Arcila's smile doesn't seem cynical or conspiratorial at all.

Maxwell shepherds the group into a break room, where the interns rush over to the machine that gives out 25-cent Cokes, then settle around a laminate table. Since Harrison got out of prison, his main avocation has simply been talking about himself.

Before Harrison has a chance to launch into his oft-told tale, Sellars interjects: "Did you run across people who are innocent, they were locked up and you kind of knew they were innocent?" To Sellars, Harrison bears an uncanny resemblance to one of his convicted relatives. He even talks like him. He leans closer because Harrison speaks softly.

"There are people I ran across that I believed were innocent. It's just that proving they're innocent, that's the hard thing to do," says Harrison.

"What was their demeanor? Was there something about them?" Sellars prods.

Harrison talks about an inmate who never really knew the facts of the crime he was convicted of committing. He only knew what was told in court. As the years passed in prison, he forgot those details and knew virtually nothing about his own case. Harrison figures if he had committed the crime, he would never have forgotten it.

"It's just the little things that go unnoticed that tell you whether this person is guilty or innocent."

Harrison segues into a description of life behind bars. Waking at 5 A.M., eating breakfast at 5:30, lining up for work detail and call at 7, school or trades at 8, or getting thrown in "the hole" for refusing to work. Once he decided to take classes, things improved a little. But he spent hours wandering in the dormitory, the TV droning every day from 4:30 to 11 P.M. Then a fitful sleep on a cot in a cell and waking up to the same damn thing the next day. Some inmates would start fights just to get a little excitement, he says.

"I would prefer that I receive a death penalty than receive another 20 years in prison," he says. "I think that would be more merciful."

What about the victim? Did you ever talk to her? Did she ever apologize?

No. Harrison says. He went back to the place where the crime occurred, near a bus stop in the Decatur neighborhood where he once lived, and marveled at how much it had changed. How much everything had changed. Folks didn't have cell phones or computers when he went into prison. His wife divorced him after he was arrested. His two children grew up without him. He is now married to a woman who befriended him and believed in him during his prison stay.

Not being bitter is something he has worked at. He blames the system, not the victim who misidentified him. But when Susan Anton, an intern from Chicago, starts quizzing him about victims, he remarks, "The most heinous crime of all is to be a victim of a victim because a victim shows no mercy."

Sellars has another question. "After 15 to 20 years—let's say it's a life sentence—do you think they would still try to get out, claiming they're innocent?"

"For a man to maintain his innocence for 15 or 20 years, it requires to be looked into," replies Harrison. "I'm not saying he could be innocent or guilty. It's our responsibility to make sure justice is always served."

FOURTH LESSON: YOU CAN'T READ INNOCENCE OR GUILT ON THEIR FACES

Reese and Arcila walk into the vast Justice Center of Clayton County, a faux historical building that looks like a supersized antebellum home, complete with portico and enormous colonnade.

The clerk in the DA's office has the file ready and ushers them into a cubicle. Reese opens the file and sees a brown paper bag, stapled shut. She fingers it. It's a cigarette butt, found near the door where the rapist waited for his victim, who was a nonsmoker. "Sweet," she says.

Yellow legal pad pages describe the case from the DA's perspective. The victim's description didn't exactly match. He was at least four inches too tall. But he had lied about when he received an eviction notice and moved out. That made his alibi weak, at best. *Ira White and his mom are absolute liars!* the DA wrote.

They flip through, focusing for a few moments on White's lineup photo, in which he is scowling. Does he look guilty? They keep hunting for anything that lists the evidence. They need some clue as to what happened to the stained pants—maybe a snip of cloth, maybe a slide of the semen. Anything with DNA.

"It's not looking too hopeful for this guy," says Arcila.

"I still have hope," says Reese.

Did not see knot on ear, the DA noted. "She double-starred that," says Arcila.

"Yeah, 'cause that's a problem for her."

She again absolutely and unequivocally IDs him in court. There is no Q in her mind. The DA hammers in on that identification in closing statements.

"In her mind, he already is the rapist whether he is or not," says Reese.

The two young women close the file, return it and move on to the microfilm room of the superior court clerk's office. They find no sign of the other evidence.

Two weeks later, Reese meets White face to face. The name in the file becomes a person, and she can't help but search for clues of guilt or innocence.

He doesn't look the way she imagined. He's too slight. He has narrow shoulders and a thin waist, and though his prison documents confirm that he is 5'11", he is far from towering. The rape victim had identified her rapist as short and slender. Now that Reese stands before inmate Ira White in a counseling office of the Autry State Prison, she wavers in her conviction that his height was a tip-off that he was the wrong guy.

When he was arrested, White had Jeri curls, but his shaved head now makes him look older. He also has at least two prison-made tattoos: a griffin (part eagle, part lion) and wolf that cover up an old marijuana leaf tattoo and a small tattoo of "13½" on his hand—"12 jurors, one judge and a half-assed chance," he explains.

In their meeting, White is almost manically elated by these women who came to visit. He hasn't slept since the day before. With so many hours in prison to ruminate over his case, he remembers specific reports by the date they were issued. He corrects Reese on details. He has collected reams of documents—including one that he says never appeared at trial showing that a hair found on the victim's panties didn't match her or him.

His voice is soft and low but rises, dripping with bitterness, as he rails at the DA: "She knew exactly what she was doing. She knew she had the wrong person, and she did not care."

Reese and Maxwell warn him that a positive DNA test would doom him to a lifetime in prison. It would be incontrovertible proof of his guilt. "If this were to come back positive, you are not going to get paroled," says Maxwell, kindly but firmly. "It's really risky. I just want to tell you."

"No worries," he says, almost cockily, shaking his head.

They promise that they will keep looking for more evidence. So far, they have just the cigarette butt. It's a start, but ideally, they want to find something more.

As they stand to leave, Maxwell asks him, "Is this what you expected?"

"Not totally—but it's more than enough," he says.

"Did you expect us to tell you we were going to get you out tomorrow?" she says teasingly.

"I was hoping so. Hoping against hope," he says, returning the smile.

"I fell disappointed," Reese confesses later, as the car whizzes past a monotony of central Georgia pine trees and dead-end diners on the four-hour ride back to Atlanta. "I guess I just wanted to go and talk to him and have no doubt in my mind." She dissects each interchange. He didn't seem aggressive or scary. But could he have been too slick? Was he lying?

"If it's him, I sat in a room with him, I shook his hand, I gave him respect, and he didn't deserve it if he's a rapist," says Reese, suddenly weighing the possibility of his guilt. "I know I shouldn't feel that way, especially if I'm going to do criminal defense. But if he did it, then I sat in a room with a rapist who did these terrible things to this woman—and I believed him. And I believed him, and I'm a fool."

"One way or another, if we find the DNA, we'll know for sure," Maxwell reassures her. "Then we'll never have to doubt."

A week later, Arcila takes a whirlwind trip to Savannah on behalf of Eric Williams, the man convicted of raping the woman in the car while her son crouched under the dashboard. The partial fingerprint is a little troublesome. But there are some problems with the prosecution's case too. The victim identified someone else in the photo lineup, but when police couldn't find that person for a live lineup, they substituted Williams instead. He had an alibi. Co-workers testified that he was driving home from work with them.

"It's so shady," says Arcila dismissively. "Typical Georgia racist justice."

The last time Arcila was in Savannah, she was wearing green and drinking green beer at a St. Patrick's Day celebration. Now, she is wearing heels and dress pants and headed for the courthouse with fellow intern Susan Anton and Lisa George, the Project's communications director (and only employee besides Maxwell). Arcila is a little on guard, expecting the district attorney's office to stonewall them.

They are ready for her. Boxes of documents rest on a cart in a conference room.

Arcila opens a thin cardboard box and peers into a translucent black bag. She catches her breath as she spies a pair of gray panties with an obvious stain. She doesn't want to touch anything, but she jostles the contents to look. She sees the door handle, a T-shirt and a pair of work pants but no sign of the lifted fingerprint.

The next day, after a night at a cheap motel outside of town, they leave Savannah's prim 19th century homes and tinseled oaks. The terrain transforms into scraggy marsh as they drive through vacant southeast Georgia towns to Ware State Prison. It is a benign-looking brick building that, without all the menacing barbed-wire fences, could resemble a converted motel. In the distance, prisoners are working in the yard.

The women hand over their driver's licenses, step through metal detectors and follow a prison guard into a lobby that looks jarringly like a school, with shiny floors and little couches and a big round clock. They must wait while the prison completes a shakedown.

Eric Williams walks in, glistening with sweat, still wearing his sunglasses. He's a stocky man with heavy jowls, close-cropped hair and a trim mustache. He smiles and shakes hands and, in fact, looks rather casual, as if he had visitors like them all the time.

Arcila gives him the usual warning about how DNA evidence could confirm his guilt and ruin his chances of ever getting parole. "Do you want us to go forward, or do you want us to stop?" George asks pointedly.

Williams looks resolute. "I have done some things. I had a temper. But I'm not a rapist."

Arcila asks him about the fingerprint. How did it get there? "I'd like to know that myself," he says. "That's something that has haunted me for 20 years."

They talk about his past—his time in the military, his previous conviction for aggravated assault. "I'll do my time for what I deserve, but this is something I did not do," he insists.

They talk about the trial, his alibi and another rape that police tried but never did pin on him. He will be eligible for parole. But that's almost beside the point. He says he doesn't want to live with the stigma of being a sex offender, with this charge of raping a schoolteacher while her son cowered in the car.

As they leave, George once again reminds him that if he's guilty, the DNA test will prove it. He shakes his head and says, once again, that he's not guilty.

Arcila walks out, buoyed, believing him, wishing that she had that fingerprint and could prove, with 21st century technology, that it wasn't his.

FIFTH LESSON: BE PATIENT

In a loft of Manuel's Tavern, the interns sit in a row on one side of a long set of tables. They look well-groomed but, with the exception of Sellars, who wears a suit, not exactly dressed up. This is the most important moment of their summer, so there's an undercurrent of nervous tension and strained casualness.

Scattered around other tables are the members of the Project's legal advisory board, a set of public defenders and criminal defense attorneys who will decide which, if any, of the interns' cases they will accept as clients. Without their okay, the Project cannot move forward to file legal motions and test DNA.

Reese rises first, with an aura of confidence and the voice of a courtroom attorney, to present the case of Ira Glenn White.

A battery of questions ensues when she says she wants to take him as client and test the cigarette butt. Have you talked to the jurors? Have you talked to the attorney in the related civil suit over the rape? What about the similar rape that was linked to the case but that he was never charged with?

"What's the next step short of testing the cigarette butt? What can we still do that won't cost us a bunch of money?" quizzes Jill Polster, one of the Project's founders.

Reese sighs heavily, impatiently. She tries again to explain. "I want to file motions. I think Aimee is with me on this. We'll be trying to get the state to pay for the DNA testing and maybe they'll produce something else."

She wishes fervently that Maxwell were there to back her up, but a death in the family has forced her to miss this meeting. Polster says bluntly. "I have a problem spending money on the cigarette butt because it's not going to walk him out the door." Reese's face reddens as Polster suggests she continue working and bring the case back in three months. "You look disappointed."

"I am, if that stands. I'm disappointed, absolutely."

"You want us to take him as a client and file motions to test the DNA," reiterates September Guy, the other co-founder.

"Yes, absolutely. Yes, I do."

"Just to get in court, we've got to show that the evidence is conclusive," Jim Bonner, who is with the Georgia Public Defender Standards Council, says didactically.

"But they admitted it as evidence!" Reese's face crumples. Her hand rightly grasps the empty chair next to hers. She takes an audible gulp of water.

"I understand that. You've got me persuaded. But I don't think it's going to open it up—"

Reese suggests the DNA on the cigarette butt might match the DNA of another convicted rapist, which would cast doubt on White's conviction. But the board members are not convinced.

"We're not saying we're not going to take him [as a client]," says Polster. "I want you to understand that. We're just saying we have to exhaust every possibility of finding the evidence that will walk him out the door."

Arcila tries to come to Reese's defense. "The biggest issue we have is finding evidence," she says. "I mean, nobody ever seems to know where it goes. You know what I'm saying? They always give you another phone number, another person, even the court reporter always dies or disappears or something happens . . ."

But it's time to move on. Reese sits down and picks at her cold tuna melt.

By the time Arcila rises to address the silenced room, she has a slim, cocky smile. Hers is not an entirely lost cause. "I'll try to get you excited about a case," she says.

"We're excited," remarks Polster.

"I actually found a pair of underwear that was introduced into evidence as the underwear the victim was wearing."

Arcila goes on to tell about Bric Williams case, his alibi, his lineup, the fingerprint. Surely, after working at a road construction site with liquid asphalt in 90-degree heat (she checked the *Farmer's Almanac*), he would have stunk—and the victim would have noticed that.

The panty stain is "nice and crusty," and Hampikian told Arcila it would be no problem to recover DNA.

She thought the fingerprint would be a major obstacle, but it turns out that these defense attorneys relish the thought of disproving a so-called fingerprint expert. In 1987, the analyst used a magnifying glass to match a partial thumbprint. Today, investigators would use a computer comparison.

"Here we have definitive evidence," says Arcila. "The question is whether we believe enough in the case to test the evidence."

"I like it. Let's take it," says Polster. "I think it's worth it on the fingerprint evidence alone."

"That would be awesome," sighs attorney Gerard Kleinrock.

Sitting in the corner, Sellars has hardly said a word. He put his greatest effort into a case that blew apart with one phone call. He thought perhaps there was something fishy about the case of an inmate convicted in the armed robbery of a liquor store. The Georgia Bureau of Investigation had uncovered a mask worn by the robber but didn't test the hairs found on the mask until two years later. Could they have mistakenly mixed up the sample hairs provided by this inmate, essentially testing the sample as the damning evidence?

The inmate insists he didn't commit the crime. Sellars believe him.

Until the day, out of curiosity, he called the inmate's ex-wife. She, too, had wanted to believe him. But then, in a doorway of their home, she discovered an empty moneybag that belonged to the liquor store. "How did it get there?" she demanded. He said he didn't know. She told Sellars her husband had been a masterful conman. She knew in her heart that he had robbed the store.

"This case was an example of how we try to filter things as carefully as possible," Sellars says serenely, as the other interns mill about at Manuel's and contemplate drinking something stronger than Coke to mark the end of their summer. The cadence of laughter and strains of music fill the room from the bar below. "We haven't closed this case, but the door is actively closing. I put all this effort because I though this guy might have something."

Sellars isn't angry about being conned. He isn't upset that he came to the Legal Advisory Board meeting empty-handed. He plans to continue working with the Innocence Project when he can, traveling from Macon.

"I feel about as excited as I was on day one, today," he declares. "The excitement hasn't waned. As long as I'm dealing with the have-nots and the innocents, that's perfectly fine with me."

Beyond the angry desperation of the letters, beyond the yearning idealism of the interns, beyond the cold scrutiny of the lawyers, Sellars has the patience to wait to find someone who need to be set free. "I've faced defeat all my life, but I've always gotten off the mat to win every time," he says. "I wouldn't doubt for one minute that I'll be part of an exoneration."

FINAL LESSON: KEEP ON SEARCHING

Just a few days later, in an effort to console Reese, Maxwell calls a Clayton County assistant DA and asks for a more thorough search for the Ira White evidence. He has a generous offer. Come and look for yourself, he says.

The evidence room is a storage space with metal shelving and boxes marked only by shelf location. Reese heads for the room with evidence slated for destruction. Maxwell takes another look at Section C2, Box 2, the location marked on the evidence sheet. The box is empty.

She scans the entire Section C, then Section B. She's about to join Reese when she randomly peers inside Box 1 in Section D2. She sees the name, "White, Ira Glenn," and like someone momentarily dazed by the opening of a window shade, she pauses. "Oh my God," she says. "I think I've got the evidence."

She asks the Clayton County investigator who accompanied them to take out the contents. An empty envelope. Some vacuum sweepings and a blue button in a plastic baggie. Then he pulls out the rape kit and a clipping from the stained black pants worn by the victim immediately after the rape.

The assistant DA offers to send the evidence to the Georgia Bureau of Investigation for testing, short-circuiting the usual legal proceedings and saving the project money. The Legal Advisory Board hastily agrees to take White as a client, through an e-mail consensus.

Maxwell and Reese call White, and the prison cooperates by bringing him to the phone. They give him one last chance to back out. He insists on going forward.

"We've already opened Pandora's box," says Maxwell. "Now we get to find out for sure."

Discussion Questions

1. Discuss how DNA analyses free some individuals who have been wrongfully convicted.
2. Explain how the "lessons" highlighted throughout the article assisted the law students in their attempt to free the wrongly accused.
3. Discuss the various ways in which individuals are wrongly convicted. What additional steps can courts take to reduce wrongful convictions? Should we take those steps?

23

Evil Twins: And How DNA Evidence Is Useless Against Them

By John Wolfson

DNA was first described by researchers in 1953 when scientists Francis Crick and James Watson identified the structure of DNA and highlighted its role as the genetic code of living organisms. Despite this significant contribution to science and society in general, it wasn't until the 1980s that those within the criminal justice system began recognizing and using DNA evidence to solve crimes and, ultimately, exonerate the innocent. DNA analysis has contributed to the conviction of many offenders. Equally important, it has also led to the acquittal of many offenders.

Many scholars tout the contributions of DNA analysis to the criminal justice system. Incorporating the hard sciences into what has traditionally been a social science arena provides much-needed confidence in our courts. DNA provides a fingerprint for each individual in the sense that everyone's DNA is unique, except in the case of identical twins. DNA testing relies on the availability of cells containing DNA. Body fluids such as blood and semen are often tested, although the tests could include saliva, hair, vaginal fluid, soft bone, and deep muscle tissue. As noted in this selection, DNA analysis, as currently used, is limited in distinguishing between identical twins. There is hope, however, that further development and study of DNA will identify differences between identical twins, thus further enhancing the utility of DNA analyses.

The selection "Evil Twins" identifies a situation in which DNA evidence provided limited direction for prosecutors. Particularly, the DNA found at a crime scene matched a set of identical twins, and little additional evidence added to the uncertainty regarding who was responsible. Although DNA analyses currently provide no differentiation between identical twins, all is not lost. The situation described in "Evil Twins" is the exception. Rarely do cases involve uncertainty regarding the criminal behavior of identical twins. And, at the very least, DNA analysis narrowed the list of suspects to two. Many detectives would welcome the opportunity to have the list of legitimate suspects in a serious crime narrowed to two.

A primary challenge when presenting DNA or any evidence in court is to ensure that all in the courtroom can follow and understand the discussion. Particularly, jurors are often unfamiliar with technical discussions of scientific analyses, and placing a DNA expert on the stand to explain how DNA works and why the evidence should be duly considered can sometimes lead to confusion. The task is to find individuals who can discuss DNA analyses in layperson terms, so jurors can comprehend the information.

The increasing popularity of DNA analyses has impacted the criminal justice system. For instance, courts can feel more confident in their decisions to convict, acquit, or set free individuals when using DNA as evidence; thus, there has been increased demand and expectation by jurors (and others) to see DNA evidence in court. In response, crime labs across the country are inundated with requests for analysis of evidence. Unfortunately, crime labs are expensive to operate and their increased use consumes substantial criminal justice budgetary resources. Those interested in careers in analyzing crime scene evidence appear to have a bright future as the courts and the criminal justice system in general continuously rely on scientific means to reduce their conviction error-rate and correct past mistakes involving wrongful convictions.

Back in the summer of 2001, Darrin Fernandez slashed himself on the jagged glass of a window he shattered while trying to break into an apartment in the Dorchester neighborhood of Boston. A woman watching television inside called the police, who made it to the building in time to arrest Fernandez, still bleeding in the yard as he tried to escape.

When investigators ran his DNA through a database, they found it to be a perfect match for the genetic material recovered from two unsolved sexual assaults, each of them committed within a few blocks of the attempted breaking and entering, and each carried out in the same fashion: a man creeping through a window and raping a woman who had been sleeping inside. Fernandez was found guilty of attempted breaking and entering for shattering the window, and eventually he would be convicted of one of the two rapes. The second rape, however, has presented prosecutors with an unexpected challenge.

The DNA match was the only substantive evidence that prosecutors had in the case. Under normal circumstances, that would likely have been enough—the DNA match should have made it billions-to-one that anyone other than Fernandez was guilty of the assault. But the DNA turned out to be a perfect match for two people: Darrin Fernandez and his identical twin, Damien.

DNA testing convicts the guilty and exonerates the innocent with unprecedented efficiency and accuracy. Yet in the rare case of identical twins—who make up about four-tenths of 1 percent of the population—a genetic match can be as much a hindrance as a help. Identical twins are born with exactly the same genes and, despite ongoing efforts by biological researchers, it remains impossible to discern one twin from the other using DNA analysis. "Everyone thinks DNA clears things up," Robert Zanello, Darrin Fernandez's lawyer, said recently. "But it has muddied the waters."

Over the course of two trials, Zanello's message to jurors has been quite simple: Damien Fernandez was as likely as Darrin Fernandez to have slipped through the window and committed the rape. The Suffolk County District Attorney's Office has nothing to link Darrin to the crime other than his DNA, no eyewitnesses, no accomplice, not even a fingerprint (which could have made a difference, since identical twins have different prints). And the DNA doesn't prove anything except that either twin could be guilty. Darrin doesn't have an alibi for his whereabouts at the time of the rapes, but neither does his brother. Damien, proclaiming his innocence, has testified that he was living in other cities at the time of the rapes, but neither he nor prosecutors have been able to account for his whereabouts on the night of the crime. "You can't put my client any closer to the crime scene than you can put the brother," Zanello said.

Rather than establishing Darrin Fernandez's guilt, genetic testing helped him establish some very reasonable doubt. After deliberating for four days, the first jury to consider the case gave up. Judge Elizabeth Donovan declared a mistrial. Eight months later, the Suffolk County D.A. tried Fernandez again. This time, Assistant District Attorney Mary Kelley took jurors to the Dorchester house where Darrin Fernandez had worked as a painter. Kelley argued that from that house, atop a ladder, Fernandez was able to case the neighborhood and select his victims. But if the visit to the scene of the crime convinced some jurors of Darrin's guilt, it did not persuade them all. Like the first, the second trial ended in a hung jury.

For all the trouble the Boston authorities have had prosecuting Fernandez, their counterparts in Grand Rapids, Mich., have had it even worse. They can't figure out which of another set of identical twins to charge with the 1999 rape of a young woman in a parking lot.

That case had gone unsolved until last year, when one Jerome Cooper, serving a five-year sentence for breaking into a home and fondling a woman, became eligible for parole. In Michigan, parole applicants are required to submit a DNA sample to be run through a database of open cases. Cooper's sample came back as a match for DNA recovered from the parking lot rape.

"I thought, 'Great, we've got our guy. He's in prison, better yet. We don't have to hunt him down,'" said detective Les Smith of the Grand Rapids Police Department. "Then it turns out he has a twin brother, Tyrone." As in the Fernandez case, there is no significant evidence in the Cooper case aside from the DNA. The victim was attacked from behind and could not provide an identification, and no fingerprints were left at the scene. Further complicating matters, both Jerome and Tyrone Cooper have prior sexual assault convictions. "You don't know who you can charge," Smith said. "Both were out of prison at the time. And it's getting hard to go back and ask somebody, 'Give me an alibi for what you were doing five years ago.' They just say it's not them."

Given the uncertainty, Smith contacted the parole board and asked them to reject Cooper's petition for early release. The board agreed, and Cooper's request was denied. As for Tyrone Cooper, he too is currently imprisoned, for failure to register as a sex offender. He would have been eligible for parole in July, but Smith got in touch with the parole board, which again refused to release a Cooper. Knowing that one of the brothers is guilty of the rape, Smith said that his department intends to do what it can to keep each of them in prison "until the technology catches up."

The technology is trying. Identical twins occur when a fertilized egg splits, producing two embryos with the same DNA. Yet some researchers believe that the genes of the individual embryos undergo tiny, unique mutations after the egg splits. If that is true, scientists might be able to create a test that could tell the difference between twins by identifying the distinct mutations.

Orchid Cellmark, a New Jersey-based company that specializes in helping states solve crimes using DNA analysis, offered to try to devise such a test to help Grand Rapids police solve the Cooper rape case. The company's researchers ran up against the limits of existing science, however, and the project ended unsuccessfully. "At this point, we've exhausted the capabilities that are currently available," said Robert Giles, Orchid Cellmark's director of United States operations. "It's basically a hypothesis that [the mutations] exist." If they do exist, Giles predicts that the technology to detect them may be available in a couple of years. The breakthrough would help close the several serious criminal cases involving twins (experts estimate there are between 3 and 10 such cases annually) as well as a similar number of paternity disputes in which twins both deny parenting a child who carries their DNA.

For now, the Suffolk County D.A. will have to find another way of convincing a jury that Darrin, and not Damien, Fernandez committed the second rape. The D.A.'s office has declined to comment, given the pending prosecution—Darrin's third trial begins in September—so it's unclear what new approach, if any, prosecutors might try. But it is safe to say that the D.A.'s office wishes it had another piece of physical evidence, something to poke a hole in Zanello's contention that either twin could be the guilty party. Something, perhaps, like the evidence the D.A. had in 2003, when it successfully prosecuted Fernandez for the first Dorchester rape. Zanello argued at that trial as well that the DNA implicated Damien as much as Darrin. The jury might have believed him then, too, had the victim not been able to positively identify the tattoo that adorns Darrin's forearm. It reads, "Twinz."

Discussion Questions

1. Do all humans have a distinct DNA makeup? Discuss.
2. Discuss the situation detailed in the article with regard to the limitations of DNA analysis. What can be done to overcome this limitation?

3. As a juror, would you expect that the prosecution and defense present DNA evidence? Would your opinion of the case likely differ if one or both neglected to reference DNA evidence?

24

Effects of Capital Punishment on the Justice System

By Brent E. Dickson

Capital punishment is one of the most intensely debated issues in society. As the most severe form of punishment in practice, the death penalty is controversial in many aspects. Some claim the death penalty deters crime; others claim it doesn't. Regardless, public support for the death penalty is often used as a litmus test to determine the public's pulse regarding crime and punishment. Critics and proponents of the death penalty intensely debate regarding the utility, morality, and practicality of the punishment.

Proponents of capital punishment cite the sense of justice that exists upon executing a murderer. Justice-based practices often assume the "eye for an eye" approach. Accordingly, it is felt that murderers should be executed. Proponents cite the sense of closure for the victim's families and the safety provided to the public as benefits of capital punishment. They add that capital punishment provides a deterrent for some who consider committing capital offenses, and the current use of DNA analyses at trial will greatly reduce the likelihood of wrongful convictions and, ultimately, wrongful executions.

Critics of capital punishment argue that it is morally reprehensible for the government to act like the murderers they execute. Furthermore, they cite the increased costs of capital murder cases, as addressed in this selection. Critics argue that capital punishment does not deter crime, it constitutes cruel and unusual punishment, and the error rate for wrongful convictions should be enough evidence to suggest there's too much uncertainty in our courts. Furthermore, it is argued that life in prison without the possibility of parole is sometimes considered a more severe form of punishment and a greater deterrent to capital offenses than is capital punishment.

The sense of finality associated with an execution and the seriousness of the penalty attract great scrutiny. Everyone involved in capital murder cases, including judges, prosecutors, and defense attorneys, puts their best foot forward as they are aware of the consequences and the great level of scrutiny involved. One mistake could mean the difference between life and death. Thus, a great deal of preparation goes into each capital offense case; preparation which takes time, costs money and may come at the expense of attention and resources devoted to other criminal cases.

Consider the role of the players involved in capital murder cases. Consider the mindset of a defense attorney who is aware that failure to perform adequately could result in a wrongful death. Or, consider the prosecutor who makes all efforts to ensure that the defendant is executed. While prosecutors are not necessarily directly executing the offenders, they certainly maintain a great deal of accountability for the punishment. Judges are also notably impacted by capital cases, for instance, they must ensure that all procedures are followed properly or wrongful death may result. Finally, consider the plight of jurors who must determine the fate of the accused. Place yourself on a jury charged with determining whether a suspect is guilty of capital murder. Your vote to find the defendant guilty may result in his or her death. The impacts associated with capital murder cases must be considered in light of the law and the offender's behavior. For some, capital murder cases pose no challenges. For others, it's quite the contrary. Such differences among individuals highlight the polarizing effects of capital punishment.

The responsibilities and work of a state court of last resort are significantly affected by the presence of capital punishment as a sentencing option in the state penal code. The effects are most apparent in decisional workload, administrative functions, and public perception of the judiciary generally.

The Indiana legislature reinstituted the death penalty in 1977,[1] following the United States Supreme Court decision in *Gregg v. Georgia,* 428 U.S. 153 (1976). During the ensuing 27 years, Indiana trial courts ordered the death penalty for 90 defendants. These cases produced 148 Indiana Supreme Court majority opinions, 45 reversals of the sentence with the defendant no longer eligible for the death penalty, but now serving a sentence other than death (life imprisonment without parole or for a specific term of years), and 16 executions. In the course of the 16 cases resulting in an execution, there were 33 state trial court proceedings (including trial, re-trial, and post-conviction hearings), 44 state Supreme Court majority opinions and substantive orders, and 25 federal court opinions.

Since 1990, death penalty cases in Indiana have been governed by a specialized rule regarding the appointment, qualifications, and compensation of trial and appellate counsel in capital cases. This rule was promulgated by the Indiana Supreme Court, which has exclusive original appellate jurisdiction in capital cases. Because trial and appellate counsel for almost all capital defendants in Indiana are appointed at public expense, Indiana's judicial experience with capital cases is best viewed in light of the practice, procedure, and results observed following the implementation of these rules.

Between the time of the rule changes in 1990 and November 15, 2005, the death penalty has been sought in Indiana trial courts against 174 defendants, of which 4 were acquitted or the charges dismissed before trial, and 30 were sentenced to death. Of these 30 defendants, 3 have been executed and 9 death sentences have been reversed with the defendant now serving a sentence other than death. Eighteen of the 30 death sentences remain in appellate review or are awaiting new trials.

Over the most recent 10-year period, from 1995 through 2004, capital opinions in Indiana (including cases on direct appeal and collateral review) accounted for approximately 7 percent of the total number of signed majority opinions issued by the court.[2] During this same period, however, the number of capital cases decided accounted for only 0.92 percent of the total number of cases decided by the court (including those on which review was denied by order). Thus, capital cases account for less than 1 percent of the court's caseload, but more than 7 percent of its number of written opinions. In the past 10 years, our court has decided an average of about 1,075 cases per year and issued an average of about 137 signed opinions per year, of which an average of 10 were capital cases opinions.

JUDICIAL TIME AND EFFORT

Each of the court's capital case opinions represented a substantially disproportionate investment of judicial time and effort. Judicial opinions in death penalty cases are characteristically more extensive than those in non-capital criminal appeals. Because of the finality of the sentence, both defense

"Effects of Capital Punishment on the Justice System" by Brent E. Dickson, as appeared in the March/June 2006 issue of *Judicature*, the journal of the American Judicature Society. Reprinted with permission.

The author acknowledges with great appreciation the valuable assistance of Greta M. Scodro, Deputy Administrator, Indiana Supreme Court, without which this writing would not have been possible.

counsel and the reviewing court endeavor to be particularly thorough and comprehensive. Courts are also inclined to address more claims on the merits and to be somewhat more hesitant to apply procedural forfeiture. It is not unusual for capital appeals to present a significantly greater number of issues than would likely be seen in non-capital cases, often including issues on which there is no basis under existing law, but wherein counsel is requesting a reexamination of precedent or seeking to preserve an issue for federal review or in anticipation of possible future modification of the law. In addition, periodic United States Supreme Court refinements in constitutional law applicable to criminal procedure and death penalty jurisprudence require particular attention in the research and crafting of capital case opinions.

To accommodate these many concerns, Indiana permits longer appellate briefs in capital cases.[3] Further adding to the burden of appellate review in capital cases, it is not unusual for the trial record in the initial appeal of a capital sentence to consist of 3,000 to 5,000 pages, or more. And the record presented in subsequent collateral review appeals is usually about twice that amount.

Appellate review in capital cases typically involves a particularly intensive review of mitigation issues, which are often quite fact specific and require detailed examination of the record. It is also not uncommon for such claims to involve expert testimony on medical and social science issues, particularly when mitigating consideration is sought for concerns related to impaired mental health or abusive childhood, which are matters not readily researched by lawyers and often require special attention.

These kinds of appellate issues usually arise not only when claims assert the ineffective assistance of trial counsel in offering evidence of mitigation, but also arise in Indiana where the state supreme court has made a separate and independent determination regarding the appropriateness of the death sentence.[4] These issues of mitigation and appropriateness in capital cases typically require a greater investment of judicial time in research, analysis, and writing than in non-capital cases.

Capital cases also take more time because of the extensive use of collateral proceedings by defense counsel. Under the Indiana Rules of Procedure for Post-Conviction Remedies, a defendant, following the affirmance of the trial court's sentencing judgment on the initial direct appeal, may again seek relief by filing a petition for post-conviction relief to assert certain types of claims not resolved on direct appeal. The resolution of such post-conviction relief petitions usually requires a full evidentiary proceeding before the trial court, replete with extensive pre-hearing discovery, and it is almost inevitably used in every capital case to claim ineffective assistance of trial and/or appellate counsel.

If post-conviction relief is denied by the trial court, the defendant may again appeal to the state supreme court, resulting in a second opinion. And if the denial of post-conviction relief is affirmed by the court, a defendant may request to file a second or successive petition for post-conviction relief, which will be authorized if the defendant's request establishes a reasonable possibility that the petitioner is entitled to relief.[5] Capital defendants make exhaustive use of these opportunities for collateral review.

Not insignificant is the additional burden upon support staff presented by the management of a capital case. In Indiana, we have assigned one appellate staff attorney to assist the court in a variety of functions related to our death penalty jurisdiction responsibilities. Her functions include tracking capital cases filed in the state trial courts and pending on appeal, answering questions from counsel, assisting with the court's review and disposition of motions, and communicating with the federal courts, the media, and the public, etc. Each year, approximately 120 hours of our staff attorney's time is routinely required for her general duties related to capital cases.

When a capital defendant's appellate recourse is exhausted and the time of execution approaches, there is almost always a further need for the substantial diversion of judicial time and resources to address last-minute requests for consideration of allegedly new or previously overlooked issues, and to do so very expeditiously. In addition to the time needed for judicial consideration, about 160 hours of additional time is spent by our staff attorney in a variety of legal and administrative functions associated with each approaching execution.

The days and hours approaching an execution require additional preparation and action. Although the exhaustion of appellate recourse is usually followed by a petition for executive clemency, the justices and court staff nevertheless make special arrangements to assure their immediate availability, if necessary, to receive and address any last-minute filings. And special security precautions are provided by the state police to assure judicial safety.

In addition to the enhanced attention required for the resolution of individual capital cases, an overriding systemic concern of the judiciary is the consistent adequacy of legal representation appropriate for the defense of capital cases. While this responsibility may reside with differing branches of government from state to state, the state judiciary must do whatever it can to assist in achieving this goal. In Indiana, we have endeavored to meet this challenge by the promulgation of Indiana Criminal Rule 24, which prescribes special procedures applicable in capital cases, requires that two trial counsel be appointed to represent each indigent capital defendant, specifies minimum qualifications and compensation for lead counsel and co-counsel, and addresses workload limits of appointed counsel. We have also worked extensively with our state legislature regarding the effective allocation of public funds for indigent criminal defense.

FINANCIAL IMPACT

The financial impact of Indiana's capital sentencing regime specifically upon the trial and appellate judicial officers has not been quantified. The cost from the capital sentencing law upon other aspects of government, however, was one of the subjects recently addressed in a comprehensive report issued by the Indiana Criminal Law Study Commission, pursuant to the request of former Indiana Governor Frank O'Bannon and the Legislative Council of the Indiana General Assembly.[6]

Based upon an analysis of 84 cases in which the death penalty was requested by the prosecution, the Commission estimated that government costs for the imposition and execution of each "typical" death sentence is $667,560. This figure includes costs for law enforcement, prosecution, jury sequestration, defense counsel legal and investigative expenses for trial and appeal, incarceration until execution following exhaustion of appellate review approximately 10.5 years later, and execution.

In contrast, the Commission estimated that in a "typical" life-without-parole case in which (a) the death sentence was never sought, (b) life-without-parole was imposed as the maximum possible sentence, and (c) the offender dies of natural causes during imprisonment 47 years later, the total cost is $551,016.[7] The difference, $116,544, indicates that the cost of a "typical" capital case is 21 percent greater than the cost of a "typical" life-without-parole case and its resulting incarceration.[8]

EFFECT ON THE PUBLIC

Finally, the care with which state courts of last resort discharge their capital sentence responsibilities may have an enormous effect on the public's perception, trust, and confidence in the judiciary generally. It is often solely through media coverage of death penalty cases that many people form their impressions regarding the operation, efficiency, fairness, and reliability of the courts. It is thus especially important for judicial opinions and orders resolving claims in capital cases to fully explain the reasons for the decision, and to do so with the objective of helping not only the parties but also the media and the general public to understand and respect the process and the result, while also fully explaining the court's analysis in the likely event that the defendant seeks recourse in the federal courts. In addition to thoughtful attention to the language of judicial opinions and orders, it can be advantageous to assign court information officers to assist media representatives in understanding substantive and procedural complexities.

Public trust and confidence can also be undermined when inefficient judicial administration or unnecessary delay is revealed in media coverage of capital cases. State courts of last resort may thus find it important to monitor carefully the progress of capital cases through the judicial system, improving procedures where necessary to eliminate issues of conflicting post-conviction jurisdiction and to assure active and expeditious case management.

The challenge of public perception takes on a different dimension when gubernatorial clemency proceedings approach and attempts are made to influence popular sentiment. This may well include efforts to portray past judicial proceedings as unfair or incomplete. Such circumstances serve to emphasize the importance of drafting opinions in capital cases in a manner that communicates the reasons for the judicial decision fully and effectively to the public and to the media.

Capital punishment can also affect the justice system when it becomes an election issue affecting judicial retention or election. Public opinions on the general subject of capital punishment, and as to its appropriateness in individual cases, are often intense. When the prosecution seeks the death penalty, an acquittal or imposition of a sentence less than death can often precipitate vindictive anger from some segments of the public. Likewise, reversing a conviction or setting aside a death sentence on appeal may sometimes also be unpopular.

On the other hand, public demonstrations protesting capital punishment often precede or accompany executions. Not surprisingly, judicial opinions on death penalty cases have become controversial issues in some judicial retention and election contests,[9] even though basing judicial retention on such issues is wholly inconsistent with principles of judicial independence. Such issue advocacy can obscure public attention to important issues of judicial performance and qualification. The resulting demands upon the time and resources of judges and the judicial system can be enormously burdensome, the consequences unfair to judicial officers, and any resulting removal of an experienced jurist very harmful to the judiciary.

The decision to employ capital punishment as a criminal sentencing option is the prerogative of the state legislature. Officers of the judicial branch, having taken an oath to uphold the constitution and laws of the state and federal governments, are obligated to apply and enforce the laws as enacted. When the ultimate penalty is at stake, trial and appellate procedures must be particularly thorough and meticulous to maximize the ascertainment of truth, to provide procedural fairness, and to assure the reliability of the resulting judgment. While capital sentencing laws impose significant burdens upon state courts of last resort and the judicial systems they oversee, the high visibility of capital cases nevertheless provides an important opportunity for the judiciary to inform, educate, and enhance public trust and confidence in the judicial system by the responsible and attentive administration of the system, and by the thoughtful crafting of informative and understandable written opinions.

Endnotes

1. The Indiana statute presently provides that, upon a conviction for murder, a defendant may be sentenced to a term of years, life imprisonment without parole, or death. The death sentence must be separately sought by the prosecution by alleging and proving in separate penalty phase trial proceedings the existence of one or more specified aggravating factors established by statute. Ind. Code § 35-50-2-9 (2004).

2. During this period, the court issued 1,378 majority opinions, of which 99 involved capital cases on direct or collateral review.

3. The 14,000 word limit for an appellant's briefs generally prescribed in Indiana Appellate Rule 44(D) results in our appellants' briefs being limited to approximately 50 pages.

In capital cases, however, double this limitation is usually permitted, resulting in appellants' briefs of approximately 100 pages.

4. *See, e.g., Lambert v. State,* 675 N.E.2d 1060, 1065-66 (Ind. 1996), *cert. denied,* 520 U.S. 1255, 117 S. Ct. 2417, 138 L.Ed.2d 181 (1977), and opinion denying leave to file successive petition for post-conviction relief at 825 N.E.2d 1261, 1263-64 (Ind. 2005); *Bivens v. State,* 642 N.E.2d 928, 957 (Ind. 1994), *cert denied,* 516 U.S. 1077, 116 S.Ct. 783, 133 L.Ed.2d 734 (1996).

5. Indiana Post-Conviction Rule PC 1(12) (2006).

6. The Application of Indiana's Capital Sentencing Law: Findings of the Indiana Criminal Law Study Commission 122A-122F (2002) (available from the Indiana Criminal

Justice Institute, One North Capitol, Suite 1000, Indianapolis IN 46204-2038). This report is also available at http://www.in.gov/legislative/bills/2003/PDF/FISCAL/HB1358.001.pdf

7. M. Goodpaster, *Cost Comparison Between a Death Penalty Case and a Case Where the Charge and Conviction is Life Without Parole*, in THE APPLICATION OF INDIANA'S CAPITAL SENTENCING LAW, *supra n.* 6.

8. It should be noted, however, that this comparison does not consider the often substantial further expenses incurred when capital convictions are vacated in collateral proceedings, on appeal, or upon federal review, and remanded for retrial either as to guilt or penalty. This is not an infrequent occurrence. During the period from 1986 through 2005, for example, opinions of the Indiana Supreme Court remanded for such further trial proceedings for 35% (30 out of 86)

of the defendants challenging their death sentences. As to four of these defendants, the state subsequently withdrew its request for the death penalty. The financial impact reported by the study also does not reflect the costs related to federal habeas proceedings, the defense costs for which are not borne by Indiana government.

9. *See, e.g.,* Paul Brace and Melinda Gann Hall, *Comparing courts using the American states,* 83 JUDICATURE 250 (2000) (citing to Hall and Brace, *Toward an Integrated Model of Judicial Voting Behavior,* 20 AM. POL. Q. 147-68 (1992); Brace and Hall, *Integrated Models of Judicial Dissent in State Supreme Courts,* 55 J. POL. 914-35 (1993); Brace and Hall, *Studying Courts Comparatively: The View from the American States,* 48 POL. RES. Q. 5029 (1995); *Traciel V. Reid, The politicization of retention elections: Lessons from the defeat of justices Lanphier and White,* 83 JUDICATURE 68 (1999).

Discussion Questions

1. Discuss the financial impact of capital punishment. How does this compare to a sentence of life in prison?

2. Discuss capital punishment in terms of judicial time and effort. Do these cases seemingly negatively impact the time and resources devoted to other cases? Discuss.

3. Explain how capital punishment impacts the general public.

IV

Corrections

INTRODUCTION

Part IV addresses the correctional aspects of the criminal justice system. Particularly, the part addresses issues such as crime and justice, Paris Hilton's experience in jail, the relationship between crime and incarceration, the use of inmates in drug trials, life sentences, the effects of incarcerating large numbers of individuals, the challenges associated with having a prison record, , and the difficulties associated with reentry.

We use the term *corrections* to refer to the component of the criminal justice system charged with administering sanctions. The term could be a bit misleading, as correcting is not always the primary goal. The criminal justice system sometimes seeks to correct; however, recently it has focused its efforts on punishment, incapacitation, and deterrence. This emphasis is noted in many of the articles presented in Part IV.

Issues surrounding all aspects of corrections interest the public. Prison life is the most intriguing; the public seemingly cannot get enough information about what it's like in prison. The first article, "The Carrot and the Sticks," was written by an inmate who provides an insider's perspective on what's wrong with criminal justice system. As someone caught up in the system, the author identifies the limitations of modern correctional efforts and offers suggestions for improvement. This insider's account contributes to the growing research literature in the field of convict criminology, or input regarding crime and justice as offered by those who have served time.

Paris Hilton. We just can't get enough of her, can we? Her involvement in the criminal justice system, particularly, in jail, and her celebrity status dictate that public attention is directed her way. Hilton was jailed for driving with a suspended license. After three days of incarceration, the sheriff operating the jail released her to home confinement with electronic monitoring. The judge in the case overturned the sheriff's decision, and Paris was returned to jail. Among other effects, the sensationalism associated with the case drew public interest toward jails and jail life.

Does incarceration reduce crime rates? One cannot deny that incarcerated offenders are less likely to commit crime. They may commit crimes while in prison, but society isn't overly concerned about that. However, does incarceration directly reduce the crime rate and, if so, to what extent? The article "Incarceration and Crime" addresses the extent to which incarceration influences crime. It is difficult to isolate the impact of crime. Nevertheless, it is argued that an over-reliance on incarceration to reduce the crime rate may not be a great idea.

Imagine you're a prison inmate making $3 a day and are three years into a fifteen-year sentence. A prison official offers you an opportunity to become a subject in an experiment testing a drug designed to reduce high blood pressure. Potential side effects of the drug are heart disease and stroke. The pharmaceutical company has agreed to pay you $1,500 for your participation; however, you must sign a waiver excusing the company from any harms that you may incur. Do you do it? It is argued that inmates have so little, that participating in pharmaceutical drug experiments is somewhat akin to winning the lottery. However, is it ethical to take most everything away from people (inmates), yet permit them to have "something" only if they participate in a risky endeavor? This and related questions are addressed in the article "Panel Suggests Using Inmates in Drug Trials."

Which is more severe: capital punishment or life in prison without the possibility of parole? While many would suggest capital punishment, some would argue that life in prison without the possibility of parole is more punitive. As noted in the article "Serving Life, with No Chance of Redemption," some offenders request capital punishment in lieu of life in prison. Why? Among other reasons, those on death row receive particular attention (especially, legal attention) that is not provided to those serving life sentences.

Many of us take the right to vote for granted. We may not vote in every election, and we likely wouldn't be too upset if authorities took away our voting privileges. Or would we? Restricting convicted felons from voting has substantial consequences, including having potentially shaped a recent presidential election. As noted in the article "Barred from Voting," the practice of preventing current and former inmates from voting could shape the direction of a country. Should felons be permitted to vote? There are strong arguments in support of and opposition to felons being permitted to vote. The article addresses the implications of preventing felons from exercising their right to vote.

The selection "Felon Fallout" highlights the current state of imprisonment. We've seen substantial increases in the incarceration rate beginning in the 1980s and continuing into the twenty-first century. Some attribute the decrease in crime rate during much of the same period to increased incarceration. Absent from such arguments, however, is discussion of the intangibles associated with incarcerating a large number of individuals. Prominent among the by-products of incarceration are the lack of rehabilitation opportunities, the spread of communicable diseases, the increased likelihood of violence, and extensive financial costs of building new prisons. As a society, we have to determine whether the benefits of increased incarceration are worth the costs.

Part IV concludes with a look at prisoner reentry. Many in society expect that those who have served their sentence are prepared to return to society. Though returning may seem to pose no problems, inmates have a poor record of readjusting to life outside of prison. Inmates leaving prison must adjust to managing life on their own and will likely have their behavior supervised in the community, which adds pressure to an already challenging period of readjustment. Some individuals will make a seamless transition from prison to society; others will need assistance. The article "Returning Home" highlights the need for additional research that focuses on reentry with the goal of ensuring that leaving prison isn't as difficult as entering prison.

The articles in Part IV highlight some of the more prominent issues in corrections. The term *corrections* encompasses many different sanctions and practices, including boot camps, electronic monitoring, incarceration, halfway houses, probation, and parole. Furthermore, critical issues are associated with each of these sanctions.

Corrections comprise the final stages of criminal case processing. Parting ways with correctional agencies signifies the end, although sometimes only temporarily, to one's involvement with the criminal justice system. For many offenders, however, the stigma and effects of having been sentenced and incarcerated stay with them—whether applying for a job or trying to get a date, one's status as a former offender stays with them for some time even though they've served their penalty. As a society, we tend to believe that wrongful behavior in the past is predictive of future wrongful behavior. Perhaps this belief is accurate. Perhaps it isn't. Such is the controversial nature of corrections.

25

The Carrot and the Sticks

By Jens Soering

EDITOR'S COMMENT

At the most basic level, criminologists study why people commit crime and the responses to those individuals and events. One critique of the field of criminology is that analyses are often conducted from offices as opposed to the streets or prisons. As a social science, criminology, it is argued, requires hands-on experience to best understand criminal behavior and responses to it. Therein lies the challenge. Working with criminals is not always easy, nor is it always legal. For instance, asking an individual if you could tag along while they rob a convenience store isn't a very good idea. Unless, of course, you wish to complement your close-up examination of criminal behavior with a close-up view of our correctional systems.

There are ways, however, to better understand criminal behavior without putting oneself at risk. Criminologists have been very creative in identifying ways to study crime without interfering with illegal behavior and/or putting themselves at great risk. For instance, riding along with motorcycle gangs and documenting, while not necessarily engaging in, their practices provides great insight regarding the behavior of such groups. Furthermore, observational studies of gang activity have largely contributed to our understanding of gang structure and behavior. Recently the field of convict criminology has provided a refreshing view of how crime and criminal justice works from an inmate's perspective. Jens Soering's work contributes to the growing research literature involving the input of individuals who have been directly exposed to the more unattractive side of the criminal justice system.

Soering highlights some of the problems contributing to the lack of effectiveness of current criminal justice practices. He cites the skewed wealth distribution in the United States as a contributing factor in high incarceration rates, and the lack of correctional system effectiveness as reasons to believe that life won't get much better for some inmates once they're released. He generally sees the good in people, arguing that social factors contribute to one's place in life. The data he uses in his analyses don't consist of survey results analyzed with advanced statistical manipulations. Instead, he bases his argument from his personal experience in prison.

Some may argue that Soering and others who have documented their experience in the criminal justice system provide a skewed version of the criminal justice system—as insiders they've been tainted through their experience. How could one remain objective regarding the criminal justice system when one is being punished? While such a concern is noteworthy, it doesn't reduce the fact that an insider's perspective contributes to our understanding of how things work. Those familiar with Jack Henry Abbott's, insightful work In the Belly of the Beast, should be aware of the significance of insights provided by those within the system.

Part of the excitement of studying crime is the creativity involved. There is no single accepted way to research crime. Criminologists are not forced to constantly look through a microscope, but use various methods to study crime and responses to it. Arguments are made regarding the merit and value of various approaches, for instance, as researchers orientated toward quantitative research methods may critique the work of qualitative researchers, and vice versa. In the end, all reliable and sound research helps us better understand human behavior, particularly as it relates to crime and justice.

PREVENTING CRIME—WHAT WORKS: WHAT DOESN'T, WHAT THE FUTURE HOLDS

Overseas, the war in Iraq has exposed the limits of American military might at an enormous and still-growing cost to taxpayers. At home, meanwhile, this nation's three-decades-long preference for hiding away social problems behind penitentiary walls has produced the ironic result that the "land of the free" now cages a greater percentage of its own citizenry than any other country in the world. From just under 100 prisoners per 100,000 population in the 1970's, the incarceration rate in the United States grew to the current world record of 715 per 100,000—compared with just 143 per 100,000 for England, 116 for Canada, 80 for France and 50 for Finland. Yet locking up so many Americans has not given this nation a crime rate appreciably lower than those of other industrialized countries. In fact, the domestic crime rate today is exactly the same as it was 30 years ago. The "big stick" of prison has proved ineffective.

Since neither the comparatively lavish welfare systems of European nations nor the enormous prison systems of the United States have had any noticeable effect on crime rates, perhaps the time has come for this country to accept a certain level of lawlessness as the standard, international price of living in an economically developed society. This is a difficult concept to accept. But the war on crime is no more likely to end with perfect peace and flower-strewn streets than the war in Iraq.

What really needs to be addressed both in the Middle East and in America's streets and courtrooms is effective problem management: minimizing the harm done to the innocent, lowering the intensity of the conflict, containing the threat and luring the next generation into compliance with authority. This last task is face-to-face, long-term work, but it can be effective if pursued patiently. I know this because for the last 18 years I have lived among those on whom such methods were never tried: my fellow prison inmates. As a long-term convict and student of criminal justice policies, I offer an insider's perspective on what definitely did not work and what might have worked if it had been tried.

INEFFECTIVE MEASURES

Threats and preaching definitely do not prevent crime, as anyone with even the slightest familiarity with teenagers, in or out of prison, knows. Participants in the first Scared Straight program, for instance, were actually more likely to end up behind bars than a control group of nonparticipants. The U.S. Department of Justice admits that having policemen lecture teens about drugs in Project DARE has been completely ineffective.

The cells around mine are filled with graduates of boot-camps and Scared Straight-type programs. In conversations with me, they express pride over having survived these trials-by-fire and emerged even tougher than before. "The man" pushed them to the limit; afterward, it was their turn to get some payback on civilians like you.

So why do such programs continue to enjoy popular support? Perhaps because they satisfy an atavistic need to see delinquent youngsters get their comeuppance at the hands of people who are stronger than they are—namely, convicts and cops. Unfortunately, at-risk youths do not enjoy being bullied any more than anyone else does, and they respond to being menaced by becoming more menacing themselves.

IMPROVING CHILDREN'S LIVES

What does work in crime prevention is the improvement of the lives of poor children while they are growing up.

In 1984, the RAND Corporation, an institution not generally thought of as politically progressive, conducted an in-depth study of the operation of the Chicago Area Project (CAP) over the previous fifty years. CAP organizes slum residents into community committees that work personally with local youths in trouble, improve the physical appearance of neighborhoods and provide recreational facilities for youngsters. According to the study, these efforts proved to be "effective in reducing rates of juvenile delinquency."

Likewise, in the Perry Preschool Program, 123 "borderline educable" mentally handicapped children from an extremely low-income black neighborhood in Ypsilanti, Mich., were enrolled in preschool two years early and visited by their teachers at home once a week for two years. Twenty-seven years later, participants were found to be only one-fifth as likely as a control group of nonparticipants to become habitual criminals, and only one-fourth as likely to be arrested for a drug-related crime. Similar results were found in Syracuse University's Family Development Research Program, another long-term pilot study that emphasized helping parents raise their children while they were still very young.

These initiatives succeed in preventing crime because they attack the root causes of crime: poverty, absent fathers and abuse.

POVERTY

When I walk out of my cell into my housing unit's dayroom, I do not see a great many people like myself, a former middle-class white kid now approaching middle age. I see instead, almost without exception, poor blacks, poor whites and poor Hispanics. Now perhaps it is just a coincidence that all these people happened to be living in slums and trailer parks when they used their free will to choose to break the law. Or perhaps there really is a link between poverty and criminal behavior.

This idea is anathema in most of America, of course. If low incomes and social deprivation really do lead to increased rates of lawlessness, then crime might be reduced by redistributing some wealth. But among social scientists, the connection between poverty and criminal behavior has been accepted for a long time: a meta-analysis that appeared in the American Sociological Review in 1981 of 224 previous studies stated that its research had "concluded rather convincingly that members of lower social classes were indeed more prone to commit crime." This finding was confirmed by later researchers as well.

A study in 1996/97 of payments made by Aid to Families with Dependent Children in 140 metropolitan areas, which controlled for all sorts of variables and took into account regional differences, found that the higher the welfare payments were, the more the burglary and homicide rates fell. And whereas Europe and the United States have a common crime rate when murder is not factored in, we find that countries spending 12 percent to 14 percent of their Gross Domestic Product on welfare have lower rates of violent crime than the United States, which spends only 4 percent of its G.D.P. on welfare.

Experiences in jail further confirm this phenomenon. What keeps convicts in line behind bars in the Virginia penitentiaries is not more prison guards or tougher rules. It is the judicious apportionment of menial jobs that pay 23 cents to 45 cents an hour. Inmates, who have no other source of income, can easily be seduced into compliance by this method, no matter how tough they pretend to be.

If that sounds terribly cynical, consider: people pay their taxes and obey the speed limit not because they actually enjoy giving their money to the I.R.S. or driving their BMW far below its capabilities, but because they have more to lose if they behave otherwise. When poor people respond to financial incentives by reducing their levels of illegal activity, they are simply obeying the same proven rules of micro-economics in capitalist societies.

The official poverty level for a family of three is $14,480 per year, or $13.22 per person per day for everything: rent, utilities, clothes, food, transportation, medical expenses, education—everything. According to the U.S. Census Bureau, 3.8 million families are so poor that some members have had to skip meals for lack of funds, and another 11 million families reported being afraid they would run out of food. Why is it considered morally offensive and economically unwise in this country to give a poor person a few dollars more than $13.22 per day, but ethically appropriate and fiscally sensible to incarcerate a poor person at an average cost of $55.18 per day?

FATHERLESS FAMILIES

Both juvenile delinquency and poverty have been consistently associated with fatherless homes since the early 19th century. But it is important to note that it is the absence of the father that is the underlying cause of the other two phenomena. Children raised by their mother alone are six times more likely to be poor than similarly situated children raised by both parents. And with only one adult to supervise and act as role model, children (overwhelmingly sons) raised without fathers make up 60 percent of rapists, 72 percent of adolescent murderers and 70 percent of all long-term inmates. For the 36 percent of all American children who grow up in single-parent families, the future looks grim.

Fathers cannot simply be forced to act responsibly toward their offspring, of course, so the question becomes: what can be done to help poor single mothers raise their children so they are less likely to turn to crime later? One answer appears to be something as simple as home visiting by public health care workers, as in a pilot program called the Prenatal/Early Infancy Project, conducted in Elmira, N.Y., or by teachers, as in the Perry Preschool Program discussed above. According to another RAND Corporation study, parent training and early intervention can reduce crime four to five times as effectively as California's three-strikes law.

In the penitentiary, practically everyone my age or younger grew up in a single-parent home on the seediest side of town. A young man I met in an inmate meditation group is typical. He came to prison at age 15 (because he was tried as an adult); and now, at age 23, he is about to finish his sentence and return "home." But his mother, who is only 38 herself, is dying from the effects of a lifetime of drug abuse. So he has no home to return to, no family or community connections of any kind. A few weeks from now, he will step through the prison gate into a world he last saw as a child and where he knows no one.

What continually surprises me is how many young men like this one tell me that they want to leave their lives of crime behind. In fact, one federal study found that over half of all youths who join gangs tried to quit, and 79 percent said they would leave if given "a second chance in life." As far as I can tell, many of my fellow prisoners never had their first chance, never mind their second.

Growing up poor and fatherless unfortunately carries an additional danger that can heighten still further a child's chances of later becoming a criminal: physical or sexual abuse. Among underclass families, reported cases of maltreatment are three times as frequent as among higher income groups, and such children are then twice as likely to be involved in serious or violent delinquency. Later, as adults, victims of abuse are 38 percent more likely to be arrested for violent crime. Among prison inmates, 16.1 percent of males and 57.2 percent of females report having been physically or sexually maltreated while growing up—rates far higher than in the general population.

Among convicts, discussing such things directly is absolutely taboo, of course. But if the dayroom television set is tuned to the local news when the arrest of some particularly odious juvenile offender is reported, one can sometimes hear prisoners discuss how the youngster in question would have behaved differently if only he had been "whooped" the way they were "whooped" by their parents. The idea that the leather-belt beatings they suffered as children may have contributed to their own later acts of violence does not seem to occur to these inmates.

THE FUTURE

According to the U.S. Census Bureau, 17.2 percent of all children—12.2 million boys and girls—now live below the poverty level. There are over one million substantiated cases of child abuse each year. And out of 32 states evaluated under the Child and Family Services Review for their "ability to protect children from child abuse," 28 states failed either all seven criteria or six out of seven.

What does the future hold for these children? It would seem that America is readying a fresh batch of prospective convicts to feed to its jails and penitentiaries. As we have seen above, at least some of those literally millions of lives could be saved.

Prison and welfare are responses to poverty. Unfortunately, in the United States over the last 30 years, the carrot of welfare has been almost totally eliminated in favor of more and larger sticks. "A growing prison system was what we had instead of an anti-poverty policy, instead of an employment policy, instead of a comprehensive drug-treatment or mental health policy," says the criminologist Elliott Currie.

In Europe, by contrast, social policies have been designed around "the internationally recognized principle of using custodial sentences only when strictly necessary," according to the Danish Prison and Probation Service. Their emphasis on welfare over prisons has had the side effect that only 4 percent of Danish and Norwegian children, and just 6 percent of French and German children, grow up in homes where earnings are less than half the country's median income.

The question, then, is this: Do you want your tax dollars to be invested early on in the cycle, when they can still improve a child's life, or at the end of the cycle, when all that is left to do is to lock the cell door after the horse of hope has bolted?

Discussion Questions

1. What does the author suggest would be a successful strategy for crime prevention?
2. How do poverty and fatherless families impact crime and justice?
3. Do you believe inmates have an unbiased perception of crime and justice? Can their input contribute to our understanding of criminal justice? If so, how? If not, why?

26

Paris Starts, Ends Week Behind Bars

By John Rogers

EDITOR'S COMMENT

Paris Hilton has a knack for attracting public attention. She has made a career of it. Whether it's starring in exotic videos, participating in reality television, or frequenting a courthouse, and more recently, jail, Hilton generates substantial public interest. Some suggest that we're intrigued by her behavior because her life is so different from the average citizen's. Being different, however, can be both a curse and a blessing. For instance, our courts have a track record of "celebrity justice" in which the rich and famous (who are different from many others who enter the criminal justice system) receive preferential treatment. More recently, however, we've seen celebrity status translate to what some consider unfavorable treatment in our courts.

In 2004 business magnate, author, editor, and homemaking advocate Martha Stewart was convicted on four counts of lying to investigators and obstruction of justice. She received a five-month prison term followed by a five-month sentence of home confinement with electronic monitoring. Stewart had insider information regarding one of her stocks, which she sold the day prior to the stock dropping 16 percent, preventing a $45,673 loss. Many thought that Stewart and her powerful attorneys would prevail in court. Few expected her to serve time in prison, particularly given her status and the court's historically lenient treatment of white-collar crime offenders. Furthermore, the case didn't involve a violent crime. Stewart, however, had bad timing. She was tried during a period of alleged intense crackdown on white-collar crime. Similar to Paris Hilton, Martha Stewart's celebrity status seemingly had little or perhaps a detrimental effect on her treatment in court. Some argued Stewart was used to exemplify society's disgust for white-collar crime.

Paris Hilton also received a more severe penalty than many anticipated. She pleaded guilty to a reckless driving charge and later was charged with driving with a suspended license. Like Stewart, Hilton did not commit a violent crime, yet she received a relatively stern sentence. It appears that Judge Michael T. Sauer, who presided over Hilton's case, seemed unappreciative of her different (celebrity) status. The judge seemed to demonstrate a zero-tolerance approach to Hilton's disregard for the law. Hilton's sentence was viewed by many as notably punitive and out of line with the expected penalties.

Of particular interest in this case is the lack of coordination between Sheriff Lee Baca, who ran the jail in which Hilton was housed, and Judge Sauer. For instance, Baca released Hilton to home confinement with electronic monitoring after three days of incarceration in jail citing a serious medical condition as the cause. However, he did not confer with Judge Sauer, who requested Hilton's return to court and subsequently her return to jail.

Many thought that Judge Sauer's initial penalty and his order for Hilton to return to court seemed unfair. With a national spotlight on his courtroom, Judge Sauer appeared not the least bit concerned that his sentence and recommitment order seemed out of line. Perhaps he was trying to make amends for the historically unfair, lenient treatment of celebrities in the courtroom by making an example of Hilton. Or, perhaps he just did not appreciate her differences. Either way, this case at the very least demonstrates that wealth and celebrity status are not always more powerful than the criminal justice system. At least not in Judge Sauer's courtroom.

L OS ANGELES (AP)—It will be a week that Paris Hilton—and a celebrity-obsessed nation— won't soon forget. What started as a graceful attempt by the 26-year-old socialite to accept her punishment for violating probation in a reckless driving case ended Friday when a disheveled and tearful Hilton was ordered back to jail to serve out the remainder of her 45-day sentence.

After Superior Court Judge Michael T. Sauer was apparently unmoved by the pleas of Hilton's three lawyers to keep their client under house arrest, the hotel heiress was led from the courtroom crying out for her mother and shouting, "It's not right!"

As Hilton sits in the downtown Twin Towers jail where she will undergo a medical and psychiatric examination, one question lingered: Was celebrity justice served?

There was no shortage of twists and turns throughout the week after Hilton made a surprise visit Sunday to the MTV Movie Awards, where she told a throng of media that she was scared but ready to face her sentence.

Hours after the event, Hilton checked herself into jail and was expected to serve only 23 days because of a state law that requires shorter sentences for good behavior.

The ensuing drama erupted Thursday when sheriff's officials released Hilton because of a medical condition and sent her home under house arrest. She had been in jail for three days.

Friday's hearing was requested by the city attorney's office, which had prosecuted Hilton and wanted Sheriff Lee Baca held in contempt for deciding to reassign Hilton to home detention despite Sauer's express order that she must serve her time in jail.

Sauer gave no explanation of his ruling to return Hilton back to jail, but his comments throughout the hearing indicated he was affronted by Baca's decision to set aside his instructions and release the celebutante to her Hollywood Hills home.

"I at no time condoned the actions of the sheriff and at no time told him I approved the actions," he said. "At no time did I approve the defendant being released from custody to her home on Kings Road."

Hilton's lawyers said the reason for her release was an unspecified medical condition. The judge suggested that could be taken care of at jail medical facilities.

Following the hearing, Baca said he decided to put Hilton under house arrest because he was concerned about a serious medical condition he could not disclose, though his further comments suggested psychological problems.

He said he had learned from one of her doctors that she was not taking a certain medication while she was in custody previously and her "inexplicable deterioration" puzzled county psychiatrists.

Baca charged that Hilton received a more severe sentence than normal, which he said would have been either no time in jail or being directly placed in home confinement with electronic monitoring.

"The only thing I can detect as special treatment is the amount of her sentence," the sheriff said.

Hilton will likely be held at the Twin Towers facility for at least a couple of days before determining what jail she will be held in, sheriff's spokesman Steve Whitmore said.

Despite being reincarcerated, she could still be released early. Inmates are given a day off their terms for every four days of good behavior, and her days in home detention counted as custody days. It appeared that Friday would count as her sixth day. Baca indicated she would serve about 18 more days.

Hilton's path to jail began Sept. 7, when she failed a sobriety test after police saw her weaving down a street in her Mercedes-Benz on what she said was a late-night run to a hamburger stand.

She pleaded no contest to reckless driving and was sentenced to 36 months' probation, alcohol education and $1,500 in fines.

In the months that followed, she was stopped twice by officers who discovered her driving on a suspended license. The second stop landed her in Sauer's courtroom, where he sentenced her to jail.

Discussion Questions

1. Do you believe Paris Hilton was the target of unfair judicial behavior? If so, how? If not, why?
2. How could the situation regarding Paris Hilton's release from jail have been better handled?

3. Do you believe celebrities receive preferential treatment from criminal justice professionals? Discuss.

27

Incarceration and Crime: A Complex Relationship

By Ryan S. King, Marc Mauer, and Malcolm C. Young

EDITOR'S COMMENT

We are currently in a dynamic period in the history of criminal justice. Incarceration rates have been steadily increasing since the 1980s while the crime rate has been consistently decreasing since the early 1990s. Based on these trends, the relationship between crime and incarceration appears pretty straightforward. Thus, it would seem that higher incarceration rates result in lower crime rates. This article, by Ryan King, Marc Mauer, and Malcolm Young of The Sentencing Project, argues otherwise. The authors cite a series of factors other than increased incarceration rates that impact the crime rate.

The incarceration rate, the economy, changes in drug markets, alterations in police practices, and community changes in response to crime are among the many factors influencing the crime rate. One cannot deny that increased incarceration rates reduce the crime rate. However, there is debate regarding exactly how great the effect is. The authors comment on several statistics that demonstrate incarceration reduces crime, though not to the extent touted by proponents of increased incarceration.

High crime rates in the 1980s were attributable to many factors. Prominent among those factors are the instability of the drug markets and the widespread introduction of crack cocaine. Many people may assume that the mind-altering effects of crack cocaine contributed to much of the drug crime. However, much of the crime associated with crack during this time pertained to the violent confrontations associated with establishing drug markets at the local level, and the crime committed by those seeking money to purchase the drug. The markets to sell crack in the inner cities were better established by the early- to mid-1990s, resulting in less crime.

A change in police styles that began in the 1980s and largely took hold in the 1990s also contributed to the decrease in crime. Community-oriented policing, a philosophy of policing in which departments are more in touch with the community, use community resources to fight crime, and assume an overall more strategic approach to policing, largely changed the manner in which police operate. Instead of being "the enemy," the police reached out to the public for support in fighting and preventing crime. The public largely responded and a seemingly more effective approach to policing evolved.

Community responses to crime also contributed to the crime rate decline. In the 1980s, many youths who witnessed the negative impacts of drug addiction and experienced the effects of the war on drugs firsthand decided to live a life free of drugs and crime and thus were deterred from engaging in drug use.

Does increased incarceration reduce the crime rate? The answer, though incomplete, is "yes." Simply responding "yes" doesn't mention how much incarceration reduces crime—a very important bit of information in light of the immense resources required to incarcerate individuals. The authors provide data regarding the extent to which incarceration impacts the crime rate. In light of these data, an in-depth cost-benefit analysis is necessary to provide greater insight regarding the effectiveness of incarceration. Perhaps some of the resources we devote to prisons and jails may be better used to address the other factors that influence the crime rate. However, it is unlikely that in the near future we will see many prison and jail resources redirected.

Over the past thirty years the United States has experienced an unprecedented rise in the use of incarceration, with the number of people in prisons and jails increasing from 330,000 in 1972 to 2.1 million today. This trend is in sharp contrast to that of the preceding fifty years, during which time there was a gradual increase in the use of incarceration that was commensurate with growth in the general population. Between 1920 and 1970 the overall population nearly doubled, while the number of people in prison increased at just a slightly higher pace. However, between 1970 and 2000, while the general population rose by less than 40%, the number of people in prison and jail rose by more than 500%. Potential explanations for this dramatic change in policy have included changing crime rates, politics, demographics, and cultural shifts.[1]

The record decline in crime during the 1990s has added an additional element to the discussion. Advocates of increased use of incarceration have contended that the significant growth in incarceration has been the primary factor responsible for this reduction. The two-pronged approach of tougher sentences and restrictive release patterns are the primary cause, proponents claim, of this sustained crime drop. Nowhere has the adoption of tougher sentencing rules and release policies been more evident than in the federal system, where mandatory minimums, sentencing guidelines, and the abolition of parole have combined to create an extremely punitive system. The Department of Justice, in supporting this approach, has stated that "tough sentencing means less crime," and that "[t]he Sentencing Guidelines have helped reduce crime by ensuring that criminal sentences take violent offenders off the streets, impose just punishment and deter others from committing crimes."[2] Despite these assertions by the Department of Justice, such a direct link is far from an accepted fact. As policymakers consider responses, including the adoption of a host of additional mandatory minimums, to the Supreme Court's 2005 remedial ruling making the federal guidelines advisory in *U.S. v. Booker*, it is important to assess what is actually known about the impact of imprisonment on crime control.

ANALYZING THE RELATIONSHIP BETWEEN INCARCERATION AND CRIME

The relationship between incarceration and crime is complex. Researchers have struggled to quantify accurately the degree to which crime reduction is attributable to imprisonment. Among the many challenges associated with the issue are the following: distinguishing between state and national trends; differing measures of crime and victimization; and, assessing various time frames for analysis. In addition to incarceration, studies have identified a range of factors which may affect crime, including general economic trends, employment rates, age, demographics, rates of drug abuse, and geographic variation. This briefing paper provides an aid to policymakers and the public by reviewing what is known about the effects of incarceration on crime.

"Incarceration and Crime: A Complex Relationship" by Ryan S. King, Marc Mauer, and Malcolm C. Young, *The Sentencing Project*, 2005. Reprinted with permission.

DIFFERING METHODS OF MEASURING CRIME RATES AND VICTIMIZATION

There are two primary measures of crime used in the United States. The Uniform Crime Reports (UCR) produced annually by the FBI measure crimes reported to the police. The UCR Index Crime measure is a composite of eight serious violent and property offenses, and is commonly referred to as the "crime rate" in the media. Victimization studies conducted by the Department of Justice measure crime through surveys of households, asking occupants about crimes committed against them and whether or not they reported them to the police (less than half of all serious crimes are reported to the police). Each means of measurement has its advantages. The victimization studies provide a broader view of total crime because they account for the many crimes not reported to the police, while the UCR provides a better sense of trends in the most serious crimes. Trends in the two measurements have been inconsistent in some time periods, but they match up about 60 to 75% of the time, depending on the type of crime measured.[3] However, most popular discussion of crime rates relies primarily on UCR data because of its focus on serious crime.

Neither of these crime measures incorporate any assessment of drug offenses, since personal drug use or drug sales, apart from those resulting in arrests, are not reported to the police or as victimizations. The proportion of arrests, convictions, and persons incarcerated for drug offenses has increased dramatically in the past two decades.[4] Accordingly, this absence of data greatly obscures the overall number of people engaged in illegal activity and skews the national perception of actual trends in criminal activity.

APPARENT TRENDS DEPEND UPON TIMEFRAME EXAMINED

While there has been a great deal of discussion and speculation regarding the crime decline since the early 1990s, a focus on this period risks employing an overly narrow view of the relationship between incarceration and crime. To be more completely analyzed, this relationship should incorporate an assessment of the unprecedented increase in imprisonment since 1972. From a combined inmate population of about 330,000 in prison and jail in 1972, there has since been a five-fold increase to a total of 2.1 million as of 2004.

This escalating growth over a 30-year period has been accompanied by sharply divergent trends in crime rates. We can see this clearly in looking at the 14-year time frame of 1984–1998. During this period, incarceration rates rose consistently, by 65% in the first seven-year period of 1984–91, and then by 47% from 1991–98. Yet crime rates fluctuated in this period, first increasing by 17% from 1984–91, then declining by 22% from 1991–98.

There were also divergent trends in crime rates among the states during the crime decline period of 1991–1998. A number of states with large increases in incarceration experienced smaller drops in crime than did states that increased their use of imprisonment at a lower rate. For example, Texas, with a 144% increase in incarceration and California, with a 52% increase, experienced considerable declines in crime (35% and 36% respectively), but New York experienced a 43% decline in crime despite an increase in incarceration of only 24%. An overview of changes in incarceration and crime in all 50 states reveals no consistent relationship between the rate at which incarceration increased and the rate at which crime decreased.

These inconsistent trends over time and among the states do not necessarily suggest that incarceration has no impact on crime, but they inform us that incarceration does not always have a uniformly positive impact on reducing crime and that, therefore, other factors significantly affect crime trends.

While the nation celebrates a reported crime rate that is near a 40-year low, it is instructive to note that despite the addition of more than one million persons to the prison population (excluding jail inmates), crime rates are only at the level at which they were at a time when the number of prisoners was just a fraction of the total today.[5]

THE CRIME DECLINE OF THE PAST DECADE

Nationally, violent crime has declined by 33% and property crime has decreased 23% since 1994. During the same period incarceration rates rose by 24%. Some commentators draw upon these two trends to support the conclusion that incarceration "works" to reduce crime. The reality is far more complex.

References to national data alone obscure the significance of the experience in the states as they utilize different strategies and achieve different results. A recent study that analyzed state prison and crime data revealed that there was no discernible pattern of states with higher rates of increase in incarceration experiencing more significant declines in crime.[6] Between 1991 and 1998, those states that increased incarceration at rates that were *less* than the national average experienced a *larger* decline in crime rates than those states that increased incarceration at rates higher than the national average.

Trends between 1998 and 2003 at the state level continue to demonstrate no significant impact of increased incarceration rates on reducing crime. Since 1998, 12 states experienced stable or declining incarceration rates, yet the 12% average decrease in crime rates in these states was the same as in the 38 states in which rates of imprisonment increased. If incarceration was having the impact on crime that proponents suggest, then those states with higher increases in incarceration rates should have experienced more substantial declines in crime rates.

Economist Steven Levitt has identified the growth in the use of incarceration as one of four primary factors leading to the decline in crime during the 1990s.[7] In a 1996 article looking at the impact of prison on crime rates, Levitt argued that each incarcerated person results in the prevention of approximately 15 crimes.[8] However, Levitt's model predicts that the majority of crime that is prevented by incarceration is comprised of "less socially costly property crimes."[9] Does this approach necessarily represent the most efficient allocation of resources? Levitt seems to think not, stating that "the social benefit of radically expanding the prison population through the incarceration of increasingly minor criminals is likely to be well below the estimates presented here."[10] Levitt's analysis suggests that about 80% of the crime prevented by the incarceration of each additional prisoner is for nonviolent offenses. In a recent article, he notes that "it seems quite plausible that substantial indirect costs are associated with the current scale of imprisonment," including the impact on the African American community, and that "further increases in imprisonment may be less attractive than the naive cost benefit would suggest."[11] This most recent caveat acknowledges the limited role of incarceration as a strategy to address crime, and recognizes the complexity of trying to base policy decisions solely on financial costs.

More recent analysis of the contributing factors to the crime decline of the 1990s suggests that about 25% of the decline in violent crime can be attributed to increased incarceration.[12] While one-quarter of the crime drop is not insubstantial, we then know that most of the decline in crime—three-quarters—was due to factors other than incarceration. Several factors stand out as key in this regard:

GROWING ECONOMY   The relatively strong economy of the 1990s produced jobs and opportunity, particularly for lower-wage workers. One study estimates that this factor was responsible for 30% of the decline in crime.[13]

CHANGES IN DRUG MARKETS   The crack cocaine epidemic of the late 1980s, combined with the availability of guns in many communities, was a significant contributor to rates of violence for several years.[14] By the early 1990s, crack use began to wane, along with much of the associated violence of the drug market, and homicide rates for young African-American males in particular dropped significantly.[15] These developments were similar to previous drug epidemics, which are typically of short duration.[16]

STRATEGIC POLICING   Law enforcement agencies in many cities adopted various forms of community policing in the 1990s. In at least some cities, these approaches are believed to have contributed to significant declines in crime. In San Diego, for example, a comprehensive model of community policing contributed to a greater than 40% decline in crime rates from 1990–1996.[17] This was the second largest drop in the country, and it occurred not through the hiring of additional officers, but by making better use of current staffing and instituting a problem-solving strategy. In Boston, a police–community partnership targeting the distribution of firearms contributed to a dramatic decline in youth homicides as well.

COMMUNITY RESPONSES TO CRIME   Witnessing the devastation wrought by drug markets and the "war on drugs" in a number of communities had a profound effect on young people in the 1990s. Seeing the impact of drug addiction on family and friends led a significant number of young people to choose to refrain from engaging in drug use or distribution in communities that had been plagued by narcotics. A study of a Brooklyn neighborhood noted that "the multiple threats of violence, crime, AIDS, and addiction" compelled many young people to "[withdraw] from the danger and [opt] for the relative safety of family, home, church and other sheltering institutions . . ."[18]

LIMITS OF INCARCERATION'S IMPACT ON CRIMINAL BEHAVIOR

For many people, the relationship between incarceration and crime rates seems intuitive. "If you lock people up, they can't commit more crime." However, the dynamics of both crime and imprisonment challenge this seemingly commonsense notion. Among the reasons for incarceration's limited impact on crime rates are:

DIMINISHING RETURNS   Expanding the use of imprisonment inevitably results in diminishing returns in crime control. This is because high-rate and serious or violent offenders will generally be incarcerated even at modest levels of imprisonment, but as prison systems expand, new admissions will increasingly draw in lower-rate offenders. This growth in lower-rate and lower-level offenders shifts the cost-to-benefit ratio, as an equal amount of resources are spent per offender, but the state receives less return on its investment in terms of declining crime rates. We have seen this trend most acutely in the federal system, where the pursuit of drug offenders has resulted in a growing proportion of low level offenders. More than half (56%) of federal drug offenders sentenced in 2002 were in the lowest criminal history category (Category I), and nearly 9 out of 10 (87%) had no weapon involvement.

LIMITED DRUG OFFENDER EFFECTS   Drug offenders have represented the most substantial source of growth in incarceration in recent decades, rising from 40,000 persons in prison and jail in 1980 to 450,000 today. Compared to other offenses, the effect of sentencing and incarceration on drug offenses is quite limited since drug selling is subject to a "replacement effect." For example, if an armed robber is convicted and sentenced to prison, the effect of incapacitation removes that person's crime potential during the period of imprisonment. But street-level drug sellers are often replaced quickly by other sellers seeking to make profits from the drug market. As criminologist Alfred Blumstein has noted, ". . . drug markets are inherently demand driven. As long as the demand is there, a supply network will emerge to satisfy that demand. While efforts to assault the supply-side may have some disruptive effects in the short term, the ultimate need is to reduce the demand in order to have an effect on drug abuse in the society."[19]

There are a number of ways to measure the prevalence of drug use, including national household survey data. Despite the fact that the number of persons in prison or jail today for drug offenses is more than ten times the number in 1980, drug use rates remain substantial, with data indicating a general increase over the past few years. Thus, during a period when the number of persons in prison for drug law violations was growing at a rate faster than other offense types, the underlying behavior appears to have experienced very little impact.

LIMITS OF FEDERAL INCARCERATION   The effect of incarceration on crime is even more limited in the federal prison system because of the offense characteristics of the federal prison population. As previously noted, the overall drop in crime was comprised primarily of declines in violent and property offenses. However, only 13% of federal prisoners have been convicted of a violent offense, while 55% are incarcerated for a drug offense (an increase from 25% in 1980). In addition, federal drug offenders are increasingly low-level. Two-thirds (66.5%) of crack cocaine offenders sentenced in 2000 were either street-level dealers or couriers/mules, as were more than half (59.9%) of powder cocaine offenders. In both cases, these proportions represent a substantial increase from the proportion of low-level offenders in 1995 (48.4% for crack cocaine and 38.1% for powder cocaine).[20]

NEGATIVE IMPACTS ON FAMILY AND COMMUNITY   The rapid growth of incarceration has had profoundly disruptive effects that radiate into other spheres of society. The persistent removal of persons from the community to prison and their eventual return has a destabilizing effect that has been demonstrated to fray family and community bonds, and contribute to an increase in recidivism and future criminality.[21] Moreover, these trends are exacerbated as prisoners are increasingly incarcerated in facilities hundreds of miles from their homes. Research by the Urban Institute in a number of cities indicates that a critical predictor of success for persons returning to the community is family connections, and prospects for employment are strengthened for persons who are able to maintain some degree of attachment to their former networks of contacts.[22] However, as the use of incarceration continues to grow, there is a resultant decline in these contacts, and a harmful impact on the individual, the family, and the community at large.[23]

IMPACT OF INCARCERATION COMPARED TO OTHER INTERVENTIONS

Estimates that about one-quarter of the drop in crime during the 1990s can be attributed to incarceration do not inform us about whether reliance upon incarceration was the *most effective way* to achieve these results. A variety of research demonstrates that investments in drug treatment, interventions with at-risk families, and school completion programs are more cost-effective than expanded incarceration as crime control measures. Regarding drug use, a RAND analysis concluded that the expenditure of $1 million to expand mandatory minimum sentencing would result in a national decrease in drug consumption of 13 kilograms, while dedicating those funds to drug treatment would reduce consumption by 100 kilograms.[24] In another analysis, researchers concluded that shifting the federal drug budget to reduce funds earmarked for supply reduction by 25% and doubling treatment funding would decrease cocaine consumption by 20 metric tons and save over $5 billion.[25] In addition, every $1 invested in drug treatment returns more than $7 in savings to society, as opposed to a net loss of nearly 70 cents for enforcement approaches.[26]

In terms of prevention, an analysis of a wide range of national programs aimed at school completion and addressing the needs of at-risk youth found similar returns on taxpayer investments, in terms of increased productivity and decreased crime, as the RAND researchers discovered with drug treatment.[27] The combined approach of prevention for juveniles and treatment for adults continues to exhibit significant cost savings and remains a viable alternative to incarceration for many individuals.

CONCLUSION: IMPLICATIONS FOR A RESPONSIBLE PUBLIC DEBATE

During the last 30 years of incarceration growth, we have learned a great deal about the financial and social costs and limited effectiveness of incarceration on crime rates. While incarceration is one factor affecting crime rates, its impact is more modest than many proponents suggest, and is increasingly subject to diminishing returns. Increasing incarceration while ignoring more effective approaches will impose a heavy burden upon courts, corrections and communities, while providing a marginal impact on crime. Policymakers should assess these dynamics and adopt balanced crime control policies that provide appropriate resources and support for programming, treatment, and community support.

Endnotes

1. For a discussion of the possible explanations for this shift in incarceration policy, see Garland, D. (2001). *The Culture of Control: Crime and Social Order in Contemporary Society.* Chicago: University of Chicago Press.

2. Prepared Remarks of Assistant Attorney General Christopher A. Wray, Response to *Booker/Fanfan,* January 12, 2005.

3. Rand, M. R. and Rennison, C. M. (2002). "True Crime Stories? Accounting for Differences in our National Crime Indicators," *Chance,* Vol. 15 (1), p. 47–51.

4. Bureau of Justice Statistics, *Drug & Crime Facts,* <http://www.ojp.usdoj.gov/bjs/dcf/contents.htm>. Accessed August 29, 2005.

5. Historical rates from Tonry, M. (1995). *Malign Neglect: Race, Crime, and Punishment in America.* New York: Oxford University Press. Pp. 22–23; current rates from Federal Bureau of Investigation. *Crime in the United States, 2003.* Washington, DC.

6. Gainsborough, J. & Mauer, M. (2000). *Diminishing Returns: Crime and Incarceration in the 1990s.* Washington, DC: The Sentencing Project. (p. 10).

7. Levitt, S. D. (2004). "Understanding Why Crime Fell in the 1990s: Four Factors that Explain the Decline and Six That Do Not," *Journal of Economic Perspectives,* Vol. 18 (1), 163–190.

8. Levitt, S. D. (1996). "The Effect of Prison Population Size on Crime Rates: Evidence from Prison Overcrowding Litigation," *The Quarterly Journal of Economics,* Vol. 111 (2), 319–351. (p. 345).

9. Ibid.

10. Ibid, p. 347.

11. Levitt, 2004, p. 179.

12. Spelman, W. (2000). "The Limited Importance of Prison Expansion," In Blumstein, A. and Wallman, J. (Eds.), *The Crime Drop in America.* Cambridge, UK: Cambridge University Press. (pp. 97–129).

13. Freeman, R. and Rodgers, III, W. (1999). *Area Economic Conditions and the Labor Market Outcomes of Young Men in the 1990's Expansion.* Cambridge, MA: National Bureau of Economic Research.

14. Levitt, 2004, pp. 179–181.

15. Ibid.

16. Musto, D. F. (1999). *The American Disease: Origins of Narcotic Control.* New York: Oxford University Press.

17. Eck, J. E. & Maguire, E. R. (2000). "Have Changes in Policing Reduced Violent Crime?: An Assessment of the Evidence," in Blumstein, A. and Wallman, J. (eds.). *The Crime Drop in America.* Cambridge: Cambridge University Press. (pp. 207–265).

18. Curtis, R. (1998). "The Improbable Transformation of Inner-City Neighborhoods: Crime, Violence, Drugs, and Youth in the 1990s," *The Journal of Criminal Law and Criminology,* Vol. 88, (4), p. 1263.

19. Blumstein, A. (1993). "Making Rationality Relevant—The American Society of Criminology 1992 Presidential Address," *Criminology,* Vol. 31, (1), p. 1–16.

20. United States Sentencing Commission. *Report to Congress: Cocaine and Federal Sentencing Policy.* Washington, DC. May 2002.

21. Clear, T., Rose, D. R., Waring, E., and Scully, K. (2003). "Coercive Mobility and Crime: A Preliminary Examination of Concentrated Incarceration and Social Disorganization," *Justice Quarterly,* Vol. 20, (1), pp. 33–64.

22. See publications by the Justice Policy Center of the Urban Institute for coverage of the reentry issue. Available online at www.urban.org

23. For a discussion of the impact of incarceration on the family and the community, see Braman, D. (2004). *Doing Time on the Outside: Incarceration and Family Life in Urban America.* Ann Arbor, MI: University of Michigan Press.

24. Caulkins, J. P., Rydell, C. P., Scwabe, W. L., Chiesa, J. (1997). *Mandatory Minimum Drug Sentences: Throwing Away The Key or The Taxpayers' Money?* Santa Monica, CA: RAND. (pp. xvii–xviii).

25. Rydell, C. P. & Everingham, S.S. (1994). *Controlling Cocaine: Supply Versus Demand Programs.* Santa Monica, CA: RAND.

26. Ibid.

27. Aos, S., Phipps, P., Barnoski, R., & Lieb, R. (2001). *The Comparative Costs and Benefits of Programs to Reduce Crime.* Olympia, WA: Washington State Institute for Public Policy.

Discussion Questions

1. What three factors have notably impacted the declining crime rate since the 1990s?

2. Discuss the impact increased incarceration rates have had on the recent decline in the crime rate.

3. Discuss the reasons why incarceration has a limited impact on crime rates.

28

Panel Suggests Using Inmates in Drug Trials

By Ian Urbina

EDITOR'S COMMENT

Imagine this scenario. You're an inmate in prison. You're approached by a pharmaceutical company that is conducting experiments for a new drug that lowers cholesterol. The company agrees to pay you a thousand dollars for your participation. Do you participate? What if the company tells you that a potential side effect of the drug is the loss of feeling in your left hand? Do you still do it? Now imagine a similar scenario in which you have no choice but to participate and you're paid nothing for doing so. Both scenarios have been played out in U.S. prisons over the years. While the unethical practice of forcing inmates to participate in experimental research has been illegal for some years, providing such opportunities is a topic of discussion in several correctional facilities, and is also the topic of this article.

Prisoners have very little freedom per the sentences they receive. Granted, inmates are entitled to basic human rights; however, what constitutes basic human rights has been debated. It wasn't until the 1960s that inmates began receiving due recognition for their claims of rights violations. Inmates' rights have been long neglected in correctional practices, and many in society wouldn't be upset if we continued to violate inmate rights. This is not to suggest that doing so is correct. Today, inmates arguably retain more rights while incarcerated than at any other period in history. Specifically, the general public often feels that inmates have too many rights, and the punishments inherent in prison are disappearing with increased recognition of inmate rights.

Negligence regarding inmates' rights was evident in earlier correctional practices when inmates were involuntarily used as subjects of research studies involving experimental drugs and psychological therapy and counseling. Needless to say, there were more than a few cases in which inmates suffered irreparable damages.

Recent debate concerns whether inmates should be granted the opportunity to participate voluntarily in experimental studies. Currently, pharmaceutical companies are having difficulty locating enough subjects to participate in research studies. The growing correctional population and the medical problems often found in the correctional population make inmates an attractive target for testing particular drugs. However, the historical mistreatment of mandating that inmates participate in research has some skeptical of current proposals to provide inmates the opportunity to participate. Given the low level of literacy amongst inmates, there's also concern that inmates may be unaware of what exactly constitutes free and informed consent. Furthermore, there's an ethical concern that inmates, who have no alternative to earn more than extremely low wages while incarcerated, may be forced to take dangerous risks in experimental research in exchange for more substantial financial compensation.

Ethical concerns are not new to the criminal justice system. For instance, police officers are often accused of acting unethically when using what appears to be too much force when arresting a subject. Judges are accused of unethical practices when they permit or deny at trial the introduction of question-able evidence. Correctional officials are accused of acting unethically when they deny inmates their basic human rights. The notable concern for ethics in the criminal justice system largely stems from the constant need for criminal justice professionals to balance crime control with due process rights.

PHILADELPHIA, Aug. 7—An influential federal panel of medical advisers has recommended that the government loosen regulations that severely limit the testing of pharmaceuticals on prison inmates, a practice that was all but stopped three decades ago after revelations of abuse.

The proposed change includes provisions intended to prevent problems that plagued earlier programs. Nevertheless, it has dredged up a painful history of medical mistreatment and incited de-bate among prison rights advocates and researchers about whether prisoners can truly make unco-erced decisions, given the environment they live in.

Supporters of such programs cite the possibility of benefit to prison populations, and the po-tential for contributing to the greater good.

Until the early 1970's, about 90 percent of all pharmaceutical products were tested on prison inmates, federal officials say. But such research diminished sharply in 1974 after revelations of abuse at prisons like Holmesburg here, where inmates were paid hundreds of dollars a month to test items as varied as dandruff treatments and dioxin, and where they were exposed to radioactive, hallucino-genic and carcinogenic chemicals.

In addition to addressing the abuses at Holmesburg, the regulations were a reaction to revela-tions in 1972 surrounding what the government called the Tuskegee Study of Untreated Syphilis in the Negro Male, which was begun in the 1930's and lasted 40 years. In it, several hundred mostly il-literate men with syphilis in rural Alabama were left untreated, even after a cure was discovered, so that researchers could study the disease.

"What happened at Holmesburg was just as gruesome as Tuskegee, but at Holmesburg it hap-pened smack dab in the middle of a major city, not in some backwoods in Alabama," said Allen M. Hornblum, an urban studies professor at Temple University and the author of "Acres of Skin," a 1998 book about the Holmesburg research. "It just goes to show how prisons are truly distinct institutions where the walls don't just serve to keep inmates in, they also serve to keep public eyes out."

Critics also doubt the merits of pharmaceutical testing on prisoners who often lack basic health care.

Alvin Bronstein, a Washington lawyer who helped found the National Prison Project, an American Civil Liberties Union program, said he did not believe that altering the regulations risked a return to the days of Holmesburg.

"With the help of external review boards that would include a prisoner advocate," Mr. Bronstein said, "I do believe that the potential benefits of biomedical research outweigh the po-tential risks."

Holmesburg closed in 1995 but was partly reopened in July to help ease overcrowding at other prisons.

Under current regulations, passed in 1978, prisoners can participate in federally financed bio-medical research if the experiment poses no more than "minimal" risks to the subjects. But a report formally presented to federal officials on Aug. 1 by the Institute of Medicine of the National Academy of Sciences advised that experiments with greater risks be permitted if they had the poten-tial to benefit prisoners. As an added precaution, the report suggested that all studies be subject to an independent review.

"The current regulations are entirely outdated and restrictive, and prisoners are being arbitrarily excluded from research that can help them," said Ernest D. Prentice, a University of Nebraska genetics professor and the chairman of a Health and Human Services Department committee that requested the study. Mr. Prentice said the regulation revision process would begin at the committee's next meeting, on Nov. 2.

The discussion comes as the biomedical industry is facing a shortage of testing subjects. In the last two years, several pain medications, including Vioxx and Bextra, have been pulled off the market because early testing did not include large enough numbers of patients to catch dangerous problems.

And the committee's report comes against the backdrop of a prison population that has more than quadrupled, to about 2.3 million, over the last 30 years and that disproportionately suffers from H.I.V. and hepatitis C, diseases that some researchers say could be better controlled if new research were permitted in prisons.

For Leodus Jones, a former prisoner, the report has opened old wounds. "This moves us back in a very bad direction," said Mr. Jones, who participated in the experiments at Holmesburg in 1966 and after his release played a pivotal role in lobbying to get the regulations passed.

In one experiment, Mr. Jones's skin changed color, and he developed rashes on his back and legs where he said lotions had been tested.

"The doctors told me at the time that something was seriously wrong," said Mr. Jones, who added that he had never signed a consent form. He reached a $40,000 settlement in 1986 with the City of Philadelphia after he sued.

"I never had these rashes before," he said, "but I've had them ever since."

The Institute of Medicine report was initiated in 2004 when the Health and Human Services Department asked the institute to look into the issue. The report said prisoners should be allowed to take part in federally financed clinical trials so long as the trials were in the later and less dangerous phase of Food and Drug Administration approval. It also recommended that at least half the subjects in such trials be nonprisoners, making it more difficult to test products that might scare off volunteers.

Dr. A. Bernard Ackerman, a New York dermatologist who worked at Holmesburg during the 1960's trials as a second-year resident from the University of Pennsylvania, said he remained skeptical. "I saw it firsthand," Dr. Ackerman said. "What started as scientific research became pure business, and no amount of regulations can prevent that from happening again."

Others cite similar concerns over the financial stake in such research.

"It strikes me as pretty ridiculous to start talking about prisoners getting access to cutting-edge research and medications when they can't even get penicillin and high-blood-pressure pills," said Paul Wright, editor of *Prison Legal News*, an independent monthly review. "I have to imagine there are larger financial motivations here."

The demand for human test subjects has grown so much that the so-called contract research industry has emerged in the past decade to recruit volunteers for pharmaceutical trials. The Tufts Center for the Study of Drug Development, a Boston policy and economic research group at Tufts University, estimated that contract research revenue grew to $7 billion in 2005, up from $1 billion in 1995.

But researchers at the Institute of Medicine said their sole focus was to see if prisoners could benefit by changing the regulations.

The pharmaceutical industry says it was not involved. Jeff Trewitt, a spokesman for the Pharmaceutical Research and Manufacturers of America, a drug industry trade group, said that his organization had no role in prompting the study and that it had not had a chance to review the findings.

Dr. Albert M. Kligman, who directed the experiments at Holmesburg and is now an emeritus professor of dermatology at the University of Pennsylvania Medical School, said the regulations should never have been written in the first place.

"My view is that shutting the prison experiments down was a big mistake," Dr. Kligman said.

While confirming that he used radioactive materials, hallucinogenic drugs and carcinogenic materials on prisoners, Dr. Kligman said that they were always administered in extremely low doses and that the benefits to the public were overwhelming.

He cited breakthroughs like Retin A, a popular anti-acne drug, and ingredients for most of the creams used to treat poison ivy. "I'm on the medical ethics committee at Penn," he said, "and I still don't see there having been anything wrong with what we were doing."

From 1951 to 1974, several federal agencies and more than 30 companies used Holmesburg for experiments, mostly under the auspices of the University of Pennsylvania, which had built laboratories at the prison. After the revelations about Holmesburg, it soon became clear that other universities and prisons in other states were involved in similar abuses.

In October 2000, nearly 300 former inmates sued the University of Pennsylvania, Dr. Kligman, Dow Chemical and Johnson & Johnson for injuries they said occurred during the experiments at Holmesburg, but the suit was dismissed because the statute of limitations had expired.

"When they put the chemicals on me, my hands swelled up like eight-ounce boxing gloves, and they've never gone back to normal," said Edward Anthony, 62, a former inmate who took part in Holmesburg experiments in 1964. "We're still pushing the lawsuit because the medical bills are still coming in for a lot of us."

Daniel S. Murphy, a professor of criminal justice at Appalachian State University in Boone, N.C., who was imprisoned for five years in the 1990's for growing marijuana, said that loosening the regulations would be a mistake.

"Free and informed consent becomes pretty questionable when prisoners don't hold the keys to their own cells," Professor Murphy said, "and in many cases they can't read, yet they are signing a document that it practically takes a law degree to understand."

During the Holmesburg experiments, inmates could earn up to $1,500 a month by participating. The only other jobs were at the commissary or in the shoe and shirt factory, where wages were usually about 15 cents to 25 cents a day, Professor Hornblum of Temple said.

On the issue of compensation for inmates, the report raised concern about "undue inducements to participate in research in order to gain access to medical care or other benefits they would not normally have." It called for "adequate protections" to avoid "attempts to coerce or manipulate participation."

The report also expressed worry about the absence of regulation over experiments that do not receive federal money. Lawrence O. Gostin, the chairman of the panel that conducted the study and a professor of law and public health at Georgetown University, said he hoped to change that.

Even with current regulations, oversight of such research has been difficult. In 2000, several universities were reprimanded for using federal money and conducting several hundred projects on prisoners without fully reporting the projects to the appropriate authorities.

Professor Gostin said the report called for tightening some existing regulations by advising that all research involving prisoners be subject to uniform federal oversight, even if no federal funds are involved. The report also said protections should extend not just to prisoners behind bars but also to those on parole or on probation.

Professor Murphy, who testified to the panel as the report was being written, praised those proposed precautions before adding, "They're also the parts of the report that faced the strongest resistance from federal officials, and I fear they're most likely the parts that will end up getting cut as these recommendations become new regulations."

Discussion Questions

1. What are the ethical and professional concerns associated with using inmates in drug trials?
2. Should inmates be permitted to serve as drug test subjects for pharmaceutical companies? Why or why not?
3. Why do drug companies target inmates for participation in drug trials?

29

Serving Life, with No Chance of Redemption

By Adam Liptak

EDITOR'S COMMENT

Which is more severe: 45 days in jail or two years probation? Six months house arrest or 15 days in jail? Capital punishment or life in prison without the possibility of parole? A primary challenge facing sentencing bodies is to determine what sentence is appropriate for each crime. The ultimate goal of any sentence is to ensure justice; however, understanding whether a select sanction serves the purpose of justice in relation to the crime is not always easy. Sentencing bodies generally have an idea of what sanctions are more severe than others, although what may seem tough for one offender may be less punitive for others. This article highlights the difficulties associated with a life sentence without the possibility of parole. To some offenders, death is preferable to being imprisoned for the remainder of their life.

Why have some offenders requested death sentences in lieu of the seemingly more lenient sentence of life in prison without the possibility of parole? To begin, inmates serving life sentences are "less important" to prisoner advocacy groups and attorneys than those sentenced to death, so they receive little attention and support. Appellate courts more closely scrutinize capital cases than the more routine life sentences, and those on death row are granted attorneys at no cost to work on their cases in federal court long after their convictions have been affirmed. It may truly be in the best interests of innocent individuals convicted of murder and sentenced to life in prison to request capital punishment because their case will draw greater attention.

Consider the mental anguish associated with a life sentence without the possibility of parole. You realize that you're never going to leave once you enter the prison. You will die inside that building. Those receiving a 25-year sentence will someday get out. You? You're here for life. While there are certainly psychological and other difficulties associated with life sentences, many in society are not sympathetic. Why? Perhaps the best answer is that such sentences are reserved for those convicted of the more heinous offenses.

For some, the psychological challenges associated with a life sentence are the most troublesome aspect of the punishment. Others fit right in behind prison walls, thus a life sentence poses few problems; the structure and resources provided by prison life are preferable to life outside of prison. To these inmates, prison is life and anything else (i.e., life on the outside) provides a struggle.

Sentencing bodies use life sentences as a sanction for the most serious crimes; life sentences serve the primary purposes of incapacitation, retribution, and deterrence. While appropriate in certain circumstances, life sentences entail long-term concerns for prisons, such as increased health care costs associated with imprisonment as inmates age. Security issues are also a concern. It is argued that releasing elderly inmates serving life sentences who no longer pose a threat to society would save precious criminal justice resources, and give lifers hope that they too may someday be released. In turn, lifers may behave better in prison.

LIVINGSTON, Tex.—Minutes after the United States Supreme Court threw out the juvenile death penalty in March, word reached death row here, setting off a pandemonium of banging, yelling and whoops of joy among many of the 28 men whose lives were spared by the decision.

But the news devastated Randy Arroyo, who had faced execution for helping kidnap and kill an Air Force officer while stealing his car for parts.

Mr. Arroyo realized he had just become a lifer, and that was the last thing he wanted. Lifers, he said, exist in a world without hope. "I wish I still had that death sentence," he said. "I believe my chances have gone down the drain. No one will ever look at my case."

Mr. Arroyo has a point. People on death row are provided with free lawyers to pursue their cases in federal court long after their convictions have been affirmed; lifers are not. The pro bono lawyers who work so aggressively to exonerate or spare the lives of death row inmates are not interested in the cases of people merely serving life terms. And appeals courts scrutinize death penalty cases much more closely than others.

Mr. Arroyo will become eligible for parole in 2037, when he is 57. But he doubts he will ever get out.

"This is hopeless," he said.

Scores of lifers, in interviews at 10 prisons in six states, echoed Mr. Arroyo's despondency. They have, they said, nothing to look forward to and no way to redeem themselves.

More than one in four lifers will never even see a parole board. The boards that the remaining lifers encounter have often been refashioned to include representatives of crime victims and elected officials not receptive to pleas for lenience.

And the nation's governors, concerned about the possibility of repeated offenses by paroled criminals and the public outcry that often follows, have all but stopped commuting life sentences.

In at least 22 states, lifers have virtually no way out. Fourteen states reported that they released fewer than 10 in 2001, the latest year for which national data is available, and the other eight states said fewer than two dozen each.

The number of lifers thus continues to swell in prisons across the nation, even as the number of new life sentences has dropped in recent years along with the crime rate.

According to a *New York Times* survey, the number of lifers has almost doubled in the last decade, to 132,000. Historical data on juvenile offenders is incomplete. But among the 18 states that can provide data from 1993, the juvenile lifer population rose 74 percent in the next decade.

Prosecutors and representatives of crime victims applaud the trend. The prisoners, they say, are paying the minimum fit punishment for their terrible crimes.

But even supporters of the death penalty wonder about this state of affairs.

"Life without parole is a very strange sentence when you think about it," said Robert Blecker, a professor at New York Law School. "The punishment seems either too much or too little. If a sadistic or extraordinarily cold, callous killer deserves to die, then why not kill him? But if we are going to keep the killer alive when we could otherwise execute him, why strip him of all hope?"

Burl Cain, the warden of the Louisiana State Penitentiary in Angola, which houses thousands of lifers, said older prisoners who have served many years should be able to make their cases to a parole or pardon board that has an open mind. Because all life sentences in Louisiana are without the possibility of parole, only a governor's pardon can bring about a release.

The prospect of a meaningful hearing would, Mr. Cain said, provide lifers with a taste of hope.

"Prison should be a place for predators and not dying old men," Mr. Cain said. "Some people should die in prison, but everyone should get a hearing."

TELEVISION AND BOREDOM

In interviews, lifers said they tried to resign themselves to spending down their days entirely behind bars. But the prison programs that once kept them busy in an effort at training and rehabilitation have largely been dismantled, replaced by television and boredom.

The lot of the lifer may be said to be cruel or pampered, depending on one's perspective. "It's a bleak imprisonment," said W. Scott Thornsley, a former corrections official in Pennsylvania. "When you take away someone's hope, you take away a lot."

It was not always that way, said Steven Benjamin, a 56-year-old Michigan lifer.

"The whole perception of incarceration changed in the 1970's," said Mr. Benjamin, who is serving a sentence of life without parole for participating in a robbery in 1973 in which an accomplice killed a man. "They're dismantling all meaningful programs. We just write people off without a second thought."

As the years pass and the lifers grow old, they sometimes tend to dying prisoners and then die themselves. Some are buried in cemeteries on prison grounds by other lifers, who will then go on to repeat the cycle.

"They're never going to leave here," said Mr. Cain, the warden at Angola, of inmates he looks after. "They're going to die here."

Some defendants view the prospect of life in prison as so bleak and the possibility of exoneration for lifers as so remote that they are willing to roll the dice with death.

In Alabama, six men convicted of capital crimes have asked their juries for death rather than life sentences, said Bryan Stevenson, director of the Equal Justice Initiative of Alabama.

The idea seems to have its roots in the experience of Walter McMillian, who was convicted of capital murder by an Alabama jury in 1988. The jury recommended that he be sentenced to life without parole, but Judge Robert E. Lee Key Jr. overrode that recommendation and sentenced Mr. McMillian to death by electrocution.

Because of that death sentence, lawyers opposed to capital punishment took up Mr. McMillian's case. Through their efforts, Mr. McMillian was exonerated five years later after prosecutors conceded that they had relied on perjured testimony. "Had there not been that decision to override," said Mr. Stevenson, one of Mr. McMillian's lawyers, "he would be in prison today."

Other Alabama defendants have learned a lesson from Mr. McMillian.

"We have a lot of death penalty cases where, perversely, the client at the penalty phase asks to be sentenced to death," Mr. Stevenson said.

Judges and other legal experts say that risky decision could be a wise one for defendants who are innocent or who were convicted under flawed procedures. "Capital cases get an automatic royal treatment, whereas noncapital cases are fairly routine," said Alex Kozinski, a federal appeals court judge in California.

David R. Dow, one of Mr. Arroyo's lawyers and the director of the Texas Innocence Network, said groups like his did not have the resources to represent lifers.

"If we got Arroyo's case as a non-death-penalty case," Mr. Dow said, "we would have terminated it in the very early stages of investigation."

Mr. Arroyo, who is 25 but still has something of the pimply, squirmy adolescent about him, said he already detected a certain quiet descending on his case.

"You don't hear too many religious groups or foreign governments or nonprofit organizations fighting for lifers," he said.

Gov. Rick Perry of Texas signed a bill in June adding life without parole as an option for juries to consider in capital cases. Opponents of the death penalty have embraced and promoted this alternative, pointing to studies that show that support for the death penalty dropped drastically among jurors and the public when life without parole, or LWOP, was an alternative.

"Life without parole has been absolutely crucial to whatever progress has been made against the death penalty," said James Liebman, a law professor at Columbia. "The drop in death sentences"—from 320 in 1996 to 125 last year—"would not have happened without LWOP."

But some questioned the strategy.

"I have a problem with death penalty abolitionists," said Paul Wright, the editor of *Prison Legal News* and a former lifer, released in Washington State in 2003 after serving 17 years for killing a man in a robbery attempt. "They're positing life without parole as an option, but it's a death sentence by incarceration. You're trading a slow form of death for a faster one."

Mr. Arroyo shares that view.

"I'd roll the dice with death and stay on death row," he said. "Really, death has never been my fear. What do people believe? That being alive in prison is a good life? This is slavery."

MURDER FOLLOWS A KIDNAPPING

Mr. Arroyo was convicted in 1998 for his role in the killing of Jose Cobo, 39, an Air Force captain and the chief of maintenance training at the Inter-American Air Forces Academy in Lackland, Tex. Mr. Arroyo, then 17, and an accomplice, Vincent Gutierrez, 18, wanted to steal Captain Cobo's red Mazda RX-7 for parts.

Captain Cobo tried to escape but became tangled in his seat belt. Mr. Gutierrez shot him twice in the back and shoved the dying man onto the shoulder of Interstate 410 during rush hour on a rainy Tuesday morning.

Although Mr. Arroyo did not pull the trigger, he was convicted of felony murder, or participation in a serious crime that led to a killing. He contends that he had no reason to think Mr. Gutierrez would kill Captain Cobo and therefore cannot be guilty of felony murder. "I don't mind taking responsibility for my actions, for my part in this crime," he said. "But don't act like I'm a murderer or violent or that this was premeditated."

That argument misunderstands the felony murder law, legal experts said. Mr. Arroyo's decision to participate in the carjacking is, they say, more than enough to support his murder conviction.

Captain Cobo left behind a 17-year-old daughter, Reena.

"I miss him so much it hurts when I think about it," she said of her father in a victim impact statement presented at trial. "I know he is in heaven with my grandmother and God is taking care of him. I want to see the murderers punished not necessarily by death. I feel sorry that they wasted theirs and my father's life."

Ms. Cobo declined to be interviewed.

Mr. Arroyo said he was not eager to leave death row, and not just because of dwindling interest in his case.

"All I know is death row," he said. "This is my life. This is where I grew up."

His lawyer sees reasons for him to be concerned about moving off death row.

"He's going to become someone's plaything in the general population," Mr. Dow said. "He's a small guy, and the first time someone tries to kill him they'll probably succeed."

That kind of violence is not the way most lifers die. At Angola, for instance, two prisoners were killed by fellow inmates in the five years ended in 2004. One committed suicide, and two were executed. The other 150 or so died in the usual ways.

The prison operates a hospice to tend to dying prisoners, and it has opened a second cemetery, Point Lookout Two, to accommodate the dead.

On a warm afternoon earlier this year, men in wheelchairs moved slowly around the main open area of the prison hospice. Others lounged in bed.

The private rooms, for terminal patients, are as pleasant as most hospital rooms, though the doors are sturdier. The inmates have televisions, video games, coffeepots and DVD players. One patient watched "Lara Croft: Tomb Raider."

Robert Downs, a 69-year old career bank robber serving a 198-year term as a habitual felon, died in one of those rooms the day before. In his final days, other inmates tended to him, in four-hour shifts, around the clock. They held his hand and eased his passage. "Our responsibility," said Randolph Matthieu, 53, a hospice volunteer, "is so that he doesn't die there by himself. We wash him and clean him if he messes himself. It's a real humbling experience."

Mr. Matthieu is serving a life sentence for killing a man he met at the C'est La Guerre Lounge in Lafayette, La., in 1983.

At Point Lookout Two the next day, there were six mounds of fresh dirt and one deep hole, ready to receive Mr. Downs. Under the piles of dirt were other inmates who had recently died. They were awaiting simple white crosses like the 120 or so nearby. The crosses bear two pieces of information. One is the dead man's name, of course. Instead of the end points of his life, though, his six-digit prison number is stamped below.

The sun was hot, and the gravediggers paused for a rest after their toil.

"I'm hoping I don't come this way," said Charles Vassel, 66, who is serving a life sentence for killing a clerk while robbing a liquor store in Monroe, La., in 1972. "I want to be buried around my family."

The families of prisoners who die at Angola have 30 hours to claim their bodies, and about half do. The rest are buried at Point Lookout Two.

"It's pretty much the only way you leave," said Timothy Bray, 45, also in for life. Mr. Bray, who helped beat a man to death for falling behind in his debts, tends to the horses that pull the hearse on funeral days, placing white and red rosettes in their manes.

WARY OF A TRANSFORMED WORLD

Not all older lifers are eager to leave prison. Many have grown used to the free food and medical care. They have no skills, they say, and they worry about living in a world that has been radically transformed by technology in the decades that they have been locked up.

Wardens like Mr. Cain say that lifers are docile, mature and helpful.

"Many of the lifers are not habitual felons," he added. "They committed a murder that was a crime of passion. That inmate is not necessarily hard to manage."

What is needed, he said, is hope, and that is in short supply. "I tell them, 'You never know when you might win the lottery,' " Mr. Cain said. "You never know when you might get a pardon. You never know when they might change the law.' "

Up the road from Point Lookout Two, near the main entrance, is the building that houses the state's death row. Lawyers for the 89 men there are hard at work, trying to overturn their clients' convictions or at least convert their death sentences into life terms. According to the Death Penalty Information Center, eight Louisiana death row inmates have been exonerated in the last three decades. More than 50, prison officials said, have had their sentences commuted to life.

But those hard-won life sentences, when they come, do not always please the prisoners.

"I have to put a lot of these guys on suicide watch when they get off death row," said Cathy Fontenot, an assistant warden, "because their chances have gone down to this."

She put her thumb and forefinger together, making a zero.

Discussion Questions

1. Why would some offenders choose to receive a sentence of capital punishment in lieu of life in prison without the possibility of parole?
2. Aside from never being permitted to leave prison, what are some of the difficulties associated with a sentence of life in prison?
3. Discuss why we should or should not impose life sentences without the possibility of parole.

30

Barred from Voting

By Katharine Mieszkowski

EDITOR'S COMMENT

You've spent the past six years in prison following an armed robbery you committed at age 18. You were messed up in drugs at the time and running with a bad crowd. While in prison, you've earned a GED, obtained some job skills, and kicked the drug habit. Perhaps most important of all, you've matured and realized the dangers of associating with troublemakers.

As you're leaving prison, a representative from the department of corrections hands you your belongings and a check for $160. You're now expected to make it on your own. Fortunately, you have family members who are willing to house you and help you get back on your feet. But what about the thousands of other inmates who aren't so fortunate? How are they going to make it? Not your problem, you say to yourself; you have your hands full worrying about how you'll make it.

Leaving prison provides significant challenges for all former inmates. Prominent among the challenges faced by the formerly incarcerated are the stigma attached to being an "ex-con" and the adjustments required in living what is often a less-structured lifestyle. Adjusting to life outside prison is difficult for some individuals, and for too many former prisoners, the challenges of living a crime-free life are too much. They return to prison where they feel most comfortable. Others, however, are able to make it outside prison.

Former inmates often complain about the treatment they receive from "non-offenders." Finding a job may be difficult, personal relations may be challenging, and, as noted in this article, former inmates are restricted from voting. Former inmates argue that they've served their penalty and should be fully reintegrated into society. As a society, however, we hold grudges, as evidenced in the restrictions on released inmates' voting rights.

Restricting or eliminating one's voting privileges may not seem all that significant, given that about 64 percent of U.S. citizens ages 18 or older voted in the 2004 presidential election. However, it has been projected that Al Gore would have won the 2000 election instead of George W. Bush if the large number of former prisoners had been permitted to vote.

Let's assume you own an air conditioning company and hire technicians. The most qualified candidate was just released from prison after serving five years for drug trafficking. Do you hire him? Why or why not? Some employers would hire him; after all, he's well qualified for the job and has paid his dues to society. He's cordial and claims to work well with others. He admits that his behavior was wrong, but he's past all that behavior. Others would be reluctant to hire the former inmate. The company's reputation is on the line, and you're not sure he's through with drugs. He may have paid his dues, but the incarceration speaks of his character. Your customers wouldn't be comfortable with an ex-con in their home.

Preventing former inmates from voting in a country that prides itself on democracy sends a message that we've not accepted former inmates back into society even though they've served their sentence. Accordingly, some inmates question whether they will ever once again be accepted back into society.

Oct. 19, 2006—When Koren Carbuccia went to prison for the second time, her son, Vaskan, was just 3 months old. Being incarcerated during the earliest years of his life changed hers. She wanted nothing more than to be home with him.

Carbuccia had gone to prison for dealing cocaine. She was just 20 years old the first time she was caught. She was working the night shift at a clothing factory while going to school during the day, studying to become an emergency medical technician. Carbuccia wasn't a user, she says; dealing just meant easy money.

But not for long. After being released from jail, Carbuccia, who lives in Pawtucket, R.I., just outside of Providence, was arrested again for possessing drugs. "Wrong company, wrong friends," she says with a sigh. This time, she'd been on leave from her restaurant job as a waitress.

Carbuccia won an early release in February 2005. Today, at 27, she is a student at Community College of Rhode Island, studying substance abuse counseling, and working toward a master's degree. While going to school and caring for her son, she also works 20 hours a week doing data entry at the Family Life Center in Providence, which provides assistance for ex-offenders and their families. Recently, she took Vaskan, now almost 5, to his first day of preschool. "I want to do the right thing," says Carbuccia, who describes herself as a PTA mom. "I want to be responsible and raise my child."

But there's one way Carbuccia isn't like other moms, and as the law in Rhode Island now stands, won't be until 2017. Only then, when she's completed both parole and probation, will she be allowed to vote. Until she's 38 years old, she'll be a second-class citizen, working, parenting, studying, paying taxes, but unable to cast a ballot. In a state of just 1 million, she's one of more than 15,000 disenfranchised voters because of prior felonies.

Across the U.S., nearly 4 million people with felony convictions, who are out of prison, have no say in their own government, and won't be going to the polls on Nov. 7. Their lost votes could make a decisive difference in close Senate and House races this fall, especially in Florida, Kentucky and Virginia, where, unlike most states, felons, even after serving their time, never regain the right to vote. Among the races that could be affected are Virginia Sen. George Allen's attempt to retain his Senate seat, despite his recently exposed history of using racial slurs, and the House race for Kentucky District 3, where polls now show Republican Anne Northup essentially tied in her attempts to keep her seat from challenger Democrat John Yarmuth.

Sociologists who have long studied the disenfranchisement of felons say that the lost votes amount to a built-in advantage for Republicans, seen most famously in the 2000 presidential race in Florida, in which Al Gore would have likely beat George W. Bush had ex-felons been allowed to vote.

The war on drugs and a trend toward tougher sentencing laws have seen the nation's prison population swell over the past few decades. In Rhode Island, for instance, some 40 percent of inmates are in prison for nonviolent drug offenses, like Carbuccia's.

What it means to be disenfranchised really hit Carbuccia one day when she was talking with mothers at her son's day care about upcoming school-board elections. "I thought, 'Oh my God. Do you mean I can't say anything? You're pretty much putting a hand over my mouth.'" She wants to be able to vote not only to influence policies that will affect her son's education, but to set a good example for Vaskan about the importance of participating. "It's not uncommon for parents to take their kids to the polls and I can't do that," she says.

"Barred From Voting" by Katharine Mieszkowski, October 19, 2006. This article first appeared in Salon.com, at www.Salon.com. An online version remains in the Salon archives. Reprinted with permission.

This year, Carbuccia joined a campaign, organized by the nonprofit where she works, to change the law in Rhode Island to allow felony parolees and probationers to go to the polls. On Nov. 7, Rhode Islanders will vote on a referendum, which if it passes would amend the state's Constitution to give ex-felons, now living on the outside, the right to vote. While Carbuccia can't vote on the measure, she is vocal about why she thinks it should pass, speaking out at rallies and appearing in ads in support of the campaign. "Voting is a responsibility of each and every citizen," she says. "We want one vote, just like everyone else."

An unlikely catalyst brought national attention to felon disenfranchisement in the United States: George W. Bush. The 2000 election debacle in Florida put a spotlight on the stringent policy in the state, where if you've been convicted of a felony, you're essentially disenfranchised for life. Despite all the attention paid to hanging chads and purged voter rolls, it was this little-known issue that really decided the election, according to sociologists Christopher Uggen of the University Minnesota, and Jeff Manza of Northwestern University.

They looked at the demographics of former felon populations—age, race, income, gender, marital status, education—to determine the likelihood of their voting at all, as well as their likely preference for Democrats or Republicans. They found that former felons were about half as likely to vote as the general population, but would have a pronounced preference for Democratic candidates, given that many of them come from working-class poor and African-American backgrounds, where people typically vote Democratic.

In a paper published in *American Sociological Review*, the sociologists concluded that Gore would have likely received some 60,000 more votes had former felons in the state been able to vote, almost certainly reversing the results, giving Gore the presidency.

Since then, the number of disenfranchised in Florida has only grown. As of the end of 2004, there were 957,000 ex-felons in Florida alone who were "off paper"—meaning they'd completed their time in prison, probation and parole—yet couldn't vote. Of those, 205,000 were African-American. According to the American Civil Liberties Union, one-third of black men in Florida cannot legally cast a ballot, either because they're in prison or once were.

It is possible to regain voting rights as an ex-felon in Florida, but only by appealing to the state's Board of Executive Clemency. At the moment, this means pleading one's case before none other than Gov. Jeb Bush. According to the American Civil Liberties Union, applicants for clemency have been asked questions such as "Do you drink?" "Do you go to church?" "Are you married?"

"I thought character tests are no longer required for voting, but they are," says the ACLU's Laleh Ispahani. A survey by sociologists Uggen and Manza found that many appeals for clemency in Florida fail.

Critics say that disenfranchising former felons is un-American because it treats voting as a privilege, not a right. "If you think about it as a further way to punish criminals, it makes perfect sense," says Uggen. "If you think about it in terms of representative democracy, as trying to get everyone's opinion, it doesn't."

Felon disenfranchisement also has significant partisan implications, and not just for the U.S. presidential election in 2000. Uggen and Manza found that "by removing those with Democratic preferences from the pool of eligible voters, felon disenfranchisement has provided a small but clear advantage to Republican candidates in every presidential and senatorial election from 1972 to 2000."

They calculate that felon voters could have made a decisive difference in as many as seven senatorial races since 1978, which they estimate would have led to the Democrats' holding majority control over the Senate from 1986 to the present. Among the Senate races that would have had different outcomes, in their estimation, are the narrow Republican victories of John Warner in Virginia, John Tower in Texas and Mitch McConnell in Kentucky.

The partisan implications of the former-felon vote are not lost on Republicans, either. In Alabama, which maintains strict restrictions on ex-felons' voting, the chair of the Republican Party Marty Connors said in 2003: "As frank as I can be, we're opposed to [restoring voting rights] because felons don't tend to vote Republican."

The roots of the concept of disenfranchising felons goes back as far as ancient Greece, when offenders deemed "infamous" weren't allowed to vote, make speeches in public or appear in court, according to Alec Ewald, a political science professor at the University of Vermont. In a 2003 paper, "Punishing at the Polls," he writes that in Renaissance Europe, some criminals were punished by being deemed "outlaws," literally outside the law, and could be killed with impunity. Later, the concept took a less literal cast, evolving into "civil death." The basic idea: a criminal could be deemed "dead in law," unable to perform any legal function, including voting.

Many U.S. states imported that European tradition in the form of laws restricting voting rights, some of which are written into state constitutions, like Rhode Island's. But in the South, in the late 1800s and post-Reconstruction period, the laws, like poll taxes and literacy requirements, were used explicitly to restrict the voting of African-Americans. "Many of these laws were made more extreme after Reconstruction to disenfranchise people of color," says Spencer A. Overton, a professor at George Washington University Law School.

For instance, in Alabama and Mississippi, not all felonies would result in disenfranchisement. At the time, certain crimes were considered "black" crimes, those thought to be committed only by African-Americans. Such crimes would result in the loss of voting rights, while even more severe offenses, thought to be committed by blacks and whites alike, would not. "In Alabama, if you were convicted of beating your wife, you would lose your right to vote," says Marc Mauer, executive director of the Sentencing Project, a nonprofit research and advocacy group. "If you were convicted of killing your wife, you would not." That law stayed on the books for 100 years.

Since the 2000 election, there have been some significant movements toward restoration of voting rights to ex-felons in several states. With the laws in flux, new questions have arisen about who is and who is not eligible to vote.

In 2001, New Mexico repealed its lifetime ban on ex-felons' voting. In 2003, Nevada restored voting rights to nonviolent first-time-offender felons immediately after they get out of prison. In 2005, Nebraska significantly reduced its former lifetime ban, so that now ex-felons are banned from casting a ballot for just two years after the completion of their sentences. The Sentencing Project estimates that in the past decade, voting rights have been restored to some 620,000 people, who'd formerly not been eligible. Just this year, 73 bills were introduced in 22 states about felons' voting rights, with the vast majority of those seeking to expand voting rights.

In Iowa, where draconian laws like those in Virginia, Florida and Kentucky are still technically on the books, Gov. Tom Vilsack issued an executive order in 2005, restoring voting rights to ex-felons. However, in Virginia, despite pressure from advocacy groups, former Gov. Mark Warner failed to do the same before leaving office. Many states, like Alaska, Arkansas, Idaho and South Carolina—and Rhode Island, at least for the moment—ban all felons on probation or parole from voting. And almost all states—48 total—don't allow felons to vote while they're in prison. Notably, Maine and Vermont, the mavericks, allow prisoners behind bars to cast ballots.

The myriad of different state laws and recent revisions leads to another form of disenfranchisement, as many felons assume they can't vote and stay home on Election Day. In fact, the laws often befuddle election officials. Sasha Abramsky, author of "Conned: How Millions Went to Prison, Lost the Vote, and Helped Send George W. Bush to the White House," found substantial differences in the ways the laws are written, and how they're implemented on the ground. "You have all these laws that in theory let ex-felons vote, but election officials at the county level didn't understand the law, and were erring on the side of not letting felons vote," he says.

Who can blame many ex-offenders for having a hard time figuring out if they're welcome at the polls? That was Joe Loya's experience.

When the former bank robber got out of federal prison, he was put on "supervisory release," essentially the federal version of parole. He asked his parole officer if he could vote. The parole officer simply didn't know. As a resident of California, it turned out he couldn't vote, but he could have if he was on probation. Now, 10 years later, Loya, a writer and memoirist, says that he's an enthusiastic voter when he goes to cast his ballot at an elementary school in Oakland.

"I love being there," Loya says. "At that moment, I get sentimental about it. I feel this is my duty. I'm participating in society. I'm no longer antagonistic with society, which I used to despise."

Loya believes that not only should ex-felons be allowed to vote when they leave prison, they should be encouraged to do so. Parole officers should not only know the law, they should be handing out voter registration information. It's a way of encouraging felons to participate in society, rather than rebel against it. "Many guys who come out want to do the right thing," Loya says. "It behooves society to invite us in. Most people will not invite us into their house for a dinner, but they can invite us into the community in multiple ways, and one of those ways is the vote."

Andres Idarraga's life has changed course dramatically since 1998, when he was arrested for drug possession and distribution, as well as gun possession, and went to prison in Rhode Island. His sentence was for 14 years but he got out in six and a half. Today, he's a junior at Brown University studying comparative literature and economics, after transferring from the University of Rhode Island. He works part-time as a writing fellow, tutoring other students, and aspires to get a Ph.D. and become a literature professor.

"There's no way when a person comes out of prison, and you're struggling to put your life back together you should be denied the right to vote," Idarraga says. He argues the implications go far beyond the individual's recovery, impacting a whole community's political clout. For instance, in South Providence, 40 percent of black males ages 18 to 34 can't vote. "When you cannot vote, it affects your family and community," he says. "Candidates have a tendency to not even go into those communities and ask, 'What are your needs?' because they don't have to."

Like Koren Carbuccia, Idarraga is campaigning for the Rhode Island measure that would restore voting rights to ex-felons on probation or parole. Under the current law, he won't be able to vote for 30 years, when he's 58 years old.

Discussion Questions

1. Discuss the effects of preventing convicted felons from voting. Why does society do it?
2. Are inmates more likely to side with Republicans or Democrats? Why? How would this orientation likely have impacted the 2000 presidential election?
3. Discuss your personal belief regarding ex-felons and voting privileges. Do you believe losing voting privileges is part of the penalty, or do you believe the penalty is restricted to the sentence served?

31

Felon Fallout

By Alan Greenblatt

EDITOR'S COMMENT

There comes a point every so often in criminal justice when society evaluates the effectiveness of the criminal justice system. We look around and realize that change is needed in how we administer justice. Sometimes the change is substantial; other times the change requires a few minor adjustments. Historically, the changes regarding our correctional practices have involved one or more of the following goals of criminal sentencing: incapacitation, deterrence, retribution, and rehabilitation. Currently, one could make a strong argument that incapacitation, retribution, and deterrence supersede rehabilitation as the primary focus of correctional practices.

This article addresses how prison systems across the United States are operating under dangerous situations. Overcrowding, the spread of communicable diseases, prison violence, the lack of rehabilitation opportunities, and the difficulties faced by ex-prisoners attempting to reenter society are among the many challenges currently facing correctional systems.

The 1980s is recognized as the decade in which the "get tough on crime" approach notably took hold. Crime control legislation and an overall "law and order" approach to crime began in the 1980s and continue today. The approach has filled our courts and correctional facilities beyond capacity in many cases. Court dockets are full, resulting in roughly 90 percent of criminal cases being plea bargained, and many of those leaving the courts end up in prison. Unfortunately, our prisons were not prepared for the overcrowded conditions. Those involved in criminal justice policy-making seemingly didn't understand or consider all of the ramifications of getting tough on crime. In response, we've released violent offenders early to make room for new inmates; we've granted community corrections to individuals who likely deserve incarceration; and we've built prisons (which are very expensive) at the expense of social services and education. There are also other related impacts stemming from increased incarceration.

Stepping back for a moment and observing our correctional system and practices is somewhat disheartening. We spend much money on corrections and the results are less than impressive. Inmates released from prison often return following a violation of their parole agreement or the commission of a crime. Strong arguments could be made that now is the time for change in justice-based practices, particularly in corrections. This article highlights many reasons why change may be imminent. Support for changes in corrections is found in the unflattering effectiveness of many sanctions, despite immense and increasing financial resources devoted to corrections. State governments are recognizing the skyrocketing costs of incarceration, and some are leading the charge to find alternatives. In contrast, one could argue that incarceration, and the criminal justice system in general, indeed works, as evidenced in the decreasing crime rate over the past 15 years. One could also argue that there are few viable alternatives to incarceration at this point. Only time will tell.

A couple of years ago, the state of California did something surprising. It changed the name of its Department of Corrections, tacking on the words "and Rehabilitation" to the agency's title. It was a small step—the modification wasn't accompanied by any sudden surge in funding for rehabilitation programs. But it was symbolically important nonetheless. Thirty years ago, the state officially recast the department's mission from rehabilitation to incarceration and punishment. Since then, the idea of rehabilitating prisoners has been a much lower priority than locking up more of them. Now, with the state's prisons bursting at the bars, that may be about to change.

California's prison system houses more than 170,000 inmates, roughly double the number it was designed to hold. Overcrowding has precipitated riots and viral outbreaks, as well as straining basic services such as water and sewer. A federal judge has given state lawmakers until June to come up with a feasible solution for handling the heavy volume or risk a court takeover of the entire system. Two other courts are also entertaining motions to put a cap on the prison population. And, in response to yet another case, a federal court has already taken control of the prison health care system, ordering changes that could cost the state as much as $1 billion. The California prison system was undeniably facing a crisis anyway, but pressure from the courts has made prison management and reform one of the most pressing issues in Sacramento this year.

"We are at the point where if we don't clean up the mess, the federal court is going to do the job for us," said Governor Arnold Schwarzenegger. He has asked lawmakers to approve an $11 billion package in response. Most of the money would go toward building more prison and jail capacity. But Schwarzenegger also aims to make good on the promise of rehabilitation suggested by the corrections agency's name change. He wants nearly double the present funding for vocational, educational and drug treatment programs.

In looking to change its approach on corrections, California is just starting to play catch-up with the rest of the country. While no one wants to be accused of being "soft" on crime, fiscal concerns in many states have helped to revive liberal notions that had been abandoned for decades. In the aggregate, state governments are now spending more than $40 billion per year on prisons—five times as much as during the mid-1980s. Corrections departments have become the largest public employers in many states. A few are even spending more on corrections than on higher education. As a result, the ground underlying the corrections debate has clearly shifted. Nearly every state has stepped up its efforts to prepare prisoners for release, hoping that at least some of them will gain the skills and attitude necessary to avoid coming back.

Granted, the word "rehabilitation" is still too charged to return to broad use. The new buzzword is "reentry," a term that tacitly acknowledges that the vast majority of inmates will return to their communities at some point. The problem is that most of them will end up behind bars again, if not for new crimes then for parole violations. In California, seven out of 10 released prisoners are re-incarcerated within three years. That's one of the worst rates in the nation. But most states recognize that if they can cut their recidivism rates by just a small fraction, they will save enormous amounts of money.

Since 2004, for example, Connecticut has been putting more money into reentry programs such as parole, housing and drug treatment. Apparently as a result, the state has seen its prison population decline after a worrisome spike upwards. Connecticut was able to avoid building more prison space, and less crowding meant the cancellation of its multimillion-dollar contract with Virginia to house 500 prisoners it previously had no room for. "Around the country, it's becoming politically safe to do this stuff," says Michael Lawlor, chair of the Connecticut House Judiciary Committee, "because there's something in it for everybody, social progressives and fiscal conservatives."

Of course, not everyone has come around to this way of thinking. The idea that has dominated state corrections policy for more than a decade—that it is better to lock up offenders than waste energy worrying about how they're treated while they're in prison—still has enormous political resonance. And although more policy makers are becoming convinced of the need for offering prisoners some choices other than staring at a wall, the notion of investing in felons for the purposes of rehabilitation still doesn't sit well with the public at large.

In California, voters have strongly indicated their continued desire for a get-tough approach. Last November, they approved one of the harshest sex-offender laws in the country—which, among other things, will put thousands more behind bars. That came on the heels of voter rejection of an attempt to soften the state's "Three Strikes" law, which puts habitual offenders away for decades or for life. "Republicans generally feel we should build more prisons," says Dick Ackerman, the party's leader in the state Senate. "The California taxpayer wants to put these people away."

THE ROOTS OF OVERCROWDING

Like most of the rest of the country, California has spent the past quarter-century on a prison-building spree. The state's prison population has increased eightfold during those years, so that despite nearly tripling the number of its prisons since 1980, the corrections department has just about run out of room. It predicts the system will reach its absolute capacity in June or July, which is just about the time a federal judge might take over the system.

The roots of overcrowding are clear. Beginning in 1976, California's legislature and voters began approving a slew of tougher sentencing laws—some 1,000 altogether, culminating with the 1994 passage of Three Strikes. Although virtually all the laws lengthened sentences, the penal code as a whole has become a hodgepodge. It's easy to sketch out scenarios under which a criminal may face any one of four or five different mandatory sentences—each carrying a different penalty—for the exact same crime.

The one thing that has become certain for virtually all prisoners, however, is the date of release. Determinant sentencing has stripped the corrections department of its former authority to make judgments about when and whether a prisoner is ready to be released. Rather than getting time off for good behavior, or shortening their sentences by completing drug treatment programs, prisoners know they will be released on a fixed day, even if they have been dangerous enough to be kept in solitary until the day of their release. "We have more stringent requirements for young people graduating high schools than we do for people being released from prison," says state Senator Mike Machado.

If prisoners have no incentive for participating in rehab programs, there aren't adequate programs available to them anyway. For instance, more than half the state's prisoners are in "high need" of drug treatment, but only about 9 percent of them are likely to be enrolled at any given time, according to the UC Irvine study. Such programs are traditionally understaffed and poorly financed, but overcrowding has meant there's literally no place for them. The state prisons have classrooms and gymnasiums, but many are filled with some of the 19,000 inmates who are sleeping not in cells but in double or triple bunks lined up in every available space. "The accusations that we became just a warehouse are true," says James Tilton, Schwarzenegger's corrections secretary.

RELEASE AND RETURN

Under Schwarzenegger's plan, counties would house more short-term prisoners and help them get access to community-based programs. His proposal includes $5.5 billion for local jails, but counties remain nervous that the state will pass too many costs and responsibilities onto them. According to the sheriff's association in the state, more than 200,000 prisoners at the county level failed in 2005 to serve any or all of their sentences because 20 county jails are under court-ordered population caps, with 12 more maintaining voluntary caps under court pressure, Tilton, undaunted, has been working to convince counties and local law enforcement officials that local programs provide an alternative to the unworkable revolving-door recidivism system currently in place. "My presentation is that, if you want the status quo, if you want an inmate who is not prepared to be in your community, then to be honest you can have that if you like."

With so many of the state's prisoners either functionally illiterate or addicted to drugs (or having a combination of both problems), it's hardly surprisingly that so many of them return to prison after a brief stint on the outside. In Kansas, says state Representative Pat Colloton, two-thirds of prison admissions are related to parole and probation violations, and 80 percent of these are due to substance abuse or mental illness. In many cases, people are going to prison for violating probation, even though they weren't sentenced to jail time for their original crime.

If their crimes weren't severe enough to warrant a prison sentence in the first place, the state doesn't want them occupying expensive beds or distracting parole officers from more dangerous offenders. Toward that end, Kansas ran a pilot program in Shawnee County that sought to coordinate housing, substance abuse, job training and other programs for parolees. It cut the usual parole-revocation rate from 80 percent to 30 percent. Colloton has introduced twin bills that aim to build on this success by offering grants to more counties. "By giving this support, we can substantially reduce the number of people coming back to jail," she says. "We think that reforming people is the way to go, rather than building more prison beds."

Colloton, a Republican, is not some '60s liberal. Her proposal, like so many among the new generation of rehab programs, would be funded with strings attached. Accountability, after all, has become another universal buzzword. In order to continue to receive funding under Colloton's legislation, a county in Kansas will have to show that it has cut its revocation rate by at least 20 percent. In Oregon, the legislature has imposed a statutory requirement on the corrections department to monitor the success rate of reentry programs. In Washington State, a legislative study found that spending $1,000 per inmate for academic and vocational training programs was a good deal, crediting such programs with savings of more than $10,000 per prisoner in the form of lower crime rates and drops in recidivism of up to 9 percent.

Because the early results look good—and there's suddenly grant money and research available from sources such as the U.S. Department of Justice and the Council of State Governments' new Justice Center—more states are willing to look hard at funding reentry programs as an alternative to spending far more on prison beds. Even in tough-on-crime Texas, which leads the nation not only in executions but also its per capita rate of incarceration, lawmakers are talking seriously about the need to increase programming in prisons and in communities to address illiteracy, drug addiction and other stumbling blocks common to prisoners and parolees. "We're trying to do the smart thing," says Jerry Madden, chairman of the House Committee on Corrections. "The answer is not just building more prisons."

LACK OF POLITICAL WILL

Governor Schwarzenegger has talked seriously about making major changes to California's corrections system throughout the course of his administration. But, according to his critics, whenever push has come to shove, he's stopped pushing. Not long after taking office, Schwarzenegger appointed a prison study commission, headed by former Governor George Deukmejian, and called for an overhaul of the state's overtaxed parole system. So confident was his administration of success with its parole changes—it promised savings of $75 million per year—that it suspended operations at the correctional officer training academy, anticipating the need for fewer officers. But neither the implementation of parole changes nor the savings ever came off.

The lack of new trained officers is just one reason why the corrections department is understaffed by about 4,000 employees. California had one of the nation's lowest guard-to-inmate ratios anyway, but the closure of the training academy has meant hefty overtime payments to those on duty; 6,000 department employees, mostly rank-and-file guards, earned six figures during the past fiscal year. Indeed, the average base salary for prison guards there is 50 percent above the national average.

The guards' main union, the California Correctional Peace Officers Association, has become one of the most powerful forces in Sacramento. It was the leading donor to Schwarzenegger's two immediate predecessors. Schwarzenegger has openly derided the union as a "special interest," sought to cut its power by changing its means of collecting political dues from members, and attempted to shut the union out from prison policy discussions for the first time in years.

The CCPOA also didn't like the fact that he suspended its members' promised pay raises during a tough budget year, or that he tried to revoke some of the managerial control over its members that the union had won from his predecessor, which allows CCPOA to determine which officers will get which jobs 70 percent of the time. After Schwarzenegger unveiled his parole plan, the union helped a victims' rights group air TV ads claiming that the plan would let murderers, rapists and child molesters roam the streets.

Last year, two corrections secretaries quit in the space of a couple of months, later testifying in court that the governor's top political aides had decided to cave in to union demands. The courts grew publicly concerned about the administration's "retreat" from prison reform, with a special master complaining about CCPOA's "disturbing" amount of clout.

But if the union is sometimes cast in the role of villain in California's ongoing prison policy drama, there is plenty of blame left for others. Schwarzenegger called a special session last summer to address the overcrowding issue, asking the legislature to approve $6 billion for prison construction. The Senate passed a heavily revised version of the governor's plan, but the Assembly balked. Legislators claimed they needed more time to address such a complex issue, but the fact that the special session was a failure—coupled with the fact that the Democrats who control the legislature have shown more interest in Schwarzenegger's proposed sentencing commission than his latest construction money request—has led Republicans to level the familiar charge that they are soft on crime and criminals.

Schwarzenegger was seeking changes to the state's sentencing structure even before the U.S. Supreme Court ruled in January that major portions of it are unconstitutional. His fellow Republicans in the legislature claim that a sentencing commission, which would aim to straighten out some of the many inconsistencies in California's penal code, is "code for early release." Sentencing commissions, which have been tried in about 20 states, have not all been successful, but neither have they universally called for shorter sentences.

In North Carolina and Virginia, commonly cited as models in California, sentences for violent crimes were significantly lengthened, although both commissions diverted funds to community-based rehab and reentry programs. But Republican legislators in California are convinced that Democrats mean to use any new sentencing commission as cover for cutting jail time. "My biggest fear is that the liberals are going to drive an agenda where they will give the governor sentencing reform," says Assembly Republican Todd Spitzer, "and will not give any additional resources for prison beds, claiming that sentencing reform is enough to solve the problem."

CHANCE OF A LIFETIME

The stop-and-start nature of California's prison debate over the past couple of years has bred plenty of cynicism. But most observers think that the threat of a court takeover will succeed in prodding the political players into finally addressing the problem. Schwarzenegger has gotten nowhere with his earlier prison reform efforts because the political stakes were too high. Now, the dynamic has changed and the penalty for inaction may have become greater than for agreement. No one wants to be blamed when a court orders the release of thousands of convicts or watch the same court freely spend billions of additional dollars from state coffers. The Department of Corrections and Rehabilitation's budget has soared 52 percent over the past five years and is set to exceed $10 billion this year. Those numbers are scary enough without risking the prospect of a court receiver backing up a truck to the state treasury. "We don't need the federal government coming in here and writing blank checks out of our general fund," says Mike Villines, leader of the Assembly Republicans.

Villines, Spitzer and other Republicans clearly mean to keep banging the "tough on crime" gong in order to pressure Schwarzenegger and Democratic legislative leaders. They may or may not succeed in their goals of keeping a sentencing commission's authority limited and prison construction spending high. But even they talk about the need for the state to do a better job with rehabilitation programs in order to cut costly recidivism. The guards' union, for its part also has embraced the need for rehabilitation programs and publicly stated that sentencing reform is going to happen in California, whether through the legislative process or via court edict.

The debate in California is just beginning, but it's clear that reconciling all the complex and politically touchy issues surrounding sentencing, parole, rehabilitation and, in all likelihood, new prison construction will be tremendously difficult. (To make things even more complicated, the guards' contract is up for renegotiation.) Yet it's quite possible that the state, having let its prison problems grow literally out of its control, will finally take a comprehensive look at solving them.

"Sometimes a crisis will drive decisions, and we are certainly in a crisis situation," says Tilton, the corrections secretary. "This really presents an opportunity that hasn't been around for the 30 years I've been in state government to work through the issues about who should be in prison versus who should be somewhere else."

Discussion Questions

1. Discuss the roots of prison overcrowding in California.
2. To what does the author refer in the section "Release and Return"?
3. What problems are associated with prison overcrowding? Is there hope that such problems can be properly addressed in the future? Why or why not?

32

Returning Home: Scholars Say More Research Is Needed on the Societal Reentry of the Formerly Incarcerated

By Ronald Roach

EDITOR'S COMMENT

The primary purposes of criminal sentences are to punish, rehabilitate, deter, and/or incapacitate. Currently, a directed focus is on punishment, deterrence, and incapacitation. The goal of criminal sanctions is often to punish individuals and deter potential criminals through the imposition and threats of long sentences, while preventing crime through keeping a large number of individuals locked up. These goals are attractive to the general public and have been promoted by more than one politician in attempts to get reelected. However, almost all inmates return to society at some point, after having served time in an institution where rehabilitation was not a primary concern. What's to suggest we've corrected the problem that led to incarceration in the first place?

The philosophical goals of correctional practices have fluctuated over time. For instance, we've seen an emphasis on punishment through incarcerating large numbers of offenders for long periods of time, and we've provided rehabilitation programs in which inmates were treated in the community. Currently, we're recognizing some of the limitations of the get-tough policies that focus on punishment, deterrence, and incapacitation through increased incarceration. This selection highlights the difficulties faced by large numbers of seemingly unprepared ex-inmates returning to society.

Let's assume you've spent the past eight years in prison. Overcrowded conditions prevented you from participating in the few rehabilitative opportunities provided, and the available programs offered you very little. You're now preparing for reentry to society. You've lost many of your connections in society since you've been incarcerated for so long, and you lack many skills needed to find a job. On top of that, your resume includes an eight-year gap, unless, of course, you choose to highlight your status as an ex-prisoner. The pool of available employment opportunities is going to be slim and is limited to low-paying positions, and finding housing may be tough, particularly since you don't have much of a financial base to begin with. You'll try hard to avoid committing crime, but for the past eight years you've associated with a variety of criminals who haven't exactly been the role models with whom your parents hoped you'd associate. You've served your penalty, yet you feel as though you'll continue to be punished.

There's a strong belief in society that criminal tendencies are permanent. High rates of recidivism suggest to some that ex-inmates are constantly going to live outside the law. Prison is probably the best place for individuals who make no attempt to live a crime-free life. However, many ex-inmates wish to avoid crime and the criminal justice system. They attempt to avoid criminal behavior, yet, the pressures associated with having been incarcerated and a lack of opportunities and financial and societal support leave them little choice but to engage in crime. The call for greater research to determine how we can mitigate the difficulties of reentry is significant, particularly at a time when so many individuals are entering and leaving our prisons. Ex-inmates have served their penalty and don't deserve to face continuous punishment, unless of course we wish to increase the likelihood that they will engage in further crime.

Since the late 1960s, politicians and policymakers have talked tough on crime and have passed tough laws to build prisons and to prescribe lengthy sentences for the criminally convicted. In the past five years, however, public attention has focused on a criminal justice issue to which politicians and other public officials previously paid little heed. That issue is the societal re-entry of the formerly incarcerated, which is documented at an unprecedented scale now as more people are leaving prisons than at any time in American history.

Since 2000, more than 600,000 people a year have been leaving prisons and jails in the United States, which is a fourfold increase over the past two decades. In comparison, the American prison and jail population rose to 2.085 million in 2003 from 503,586 in 1980, according to the U.S. Bureau of Justice Statistics.

"The Justice Department has predicted that 630,000 individuals are going to be released from prison this year. Unfortunately, as a nation, we have not prepared for these individuals as they come back to neighborhoods and communities. We must take a serious look at our correctional system and a serious look at what it takes to reform, to rehabilitate and to prepare people for re-entry into normal society once they are released from correctional facilities and institutions," says U.S. Rep. Danny K. Davis, D-Ill.

Davis, a member of the Congressional Black Caucus, has been the author of the Public Safety Ex-Offender Self Sufficiency Act and a chief cosponsor of the Second Chance Act of 2004: Community SafEty [*sic*] through Recidivism Prevention. The bills, which will be reintroduced this year, are legislative measures to provide supportive services and opportunities for the formerly incarcerated. Though officials such as Davis have been pushing the federal government to address the re-entry issue, the burden has fallen squarely on localities and states to provide the necessary social services and training for ex-offenders.

Officials know that people leaving prison present a challenging profile for states and localities because such individuals have a legion of complex needs. Three-quarters of those released from prison and jail have a history of substance abuse, two-thirds have no high school diploma, and 55 percent of reentering adults have children under 18, according to the Re-Entry Policy Council, a policy advisory group established to advise state governments. Nearly half of those leaving jail earned less than $600 per month immediately prior to their incarceration, and their opportunities for employment are significantly diminished once they have a criminal record, the policy council reports. In addition, more than a third of jail inmates report having some physical or mental disability.

"Returning Home: Scholars Say More Research is Needed on the Societal Re-entry of the Formerly Incarcerated" by Ronald Roach, *Diverse: Issues In Higher Education*, February 24, 2005, www.diverseeducation.com. Reprinted with permission.

Criminal justice reform advocates and some scholars say that in addition to their personal disadvantages and problems, such as low education and high rates of a history of substance abuse, the formerly incarcerated are unjustly saddled with a depth of social stigma, discrimination and political disenfranchisement that manifests as "social death." There's also concern over what many perceive as the loss of rehabilitation as a goal in the U.S. criminal justice system.

"Unless prisons and corrections systems truly adopt the rehabilitative model while prisoners are incarcerated, unless our society is willing to have faith in the fact that these men and women have been rehabilitated, unless there's a demonstration on the part of a society to have a willingness to use those coming out of the jails in a productive way, we're going to continue to see higher recidivism," says Dr. Ramona Brockett, a professor of criminal justice at the University of Maryland-Eastern Shore.

"The time has been served for some of these drug offenses and other offenses, and these people are coming out," explains Dr. Everette B. Penn, a criminology professor at the University of Houston–Clear Lake. "These people have now been labeled as felons, and although they did wrong before by that definition they have served their time and now they're back in society. The question becomes 'is society ready to accept them back?'"

"And I would say at this time with some of the laws that currently exist, (with) the loss of voting privileges and the constant reminder on job applications that this person was a felon and continues to be labeled as a felon limits the opportunities for these people," he adds.

COMBATING SOCIAL DEATH

Scholars say that while there hasn't been much research produced specifically around the re-entry issue, there is considerable activity devoted to interpreting and explaining what some consider to be an incarceration crisis in the United States. Some scholars have argued that with the last three decades of building prisons, the passage of harsh sentencing laws and aggressive treatment of Black and Latino defendants in the courts' local and national leaders have redefined governance largely by their response to crime.

Emerging in the aftermath of the civil rights movement, the impulse towards "governing through crime" gave rise to the "War on Drags" and aggressive law enforcement with the passage of laws such as mandatory-minimum sentencing. Mandatory-minimum sentencing permits no room for judges to exercise discretion in sentencing. Those found guilty of a crime are automatically locked up for a set amount of time.

By the early 1990s, the federal government and numerous states took the mandatory-minimum sentencing idea to another level, by passing "three strikes" laws mandating prison sentences of 25 years to life for third felonies. In addition, the establishment of disparate sentences for crack and powder cocaine possession garnered criticism because it was seen to demonstrate criminal justice bias against minorities.

When researchers look at the re-entry issue, it's important they do it in the context of what initially led to the removal or incarceration of people from their respective communities, says Dr. Todd Clear, a distinguished professor in the John Jay College of Criminal Justice, City University of New York.

"One thing that is consistent in the research is that when ex-offenders return to home communities unable to offer them assistance and opportunities, their likelihood of getting into trouble with the law increases," Clear says.

"Researchers have really been late to this (re-entry) issue," says Dr. Geoff Ward, an assistant professor of criminal justice at Northeastern University. "I think it's safe to say that it's really only been in the last five years that really significant research has been committed to not the issue of re-entry generally, but how mass imprisonment has introduced unprecedented social, political, economic havoc on communities. . . . The scale of the re-entry issue has been increased by the problem of mass imprisonment over the last couple of decades," he says.

One issue said to be generating a symbolic as well as widespread image for the formerly incarcerated is the national debate over convicted felons and the right to vote. Nearly five million Americans are barred from voting by a complicated spectrum of state laws that deny those convicted as felons of the right to vote, sometimes temporarily, but often for life. Criminal justice reform advocates have long contended that such laws have neither correctional nor rehabilitative function, yet represent a clear example of imposing social or civic death on the formerly incarcerated.

"First and foremost programs, activists and organizations and government programs should see to the immediate needs of the formerly incarcerated," says Laurent Alfred, director of the Africana Criminal Justice Project at Columbia University. "With that being said, none of that will happen if this population is so politically disenfranchised. It's a population that lacks any political voice whatsoever in many states because of permanent disenfranchisement."

Number of Sentenced Prisoners Under State or Federal Jurisdiction, 2003

	Males			
	Total*	**White****	**Black****	**Hispanic**
Total	1,316,495	454,300	586,300	251,900
18–19	25,200	7,100	12,600	4,900
20–24	208,300	59,400	99,900	46,200
25–29	231,400	63,100	111,400	54,700
30–34	221,000	70,300	100,000	47,900
35–39	209,400	75,400	91,900	37,800
40–44	182,300	71,700	78,100	27,900
45–54	178,400	74,800	73,900	24,800
55 or older	57,700	31,900	17,200	7,200

	Females			
	Total*	**White****	**Black****	**Hispanic**
Total	92,785	39,100	35,000	16,200
18–19	1,100	400	500	200
20–24	11,100	4,400	4,200	2,300
25–29	13,900	5,600	5,300	2,600
30–34	17,200	7,200	6,500	3,100
35–39	18,800	7,800	7,300	3,200
40–44	15,600	6,800	5,800	2,500
45–54	12,400	5,400	4,700	1,800
55 or older	2,600	1,400	700	300

NOTE: Based on custody counts by race and Hispanic origin from national prisoner statistics (NPS-1A) and updated from jurisdiction counts by gender at year end. Estimates by age were derived from the National Corrections Reporting Program, 2002. Estimates were rounded to the nearest 100.

*Includes American Indians, Alaska natives, Asians, native Hawaiians, and other Pacific Islanders.

**Excludes Hispanics.

Educational Programs Offered in State, Federal and Private Prisons and Local Jails

	State Prisons		Federal Prisons		Private Prisons	
	2000	**1995**	**2000**	**1995**	**2000**	**1995**
With an Education Program	91.2%	88.0%	100.0%	100.0%	87.6%	71.8%
Basic Adult Education	80.4%	76.0%	97.4%	92.0%	61.6%	40.0%
Secondary Education	83.6%	80.3%	98.7%	100.0%	70.7%	51.8%
College Courses	26.7%	31.4%	80.5%	68.8%	27.3%	18.2%
Special Education	39.6%	33.4%	59.7%	34.8%	21.9%	27.3%
Vocational Training	55.7%	54.5%	93.5%	73.2%	44.2%	25.5%
Study Release Programs	7.7%	9.3%	6.5%	5.4%	28.9%	32.7%
Without an Education Program	8.8%	1.2%	0.0%	0.0%	12.4%	28.2%
Number of Facilities	1,307	1,278	x	x	242	110

	Local Jails
	1999
With an Education Program	60.3%
Basic Adult Education	24.7%
Secondary Education	54.8%
College Courses	3.4%
Special Education	10.8%
Vocational Training	6.5%
Study Release Programs	9.3%
Without an Education Program	39.7%
Number of Facilities	2,819

NOTE: Detail may not add to total because facilities may have more than one educational program.

X: Changed definitions prevent meaningful comparisons of the numbers of federal facilities, 1995 and 2000.

Number and Percentage Change for Female Inmates in State or Federal Prisons and Local Jails

	% Change from 1999 to 2003	2003	% Change from 2001 to 2003	2001
Total	18.16%	176,300	9.37%	161,200
18–19	16.22%	4,300	4.88%	4,100
20–24	35.11%	25,400	20.95%	21,000
25–29	−9.41%	26,000	−16.93%	31,300
30–34	−11.26%	33,100	−17.46%	40,100
35–39	21.09%	35,600	11.95%	31,800
40–44	66.26%	27,100	56.65%	17,300
45–54	73.91%	20,000	65.29%	12,100
55 or older	52.00%	3,800	46.15%	2,600

Source: Percentages done by BIHE using data from the Bureau of Justice Statistics–Prison and Jail Inmates at Midyear 1999, 2001, and 2003: http://www.ojp.usdoj.gov/bjs/jails.htm

* Includes American Indians, Alaska natives, Asians, native Hawaiians, and other Pacific Islanders.

** Excludes Hispanics.

Number of Female Inmates in State or Federal Prisons and Local Jails

	30-Jun-03			
	Total*	**White****	**Black****	**Hispanic**
Total	176,300	76,100	66,800	28,300
18–19	4,300	1,700	1,500	1,000
20–24	25,400	11,000	8,900	4,900
25–29	26,000	10,900	9,800	4,700
30–34	33,100	14,000	12,600	5,400
35–39	35,600	15,600	13,800	5,100
40–44	27,100	11,800	11,100	3,600
45–54	20,000	8,900	7,800	2,800
55 or older	3,800	2,100	900	700

NOTE: For 2003 data—Based on custody counts from National Prisoners Statistics (NPS-1A), 2003, and annual Survey of Jails, 2003. Estimates by age were obtained from survey of inmates in local jails, 2002, National Corrections Reporting Program, 2001, and Federal Justice Statistics Program (FJSP) for Inmates on September 30, 2002. Estimates were rounded to the nearest 100.

*Includes American Indians, Alaska Natives, Asians, Native Hawaiians and other Pacific Islanders.

**Excludes Hispanics.

Source: Bureau of Justice Statistics—Prison and Jail Inmates at Midyear 1999, 2001, and 2003; http://www.ojp.usdoj.gov/bjs/jails.htm

Education for State Prison Inmates, 1997

	Male	**Female**	**White**	**Black**	**Hispanic**
Educational Attainment					
8th Grade or Less	14.3%	13.6%	10.9%	11.7%	27.9%
Some High School	25.3%	28.2%	16.3%	32.4%	25.1%
GED	28.9%	22.3%	35.2%	24.8%	24.7%
High School Diploma	20.4%	21.6%	22.8%	2.1%	14.9%
College	8.8%	11.2%	11.4%	8.4%	5.5%
College Graduate	2.3%	3.1%	3.5%	1.6%	1.9%
High School Completion					
Completed High School	25.2%	30.3%	29.9%	25.5%	17.2%
Earned GED	35.2%	27.9%	42.9%	30.4%	29.7%
In Prison/Jail	26.3%	15.9%	30.0%	23.2%	23.4%
Outside Prison/Jail	8.9%	11.9%	12.9%	7.2%	6.3%
Educational Programs					
Total	5.2%	50.1%	48.8%	53.8%	52.6%
Basic	3.1%	3.3%	2.1%	3.3%	4.8%
GED/High School	23.6%	21.3%	18.7%	26.1%	25.4%
College	10.0%	9.1%	12.4%	0.9%	7.1%
English as a Second Language	1.2%	0.5%	0.1%	0.1%	6.4%
Vocational	32.4%	29.5%	32.0%	33.7%	29.1%
Other	2.5%	3.8%	3.0%	2.5%	1.8%
Number of Prison Inmates	989,419	66,076	351,742	490,384	179,301

NOTE: Detail may not add to total due to rounding or inmates' participation in more than one educational program.
Source for these: U.S. Department of Justice Statistics, Office of Justice Programs, Bureau of Justice Statistics Special Report Education and Correctional Populations; http://www.ojrusdoj.gov/bjs/pub/pdf/ecp.pdf

Participation in Educational Programs Since Most Recent Admission, by Educational Attainment, 1997

State prison inmates with—	Less than high school diploma	GED	High school diploma	Post secondary/college
Total	53.5%	60.4%	4.2%	42.8%
Basic	6.4%	1.4%	0.8%	0.4%
GED/High School	36.1%	28.0%	4.6%	2.0%
College Courses	0.7%	16.5%	13.5%	18.9%
English as a Second Language	2.0%	0.6%	0.9%	0.6%
Vocational	24.3%	43.7%	31.8%	31.6%
Other	1.5%	3.1%	3.3%	4.2%
Number of Prison Inmates	413,759	298,912	214,439	119,027

NOTE: Detail may not add to total due to rounding or inmates' participation in more than one educational program.

Discussion Questions

1. What are some of the problems facing inmates returning to society?
2. Discuss how prisons and jails can better prepare inmates for reentry to society.
3. What characteristics often found among those leaving prisons and jails suggest they will have a difficult time adjusting to society?

V

Juvenile Justice and Emerging Issues in Criminal Justice

INTRODUCTION

Part V consists of two primary categories of topics: issues pertaining to juvenile offenders, including the problems associated with troubled teens, life sentences for juveniles, teen prostitution, and the challenges facing the children of the incarcerated, and emerging issues in criminal justice, including the use of technology in the form of biometrics and GPS tracking, immigration and its impact on crime, and the impact of the popular television show *CSI*.

Juveniles are processed in a system distinct from the criminal justice system. Beginning with the turn of the twentieth century, specific courts were designated to process juvenile offenders. Having a system separate from adults does not preclude juveniles from facing controversial and critical issues. The article "The Trouble with Troubled Teen Programs" highlights the challenges associated with imposing tough-love justice on juveniles. Historically, society has attempted to nurture and protect juveniles. Recently, however, such attempts have given way to punishment and deterrence. Some of the "get tough" punishments given to young adults provide evidence of the public's frustration with juvenile delinquency.

Imagine you're a 17-year-old out having fun with your friends. Alcohol is involved. You wake up in the morning and you're in jail. As you wake up a jailer approaches you and says, "you messed up boy." Later, you find out that you got into a fight and stabbed someone to death. You're eventually transferred to the adult justice system and are tried as an adult. In light of the seriousness of the crime, you receive a life sentence without the possibility of parole—and, you haven't even graduated high school. Locking up young adults/teenagers for life may seem appropriate in select circumstances; however, the United States is one of the few countries that has and uses such legislation. The article "Jailed for Life After Crimes as Teenagers" addresses the uniqueness of giving up on such young individuals.

Prostitution seems harmless enough. Two people willing to engage in sexual relations for a specified amount of money. She gets money, he gets satisfaction, as it usually goes. However, the situation is not always so simple. As the article "Young Lives for Sale" notes, teenagers engaged in prostitution shed an increasingly seedy light on an already questionable practice. Society often perceives those engaging in prostitution as willing participants. We often don't consider the histories or current situations of those involved in the trade. If we did, however, we may recognize the youthfulness and innocence of some prostitutes and our opinion of prostitution might change.

Increased incarceration rates arguably contribute to decreased crime rates. The more criminals in prison, the less crime outside prison, or so the theory goes. However, increased incarceration brings with it many intangibles that people often overlook. For instance, consider the number of single-parent families resulting from one parent serving time in prison. Or, consider the plight of children with both parents in prison. Society has demonstrated little concern for the children of incarcerated parents, as evidenced in the article "Stepchildren of Justice." Unfortunately, these same children are at substantial risk of following in their incarcerated parents' footsteps.

Technology has changed criminal justice practices, as evidenced in the articles "Biometric Basics" and "GPS Offender Tracking and the Police Officer." These articles demonstrate how the introduction and incorporation of technology in the criminal justice system have influenced crime control and prevention. The intriguing aspect of discussing the incorporation of technology into any field is wondering where it will end—what are the limits regarding the contributions technology can offer to the criminal justice system? Should we expect that technology will assume an even greater role in the criminal justice system? The obvious answer is "yes." And, based on recent developments, we should welcome such changes.

Immigration is one of the more debated issues in society. Some feel that increased immigration will lead to additional or enhanced social problems. For example, many believe that immigrants are responsible for a disproportionate amount of crime. The article "Do Immigrants Make Us Safer" addresses this issue, offering the nonconventional argument that immigrants may actually make our society safer. Fear of involvement with the criminal justice system and the goal of attempting to "fit in" prevent many immigrants from engaging in illegal activity.

The final selection of this book examines how the TV show *CSI* has impacted the criminal justice system, and justice studies in general. *CSI* has encouraged more than one individual to seek a career in criminal justice. Accordingly, universities and colleges have seen increases in the number of students hoping to attain careers in crime scene investigation and thus majoring in criminal justice. The show has also impacted courtroom practices in that some jury members have expectations that all evidence is, or should be scrutinized to the extent that it is on the show. *CSI* is not the first, nor will it be the last television show to influence the study and practice of criminal justice.

There are many other topics that could have been discussed in this text. Accounts of crime and justice consume much of our daily lives and address a variety of issues—interesting issues worthy of public attention. As a discipline criminal justice is fortunate to involve the combination of interesting and important issues. I guess that's why it attracts such extensive public attention.

33

The Trouble with Troubled Teen Programs

By Maia Szalavitz

EDITOR'S COMMENT

Addressing troubled teens is particularly challenging for justice officials. Much of the difficulty stems from society's uncertainty regarding how to confront teen wayward behavior. Historically, the juvenile justice system has operated under the belief and assumption that juveniles are impressionable and in need of guidance, nurturance, and protection. More recently, the system has gotten tough on juvenile offenders and began abandoning efforts to protect and nurture our troubled youth. So, what to do with a troubled teen? There are many approaches to helping today's youth. Unfortunately, there's little agreement on the most appropriate approaches.

As noted in this article, the tough-love approaches taken by some jurisdictions to address troubled youth are sometimes unpredictable and dangerous. Society is tired of hearing accounts of young adults, and sometimes young children committing serious crimes and receiving little punishment. The popularity of boot camp programs exemplifies a response to the public's concern. Boot camps are designed primarily to encourage pro-social behavior through breaking down an individual, typically a young adult, through military-like exercises and drill instruction. The goal is to then "re-build" the individual through enhancement approaches such as education, self-esteem, and counseling. Thus, boot camps combine punishment with positive reinforcement.

Much of the general public is encouraged by efforts to both punish and improve the behavior of young offenders. Unfortunately, the emphasis on punishment sometimes far exceeds the emphasis on reconstruction. As a result, we get an angry individual with experience in the juvenile justice system and without proper rehabilitation. Boot camps and other tough-love sanctions serve a purpose. Some individuals respond positively to the challenging situation. Others, however, leave the programs and continue to misbehave. This problem of uncertain outcome is not restricted to juveniles.

Getting tough on crime and delinquency is politically popular and effective in some cases. In other cases, this approach fails to correct existing problems and may create new ones. Failure to achieve the desired results with a get-tough approach is more harmful to juveniles than to adults. For example, unrehabilitated young adults have more time to commit crime because they are just entering the crime-prone ages of 18–24.

The difficulty with troubled-juvenile programs, and all correctional programs for that matter, is to determine what works best for each individual. Blanket approaches designed to address "crime" or "delinquency" without consideration of what type of offense is involved and why it occurred are doomed to fail. Officials must effectively determine what caused or prompted a teen's involvement in the justice system and locate programs that appear to properly address such problems. For instance, getting tough may work for middle-class drug users, yet not for more impoverished drug users. Our justice systems do consider the issue of "what works best for whom," yet much work remains in understanding who should receive what sentence.

Along these lines, researchers are encouraged to continue assessing the effectiveness of various sanctions. Such research should continue to closely examine the variables influencing a youth's involvement in crime and delinquency, and consider those factors in relation to current sentencing options. As "protectors of our youth" adults in society should have a firm grasp of how to best correct the wayward behavior of our youth.

The state of Florida tortured 14-year-old Martin Lee Anderson to death for trespassing. The teen had been sentenced to probation in 2005 for taking a joy ride in a Jeep Cherokee that his cousins stole from his grandmother. Later that year, he crossed the grounds of a school on his way to visit a friend, a violation of his probation. His parents were given a choice between sending him to boot camp and sending him to juvenile detention. They chose boot camp, believing, as many Americans do, that "tough love" was more likely to rehabilitate him than prison.

Less than three hours after his admission to Florida's Bay County Sheriff's Boot Camp on January 5, 2006, Anderson was no longer breathing. He was taken to a hospital, where he was declared dead early the next morning.

A video recorded by the camp shows up to 10 of the sheriff's "drill instructors" punching, kicking, slamming to the ground, and dragging the limp body of the unresisting adolescent. Anderson had reported difficulty breathing while running the last of 16 required laps on a track, a complaint that was interpreted as defiance. When he stopped breathing entirely, this too was seen as a ruse.

Ammonia was shoved in the boy's face; this tactic apparently had been used previously to shock other boys perceived as resistant into returning to exercises. The guards also applied what they called "pressure points" to Anderson's head with their hands, one of many "pain compliance" methods they had been instructed to impose on children who didn't immediately do as they were told.

All the while, a nurse in a white uniform stood by, looking bored. At one point she examined the boy with a stethoscope, then allowed the beating to continue until he was unconscious. An autopsy report issued in May—after an initial, disputed report erroneously attributed Anderson's death to a blood disorder—concluded that he had died of suffocation, due to the combined effects of ammonia and the guards' covering his mouth and nose.

Every time a child dies in a tough love program, politicians say—as Florida Gov. Jeb Bush initially did on hearing of Anderson's death—that it is "one tragic incident" that should not be used to justify shutting such programs down. But there have now been nearly three dozen such deaths and thousands of reports of severe abuse in programs that use corporal punishment, brutal emotional attacks, isolation, and physical restraint in an attempt to reform troubled teenagers.

Tough love has become a billion-dollar industry. Several hundred programs, both public and private, use the approach. Somewhere between 10,000 and 100,000 teenagers are currently held in treatment programs based on the belief that adolescents must be broken (mentally, and often physically as well) before they can be fixed. Exact numbers are impossible to determine, because no one keeps track of the kids in these programs, most of which are privately run. The typical way to end up in a government-run program, such as the camp where Martin Lee Anderson was killed, is for a court to give you the option of going there instead of prison. The typical way to end up in a private program is to be sent there by your parents, though judges and public schools have been known to send kids to private boot camps as well. Since they offer "treatment," some of the private centers are covered by health insurance.

"The Trouble With Troubled Teen Programs" by Maia Szalavitz, *Reason*, January 2007. Reprinted by permission of the Reason Foundation.

In the nearly five decades since the first tough love residential treatment community, Synanon, introduced the idea of attack therapy as a cure for drug abuse, hundreds of thousands of young people have undergone such "therapy." These programs have both driven and been driven by the war on drugs. Synanon, for example, was aimed at fighting heroin addiction, its draconian methods justified by appeals to parents' fears that drugs could do far worse things to their children than a little rough treatment could. The idea was that only a painful experience of "hitting bottom" could end an attachment to the pleasures of drugs.

But like the drug war itself, tough love programs are ineffective, based on pseudoscience, and rooted in a brutal ideology that produces more harm than most of the problems they are supposedly aimed at addressing. The history of tough love shows how fear consistently trumps data, selling parents and politicians on a product that hurts kids.

ATTACK THERAPY UTOPIA

Synanon was a supposedly utopian California community founded in 1958 by an ex-alcoholic named Chuck Dederich. Dederich believed he could improve on the voluntary 12-step program of Alcoholics Anonymous. Rather than rely on people choosing to change, Synanon would use extreme peer pressure and even physical coercion to impose the confession, surrender, and service to others that 12-step programs suggest as the road to recovery.

At the time, heroin addiction was seen as incurable. But when a heroin addict kicked drugs after participating in Dederich's brutally confrontational encounter groups, the founder and other members began living communally and promoting Synanon as an addiction cure.

The media took note, and soon state officials from across the country were visiting and setting up copycat programs back home to treat addicts. Only New Jersey bothered to do an outcome study before replicating Synanon. The investigation, released in 1969, found that only 10 to 15 percent of participants stayed in the program for more than a few months and actually ended their addictions, a rate no better than that achieved without treatment. A 1973 study of encounter groups by the Stanford psychiatrist Irvin Yalom and his colleague Morton Lieberman found that 9 percent of participants experienced lasting psychological damage and that Synanon groups were among those with the highest numbers of casualties.

But the research didn't matter. To both the media and the politicians, anecdote was evidence. The idea that toughness was the answer had a deep appeal to those who saw drug use as sin and punishment as the way to redemption. And Synanon produced testimonials worthy of a revival meeting. Indeed, it eventually recast itself as the "Church of Synanon."

By the early 1970s, the federal government itself had funded its own Synanon clone. It was located in Florida and known as The Seed.

In this program, teenagers who were using drugs or who were believed to be at risk of doing so would spend 10-to-12-hour days seated on hard-backed chairs and waving furiously to catch the attention of staffers, most of whom were former participants themselves. Like Arnold Horshack in Welcome Back, Kotter but with more desperate urgency, they would flutter their hands, begging to be called on to confess their bad behavior. Even before the excesses of the '80s, parents were so frightened of drugs that they were willing to surrender their children to strangers for tough treatment to avoid even the possibility of addiction; some parents even hit their children themselves at Seed meetings, following the instructions of program leaders.

When kids entered The Seed, they lived in "host homes"—houses of parents of other program participants that had been specially prepared to incarcerate teenagers at night. If these "newcomers" didn't give convincing enough confessions in group sessions, they would not be allowed to "progress" in the program and return to home and school.

In 1974 Sen. Sam Ervin, the North Carolina Democrat best known for heading the congressional committee that investigated Watergate, presented a report to Congress entitled "Individual Rights and the Federal Role in Behavior Modification." Ervin and other members of Congress were concerned about federal funding for efforts to change people's behavior against their will, seeing a fundamental threat to liberty if such efforts were successful. The report cited The Seed as an example of programs that "begin by subjecting the individual to isolation and humiliation in a conscious effort to break down his psychological defenses." It concluded that such programs are "similar to the highly refined brainwashing techniques employed by the North Koreans in the early 1950's."

THE SEED GERMINATES

Ervin's report led Congress to cut off The Seed's funding. But The Seed had produced two important true believers: Mel Sembler, who went on to serve as campaign finance chairman for the Republican Party during the 2000 election season and as U.S. ambassador to Italy from 2001 to 2005, and Joseph Zappala, who would go on to serve under the first President Bush as ambassador to Spain and who at the time was also a major Republican campaign donor.

In 1976 Sembler and Zappala founded a program virtually identical to The Seed, staffed by former Seed parents and participants (including some who had become Seed staffers). They named it Straight Incorporated. The federal agency that had funded The Seed, the Law Enforcement Assistance Agency, had been barred from funding further human experiments because neither the agency nor projects like The Seed had procedures for informed consent. Despite that fact, and despite the congressional critique of The Seed, Straight soon received federal money from the same agency. It, too, never informed parents that it was experimental.

Straight expanded rapidly in the '80s, around the same time newspapers, TV, and other media were filled with dire warnings about the dangers of crack. Nancy Reagan called it her "favorite" drug program. In fact, it was a visit to Straight, suggested by Sembler, that had inspired the first lady to make drugs her cause.

An undated issue of Straight's newsletter, *Epidemic*, from around this time carried a photo of the legs of a young-looking corpse with a tag on one toe: "Cocaine, crack and kids." The accompanying article said crack was "almost instantaneously addictive"—"the most addictive drug known to man"—and passed along the tale of a 16-year-old girl who had recently tried smoking cocaine. "One night I noticed a big lump on my back," she wrote. "I was rushed to the hospital and operated on and had two tumors removed. The tumors were caused by impurities in the coke which built up in my blood and got infected." Such a story, if true, would have made medical history.

But for the media, drugs act as an anti-skeptic; the scarier the consequences, the bigger the story, the higher the ratings, and the lower the incentive to qualify extreme claims. The 1986 documentary 48 Hours on Crack Street purported to show the crack menace spreading ineluctably to the middle class. It drew one of the largest TV audiences ever for a news program.

Between 1981 and 1989, Straight opened sites in Atlanta; Cincinnati; Orlando; Boston; Detroit; Yorba Linda, California; and Springfield, Virginia. Former employees opened virtually identical programs in New Jersey, Kentucky, Utah, New Mexico, and Florida in the late '80s and early '90s.

SPANKING AND MOTIVATING

As far back as 1978, however, employees had begun to quit Straight and contact regulators, reporting beatings and other maltreatment. "The program was getting . . . so bad that I felt it was hurting more kids than it was helping," one anonymous former staffer told the *St. Petersburg Times* that year. Miller Newton, Straight's national clinical director, admitted to authorities in 1982 that he had kept teenagers awake for 72-hour periods, put them on peanut butter–only diets, and forced them to crawl through each other's legs to be hit in a "spanking machine."

At Straight, The Seed's hand-waving procedure to get staff attention during group sessions mutated into "motivating," in which kids flapped their arms so vigorously it looked like they were trying to fly away. The movements were so violent that more than once teenagers hit those sitting next to them, resulting in broken bones.

Richard Bradbury, whose activism eventually helped shut Straight down, was forcibly enrolled in the program in 1983, when he was 17. His sister had had a drug problem, and Straight demanded that he be screened for one as well. After an eight-hour interrogation in a tiny room, Bradbury, who was not an addict, was nonetheless held. He later described beatings and continuous verbal assaults, which for him centered on sexual abuse he'd suffered as a young boy. Staffers and other participants called him a "faggot," told him he'd led his abusers on, and forced him to admit "his part" in the abuse.

Straight ultimately paid out millions of dollars in dozens of lawsuits related to abuse and even kidnapping and false imprisonment of adults. But the Straight network remained in operation until 1993. Even today, at least nine programs in the U.S. and Canada still use tactics, such as host homes and "motivating," that come directly from Straight. Some are run by former Straight employees, sometimes in former Straight buildings. Among them: SAFE in Orlando; Growing Together in Lake Worth, Florida; Kids Helping Kids in Cincinnati; the Phoenix Institute for Adolescents in Marietta, Georgia; Turnabout/Stillwater Academy in Salt Lake City; Pathway Family Center in Detroit; the Alberta Adolescent Recovery Center in Calgary, Alberta; and Love in Action, a program aimed at "curing" homosexual teenagers, located near Memphis. The Straight Foundation itself, which coordinated the organization and doled out the money, never died; it simply renamed itself the Drug Free America Foundation, which to this day works to promote student drug testing and to oppose efforts to end the drug war. Its website lists Mel Sembler and his wife Betty as "founding members."

Meanwhile, other organizations found they could profit from tough love with legal impunity. As negative publicity finally began to hurt Straight and skepticism about the drug war itself grew, other groups began to use similar tactics, all converging on a combination of rigid rules, total isolation of participants from both family and the outside world, constant emotional attacks, and physical punishments. These programs were sold as responses not just to drug use but to teenage "defiance," "disobedience," "inattention," and other real or imagined misbehavior.

Military-style "boot camps" came into vogue in the early '90s as an alternative to juvenile prison. The media spread fears of a new generation of violent teenaged "super-predators," and this solution gained political appeal across the spectrum. Liberals liked that it wasn't prison and usually meant a shorter sentence than conventional detention; conservatives liked the lower costs, military style, and tough discipline. Soon "hoods in the woods" programs, which took kids into the wilderness and used the harsh environment, isolation, and spare rations to similar ends, also rose in popularity, as did "emotional growth" schools, which used isolation and Synanon-style confrontational groups.

Again, little evidence ever supported these programs. When the U.S. Department of Justice began studying the boot camps, it found that they were no more effective than juvenile prison. For a 1997 report to Congress, the department funded a review of the research, which found that the boot camps were ineffective and that there was little empirical support for wilderness programs. In late 2004 the National Institutes of Health released a state-of-the-science consensus statement on dealing with juvenile violence and delinquency. It said that programs that seek to change behavior through "fear and tough treatment appear ineffective."

THE WAY OF WWASP

But as the Martin Lee Anderson case makes clear, tough love continued to thrive. Indeed, the *New York Times* business section reported on tough teen programs as an investment opportunity last year, saying the number of teenagers attending residential programs to deal with drug and behavior problems had quadrupled since 1995. Exposés of programs like Straight or Florida's government-run boot camps almost always include positive anecdotes along with the accounts of abuse. As a result, for parents terrified of drugs, these stories seem to portray the programs as the only ones tough enough to "do what works." Since the media play positive anecdote against negative anecdote, often without citing the negative research data, exposés can actually serve as advertisements. The suggestion that the programs work serves to justify any abuse. In 2004, for example, Time quoted a father who said a tough-love program "improved his [son's] attitude and sense of responsibility," even as it reported that the family removed the child after finding some of the program's disciplinary measures too harsh.

One of the largest chains of currently operating tough love schools is known as the World Wide Association of Specialty Programs (WWASP), sometimes called the World Wide Association of Specialty Programs and Schools. Like Straight, it took tactics from Synanon; its ideology, the language it uses, and its methods for discrediting teens' complaints are eerily similar.

Variously claiming to hold 1,200 to 2,500 teenagers and reporting 2003 revenues of $80 million, the group currently has at least eight affiliates, in Jamaica (Tranquility Bay), South Carolina (Carolina Springs Academy), Nevada (Horizon Academy), Utah (Cross Creek Programs, Majestic Ranch Academy), Georgia (Darrington Academy), Mississippi (Respect Camp), and Iowa (Midwest Academy). WWASP is a series of limited liability corporations that frequently switch corporate officers and names. This strategy is often used to limit losses from lawsuits by disgruntled customers, and until very recently, WWASP has been successful in deterring major law firms from pursuing such cases against it.

Through its public relations representative, James Wall of Freeman Wall Aiello, WWASP denies charges of abuse. But nine of its affiliates have closed following abuse allegations and government investigations. Mexico has shut down three programs since the late '90s; at one, police shot video of teenagers held in outdoor dog cages. (That program currently faces a civil suit by a boy who claims he not only was kept in a dog cage but was sexually assaulted and forced to eat vomit.) In 1998 the U.S. State Department found "credible allegations of physical abuse" at WWASP's facility in Samoa, citing "beatings, isolation, food and water deprivation, choke-holds, kicking, punching, bondage, spraying with chemical agents, forced medication, [and] verbal abuse." It called for an investigation by the local government, which resulted in the program's closure. The man who ran that program, who once admitted to 48 Hours that teens had been bound with duct tape at the Samoa site, now operates the WWASP facility in Iowa.

In 2003 Costa Rican child welfare authorities raided WWASP's Dundee Ranch Academy. They found staff "unqualified to attend to needs of children," "inadequate food and meal portions," and "some punishments [that] qualify as physical and psychological abuse." The owner of the facility was arrested for human rights violations, and a source in the Costa Rican government says a prosecution is imminent. Yet Pillars of Hope Academy, an affiliated program for young adults run by Dundee Ranch's owner, operates in the same building; it is not subject to Costa Rica's regulations for programs aimed at minors.

Last year one WWASP program in upstate New York, the Academy at Ivy Ridge, was forced by the state attorney general to return nearly $2 million for fraudulently claiming to offer New York high school diplomas. It says it is no longer affiliated with WWASP, but it has changed neither its staff nor its treatment methods. (It is currently facing a $100 million class action suit for educational fraud.) Another WWASP affiliate, Spring Creek Lodge in Montana, likewise claims to be independent now, although it has the same staff and still gets referrals through the WWASP phone line and websites. In July a press release announced a new website, troubledteenprograms.org, linking all of the WWASP-associated programs under the name "Teen Revitalization."

WWASP seems to have learned Straight's P.R. lessons well: Deny abuse; smear kids who report problems as drug addicts, liars, and manipulators; insist that the media "balance" negative stories with positive anecdotes; and when the charges begin to stick and the press and regulators have thoroughly discredited a program, simply change its name and reopen, changing location only if necessary.

In an email message, James Wall, the WWASP publicist, says: "Clearly you can speculate about similarities between Straight and WWASPS. However, the two are completely separate organizations with no links whatsoever. You should also note that WWASPS and associated organizations continue to thrive (in terms of growth) despite continued attacks from individuals (online, etc.) and the media."

WWASP seems to have learned from Straight's political and regulatory strategies as well. Since the 2002 election, founder Robert Lichfield, his family members (some of whom run WWASP programs), and their various business entities have donated more than $1 million to the Republican

Party and its candidates. Together the Lichfields and their businesses are the third largest Republican donor in WWASP's home state of Utah, according to the Deseret News. WWASP has moved to block or water down state legislation aimed at reigning in tough love programs in at least two states, Utah and Montana.

In 2004 Marty Stephens, speaker of the Utah House of Representatives, used a procedural maneuver to block a vote on legislation, which backers say had more than enough support to pass, imposing stricter controls on a WWASP facility near Randolph, Utah. Six days later, he received a check from Robert Lichfield for his gubernatorial campaign. Lichfield insisted to the Salt Lake Tribune that "that check had nothing to do with" the bill's blockage. He added: "I'd like to use my means and resources to bless people's lives. Does that also imply influencing policy makers to make good policies that support good family values, quality education, and the things I believe in? Definitely."

Prior to 2005, Montana didn't require teen programs to let the state know they existed, let alone impose regulation. But local and national exposés led to calls for greater oversight. In the 2005 legislative session, Spring Creek Lodge registered five lobbyists and spent at least $50,000 to block a bill that would have imposed strict state rules, according to the *Missoula Independent*. The legislation died in the state House of Representatives. An alternative bill, sponsored by Spring Creek's competitors, passed. It created a governor-appointed board with five members—three of whom represent the industry. One of the members is the "principal" of Spring Creek Lodge.

THE TIDE TURNS?

Thanks to the potent combination of political influence, industry and government fear-mongering, and media malpractice, tough love has so far survived its detractors. But Martin Lee Anderson's death may have marked a turning point.

The case has revealed the politics of tough love in one of its home states, and has turned a new spotlight on the data. In a departure from the usual journalistic pattern, the early coverage of the case consistently cited the research finding boot camps to be no more effective than juvenile prison, and editorials mainly called for their closure.

The movement toward "evidence-based" social policy has been growing since the early '90s, as insurers, patient advocates, and government agencies alike demanded proof that expensive policies produce demonstrable results. It also seems to have spurred at least some journalists to view scientific data as superior to anecdotes when assessing the performance of tough love programs. This has reduced the false balance in prior coverage that simply played success stories against abuse accounts. Some Florida papers even noted how the research and prior abuse scandals had led other states to shut down their government-run boot camps. They cited a Maryland scandal in which the *Baltimore Sun* photographed guards at a state-run boot camp openly beating inmates, which led that state to drop such programs. They also mentioned a similar scandal that prompted a federal investigation of Georgia's public boot camp programs, leading to their closure. Some coverage of the Anderson case noted the 1999 death of 14-year-old Gina Score at a South Dakota boot camp following forced exercise similar to that endured by Anderson, an incident that led that state to shutter its programs.

As the Florida case unfolded, political missteps dogged boot camp supporters. First, the state refused to release the videotape of the boy's beating to the media, leading to an outcry and greater media attention. Guy Tunnell, who had founded and staffed the sheriff's boot camp in which Anderson died, had gone on to head the Florida Department of Law Enforcement; as a result, he was initially in charge of investigating the death. Email messages from Tunnell—who serves on the board of the Drug Free America Foundation—showed that he supported the boot camp he was supposed to be objectively investigating, and that he had adamantly resisted releasing the video. The revelations prompted the appointment of a special prosecutor, generating yet more media attention. No criminal charges have been filed so far, but Anderson's family has filed a $40 million lawsuit against the state.

Because Anderson was African-American, some activists raised the question of racism. (Most teens killed in these programs have been white, since blacks are less likely to be able to afford the private camps and more likely to be incarcerated instead of diverted to public boot camps.) On April 19, students occupied the governor's office in an attempt to spur the arrest of the guards responsible for Anderson's death. Two days later, more than 1,500 people attended a rally at the state Capitol in Tallahassee calling for the state to shut down its boot camps. (Full disclosure: I spoke there about the dangers of the tough love approach.) The event was also aimed at keeping pressure on prosecutors to indict the guards and the nurse who didn't stop the beating. At the rally, two Florida legislators spoke in favor of legislation that would shut down the boot camps. Tunnell was forced to resign as head of the Florida Department of Law Enforcement after he mocked two men invited to speak at the rally, referring to Jesse Jackson as "Jesse James" and to Illinois Sen. Barack Obama (who ultimately did not attend the event) as "Osama bin Laden."

This series of events has placed an unusual spotlight on tough love, connecting it not with re-habilitation but with death, cronyism, and bigotry. Previous deaths haven't generated anywhere near as much activism.

To his credit, Jeb Bush recently signed into law a bill that shuts down the state's youth boot camps. The replacement programs it creates are prohibited from using physical punishment or "harmful psychological intimidation techniques," including humiliation and attempts to "psycho-logically break a child's will." But the kinder, gentler programs will still be run by the county sheriffs, and the regulations (which are limited to Florida, of course) do not apply to the majority of pro-grams, which are private. Right now, children sent to private tough love programs have fewer rights than convicted prisoners. A parent can send a child to a private program where he can be held in-communicado until he turns 18, without any medical diagnosis or rationale for the treatment and without any oversight or means of appeal.

In both public and private programs, policies on the use of force are far less stringent than they are for adult prisoners or psychiatric patients. At the government-run boot camp where Anderson died, for example, restraint, punches, and kicks were routinely applied to teens to punish them for not completing exercise, for "whimpering," or for "breathing heavily." Administrators who reviewed 180 "use of force" reports found inappropriate actions in only eight cases, even though most people would think that beating someone for "breathing heavily" is not acceptable. In a prison or mental hospital, by contrast, force is officially permitted only if the prisoner or patient is an immediate threat to himself or others. Parents who engaged in such practices could be charged with child abuse.

And the parents who send their kids to these camps? For the most part, they are uninformed about the absence of evidence supporting tough love programs and often desperate to save their kids from drugs and delinquency. Until we figure out a better balance between the right of parents to place their kids in whatever programs they choose and the right of kids to be free from inappropri-ate punishment by agents of their parents or the state, the abuse will continue. The shame of it all is that we know hurting kids doesn't help them.

Discussion Questions

1. Discuss the limitations of and controversy surrounding "tough-love" programs for juvenile offenders.
2. Why did boot camps as a sanction for juvenile offenders initially appeal to both Republicans and Liberals? What events regarding boot camps changed the opinion of some?
3. What is WWASP, and why is it discussed in an article on tough-love approaches for juvenile offenders?

34

Jailed for Life After Crimes as Teenagers

By Adam Liptak

EDITOR'S COMMENT

There comes a point in every sentencing decision when sentencing bodies consider the offender's future. Are we going to try to save or rehabilitate the individual? Are we going to try to protect society from this person? Should this individual be punished? These and related questions are asked, perhaps not externally but certainly internally by those tasked with sentencing offenders. There are times when the decision is to give up on an individual and a life sentence, or perhaps capital punishment, is in order. Such is the focus of this selection, in which author Adam Liptak discusses society giving up on teenagers. Historically, society has been reluctant to give up on youth, as they were often viewed as salvageable.

We all make bad decisions sometimes. Typically, however, our bad decisions don't involve criminal or delinquent behavior. Our bad decisions that fall outside the law are rarely brought to the attention of authorities, so we don't get caught. Speeding in traffic is an example. It is illegal. However, drive on any major highway and it is likely that many drivers will exceed the speed limit. Some get ticketed, most won't. Historically when juveniles have made bad decisions to break the law, the penalty has been mitigated in light of age and maturity considerations. Lately, however, we've increasingly seen teens and young adults held accountable for their bad decisions. We expect better decisions from our youth, largely in response to our concern for crime.

There are some individuals who see no good in select individuals. Others believe there's something good in everyone. Life sentences have long been used in corrections throughout the world. However, sentencing teens to life in prison is largely restricted to the United States. Although a few other countries maintain the possibility of sentencing juvenile offenders to life in prison and even fewer actively choose the option, the United States has witnessed a notable number of young adults being sentenced to life in prison. The practice is controversial for obvious reasons; however, the controversy has not discouraged sentencing bodies from imposing the sentence.

Legislators create the laws by which we must abide. They also pass legislation that affects criminal justice practices. Sentencing practices are often influenced by legislative action. Legislators do not act alone, however. We elect individuals into office as our representatives. They are our voice in politics and policy making. Legislators hopefully respond to our wants and wishes. At some point legislators decided that juveniles in the United States should face the possibility of life in prison, that some youth are irreparable. Herein lies the controversy, as some would argue that everyone, especially juveniles, is reparable.

Sentencing a teenager to life in prison sends the message that the individual is hopeless. Are there individuals, particularly young adults, whose actions suggest they are clearly unfit for life in a free society? Strong arguments could be made either way. Victims of violent crimes and their families would likely suggest that the offender be put away for an extended period. Those distanced from the direct effects of the crime may argue otherwise. Giving up on someone, including a juvenile offender, sends a strong message to the public and potential offenders that the criminal justice system is tough on crime, and it tells victims and their families that their interests, and justice, will be served. However, many hope that such a severe penalty is used in moderation and with due caution.

OCALA, Fla.—About 9,700 American prisoners are serving life sentences for crimes they committed before they could vote, serve on a jury or gamble in a casino—in short, before they turned 18. More than a fifth have no chance for parole.

Juvenile criminals are serving life terms in at least 48 states, according to a survey by The *New York Times*, and their numbers have increased sharply over the past decade.

Rebecca Falcon is one of them.

Ms. Falcon, now 23, is living out her days at the Lowell Correctional Institution here. But eight years ago, she was a reckless teenager and running with a thuggish crowd when one night she got drunk on bourbon and ruined her life.

Ms. Falcon faults her choice of friends. "I tried cheerleaders, heavy metal people, a little bit of country and, you know, it never felt right," Ms. Falcon said. "I started listening to rap music and wearing my pants baggy. I was like a magnet for the wrong crowd."

In November 1997 she hailed a cab with an 18-year-old friend named Clifton Gilchrist. He had a gun, and within minutes, the cab driver was shot in the head. The driver, Richard Todd Phillips, 25, took several days to die. Each of the teenagers later said the other had done the shooting.

Ms. Falcon's jury found her guilty of murder, though it never did sort out precisely what happened that night, its foreman said. It was enough that she was there.

"It broke my heart," said Steven Sharp, the foreman. "As tough as it is, based on the crime, I think it's appropriate. It's terrible to put a 15-year-old behind bars forever."

The United States is one of only a handful of countries that does that. Life without parole, the most severe form of life sentence, is theoretically available for juvenile criminals in about a dozen countries. But a report to be issued on Oct. 12 by Human Rights Watch and Amnesty International found juveniles serving such sentences in only three others. *Israel* has seven, *South Africa* has four and *Tanzania* has one.

By contrast, the report counted some 2,200 people in the *United States* serving life without parole for crimes they committed before turning 18. More than 350 of them were 15 or younger, according to the report.

The Supreme Court's decision earlier this year to ban the juvenile death penalty, which took into account international attitudes about crime and punishment, has convinced prosecutors and activists that the next legal battleground in the United States will be over life in prison for juveniles.

Society has long maintained age distinctions for things like drinking alcohol and signing contracts, and the highest court has ruled that youths under 18 who commit terrible crimes are less blameworthy than adults. Defense lawyers and human rights advocates say that logic should extend to sentences of life without parole.

Prosecutors and representatives of crime victims say that a sentence of natural life is the minimum fit punishment for a heinous crime, adding that some people are too dangerous ever to walk the streets.

In the Supreme Court's decision, Justice Anthony M. Kennedy said teenagers were different, at least for purposes of the ultimate punishment. They are immature and irresponsible. They are more susceptible to negative influences, including peer pressure. And teenagers' personalities are unformed.

"Even a heinous crime committed by a juvenile," Justice Kennedy concluded, is not "evidence of ir-retrievably depraved character."

Most of those qualities were evident in Ms. Falcon, who had trouble fitting in at her *Kansas* high school and had been sent by her mother to live with her grandmother in *Florida*, where she received little supervision. She liked to smoke marijuana, and ran with a series of cliques. "I was looking for identity," she said.

Like many other lifers, Ms. Falcon is in prison for felony murder, meaning she participated in a serious crime that led to a killing but was not proved to have killed anyone.

In their report, the human rights groups estimate that 26 percent of juvenile offenders sentenced to life without parole for murder were found guilty of felony murder. A separate Human Rights Watch report on *Colorado* found that a third of juveniles serving sentences of life without parole there had been convicted of felony murder.

The larger question, advocates for juveniles say, is whether any youths should be locked away forever.

At the argument in the juvenile death penalty case, Justice Antonin Scalia said the reasons offered against execution apply just as forcefully to life without parole. Justice Scalia voted, in dissent, to retain the juvenile death penalty.

"I don't see where there's a logical line," he said at the argument last October.

When it comes to Ms. Falcon, the prosecutor in her case said she does not ever deserve to be free. Indeed, she is lucky to be alive.

The prosecutor, Jim Appleman, is convinced that she shot Mr. Phillips. "If she were a 29-year-old or a 22-year-old," he said, "I have no doubt she would have gotten the death penalty."

Ms. Falcon dressed up, as best one can in prison, to meet two journalists not long ago. There was nothing to be done about the plain blue prison dress, with buttons down the front. But she wore gold earrings, a crucifix on a gold chain and red lipstick. Her dark hair was shoulder length, and her eyes were big and brown.

She said her eight years in prison had changed her.

"A certain amount of time being incarcerated was what I needed," she said. "But the law I fell under is for people who have no hope of being rehabilitated, that are just career criminals and habitually break the law, and there's just no hope for them in society. I'm a completely different case."

"My sentence is unfair," she added. "They put you in, and they forget."

TAGGING ALONG ON A HORRIFIC NIGHT

The case of another Florida teenager, Timothy Kane, demonstrates how youths can be sent away for life, even when the evidence shows they were not central figures in a crime.

Then 14, Timothy was at a friend's house, playing video games on Jan. 26, 1992, Super Bowl Sunday, when some older youths hatched a plan to burglarize a neighbor's home. He did not want to stay behind alone, he said, so he tagged along.

There were five of them, and they rode their bikes over, stashing them in the bushes. On the way, they stopped to feed some ducks.

Two of the boys took off at the last moment, but Timothy followed Alvin Morton, 19, and Bobby Garner, 17, into the house. He did not want to be called a scaredy-cat, he said.

"This is," he said in a prison interview, "the decision that shaped my life since."

The youths had expected the house to be empty, but they were wrong. Madeline Weisser, 75, and her son, John Bowers, 55, were home.

While Timothy hid behind a dining room table, according to court records, the other two youths went berserk.

Mr. Morton, whom prosecutors described as a sociopath, shot Mr. Bowers in the back of the neck while he pleaded for his life, killing him. Mr. Morton then tried to shoot Ms. Weisser, but his gun jammed. Using a blunt knife, Mr. Morton stabbed her in the neck, and Mr. Garner stepped on the knife to push it in, almost decapitating her.

"I firmly believe what they were trying to do was take the head as a kind of souvenir," said Robert W. Attridge, who prosecuted the case.

Mr. Morton and Mr. Garner did succeed in cutting off Mr. Bowers's pinkie. They later showed it to friends.

Mr. Morton was sentenced to death. Mr. Garner, a juvenile offender like Mr. Kane, was given a life sentence with no possibility of parole for 50 years.

Mr. Kane was also sentenced to life, but he will become eligible for parole after 25 years, when he will be 39. However, he is not optimistic that the parole board will ever let him out. Had he committed his crime after 1995, when Florida changed its law to eliminate the possibility of parole for people sentenced to life, he would not have even that hope.

Florida is now one of the states with the most juveniles serving life. It has 600 juvenile offenders serving life sentences; about 270 of them, including Ms. Falcon, who committed her crime in 1997, are serving life without parole.

Data supplied by the states on juveniles serving life is incomplete. But a detailed analysis of data from another state with a particularly large number of juvenile lifers, *Michigan*, shows that the mix of the life sentences—those with the possibility of parole and those without—is changing fast.

In Michigan, the percentage of all lifers who are serving sentences without parole rose to 64 percent from 51 percent in the 24 years ended in 2004. But the percentage of juvenile lifers serving such sentences rose to 68 percent from 41 percent in the period. Now two out of three juvenile lifers there have no shot at parole.

The *Times*'s survey and analysis considered juvenile lifers generally, while the human rights report examined juveniles serving life sentences without parole. Both studies defined a juvenile as anyone younger than 18 at the time of the offense or arrest. For some states that could not provide a count based on such ages, the studies counted as a juvenile anyone under the age of 20 at sentencing or admission to prison.

Juvenile lifers are overwhelmingly male and mostly black. Ninety-five percent of those admitted in 2001 were male and 55 percent were black.

Forty-two states and the federal government allow offenders under 18 to be put away forever. Ten states set no minimum age, and 13 set a minimum of 10 to 13. Seven states, including Florida and Michigan, have more than 100 juvenile offenders serving such sentences, the report found. Those sending the largest percentages of their youths to prison for life without parole are *Virginia* and *Louisiana*.

SOME DISMAY OVER SENTENCES

Juvenile lifers are much more likely to be in for murder than are their adult counterparts, suggesting that prosecutors and juries embrace the punishment only for the most serious crime.

While 40 percent of adults sent away for life between 1988 and 2001 committed crimes other than murder, like drug offenses, rape and armed robbery, the *Times* analysis found, only 16 percent of juvenile lifers were sentenced for anything other than murder.

In those same years, the number of juveniles sentenced to life peaked in 1994, at about 790, or 15 percent of all adults and youths admitted as lifers that year. The number dropped to about 390, or 9 percent, in 2001, the most recent year for which national data is available.

Similarly, the number of juveniles sentenced to life without parole peaked in 1996, at 152. It has dropped sharply since then, to 54 last year. That may reflect a growing discomfort with the punishment and the drop in the crime rate.

It is unclear how many juveniles or adults are serving life sentences under three-strikes and similar habitual-offender laws.

Human rights advocates say that the use of juvenile life without parole, or LWOP, is by one measure rising. "Even with murder rates going down," said Alison Parker, the author of the new report, "the proportion of juvenile murder offenders entering prison with LWOP sentences is going up."

The courts that consider the cases of juvenile offenders look at individuals, not trends. But sometimes, as in Mr. Kane's case, they express dismay over the sentences that are required.

"Tim Kane was 14 years and 3 months old, a junior high student with an I.Q. of 137 and no prior association with the criminal justice system," Judge John R. Blue wrote for the three-judge panel that upheld Mr. Kane's sentence. "Tim did not participate in the killing of the two victims."

These days, Mr. Kane, 27, looks and talks like a marine. He is fit, serious and polite. He held a questioner's gaze and called him sir, and he grew emotional when he talked about what he saw that January night.

"I witnessed two people die," he said. "I regret that every day of my life, being any part of that and seeing that."

He does not dispute that he deserved punishment.

"Did I know right from wrong?" he asked. "I can say, yes, I did know right from wrong."

Still, his sentence is harsh, Mr. Kane said, spent in the prison print shop making 55 cents an hour and playing sports in the evenings.

"You have no hope of getting out," he said. "You have no family. You have no moral support here. This can be hard."

Mr. Attridge, the prosecutor, who is now in private practice, said he felt sorry for Mr. Kane. "But he had options," Mr. Attridge said. "He had a way out. The other boys decided to leave."

In the end, the prosecutor said, "I do think he was more curious than an evil perpetrator."

"Could Tim Kane be your kid, being in the wrong place at the wrong time?" he asked. "I think he could. It takes one night of bad judgment and, man, your life can be ruined."

DIFFERENT ACCOUNTS OF A CRIME

Visitors to the women's prison here are issued a little transmitter with an alarm button on it when they enter, in case of emergency. But Ms. Falcon is small and slim and not particularly threatening.

She sat and talked, in a flat Midwest tone married to an urban rhythm, on a concrete bench in an outdoor visiting area. It was pleasant in the shade.

Her mother, Karen Kaneer, said in a telephone interview that her daughter's troubles began in Kansas when she started to hang around with black youths.

"It wasn't the good black boys," Ms. Kaneer said. "It was the ones who get in trouble. She started trying marijuana."

Not pleased with where things were heading, Ms. Kaneer agreed to send Rebecca away, to Panama City, Fla., to Rebecca's grandmother. "It was my husband's idea," Ms. Kaneer said ruefully, referring to Ms. Falcon's stepfather. "Her and my husband didn't have the best of relations."

Ms. Falcon received a piece of unwelcome news about an old boyfriend on the evening of Nov. 18, 1997, and she hit her grandparents' liquor cabinet, hard, drinking a big tumbler of whiskey. Later on, when she joined up with her 18-year-old friend, Mr. Gilchrist, she said, she did not suspect that anything unusual was going to happen. She thought they were taking the cab to a party.

"I didn't know there was going to be a robbery at that time," she said. "I mean, Cliff said things like he was going to try out his gun eventually, but as far as right then that night in that situation I didn't know."

Asked if she played any role in the killing, Ms. Falcon said, "No, sir, I did not."

In a letter from prison, where he is serving a life term, Mr. Gilchrist declined to comment. At his trial, both his lawyer and the prosecutor told the jury that Ms. Falcon was the killer.

The medical evidence suggested that the passenger who sat behind Mr. Phillips killed him. But eyewitnesses differed about whether that was Ms. Falcon or Mr. Gilchrist.

Several witnesses did say that Ms. Falcon had talked about violence before the shooting and bragged about it afterward.

"On numerous occasions she said she wanted to see someone die," Mr. Appleman, the prosecutor, said. Ms. Falcon said the evidence against her was "basically, that I was always talking crazy."

The testimony grew so confused that at one point Mr. Appleman asked for a mistrial, though he later withdrew the request.

Though their verdict form suggested that they concluded that Mr. Gilchrist was the gunman, the jurors remain split about what was proved. "There was no evidence presented to confirm who was the actual shooter," said Mr. Sharp, the jury's foreman.

But Barney Jones, another juror, said he believed Ms. Falcon shot the gun. "She was confused," he said. "She was probably a typical teenager. She was trying to fit in by being a violent person. The people she hung out with listened to gangster rap, and this was a sort of initiation."

Whoever was to blame, Mr. Phillips's death left a terrible void. "Each day we see a cab, the memories of our son and the tragic way he died surfaces," his father and stepmother, Roger and Karen Phillips, wrote at the time of the trial in a letter to Mr. Gilchrist, according to an article in The News-Herald, a newspaper in Panama City.

At the prison here, as Ms. Falcon talked, a photographer started shooting, and she seemed to enjoy the attention, flashing a big smile at odds with the grim surroundings.

It was a break, she explained, from the grinding monotony that is the only life she may ever know. She reads to kill time and to prepare herself in case a Florida governor one day decides to pardon her.

She had just finished a book on parenting.

"If God lets me go and have a kid," she said, "I want to know these things so I can be a good mother."

Discussion Questions

1. Discuss the arguments both in support of and against the use of life sentences without the possibility of parole for juvenile offenders.
2. Do all states allow offenders under age 18 to be sentenced to life in prison without the possibility of parole? Discuss the breakdown of states in relation to their use of the sentence.
3. Should the sentence of life without the possibility of parole for juvenile offenders be restricted to murder cases?

35

Young Lives For Sale

Why More Kids are Getting into the Sex Trade—and How the Feds are Fighting Back

By Bay Fang

EDITOR'S COMMENT

The term crime constitutes many different actions and behaviors. A crime can involve one person murdering another, someone stealing from a grocery store to feed his or her kids, or a prostitute selling sex for money. The motivations for committing crime also vary. Although crimes are often committed for financial reasons, hatred, excitement, and illness could also explain criminal behavior, as can other factors. There is a perception regarding the severity of various types of crime in society. For instance, we all likely agree that murder is the most serious offense; however, there is less agreement with less serious crimes. What would you consider worse: stealing a bicycle or vandalism? Some would say vandalism; others believe stealing a bike is worse.

Some consider prostitution a crime without a victim. Some believe there are crimes that don't involve victims, others believe every crime has a victim. Other examples of alleged victimless crimes include illegal gambling and drug use. It is argued that while there may not be an immediately identifiable victim in each of these crimes, there are certainly individuals who suffer as a result of their occurrence. For instance, the sale of untaxed drugs and the social irresponsibility associated with drug use suggest that all in society could be considered victims of drug use. Illegal gambling also results in untaxed profits and leads some individuals to abandon their social responsibilities when they lose money. Prostitution is viewed by some as the exploitation of women for sex and money.

Counter to these arguments, however, is the argument that such victimless crimes involve consensual acts. The gambler chooses to gamble, the drug user chooses to use drugs, and the prostitute chooses to engage in prostitution. Nobody is forcing these offenders to potentially harm themselves. Or are they? This article by Bay Fang highlights the discouraging underbelly of teenage prostitution. What may seem to some as a victimless crime, prostitution sometimes involves young females being exploited and controlled by pimps and madams.

The exploitation of females through prostitution is disheartening to say the least. The situation is even more troubling when the prostitutes are teenagers who have few other options in life. They may have nobody to care for them, or they may have run away from home and, needless to say, got caught up in a very difficult situation. The challenge for society is to figure out how to prevent the perpetuation of teenage prostitution and how to best help address the exploitation of females in general.

One of the more radical approaches to many victimless crimes is to decriminalize or legalize such practices. Decriminalization refers to maintaining penalties, yet making them so inconsequential that the laws pertaining to the action are rarely enforced.

Legalization refers to legalizing a particular behavior. Some suggest decriminalizing or legalizing some or all victimless crimes. This argument is based on the belief that decriminalization or legalization eliminates the criminal element and can generate substantial government resources in taxes. For instance, pimps would be out of a job if prostitution was legalized, and drug dealers would be taxed and have to compete with commercial enterprises. It is unlikely that the legalization or even decriminalization of all victimless crimes will be fully recognized any time soon. There are hints of change, however, in the legalization of prostitution in areas within Nevada, in proposals to legalize marijuana making it to the ballot during elections in several states, and in the increased presence of casino gambling throughout the United States. For better or for worse, the offenses deemed victimless crimes may soon not be considered offenses or crimes at all.

LOS ANGELES—Kristie was 13 when she met the first of her four "daddies." She had run away from home in the Southwest, and friends introduced her to a tall, good-looking man, who said the red-haired teenager was sexy and had potential. Pretty soon, he had her prostituting herself on the streets of Las Vegas—and then Los Angeles, Atlanta, and Phoenix. She and her "wifies," the other girls working under the same pimp, most of whom were also in their teens, would be brought to a city, work from 7 P.M. until sunrise, then move on. The now 15-year-old (who, like the other girls, doesn't want her real name used) stopped only after she was arrested, in July. From the beginning of the year until then, she estimates, she had over 100 sex partners—but she had long since stopped counting.

The trafficking in children for sex was once thought to be a problem beyond America's borders. But the FBI and the Justice Department have now started focusing intently on the issue—and what they've found is shocking. Thousands of young girls and boys are falling victim to violent pimps, who move them from state to state, which makes it a federal matter. The younger they are, the more they're worth on the street. "There is a greater and greater demand for younger and younger kids," says Ernie Allen, president of the National Center for Missing and Exploited Children. "America doesn't look. People are shocked and horrified when they hear these girls' stories. They say, 'That doesn't happen here. It happens in Thailand. Or the Philippines.' But once you start shining a light on it, you find it everywhere."

GETTING SERIOUS

Two years ago, the FBI and the Justice Department launched something called the Innocence Lost initiative. More than 40 FBI agents have been dedicated to task forces in the 14 cities with the highest incidence of child prostitution—places like Atlanta, Detroit, and Minneapolis. Since the campaign's inception, the feds have obtained almost 40 federal indictments of accused sex traffickers and pimps. Earlier this month, a federal grand jury indicted Jaron Brice, 29—also known as "Jay Bird" and "Daddy"—in Washington, D.C., on 17 counts related to the sex trafficking of minors. And "in a few months," says David Johnson, director of the Crimes Against Children unit of the FBI, "there will be a round of cases that is bigger than anything that's happened before. We are not looking just to do a quick arrest; we are trying to remove an entire enterprise."

The roots of Innocence Lost can be found in investigations begun in Oklahoma City back in 2003, after a series of murders of prostitutes who worked at truck stops. "We went out and said, 'Is there some federal intervention we could do to combat all this violent crime?'" says Mike Beaver, the FBI Crimes Against Children coordinator in Oklahoma City. "The more we looked, the more we determined that we needed to work child prostitution." The investigations led to the discovery of a loose network of more than 45 pimps and over 100 prostitutes, who recruited girls from Oklahoma City

---

and followed trucking routes to Denver, Miami, Houston, and Dallas. Fourteen pimps have since been convicted on federal charges as a result of the Oklahoma City probes, with sentences as long as 210 months. Three major interstates cross Oklahoma City, and the truck stops here, such as Pilot and TravelCenters of America, are like little cities, with everything from restaurants to TV lounges. The parking lots can cover acres. The back row of each lot is known as "Party Row," and the truckers know that's where the girls are. Law enforcement officers monitoring CB radio traffic regularly hear girls ask, "Hey truckers, anyone want some commercial company?" If someone responds, they switch to a different frequency, then get down to business. "I'm blond-haired, blue-eyed, 34C . . . if you want to play with this baby doll, tell me what color your house is," she will say, referring to his truck. He will often flash his lights so she knows where to go. A girl can have dozens of "dates" a night but will not stop until she has made her "trap," the amount of money she has to bring home to her pimp.

OWNERSHIP

Cindy (not her real name) is 14, with dyed blond hair and an $800 trap. Her pimp was Michael Thomas, FBI officials say, whose street name was "1-8," a reference to time in an Oklahoma City gang. He had tattooed on his girls' bodies the letters POE, for "Pimpin' One Eight." He would buy girls from other pimps, for as little as $50, give them names like Orgasm, and send them out to truck stops, charging $60 for oral sex, $80 for intercourse, and $100 for both. When Cindy told Thomas she wanted to leave his "stable," he had another girl stab her in her arms and hands, according to the FBI.

A University of Pennsylvania study from 2001 estimates that close to 300,000 children nationwide are at risk of falling victim to some sort of sexual exploitation. Outreach workers concur, saying that of the 1 million to 1.5 million runaway children in the country, about a third have some brush with prostitution. "When we began initiating investigations around the country," says Johnson, "we found it everywhere we looked."

On the "strolls" of Sunset Boulevard and Figueroa, in South-Central Los Angeles, girls step out from the shadows in tiny skirts and stiletto heels. Detective Keith Haight sizes them up. He doesn't bother stopping unless they look underage, but it's hard to tell nowadays. Haight has been working these streets for 25 years and has seen the girls getting younger. This drop in age is due both to the rise of the Internet, which provides ready access to child pornography, and to the fear of HIV/AIDS. "Back then, if you found a 15- or 16-year-old, that was a big deal. But now, they're 11 or 12," he says. "If you go to the bus station, you can see the runaways coming off the buses, and you can tell the pimps waiting for them."

Many of today's pimps have gang ties, and they've moved from murder and robbery to pimping. "There has been a trend of organized crime moving away from traditional commodities like drugs, tobacco, and arms, to kids," says NCMEC's Allen. "They are reusable, inexpensive, with a huge consumer market that is enormously profitable with next to no risk. Nobody cares. Nobody is looking for them. They are the forgotten."

Kristie has a ponytail and eyes that dart around the room. Sometimes, it's easy to forget that the articulate teenager prowling for johns is just that—a teenage girl. She glibly instructs a visitor on how to outsmart the vice cops. "You never offer anything until you're up in the room with him," she says. "You tell them you're a private dancer. When you hug him, make sure he only has one wallet— if he has another lump, it could be a badge. Check to see that there's luggage in his room, with the tags still on it. And always, always, say you're 18."

EYES AND SMILES

At truck stops in California, girls often wear jeans and carry a backpack, looking as if they're studying. "But there is something about their eyes, and the way they smile at you, that tells you they're not just regular kids," says James Morrow, an outreach worker for a nonprofit called Children of the Night, who used to frequent truck stops to educate both the girls and the truckers—until threats from the pimps made that too dangerous. Sometimes the same girls will travel to Texas, Arizona, and Oklahoma, greeting truckers in each place by name.

The girls' stories sound scarily similar. Kristie's parents are divorced, and she was raped at the age of 8 by one of her mother's boyfriends. Linda, a 14-year-old from Arizona, never met her father. She was raped repeatedly by her stepbrothers when she was 6 and 7, and she fell in with a pimp who convinced her to start prostituting herself when she was 13.

Because of their backgrounds, many of the girls just crave attention. "I wanted someone to look out for me," says Fay, who grew up in a wealthy family in New York City but was left by her parents to be brought up by strict grandparents. "I needed a father—someone older, who could figure out my little tricks." Pimps play mind games to make their prostitutes compete with one another for attention. "I felt wanted all the time—by somebody," explains Kristie. "I felt like I was good at something."

BAPTIZED

Pimps also use the promise of riches to entice girls into "the Game." But while the girls can make thousands of dollars a night, they never keep much of it. If they do, they get "baptized," or beaten by their pimps. Kristie's pimp would rape her if she did not bring in enough money, saying things like, "I know you don't want Daddy to do it like this, but you have to be punished." "The average life expectancy of a child after getting into prostitution," says Johnson, citing homicide or HIV/AIDS as the main causes of death, "is seven years." Tom O'Brien, the criminal division chief of the Los Angeles U.S. attorney's office, describes a conversation he had with one 14-year-old prostitute who was testifying against her pimp. "I told her, 'When I was your age, I thought I'd live forever.' She looked me in the eye and said, 'Mr. O'Brien, I'll be dead before I'm 21.' "

Children of the Night is housed in a nondescript building in the San Fernando Valley. A big teddy bear on the counter greets visitors, and the dorm-like rooms are plastered with posters of pop stars. The difference between this and a regular boarding school is that the teenagers here are all former prostitutes. They have parole officers, social workers, therapists. They are tested every week for HIV/AIDS. A list in the office keeps track of when and where each girl has to testify against her pimp. When Lois Lee started this program 26 years ago, local government social services agencies told her they couldn't take in prostitutes. She says that the new federal interest is a step in the right direction." But what do you do with them once you've got them?" she asks. "Where's the love, the family, the programs, the schools?"

Kristie has been at the shelter for three weeks, and she says, with a toss of her head, that she thinks she'll stay. She has been arrested twice, she says, but the first time, she said to her parole officer, "I'm not going to stay here. I know California like the back of my hand. You won't be able to find me." When she was released from juvenile detention hall, she immediately cut off her parole bracelet and ran away, back to the streets. Haight, sitting in his car on Sunset Boulevard, says he has seen hundreds like her—and more coming in every day. "It's like America has lost its innocence," the detective says. "Little girls just aren't little girls anymore."

Discussion Questions

1. What can be done to address the problem of teenage prostitution? What steps could be taken to address prostitution in general?

2. Discuss the anticipated effects associated with legalizing prostitution. How would this impact the young girls involved in the trade?

3. Why do some teenage girls become involved in prostitution, and what are the risks? In lieu of the harms involved, why don't the girls simply quit?

36

Stepchildren of Justice

By Carl M. Cannon

EDITOR'S COMMENT

The incarceration rate in the United States has increased dramatically beginning in the early 1980s. The "get-tough" and "lock 'em up" approach to crime control has had both positive and negative conse- quences. The increased incarceration rate has contributed, in part, to the declining crime rates in recent years. Our willingness to incarcerate so freely has deterred more than one offense. On the other hand, increased incarceration rates contribute to many significant social problems, including the lack of reha- bilitation programs offered in prisons that help offenders who have difficulty reentering society; the resources spent on prison that could be used for education, health care, and other means of social well-being; and the increase in the number of single- or no-parent families. The latter is the topic of this selection.

Imagine you're an eight-year-old, inner-city child with a 12-year-old sister and a 6-year-old brother. Your father has been in prison since you were three. Mom has raised you and your siblings during most of your life. Times have been tough, as living on one, low-wage income makes for trying times. As fate would have it, your mother was recently arrested for selling drugs. Yesterday she began a six-year sentence. You and your siblings have just been turned over to the custody of the state.

What is the likelihood of you later committing delinquency and/or crime? You grew up in an impoverished neighborhood where drug use, crime, and general disorder were accepted and expected. The answer is that you're much more likely to engage in crime than are your counterparts who were raised in environments in contrast to yours. Several of the more prominent criminological theories, including social disorganization theory, labeling theory, and differential association theory offer suggestions as to why.

What should we do with children of incarcerated parents? Put them on an "at-risk for crime" list and keep close tabs on them? This article discusses the feasibility of mentoring children of incarcerated parents in what could be considered a preemptive strike to prevent future criminal behavior. Such pro- grams seem to offer hope for abstinence from crime and, at the very least, provide extra attention for chil- dren facing the challenges of growing up in a single-parent family and likely no other source of income.

Yet, is a mentorship program that speculates that parental involvement in the criminal justice sys- tem will lead to a child's involvement in the system an overreaction? There are many children who will not resort to a life of crime, even though they have an incarcerated parent. Couldn't the resources be bet- ter used elsewhere? Crime prevention efforts typically involve a sense of uncertainty as we cannot always accurately predict who will engage in crime and when and where a crime will occur. For instance, the locks we have on our doors may be a waste of resources as it is likely that nobody is trying or has tried to break into our house. Yet, we keep the locks because our investment will pay off after that one time some-one tries to break in and is deterred by a locked door. The same argument could be made for mentorship of at-risk children. The resources we save from preventing one child from entering the criminal justice system will free up resources to continue the mentorship programs.

The financial savings, however, are not the true benefit of targeting and mentoring children of incarcerated parents. Positively impacting a potentially troubled life is the true benefit.

Jessica Bailey, like all other sixth-graders in her Nevada school district, heard the spiel from a local police officer on resisting peer pressure to do drugs. But Jessica knows as much as any cop about the human cost of addiction—and about the profound implications of getting caught in the criminal-justice system. Jessica's mother was in prison on drug charges when the D.A.R.E. officer visited her school, and her father is out of the picture. At night Jessica cuddles up with her stuffed pink bunny rabbit and by day she pursues a black belt in tae kwon do. Her grandfather, who has custody of her, says that at 11 years of age, she can already spot a drug buy going down on Reno's streets.

For help in life, Jessica attends group counseling sessions for the children of inmates that is run by a local community organization on a shoestring budget, and she goes on outings with Janet Walford, her mentor in the Big Sisters program. "She's a good listener," Jessica says, "and a good friend."

At least someone is paying attention. The government does not keep track of such children, or even know how many there are. Social scientists have an idea, however, and the numbers are staggering. Moreover, various studies show a pronounced, if hard-to-measure, correlation between a parent in prison and a child later turning to crime.

"The significance of that" correlation, says Denise Johnston, co-founder of the Center for Children of Incarcerated Parents, "is that the next generation of prisoners is going to come from the current generation of prisoners."

In Washington, and a handful of state capitals, this message is beginning to sink in. The question is, What should government do about it? Many of the nation's most prominent criminologists have lined up behind one obvious solution—cut back on the long-term incarceration of so many drug offenders. But repealing harsh sentencing laws is politically harder than passing them.

Social scientists champion another approach that raises fewer hackles: mentoring the children of inmates. President Bush has saluted these efforts several times, including once in a State of the Union address. "It is a necessary program," Bush said last year, lauding a mentor in an organization called Amachi.

And it's cheaper: about $1,000 a year to mentor an inmate's child versus $26,650 a year to incarcerate a prisoner. Three years ago, the Health and Human Services Department dispersed about $9 million in grants for mentoring. In the current fiscal year, that number will approach $50 million, which represents a big increase, but only a fraction of the need.

"ALL THE KIDS SHOULD COUNT"

A generation ago, the United States embarked on a vast social experiment. Facing soaring crime rates and armed with research indicating that a small number of habitual criminals were responsible for a large share of the mayhem, state legislatures and Congress, backed by governors and presidents from both parties, enacted a montage of measures, including "mandatory minimums" for drug and gun offenses, "three-strikes-and-you're-out" laws, and "truth-in-sentencing" decrees that virtually abolished parole.

A prison population already on the rise ballooned. In 1970 on any given day, 200,000 people were locked up in America's state and federal prisons. Thirty-six years later, that figure has increased to more than 1.4 million. When the 700,000 in local jails are added, the number of people behind bars comes to 2.1 million—four times the average per capita rate in previous decades.

Victims' advocates are quick to say that the effects on the nation's streets were even more dramatic: In the past decade, murder, rape, robbery, and assault have declined annually, not just per capita but in raw numbers as well. Consequently, these laws remain popular with the public and with legislators. But many of the nation's most prominent criminologists maintain that the real causes for declining criminal activity are a robust economy, better policing techniques, and the end of "Baby Boom II." The return to demographic norms means that fewer young males—the key crime cohort—are out on the streets.

This debate will not be reconciled anytime soon. But both sides agree on a couple of things: The children of these inmates are innocent of any crime, and a society that locks up parents has some obligation to their children. Both a moral component and a self-interested one attach to this equation. The altruistic rationale for action is that the children of offenders are also victims, and often come from the most-disadvantaged families in American society. The self-preservation component stems from that same point. Without policies to break the cross-generational recidivism rate, any social policy that puts more people behind bars is intrinsically self-defeating because it practically ensures future generations of offenders.

Calculating by the average number of children per inmate shows that at least 2.8 million minors in this country have a parent behind bars. Only about half of them were living with those parents when they were arrested, but that is scant consolation. In fact, 2.8 million children is a vast undercount. The reason is that most of the people incarcerated in the United States in any given year are in local jails, not prisons—and jails have revolving doors. The annual inmate counts, taken on June 30 and December 31, provide only one-day snapshots of how many people are behind bars at that moment. What they don't reveal is how many people were locked up for some period of time during the calendar year. Johnston, a Southern California pediatrician who has worked with inmates' children for two decades, points out that the Los Angeles County jail system housed more than 100,000 inmates in 2004. Yet the census counted only 22,000, Johnston says.

"So if you do it that way, you're missing 80,000 people in Los Angeles County alone, and if you're talking about the effects on children, you have to consider the mother of preschoolers who served three months in jail—and missed being tallied," Johnston said. "All the kids should count."

She estimates that the number of children whose parents have been jailed or imprisoned sometime in their child's life surpasses 10 million. Using different criteria, W. Wilson Goode, the head of a Philadelphia-based mentoring group, estimates that 7.3 million children in the United States have a parent who is behind bars, on parole, or under supervision by the criminal-justice system. It is those numbers that make the stakes so high.

"I'm here on behalf of your children," was the way that Goode put it to inmates in a Hampton, Fla., jail. "The reason is that if we do nothing—if we do nothing—seven out of 10 of your children will end up where you are."

ANOTHER PHILADELPHIA STORY

"City of Brotherly Love" is not Philadelphia's civic slogan. It's that the word "Philadelphia" means in Greek, a name that William Penn, the founder of the colony of Pennsylvania, chose to promote a sense of community. Those who follow sports know that Philadelphians often mock Penn's vision. Philadelphia is where they boo the home team, and where Eagles fans once threw snowballs at a guy dressed up as Santa. Phillies fans booed Mayor John Street at the ceremonies for a new baseball park that opened in 2004.

But when it comes to helping the children of prison inmates, most roads lead to Philadelphia. The first modern American "penitentiary"—its religious roots and redemptive goals are revealed in that word—was operated by the Quakers, who refitted Philadelphia's Walnut Street jail in the late 1700s. One of their initial reforms was to remove children from the prison. That sensibility remains alive in Philadelphia, where brotherly (and sisterly) love is on display at the national headquarters of Big Brothers Big Sisters of America.

Big Brothers got its start in the earliest days of the 20th century after an Ohio-born New York City newsman, Ernest K. Coulter, helped his paper launch a crusade for a juvenile court system. The campaign succeeded, and in 1902, New York created its first Children's Court. Judge Julius Mayer, appointed to preside over it, noticed that a huge percentage of the troubled boys in the system had no father at home. The concept of mentoring young people from outside their own families had been catching on in the world of social service, and Mayer personally recruited New Yorkers to mentor the wayward boys who came through his courtroom. This effort impressed Coulter, who left the news business to clerk in Mayer's court (while attending law school). In 1904, Coulter was invited to speak at a luncheon at the Men's Club of the Central Presbyterian Church of New York.

"There is only one possible way to serve that [troubled] youngster," Coulter said at the luncheon. "And that is to have some earnest, true man volunteer to be his big brother, to look after him, help him do right; make the little chap feel that there is at least one human being in this great city who takes a personal interest in him, who cares whether he lives or dies. I call for a volunteer."

As he made that request, Coulter raised his own hand. Thirty-nine Presbyterian men were in the audience. Thirty-nine hands rose along with Coulter's. "Big Brothers" was launched. In time, it became a national movement, relocated to Philadelphia, and merged with Big Sisters. Their famous formula was well known, and simple: At least one hour a week (and two hours twice a month) of quality time between an adult and a child, for at least one year.

But did the program make a difference in the lives of the young people being mentored? Big Brothers Big Sisters was convinced that it did, and in the mid-1990s, the group took a rare step in the nonprofit world: It hired an outside authority to evaluate its approach.

The organization chosen was another Philadelphia nonprofit, Public/Private Ventures, chartered to improve the effectiveness of social programs for the needy. With grant money from the Pew Charitable Trusts (also based in Philadelphia) and others, P/PV tapped two scholars on its staff, Joseph P. Tierney and Jean Baldwin Grossman, to design and administer a study comparing the behavior of kids being mentored by a Big Brother or a Big Sister with their peers on a waiting list.

"Big Brothers Big Sisters was supremely confident that what they were doing was right," Tierney recalled. "I was not."

He and Grossman compared rates of school attendance, academic performance, aggressive behavior, relationships with friends and family members, and the avoidance of drugs and alcohol. "We ran the models, and the results came in: positive, positive, positive, positive, positive," Tierney said. "I nearly fell out of my chair."

Tierney had empirical proof that Judge Mayer's intuition was right. Little Brothers and Little Sisters were 46 percent less likely to initiate drug use than their peers, and 27 percent less likely to begin using alcohol. They were one-third less likely to hit a classmate, and half as likely to skip classes. Their grades were better. The study attracted scant attention from the mainstream press, but its significance was not missed in social-science circles.

"These findings were extraordinary," recalls University of Pennsylvania political scientist John Dilulio, the former head of the White House Office of Faith-Based and Community Initiatives, "and the implications even more so."

THE EDUCATION OF "BIG JOHN"

Dilulio is a stout, gregarious South Philly guy who, after earning his Ph.D. from Harvard in political science, made a name for himself in academia in the late 1980s and early 1990s by advancing the theory that America's then-soaring violent crime rates resulted from the coddling of criminals.

He promoted his view in outlets ranging from *The Wall Street Journal* to *The New York Times* under memorable headlines such as "Prisons Are a Bargain" and "Let 'Em Rot." In a provocative 1995 essay in *The Weekly Standard,* Dilulio warned that falling crime rates were illusionary, because "the demographic fuses of America's ticking crime bomb are already burning." Who would bring this impending crime wave? According to Dilulio, the answer was America's increasingly remorseless juvenile delinquents. The headline said it all: "The Coming of the Super-Predators."

It was a choice of words that Dilulio would come to regret. For starters, the predicted wave of violence never materialized. Instead, even as Republican presidential nominee Bob Dole used "super-predators" imagery in his 1996 White House bid, crime rates kept falling. A second factor that gave Dilulio pause was his own scholarship. While conservative social critics—and politicians of both parties—were quick to credit the rise in the incarceration rate with lowering the violent-crime rate in the United States, Dilulio and his research partners were discovering that a large percentage of those being locked up—many for very long prison terms—were first-time drug offenders who posed little threat to anyone except themselves.

As the evidence accumulated that the United States was incarcerating record numbers of people who were essentially drug addicts, Dilulio's own views evolved. He publicly questioned the wisdom of mandatory drug sentences and began referring to juvenile offenders as "kids" instead of "predators." Kids, he said, need love and guidance from a mature adult—adding that they were unlikely to find such role models in prison. By 1999, Dilulio was writing op-ed pieces with headlines such as "Drug Sentences Run Amok" and "Two Million Prisoners Are Enough." New research and new facts had convinced Dilulio that a different direction was needed.

The emphasis, he believed, must be on breaking a self-perpetuating cycle that shoved the same individuals—and the same families—through the pitiless revolving doors of the criminal-justice system year after year. The Tierney study had shown that mentoring the children of inmates was one obvious solution. Doing it on a national scale would entail enlisting government, faith-based community groups, private-sector donors, philanthropies, and individual volunteers in the same efforts.

This principle was not strictly conservative, and it wasn't partisan either. In 1996, President Clinton signed a welfare reform measure that encouraged states to allow community and faith-based groups to provide federally funded services to the needy. In his bid to succeed Clinton, Vice President Gore warned his party against embracing hollow secularism," while in Texas expanding the opportunities of faith-based organizations to serve the poor became the rhetorical cornerstone of Gov. George W. Bush's "compassionate conservatism."

Bush began by reaching out to a professor from Philadelphia: Dilulio was invited to Austin in February 1999 for a meeting with a small group of social policy experts. Bush took a liking to Dilulio, often giving him the last word on a topic.

At one point, the governor asked the group for "one big new idea on compassion." Dilulio replied that America was a land where, on any given day, 2 million children had a mother or father in prison or jail. The best way to address this predicament, he told Bush, would be a national initiative "matching low-income children of prisoners with loving, caring, year-round, lifelong adult mentors mobilized from inner-city churches." Bush seemed stunned by the number of children involved, and was impressed with Dilulio's proposed solution. Before Dilulio left Austin, Bush gave him a bear hug and a nickname.

By the summer of 1999, the Bush campaign's domestic policy shop had brought "Big John" into the loop on social issues, and he was drafting speeches on compassion for the governor. Dilulio believed that faith-based volunteer groups, in general, and the mentoring of at-risk kids, in particular, were a big part of the answer to America's social pathologies. Narrowing the focus even further, Dilulio proposed establishing a systematic model to mentor the children of prison inmates.

Dilulio and Tierney were more interested in faith-based groups than ones that depended on government grants, so they looked for a way to adopt the mentoring techniques of Big Brothers Big Sisters of America without being part of it. Big Brothers Big Sisters is a secular organization and, as such, has easy access to local, state, and federal money.

They considered partnering with Angel Tree, which gives Christmas presents to the children of inmates. But for all of the goodwill that Angel Tree sows, it is not a mentoring group—it's an evangelizing Christian program run by Prison Fellowship Ministries. This wasn't a perfect fit, either.

Tierney and Dilulio then attempted to spin off an organization from the pastors and lay leaders in Philly's inner-city churches, but this approach quickly bogged down in local politics. Finally it dawned on Dilulio and Tierney that if they wanted a faith-based (but ecumenical) community group to mentor inmates' children, they would have to start one. So they did. After picking up some seed money and office space, they opened their doors in September 2000.

There was one catch, though: Where could they find a dynamic leader to run their group?

WHO KNOWS WHAT GOD HAS BROUGHT US?

At the beginning of this decade, Wilson Goode tended to be remembered outside Philadelphia—if he was remembered at all—as the mayor who authorized the 1985 bombing of a row house occupied by an armed back-to-nature cult known as MOVE. Philadelphians remembered that incident, too, but they knew more about Goode: that the MOVE tragedy happened in his second year in office; that he served two more years, ran for re-election, and served another four; that when he left office, Philadelphia's bond rating had been restored; and that Goode had gone on to serve in the Clinton administration's Education Department and, while doing so, had prepared himself for a second career in the ministry by earning a doctorate in theology.

But there were things about Goode that not even his close friends knew. One of them was that he was the son of an incarcerated father. And that, as a kid, Goode was headed for trouble himself until the intercession of a pastor and his wife. "They became my Big Brother and Big Sister," he recalled. "When John Dilulio came to me, the question that he was really posing was, 'Did I want to use the influence and knowledge I'd accumulated to enrich myself—or to enrich the lives of others?' It took me about 30 seconds to decide."

The group Goode agreed to lead is Amachi—its name the inspiration of Tim Merrill, a Baptist pastor from Camden, N.J., who helped get the program running. Merrill was on the Internet one day when he came across the word "amachi," defined in the Ibo language (which is spoken in Nigeria) as meaning "who knows what God has brought us through this child?"

Amachi also turned to Big Brothers Big Sisters of America, the mentoring group that had originally inspired Dilulio and is headquartered in the city.

When Dilulio paid a personal call on Judy Vredenburgh, the president and chief executive officer of BBBSA, he couldn't have found a more receptive audience.

"I told John, 'Put your sales materials away,'" Vredenburgh recalled. "Mentoring children whose families are in the criminal-justice system is so deep in our history and culture. Remember, it started with Ernest Coulter—in juvenile court!"

Big Brothers Big Sisters was the logical group for Amachi to tap into. It already knew how to match mentors and kids, and it already was mentoring thousands of kids with parents in prison. Second, Big Brothers Big Sisters could show faith-based groups how to avoid church-state pitfalls.

"Although a lot of our volunteers are religious people, Big Brothers Big Sisters is a completely secular organization—and that's precisely why we're important in this formula," says Vredenburgh.

If mentoring is an ecumenical calling, it's a bipartisan one as well. Sen. John Ensign, a conservative Nevada Republican, is a Big Brother. So is Rep. Adam Schiff, a liberal California Democrat. The two have sponsored joint resolutions in support of Big Brothers Big Sisters. Last summer, they quietly encouraged their colleagues on Capitol Hill to become mentors.

"Having a Little Brother has made a tremendous impact on *my* life," Ensign said at a June event marking the group's 100th anniversary. He then introduced his "Little," a high school senior named Donzale Butler whom Ensign has mentored since the boy was 9. Schiff told of being matched with a boy named David McMillan, then 7 years old, who filled out a questionnaire saying that his three wishes were a Big Brother, a puppy, and "a beautiful world." That was two decades ago. Schiffs "Little" isn't so little anymore. McMillan graduated from Yale and wrote for *Judging Amy,* a CBS television drama about a single mom who worked as a juvenile court judge.

GOING TO JAIL

One hurdle for Amachi is that inmates' children often come from rough neighborhoods. A second dilemma is that the children of inmates are an especially vulnerable population. Goode worried that volunteers would sign up with the best of intentions but quit when the demands of this extra-challenging group of kids and their caregivers got to be too much. His concerns led Goode to the sanctuary of the inner city, to predominantly African-American churches where the mentors would already know the neighborhood—and know the score.

In recruiting sessions, Goode bluntly told the would-be mentors that if they weren't sure they could stick with the program for a year, not to bother, because if they faded away they would inflict more heartbreak on the children. Goode is convinced that the children of inmates are even more susceptible to feelings of abandonment, and for that reason, Amachi reverses the order by which matches are made.

"Big Brothers Big Sisters says you get the children first, then you get the volunteers," Goode told a group of pastors and social workers in Hampton. "My philosophy is that you get the volunteers first—*for this group of children.* If you find a child who wants a mentor and it takes six months to find a volunteer, you've exacted another stress on that family. In Philadelphia, we had 450 volunteers before we had a single child."

Another singular obstacle facing Amachi is obtaining parental permission. Simply put, if you want to mentor the children of inmates, you need to go where the inmates are—the cell blocks of prisons and jails—and get signed permission. That's not easy, particularly among the men, who typically were not the caregivers of their children before going to prison. These men, moreover, often fathered multiple children with different women and faced questions of paternity.

Some inmates have trouble envisioning other people mentoring their sons and daughters. It's common for an inmate to tell Goode: "What you need to do, Reverend Goode, is get me out of here so I can go home and mentor my own kids." Goode is not unsympathetic, but he urges them to be realistic and to think of their children's future.

Some inmates bring that up themselves, quite poignantly. In one Pennsylvania penitentiary, Goode met a man serving a long stretch who said he'd met his father for the first time in the prison yard—his dad was an inmate in the same facility. "I have a son who I have not seen," this prisoner added in tones of resignation. "I guess I will see him for the first time in jail, too."

During another prison recruiting trip, a female inmate introduced Goode to her cellmate—her own daughter.

On his visit to Hampton, Goode is scheduled to take two dozen volunteers—and one journalist—inside the local jails. Eighteen sullen men, 14 of whom are black, file into a room in their orange jumpsuits. About half of them raise their hands when asked if they have children. But only four or five agree to fill out the card that could give their kids a mentor. A young inmate who has five children—he can't be older than 24—is not one of them. Tall and handsome, sporting dreadlocks and a tight smile, he pushes the paper away.

Goode confesses later that he'd rather do this work only in women's prisons, but adds, "You have to reach some of the men. But it's hard."

Afterward, Goode takes a smaller group to a lockup across town to meet with nine female inmates. Their racial ratio is the same as the men's—two are white—but everything else about this encounter is different.

"How many of you have children?" he asks. Every hand goes up. This time the women are rapt while Goode tells his personal story. When he explains what "Amachi" means, one murmurs, "Amen!"

When he asks who wants to fill out a card, they all reach out. "My son is 3. Is that too young?"

"My boy is 24," adds another. "He's in the service. He's doing OK. But my 19-year-old—"

As he walks out of the cell block, all nine women break into applause. In the elevator, Goode is shown the cards with the children's names on them, and he smiles wanly and lets out a deep sigh.

LOVE IS WHERE WE FIND IT

A central underlying tension in the mentoring movement is that the mere presence of an unrelated adult in a youngster's life can serve as a constant, if unspoken, rebuke of the person who is supposed to give children direction—the parent.

For this reason, mentoring advocates are careful to emphasize studies suggesting that successful Big Brother and Big Sister matches bolster the bond between a parent and a child. "We're not here trying to replace the parent," Goode tells inmates and mentor volunteers alike. "Research shows that when there is a mentor in the life of the child, the relationship between the parent and child becomes stronger."

Still, that persistent challenge to Goode from inmates—*"Get me out of here so I can mentor my own kids"*—haunts this issue.

Since the closing of the District of Columbia's Lorton Prison in Northern Virginia four years ago, Carol Fennelly, a longtime Washington activist on behalf of the poor and dispossessed, has worked tirelessly to keep the District's children connected to fathers who were sent to far-flung prisons in other states.

Fennelly's imaginative solutions include teleconferencing from behind prison walls; "Summer Camp Behind Bars," in which kids visit their inmate fathers in the penitentiary (often for the first time); and the Father to Child Reading Program. Fennelly herself goes into prison, tapes an inmate father reading a book, and then mails his child the tape and the book.

Late last summer, Fennelly hosted a picnic for some of these children, and some recently paroled dads. Jasmine Vivian Williams, 8, of Temple Hills, Md., showed up wearing a bright yellow outfit, along with her brother and mother—and, best of all, her father, Irn Williams. The girl volunteers that the books her dad read on tape were *The Popcorn Book* and *When the Wind Stops*.

"What's the best part of today?" she asks, repeating the question. "Just having him here."

But inmates' homecomings do not always have happy endings, and sometimes loving adults find themselves picking up the pieces. Out in Reno, Jessica Bailey got her mom back on New Year's Eve; she had been released from prison a few weeks early. But Jessica's joy was short-lived. Earlier this month, her mother was dropped off at the local Department of Motor Vehicles and just vanished, apparently into die swamp of drugs and mental distress.

"We haven't heard from her, and that's not usually a good sign," says Don Bailey, Jessica's grandfather.

"Jessica is devastated," says Elaine Voigt, who founded My Journey Home, a faith-based support group for the families of inmates. "Thank God, she has her grandfather."

Her grandfather is thankful, in turn, for the presence in Jessica's life of a woman unrelated to them. He thinks his granddaughter is doing all right, considering. She has taken up a new sport, gymnastics, and thanks to the adults around her, she realizes that her mother's problems and actions are not her fault. She also takes solace in the company of "Big Sister." Last Monday, Janet took Jess to see *Nanny McPhee,* a movie Jessica enjoyed so much that she made her grandfather take her again.

"Jessica just loves being with her," Don reports. "It's good."

Discussion Questions

1. What options and/or programs are available to assist children of incarcerated parents?

2. Does the government have a moral obligation to address the needs of children of incarcerated parents? Explain your response.

3. Discuss what the author refers to in the section "The Education of 'Big John.'"

Biometrics Basics

By Law and Order Staff

EDITOR'S COMMENT

"Resident R84B please put your eye up against the sensor and state your last name. Thank you. Now, please step forward into the personal spacecraft and prepare for departure to the psychiatric counseling ward. You have two years, six months, and fourteen days left on your sentence." As Resident R84B departs for the psychiatric counseling ward, another resident (formally known as inmate) steps before the large screen. "Resident L6YR, please put your eye up against the sensor and state your last name. Thank you. Now, please step forward into the personal spacecraft and prepare for departure to the vocational training ward. You have six months and four days left on your sentence." And so it goes. Another day in world of corrections in the year 2050.

This fictitious account of what the future of criminal justice may hold hopefully generates thoughts about the future. How will our system of criminal justice look in 20 years, 50 years, or 100 years? Will future societies reflect on our system of justice and marvel at the inadequacies and inaccuracies, much in the same manner that we currently look at the history of criminal justice and wonder how such practices could be considered justice? For instance, consider the injustices inherent in earlier criminal justice systems. Corporal punishment and trial by torture are but a few of the historical means by which justice was allegedly achieved. Will society in the twenty-second century look back at our body of work and wonder how we could have rightfully considered our actions in line with justice?

Technological changes have already transformed our criminal justice system, as evidenced in this article. Technology is used to control, prevent, and commit crime. Computers have had both positive and negative influences on criminal justice practices. Cyber crime has provided specific challenges that law enforcement is ill-prepared to meet. For instance, local law enforcement agencies do not always have the resources to staff a computer crime division nor the technology to keep pace with high-tech crime. However, computers are often used to track offenders, provide quick access to various information and data, and generally make the job of criminal justice professionals much easier.

Entrepreneurs with an interest in criminal justice have a bright future. The general public is constantly fearful of crime. The criminal justice system is always searching for ways to save resources, maintain public safety, and ensure justice. Creative thinkers have seemingly endless opportunities to incorporate technology into the criminal justice system while meeting the needs of both the public and the criminal justice system. We're in a transitional period in criminal justice, as technology is increasingly assuming its place. The challenge is to identify technological means to best improve justice-based efforts.

The possibilities for using technology to address the public's fear of crime also provide potentially lucrative opportunities for creative individuals. The public is often willing to consider ideas regarding how to best find protection from criminal victimization. The popularity and simplicity of "The Club," a locking device that secures one's automobile steering wheel, demonstrates the potential for creating and marketing items used for crime prevention. One can only hope that crime and the need for criminal justice will become obsolete following extensive societal focus on crime control and prevention, and visions of Residents R84B and L6YR will truly remain fictitious.

One of life's rites of passage is the first time that we are given a key to something. Having a key means that we are trusted enough to have access to something that is kept secure from others, and it also suggests that we now have an increased expectation of privacy in whatever that key helps protect. It is an inevitable rite of passage that we will eventually lose that key, and usually several others, and create a security problem.

Is the person that finds the key likely to know what lock it fits? Should we change the lock? How many keys and people will be involved in the change, and what is the risk-versus-rewards calculation? Keys are necessary, but they are also a nuisance. We collect so many of them that we eventually forget what locks they all fit.

What if your keys were contained in the physical characteristics of your body? You would always have your "keys" with you, so they couldn't be accidentally lost, and no one could have a duplicate. This premise is the essence of biometric security technologies. By keying locks to buildings, cars, safes, computers, documents and all of the other things we want to secure to physical characteristics, we ensure that these resources cannot be accessed unless the person authorized to do so is physically present.

Biometric technologies work against the bad guy in another way. Certainly, crooks want to get access to things they aren't supposed to, but almost as commonly, they want to conceal their own identities. Sometimes they are looking to avoid capture and avoid being held accountable for their crimes, but increasingly, they are trying to impersonate others in a variety of schemes that have come to be grouped under the heading "identity theft."

Identity theft crimes are often a nightmare of red tape for the victim, even if the monetary loss is minimal or covered by insurance and various protection plans. Victims spend weeks or months contacting creditors, trying to convince them that either they are who they say they are, or that someone else wasn't them.

Traditionally, our system of identifying people for civil purposes has been based on a few foundation documents: birth certificates, Social Security cards, and the ubiquitous driver's license. Skilled identity thieves who get control of any one of these documents often can parlay it into a full set of credentials, sufficient to file address changes, apply for credit cards and loans, and generally misrepresent themselves. If the foundation credential was, instead, a unique, nonreplicable physical identifier, such as a fingerprint, it would be much more difficult to establish an identity other than the one you were born with.

Because fingerprints are more or less the gold standard of identification, that is where manufacturers of biometric systems have put most of their efforts. There are a number of physical characteristics that are as unique as fingerprints, but they are not as well-known, and scanning them is usually more awkward and invasive.

The pattern of blood vessels on the retina, distribution of pigment in the iris, hand geometry, voice patterns, and handwritten signatures are all forms of biometric identifiers. Fingerprints, retinal and iris patterns, and hand geometry are physiological biometrics, as they cannot be altered by the possessor, while voices and handwritten signatures are behavioral biometrics. Behavioral biometrics change all by themselves over time, can be altered by the possessor, and can even be duplicated by a skilled imitator.

Another standard of biometric identification is facial recognition, which is a physiological biometric, but is not unique to the individual. Facial recognition has its place in the biometric arsenal, but it is insufficiently reliable to be used as a positive identification method.

"Biometrics Basics", *Law and Order*, April 2007. Reprinted with permission of Reprint Management Services.

As with illegitimate issuance of conventional identification documents, faulty initial recording of the biometric information or associating that information with the wrong person can make the system worse than useless. The administrators of these systems have to use special care to ensure that identification of all parties is fully documented and matched with the right records in the system database. The process of initial matching of biometric signatures with the records of the people to whom they belong is called enrollment.

TYPE I AND TYPE II ERRORS

Biometric engineers make reference to Type I and Type II errors, terminology that is normally used in discussing statistics. A Type I error, also known as a False Acceptance Error, occurs when the system incorrectly matches the biometric signature provided to a record in the database, providing access to the wrong person. The rate of Type I errors is called the False Acceptance Rate or FAR. A high FAR indicates an unreliable system that does not provide adequate safeguards for the resource to be protected.

A Type II Error, or False Rejection Error, occurs when the biometric signature presented to the system does in fact match a record in the enrolled database, but the system fails to match the sample and the record successfully, denying access to the authorized user. The incidence of Type II Errors is called the FRR, or False Rejection Rate. No biometric system can promise FARs and FRRs of zero.

In evaluating the acceptable rates of error, the nature of the application has to be considered. A biometric system to screen jail inmates picking up their meal trays could tolerate a high FRR, as the maximum consequence would be that the inmate got his meal a few minutes later than usual. However, consider a product that didn't quite make it to market a few years back. A gun leather manufacturer produced a sidearm holster that released the gun only after it recognized the fingerprint of an authorized enrolled user. A False Rejection Error would keep the officer's gun in the holster when he needed it, and the maximum consequence could be extremely grave.

PATTERN RECOGNITION

Humans are much better at pattern recognition than are computers. A human can see the older script logo of Coca-Cola and not only recognize it for what it is, but read the text and pick out individual letters, if needed. A computer would see a graphic and would probably not be able to render the words into its component letters. Much of pattern recognition for people is contextual.

If you were to see your dentist at the grocery store, you might find his face familiar, but not recognize it at first. This is because you didn't expect to see the face in that context, and because most of the time that you see the face, it is upside down to you. If the dentist speaks to you, the voice supplies another characteristic of pattern recognition that assists in identifying the appropriate "record" in your cerebral "database."

People consider the entire impression first, then move to analysis of particular details (voice, facial hair, clothing, gait) for refinement of the identification. A substantial amount of the information normally available for identification can be missing, and yet people still will be able to match what they see with what they remember.

Computers generally, and biometric systems in particular, have to first resolve the information presented to them into a mathematical model. A biometric system usually maps landmarks of the biometric sample presented to it, then renders the arrangement of those landmarks into a number.

With fingerprints, the system first identifies the minutiae (properly pronounced "my-NOO-she-ee," but commonly said as "min-NOO-sha") present in the sample (the location of crossovers, bifurcations, deltas, and so on) then uses a procedure called an algorithm to convert that pattern into a number or numbers. These numbers are compared against the results of calculations already recorded in the database during the enrollment process.

If there's a match, then the system grants access to the person requesting it. The match is seldom exact. In most cases, the match will be expressed as a percentage indicating confidence in the match, e.g. 99%, 90%, etc. Lower confidence levels occur when the sample doesn't exactly match an enrolled record but is close, or the sample is of poor quality because of haste, malfunction, or dirt on the scanner.

The system administrator has to determine in advance what level of confidence is acceptable for the application. Setting too high a level of acceptable confidence will increase the number of Type I errors significantly, while setting it too low will increase the Type II errors.

In Automated Fingerprint Identification Systems (AFIS), where the necessity to maintain 100% confidence in identifications is critical, the final identification is always done by a human fingerprint examiner. An AFIS may spit out a hundred or more "possibles," ranked in order of confidence, and most of the time, the appropriate record will be one of those near the top. But users of these systems know that the computers are not 100% reliable, and that is why we always keep a human in the loop. The humans still use old-fashioned pattern recognition, which will remain the gold standard for the foreseeable future.

Because no system can be 100% accurate, it often makes sense to configure biometric systems used for security applications as verification systems, rather than identification systems. An identification system must match the biometric sample provided with the correct record in the entire database, with no "hints" as to whom the submitted sample belongs.

Type II or FRR errors are likely to be common, especially if the confidence level is set high. In a verification system, the user submits his biometric signature, and at the same time, swipes a card and/or keys in a passcode that tells the system "I am Bill Jones." If the biometric signature matches the one on file for Bill Jones to the preset confidence level, Jones is given access. This method is reasonably convenient and drastically reduces Type II errors.

When biometric security systems need to be identification systems (such as those used to verify the identity of inmates before release), it is almost mandatory to have a human operator in the loop. The operator, probably a corrections officer, would verify the inmate's identity against the most likely match made by the biometric system, usually by a photo or by personal knowledge of the inmate. Systems used in the field are somewhat more problematic because of the delays typically encountered by wireless transmission of the biometric data, but officers have been negotiating this sort of problem ("No, that's not me, that's somebody else with my name") for many years without the aid of biometric systems.

FINGERPRINT SYSTEMS

Past practice is not the only reason that fingerprint-based biometric systems are the most commonly used. It's usually much easier to place a finger onto a scanning plate than it is to hold your face in front of an iris or retinal scanner or submit most of the other biometric signatures that are in use.

People tend to believe that biometric systems that use fingerprints store the fingerprint itself and compare the scanned image with the one on file. Although there may be a stored graphic image of the enrolled fingerprint in the database, the comparison is actually performed against a mathematical model of the minutiae identified in that scanned image. When a sample fingerprint is presented to the system for comparison against the database, the system identifies the minutiae of the sample, calculates the mathematical representation based on that set of minutiae, and compares that against the models in the database. The number and type of minutiae can vary from scan to scan, depending on a number of factors, so the match is almost never an exact one.

There are four types of fingerprint scanners in widespread use. Optical scanners are by far the most common. In optical scanning, light is reflected from the finger surface through a prism. Wet fingers or dirt on the fingers or the scanner may degrade the quality of the scan. Thermal scanning records a thermograph of the finger image. Capacitance sensing uses a CMOS sensor to create an image of the fingerprint from the electrical pathways created by the friction ridges. Finally, ultrasound sensing uses high-frequency sound waves to scan the finger surface. This last method isn't affected by dirt or moisture, but the equipment is bulky, and the process takes considerably longer than the others, so it is not widely used.

In the movies, the diabolical bad guy severs a finger from his victim and uses the finger to gain access to the vault/computer/secret spy headquarters. If you see this as a realistic scenario, you have some truly serious security problems. However, a far more likely scenario is that a fake finger, complete with fingerprint, can be made and used to spoof a fingerprint scanner. A Japanese cryptographer by the name of Tsutomo Matsumoto published a paper documenting several methods that he used for making "gummy fingers" out of silicon compound. The fingerprint dummies were of sufficiently good quality to fool most scanners, both for enrollment and for identification/verification purposes, and the materials cost less than $10.

Other methods of defeating fingerprint scanners seem to be dependent on the type and even the manufacture of the scanner in use. Fingerprint reactivation uses the latent image of a print placed on the scanner by a previous legitimate user. The print can be "reactivated" by merely breathing on the scanner plate, in some instances. The warmth and moisture in the exhaled breath is enough to reveal the image left by the friction ridges and spoof the scanner. Experimenters have also been successful in using a latent print that was developed and lifted onto a plastic carrier, then applying the latent print image onto the scanner with a plastic bag of warm water on top. The warm water supplies "body heat" sufficient to fool a thermal scanner and accepts the fake.

RETINAL AND IRIS SCANNING

Up until a few years ago, retinal scanning was far more commonplace than iris scanning. In retinal scanning, an optical device not unlike an opthalmoscope (the little flashlight gizmo that doctors shine into your eyes) is used to capture an image of the patterns of blood vessels on the retina on the rear wall of the eyeball. These patterns are believed to be random and unique for every individual, and they remain static through one's lifetime. Obviously, if the scanner is not positioned just right, the retinal image won't be scanned correctly. Iris scanning is now more common, as the iris is visible to the naked eye and is more accessible. Close examination of the iris shows that there is a complex design of colors contained there that is also believed to be unique for each person.

Retinal scanning is used for access to very high-risk facilities, such as military installations and nuclear power plants. Some experts consider it to be the most reliable and foolproof biometric method available today. However, the hardware is expensive, and both the enrollment and verification process tedious. It is probably not practical for most applications.

Iris scanning is far more commonplace. Users facing an iris scanner need not stand as close to the device (some work from as far away as 2 feet), and many don't require the removal of eyeglasses. Experiments indicate that most iris scanners can be fooled, however, with a photograph or a high-resolution video clip of the user's face. Like most security systems, manufacturers have reacted to these spoofing methods by incorporating refinements such as varying light levels during scanning, with concurrent monitoring for reactive pupil dilation. By randomizing the light intensity variances, advance production of a properly reactive video clip would be that much more difficult.

Because the scanning equipment does not have to come into physical contact with the person being scanned and can thus be secured behind a protective sheet of glass, iris scanning may be the biometric of choice for ATMs and other unattended premises where identity needs to be verified.

FACIAL RECOGNITION

The computers that run facial recognition routines don't "see" faces in the same way that you or I do. An image of the face is captured, and the computer identifies the minutiae of the face in much the same way as a fingerprint scanner does for friction ridge detail. The location of the eyes, nose, corners of the mouth, chin and crown of the head, and jaw points are mapped, and a mathematical representation of the proportions of these landmarks is created. This numeric string is then compared against a database of people of interest, whether they be people enrolled and entitled to be admitted to a facility, or known terrorists or wanted persons. In the latter case, possible matches are presented to a human operator for evaluation and follow up.

Performance of these systems in large-scale environments hasn't been spectacular. A few years back, people attending the Super Bowl in Tampa, FL were unknowingly scanned by a facial recognition system as they entered the stadium. Local police had stored images of wanted persons into the database, and a few positive identifications were made (along with just as many incorrect identifications). The systems have shown similar reliability in experimental deployments at airports and mass transit facilities. They may be better suited for environments where the system can consider one image at a time, such as in a police station or booking area.

The Los Angeles County Sheriff's Department has been using a facial recognition package for some years to help verify the identity of persons coming into their booking facilities, and who are prone to providing false names in order to avoid warrants and other court processes.

In access control applications, facial recognition systems have been defeated by showing the camera a photo of the enrolled person, or by playing a video clip of their face. Some of the more sophisticated systems use a 3-D method called elastic graph matching to record information that can be perceived only if the subject is scanned from multiple angles. Although early models could be defeated by displaying a video clip of the person moving his head slightly, refinements require the person to smile or move his head in a specified way on command, so the video clip is less likely to work.

SPEECH RECOGNITION

In this context, speech recognition seeks to match a voice pattern with one stored in the enrolled database. Other speech recognition applications convert the spoken word into machine-readable text, using the voice as the interface instead of a keyboard. Speech patterns may be among the easiest biometric keys to imitate, as evidenced by the career of Rich Little and other entertainers. Most of us have had the experience of answering a telephone call and mistaking the voice of one person for that of another.

Early speech recognition systems merely recorded a passphrase that the user had to repeat into a microphone in order to gain access. In most cases, a reasonably high quality recording of the person speaking the same passphrase would be enough to get past the access protection. Current speech recognition systems require the user to record a variety of words and phrases during enrollment.

When the user desires access to the resource, the system displays a random assortment of these phrases that have to be spoken in the correct order. Still another refinement is the monitoring and recording of high and low frequencies in the user's speech. Only very high quality playback devices can faithfully reproduce these frequencies, so the use of most common tape recorders and other portable players is not practical.

Speech recognition systems can reject authorizer [*sic*] users' attempts to gain access (Type II errors) if the user has a cold, has strained his voice, or has some other affliction that changes the sound of his speech. These systems are also perceived as being less convenient because people often resist being required to talk to a computer.

Biometric security applications are probably going to become more commonplace in the future as we move closer to a paperless business model and require increased verification of identity to reduce fraud and theft. Even though most of the biometric standards described above can be defeated, given enough effort and expertise, they still represent better protection than a paper identity document or a password that can be guessed, copied, or stolen. If you build a better mousetrap, you eventually get a smarter mouse. So long as manufacturers are building these systems, malefactors will be looking for ways to defeat them, and the industry will respond with countermeasures. The key is not to become complacent or believe that you have a truly impregnable system.

The best application of biometrics is most likely in conjunction with other security measures, such as a paper or plastic identity document, a password, or a "smart card" that contains a complex passcode that is difficult to duplicate. While any one of these methods can be compromised, it would be difficult to compromise all of them at the same time. Further, the flagging of any one of the criteria in the master database would alert the human in the loop (and there should always be a human in the loop) that this person's identity had possibly been compromised and to give any credentials presented greater scrutiny.

There is also a fear, for lack of a better word, that we are moving toward a national identity document that all people would be required to have in order to access even the most basic resources of civilization. Biometric standards would almost certainly be a part of any such credential. While a national identity card might make the job of police officers considerably easier, it invites a whole new discussion of civil liberties and the intrusion of government into one's personal affairs. People want the government to intervene to catch the offender when their personal credentials have been compromised, but not until that happens.

Discussion Questions

1. What are biometrics, and how can they be used to impact crime and justice?
2. Discuss the difference between Type I and Type II errors. Which have more severe implications for the criminal justice system? Why?
3. Identify and discuss the different types of biometrics. Which type can provide the greatest assistance to the criminal justice system? Discuss.

38

GPS Offender Tracking and the Police Officer

By Patrick Hyde and Nicole DeJarnatt

EDITOR'S COMMENT

This article describes how GPS offender tracking, which has historically been the sole concern of corrections officials, should also be considered by police officers. The article highlights some of the contributions technology has made to the criminal justice system, and the need for the primary components of the criminal justice system to work harmoniously as opposed to independently. The article also provides interesting insight regarding how officers should respond to offenders wearing tracking devices.

Current criminal justice practices are conducted in perhaps a more professional manner than at any other point in history. Consider our justice system 50 years ago. No computers, limited exchange of information, no databases, and so on. Consider today's criminal justice system. Police officers have computers in their cars, and departments can more easily communicate with each other and share information. Our court systems have improved as a result of technological advancements, for instance, attorneys are able to more effectively present evidence (e.g., via computer simulation); attorneys also have access to a wealth of legal research at the touch of a keyboard; and judges can more easily review case-related material during the course of a trial. In corrections, prisons have benefited through the incorporation of technology, offenders are more easily tracked via technology, and electronic monitoring is used to keep tabs on some offenders living in the community. The criminal justice system has changed to a large extent in recent times, particularly as a result of technological innovations.

It is important for police officers to be aware of how to process individuals wearing a tracking bracelet following an arrest. A sentence involving electronic monitoring is imposed by the courts and carried out by correctional agencies. Unfortunately, some of the same individuals on electronic monitoring end up under arrest. The police should understand how to treat the individual (e.g., contact a probation or parole officer), what to do with the bracelet (e.g., store it, dispose of it, return it), and related issues. Greater cooperation among the police, courts, and corrections would reduce the likelihood of confusion that may follow an arrest of someone being monitored in the community.

Some question whether electronic monitoring, which is often used in conjunction with house arrest, serves a viable purpose. For example, those confined to their home yet free to leave for work or school each day have many opportunities to engage in criminal behavior. Furthermore, in some instances, sentencing offenders to their home doesn't seem like much of a sanction. Earlier, Martha Stewart received a sentence of home confinement with electronic monitoring. To many, sentencing one to stay within the confines of a luxurious home with all the amenities and no financial worries provides little deterrence, retribution, rehabilitation, or incapacitation: the four goals of criminal sentences. However, it would seem unfair not to provide the rich and famous the same opportunity to house arrest with electronic monitoring as others.

In the end, GPS tracking holds much promise for the criminal justice system, primarily through its potential to save resources and provide offenders the opportunity to serve their sentences in the community.

GPS criminal offender supervision has been around for awhile, but it made national news a few months ago when Martha Stewart donned an electronic monitoring bracelet to track her movements during a five-month house arrest at her 153-acre estate. The monitoring system allows police to track Stewart's movements both at her $16 million estate and during the 48 hours a week she is allowed to leave her home to shop or carry out other approved errands.

While not every offender will have the prominence of Martha Stewart, recent innovations in technology combined with the U.S. Military's Global Positioning System (GPS) have pushed GPS criminal offender supervision to the forefront for community corrections agencies, typically charged with monitoring probationers, parolees and pretrial defendants. Such advancements have many community corrections agencies taking a second look at GPS tracking.

GPS offender tracking, as with more traditional house arrest electronic monitoring systems, is being used for community supervision and as a viable sanction for judges seeking an alternative to incarceration. It is also for community corrections agencies wanting an extra layer of detail about a person's activities when they are being supervised in the community. In general, offender monitoring has grown in importance over the last few years due to increasingly tighter budgets, overcrowded prisons and jails, and a shift toward moving nonviolent offenders back to the community, where they can be closely supervised using modern technology, versus the much more costly alternative—incarceration.

GPS tracking takes offender supervision to the next level. When police officers encounter a suspect wearing one of these devices, it makes sense for them to understand what these systems are, how they operate, what they can and cannot do, and finally, what procedures agencies using these systems would suggest you follow.

COMMON GPS SYSTEM COMPONENTS

GPS offender tracking systems have many common components. To date, all GPS tracking systems have a GPS tracking unit worn by the offender on a belt when they leave home, an ankle bracelet transmitter, a charging base station in the individual's home and a central monitoring computer system.

- *GPS tracking unit.* These units vary in size and weight, with some original tracking units weighing almost 5 pounds. These units have been shrinking, though, with the newest GPS tracking unit on the market, BI ExacuTrack, weighing in at 9 ounces. All systems gather GPS data points while the offender moves about the community. The GPS tracking unit must be "visible" to three GPS satellites at one time to provide an accurate position for the offender. Typically, eight to 12 of the 24 satellites in the U.S. Military's constellation of GPS satellites are visible at any one time to the GPS tracking unit, providing many redundant observation vantages. When the person leaves home, the GPS tracking unit must not become separated from the ankle bracelet transmitter or an alert is issued.
- *Ankle bracelet transmitter.* The ankle-mounted bracelet transmitter is an extension of traditional, proven technology—radio-frequency electronic monitoring systems that monitor the

---

"GPS Offender Tracking & the Police Officer" by Patrick Hyde and Nicole DeJarnatt, *Corrections Technology*, Vol. 32, #6, June 2005. Reprinted by permission of Patrick Hyde.

absence or presence of a person, usually at home. When the GPS tracking unit is added to the mix, the ankle bracelet creates an electronic bond to this device. The ankle transmitter is tamper-resistant. That doesn't mean an offender cannot remove it; it simply means if it is tampered with, monitoring specialists will know and can then notify the community corrections agency.

- *Charging base station.* The charging base station, sometimes called a docking station, is plugged into an AC power outlet and a standard phone jack in the offender's residence. It appears similar to a home telephone system. The system can both download and relay GPS data points to the central monitoring computer.
- *Central computer and monitoring corrections.* The central monitoring computer maintains offender details and schedules for each person on GPS tracking. Agencies will define geographic zones the offender may or may not enter (called "inclusion" and "exclusion" zones). The monitoring computer will issue violation alerts, if necessary, when a person breaches the conditions of release. The corrections also must be able to translate an offender's GPS data points logged as he or she moves through the community and overlay those onto an easy-to-read mapping system.

ACTIVE AND PASSIVE GPS

Sometimes, violations to the parameters laid out for the offender can be noted and forwarded to the agency within minutes—this type of system has been labeled an "active" GPS system—while other systems log GPS data points while the person travels through the community then downloads that information to be analyzed when the person returns home and places the GPS tracking unit in the charging base station. Each system has pros and cons, but usually the systems that download the data once or twice a day provide sufficient detail for uncovering the patterns of activity that the supervising officer must address with the offender.

On the surface, it may seem most helpful for agencies to know within minutes if an offender has violated their conditions of release by leaving an inclusion zone or entering an exclusion zone. However, some agencies are leery of active GPS systems. So much information, they say, can lead to "data overload" that can have the agency responding daily to continuous violation notifications, some of which are simply nuisance violations. To the police officer on the street, there will be little if any noticeable difference to these systems, other than size.

A major drawback voiced about active GPS systems is the misperception that a community corrections or police officer can intervene to thwart criminal activity. That is simply not the case, as few agencies have dedicated resources waiting for such a call nor could they move from office to "potential" crime location before a crime is committed.

What both active and passive GPS systems can provide, though, is important and concrete details about offender behavior while they move within the community. As a result, patterns in behavior can be detected and addressed, with the hope that future crime can be prevented. GPS systems can provide correlation to crime scenes and can alert local police officers if offenders are associating with other GPS-tracked individuals while in the community.

ENCOUNTERS WITH OFFENDERS

Most community corrections agencies have outlined procedures and protocols for what local police should do when encountering an offender on GPS tracking, according to Jim Buck, a senior product manager for BI Inc., a Boulder, Colorado, provider of electronic supervision equipment and services. Buck, who heads up BI's GPS product development team, has helped agencies educate local police officers on what these systems are—and are not—and best practices for managing offenders being monitored with GPS.

For example, if a police officer encounters a person on GPS, it will be fairly apparent the person is on some type of monitoring system. The officer will probably notice an ankle bracelet or belt-mounted GPS tracking unit, or the individual may simply offer this information. If the officer decides to detain the person, it is important to identify what agency is supervising the individual and the person's supervising probation or parole officer. Individuals on GPS tracking will know their supervising officer's contact information, according to Buck.

If the person is to be booked, as with traditional electronic monitoring equipment, the GPS equipment will typically be removed before the individual is processed for secure detention. Contacting that supervising officer is a best first step, even before processing the suspect. The equipment does not need to be removed if the person is not going to be detained, Buck suggests.

In the event a suspect is processed for arrest, officers should understand that none of the equipment poses a danger or threat to the individual or to the officer. "Officers should not have any concerns about cutting the ankle bracelet, provided it can be safely stored along with the GPS tracking unit until returned to the overseeing authority," Buck says. If the offender is uncooperative in identifying their supervising agency, contact the equipment's manufacturer, which can identify the agency.

If police opt to remove a person's ankle bracelet or GPS tracking unit, it is easier to remove the equipment in a secure facility, where the officer can control the environment. Removing the system in the field or transporting a suspect through a location they are not supposed to go, such as near a school, may trigger an audible alert or alarm. "Officers should not be alarmed in either case," says Buck. "Simply contact the supervising agency and they can deactivate the system."

Upon returning the equipment to the overseeing agency, a verifiable account of the individual's GPS trail can be downloaded by docking the GPS tracking unit to the charging base station in the offender's home. This can actually provide valuable information to police, such as whether a suspect was within the vicinity of a crime scene, since the GPS data points can be precisely matched to street locations within meters. This data is court admissible, if needed.

As with any system, though, each corrections or law enforcement agency will follow protocols that work for their situation. In Roanoke County, Virginia, the sheriff's department has used electronic monitoring to help reduce jail overcrowding. Today, the Roanoke Home Detention Program, using both GPS and traditional electronic monitoring, includes almost 10 percent of its jail's population. These individuals are community-based prisoners who have been released to community supervision to relieve overcrowding, produce savings for the community, and allow these individuals to work and support their families versus taking up valuable jail space.

Sgt. Brian Keenum, who oversees the Roanoke Home Detention Program, says GPS tracking is used for individuals released to the community who need an extra level of accountability. He encourages law enforcement officials who encounter an individual on GPS tracking to contact his department immediately if a person is to be detained. Once contacted by an arresting officer, jail or booking agent, Keenum will meet the suspect and arresting officer at the designated location and remove the equipment with a specific unlocking tool, thereby preventing a trip to the manufacturer for replacement or repair. He will also go to the individual's home, insert the GPS tracking unit in the charging base station and download that offender's GPS data points.

Roanoke officials like the GPS tracking system, and use the GPS maps to discuss a person's behavior and patterns of activity with local judges and the offender's themselves. Importantly, Keenum's department has begun—and hopes to expand—educational training seminars about GPS systems locally. These outreach efforts will include communicating with local police. "We need to do more training for local departments on the program's abilities, what offenders are on these systems and who to contact for more information," he explains.

In Boulder County, Colorado, the local sheriff's office also operates a home detention program that includes the use of electronic supervision technology. The department recently tested GPS offender tracking. Deputy Sheriff Bill Weiss says most police officers in the region who come in contact with a person on electronic monitoring or GPS will know to contact the sheriff's department. The officer can find out who is supervising the individual through a statewide database of all offenders, current and past. "We encourage police officers to contact us first, before trying to remove the equipment," Weiss says. "Officers really don't need to do anything differently for a person on one of these systems, simply contact us and we will meet them and determine if equipment should be removed."

GPS systems for offender supervision are an important tool for community corrections agencies. These systems will help deliver information not previously available, namely a verifiable, accurate record of an offender's movement during each day. It is important for local police to be able to recognize these systems, be familiar with their capabilities and know who to contact if they need more information about them. This understanding should reap rewards for the community corrections agency, local police and public safety efforts.

Discussion Questions

1. Identify and discuss the common GPS system components.
2. Discuss the differences between active and passive GPS systems. Which has more to offer the criminal justice system? Why?

3. Why do police departments and law enforcement officers need to be aware of GPS and how to approach offenders on GPS?

39

Do Immigrants
Make Us Safer?

By Eyal Press

EDITOR'S COMMENT

Many factors have contributed to the recent declining crime rates in the United States. Prominent among them are a strong economy, the increased rate of incarceration, tougher sentencing, and community policing. Rarely have discussions surrounding the decreased crime rate referenced immigration as a contributing factor. However, the possibility that immigrants create a safer United States is addressed in this article.

The United States is known as a "melting pot" and "the land of opportunities." The diversity within the United States is one of the country's many strengths. It is also a source of great tension. The interaction and assimilation of the many groups living in the United States has provided significant challenges. Among those challenges is the belief that immigrants and the undocumented commit a disproportionate amount of crime. Some accounts suggest this belief is misguided. For instance, the fear of being brought to the attention of authorities encourages those new to the United States to stay clear of the criminal justice system.

The multicultural makeup of the United States generates conflict among cultures. Historically, new challenges arose as new waves of immigrant groups arrived. Each group has had its share of struggles, and many groups continue to struggle to find acceptance. Racism, genderism, ethnocentrism, and plain bigotry have contributed to differences among groups in society. Professionals working within the criminal justice system need to be cognizant and respectful of cultural differences, as those entering the system come from a variety of backgrounds. Minority groups, particularly African Americans, are largely overrepresented in crime statistics. Why? Two particular answers are often offered: poverty and related social issues.

Another explanation for the overrepresentation of African Americans and other minorities in the criminal justice system has to do with criminal justice practices. The question "Is the criminal justice system racist?" is often asked, The simple answer is "No." There are not specially designed, more punitive paths for minorities during criminal case processing. However, one could argue that some individuals working within the criminal justice system are biased and show favoritism toward particular groups. The term racial profiling has become common in many discussions of police patrol practices. Some see racial profiling, or targeting individuals based on their race, as an effective law enforcement tool. Others view it as discriminatory policing that contributes to the overrepresentation of specific groups within the criminal justice system.

Debate regarding immigration and crime will not soon end, nor will culture conflict. Our best hopes are to make all efforts toward promoting tolerance and respect for one another, and recognize that one's race, gender, sexual preference, or cultural background does not suggest a direct link to crime involvement. It is imperative that knowledge, tolerance, and understanding guide our actions.

Although the midterm election failed to render a clear verdict on illegal immigration, the new Democratic Congress may enact sweeping legislation tightening border controls and allowing more guest workers next year. If that happens, the rancorous debate about how undocumented workers affect jobs and wages in the United States will be rejoined. So, too, will an equally rancorous, if less prominent, debate: Do immigrants make the U.S. more crime-ridden and dangerous?

In an age of Latino gangs and Chinese criminal networks, the notion that communities with growing immigrant populations tend to be unsafe is fairly well established, at least in the popular imagination. In a national survey conducted in 2000, 73 percent of Americans said they believe that immigrants are either "somewhat" or "very" likely to increase crime, higher than the 60 percent who fear they are "likely to cause Americans to lose jobs." Cities like Avon Park, Fla., have considered ordinances recently to dissuade businesses from hiring illegal immigrants, whose presence "destroys our neighborhoods." Even President Bush, whose perceived generosity to undocumented workers has earned him vilification on the right, commented in a speech this May that illegal immigration "strains state and local budgets and brings crime to our communities."

So goes the conventional wisdom. But is it true? In fact, according to evidence cropping up in various places, the opposite may be the case. Ramiro Martinez Jr., a professor of criminal justice at Florida International University, has sifted through homicide records in border cities like San Diego and El Paso, both heavily populated by Mexican immigrants, both places where violent crime has fallen significantly in recent years. "Almost without exception," he told me, "I've discovered that the homicide rate for Hispanics was lower than for other groups, even though their poverty rate was very high, if not the highest, in these metropolitan areas." He found the same thing in the Haitian neighborhoods of Miami. In his book "New York Murder Mystery," the criminologist Andrew Karmen examined the trend in New York City and likewise found that the "disproportionately youthful, male and poor immigrants" who arrived during the 1980s and 1990s "were surprisingly law-abiding" and that their settlement into once-decaying neighborhoods helped "put a brake on spiraling crime rates."

The most prominent advocate of the "more immigrants, less crime" theory is Robert J. Sampson, chairman of the sociology department at Harvard. A year ago, Sampson was an author of an article in The *American Journal of Public Health* that reported the findings of a detailed study of crime in Chicago. Based on information gathered on the perpetrators of more than 3,000 violent acts committed between 1995 and 2002, supplemented by police records and community surveys, it found that the rate of violence among Mexican-Americans was significantly lower than among both non-Hispanic whites and blacks.

In June, Sampson and I drove out to a neighborhood in Little Village, Chicago's largest Hispanic community. The area we visited is decidedly poor: in terms of per capita income, 84 percent of Chicago neighborhoods are better off and 99 percent have a greater proportion of residents with a high-school education. As we made our way down a side street, Sampson noted that many of the residents make their living as domestic workers and in other low-wage occupations, often paid off the books because they are undocumented. In places of such concentrated disadvantage, a certain level of violence and social disorder is assumed to be inevitable. As we strolled around, Sampson paused on occasion to make a mental note of potential trouble signs: an alley strewn with garbage nobody had bothered to pick up; a sign in Spanish in several windows, complaining about the lack

---

of a park in the vicinity where children can play. Yet for all of this, the neighborhood was strikingly quiet. And, according to the data Sampson has collected, it is surprisingly safe. The burglary rate in the neighborhood is in the bottom fifth of the city. The overall crime rate is nearly in the bottom third.

The safety of neighborhoods like these has received little attention in the debate about immigration—or, for that matter, the debate about crime. Ever since cities like New York began cracking down on panhandling and loitering in the mid-1990s, a move that coincided with a precipitous drop in violence, policy makers have embraced the so-called broken-windows theory, which emphasizes the deterrent effects of punishing such minor offenses. Lately, though, scholars have begun to question whether "broken windows" deserves all the credit for diminishing crime after all. Some researchers have linked progress to the cessation of the crack epidemic. Others point to an improved economy, community-policing initiatives or even the legalization of abortion, which reduced the number of poor, unwanted children growing up in high-risk neighborhoods.

Sampson's theory may be the most provocative yet. Could America's cities be safer today not because fewer unwanted children live in them but because a lot more immigrants do? Could illegal immigration be making the nation a more law-abiding place?

There are, to be sure, scholars who take issue with this rosy picture. Wesley Skogan, a political scientist at Northwestern University, has spent the past 13 years tracking violence and social disorder in the white, black and Latino communities in Chicago. In a new book, "Police and Community in Chicago: A Tale of Three Cities," just out from Oxford University Press, Skogan concludes that the big success story took place not in immigrant areas but in African-American ones, where participation in community-policing programs was highest and violence fell the most. "About two-thirds of the crime decline in Chicago since 1991 took place in black neighborhoods," Skogan says. In Hispanic communities, by contrast, Skogan found that the fear of crime, as measured in surveys of residents, and real social disorder—gang activity, loitering—actually became worse as the foreign-born population increased. Skogan acknowledges that Hispanic immigrants don't show up much in arrest records, but he says he believes part of the explanation for this rests in the fact that those who are undocumented go to enormous lengths to "stay off the radar." Many also come from a country, Mexico, where distrust of law enforcement is endemic, which is why he suspects they underreport crime and participate less in community-policing programs, as his study found.

Sampson doesn't deny that crime may be underreported in immigrant neighborhoods. Nonetheless, he is quick to note that as the ranks of foreigners in the United States boomed during the 1990s—increasing by more than 50 percent to 31 million—America's cities became markedly less dangerous. That these two trends might be related has been overlooked, he says, in part because immigrants, like African-Americans, often trigger negative associations regardless of how they actually behave. Not long ago, Sampson and Stephen W. Raudenbush, a sociologist who teaches at the University of Chicago, conducted an experiment to test this idea. The experiment drew on interviews with more than 3,500 Chicago residents, each of whom was asked how serious problems like loitering and public drinking were where they lived. The responses were compared with the actual level of chaos in the neighborhood, culled from police data and by having researchers drive along hundreds of blocks to document every sign of decay and disorder they could spot.

The social and ethnic composition of a neighborhood turned out to have a profound bearing on how residents of Chicago perceived it, irrespective of the actual conditions on the streets. "In particular," Sampson and Raudenbush found, "the proportion of blacks and the proportion of Latinos in a neighborhood were related positively and significantly to perceived disorder." Once you adjusted for the ethnic, racial and class composition of a community, "much of the variation in levels of disorder that appeared to be explained by what residents saw was spurious."

In other words, the fact that people think neighborhoods with large concentrations of brown-skinned immigrants are unsafe makes sense in light of popular stereotypes and subliminal associations. But that doesn't mean there is any rational basis for their fears. Such a message hasn't sat well with everyone. As the debate about immigration has grown more heated and polarized, Sampson has found himself barraged with hate mail. "Vicious stuff," he told me, "you know, thinly veiled threats, people saying, 'You should just come and look at the Mexican gangs here.' " But Sampson has also won some far-flung admirers. In Mexico, one of the nation's leading dailies, *La Reforma*, published a story hailing his findings, under the triumphal heading, "Son barrios de paisanos menos violentos que los blancos" ("Neighborhoods of our countrymen are less violent than white ones").

If immigrants really are making America safer, why is this so? "That," Sampson says, "is the $64,000 question." In discussing the persistence of poverty and the causes of crime, sociologists on the left often emphasize the importance of "structural" factors like unemployment and racism, while scholars on the right tend to focus on individual behavior like having an illegitimate child and using drugs. Sampson prefers to focus on the nature of the social interactions taking place in particular neighborhoods. At one point in Little Village, we strolled past a house where a couple of young girls were playing outside. It didn't seem that anybody was supervising them. Next door, however, an elderly woman was standing just inside the window. The window was open, and as Sampson and I passed by, her eyes did not leave us. "Did you notice that?" asked Sampson as we proceeded down the block. She was making sure the two strangers who had appeared weren't dangerous. It was an example of the kind of informal social control that Sampson says can prevent even the poorest neighborhoods from spiraling into chaos and that he suspects may distinguish many tightknit immigrant communities.

But Sampson also notes the importance of another factor, one often stressed by conservatives: Mexicans in Chicago, his study found, are more likely to be married than either blacks or whites. "The family dynamic is very noticeable here," Sampson remarked as we passed a girl with long braided hair clutching her mother's hand. Her father followed a few steps behind. Sampson does not believe family structure explains everything: the data showed that in immigrant neighborhoods, even individuals who are not in married households are 15 percent less likely to engage in crime. Yet neither did he discount its significance.

To the extent a strong family structure does play a role, it has left Sampson understandably mystified why the most strident opponents of immigration so often come from the right. Shouldn't conservatives concerned about the breakdown of traditional values be celebrating these family-oriented newcomers? This is indeed what David Brooks argued not long ago in a column in The *New York Times*, gently chiding his fellow conservatives for reflexively assuming foreigners have had a corrosive impact on the nation's moral fiber. "As immigration has surged, violent crime has fallen 57 percent," Brooks noted in the column, which was titled "Immigrants to Be Proud Of."

Sampson wrote Brooks a note complimenting him on the piece. But he is under no illusions that his views on crime and immigration will endear him to Republicans clamoring for America's borders to be sealed. On the other hand, it might not make his colleagues on the left any happier. The flip side of the impulse to demonize immigrants is, after all, the tendency to romanticize them as hard-working Horatio Alger types who valiantly lift themselves out of poverty—with the implication that if they can avoid falling victim to drugs, gangs and other inner-city scourges, those who succumb to these forces have only themselves to blame. In calling attention to the virtues of immigrant communities, there is a risk that Sampson's work will be taken by some as a commentary on the high crime rate in some poor African-American communities.

Of course, comparing the experiences of Mexican immigrants and African-Americans may seem grossly unfair, not least because studies have shown that many employers are willing to hire foreigners (on the assumption they work hard) but not blacks (on the assumption they don't). Yet the fact that it is unfair hardly means such comparisons won't be made—even though immigrants commit less crime not only than African-Americans in inner-city neighborhoods but less than American-born white people as well.

Before anyone rushes to conclude that crime would vanish from America's cities if only more foreigners moved here, it is worth considering something else Sampson's study uncovered. It is a finding as troubling as his basic thesis about immigrants is hopeful. Second-generation immigrants in Chicago were significantly more likely to commit crimes than their parents, it turns out, and those of the third generation more likely still.

Opponents of immigration frequently charge that Mexican immigrants threaten America's national identity because of their failure to assimilate. A more reasonable concern might be the opposite of this: not that foreigners in low-income neighborhoods refuse to adopt the norms of the native culture but that their children and grandchildren do.

The sociologists Alejandro Portes and Rubén G. Rumbaut conducted a multiyear longitudinal study of immigrant children in Miami and San Diego. The offspring of foreigners who grow up in impoverished ghettos, they have argued, particularly Mexican-Americans exposed to racial as well as economic discrimination, often lose the drive and optimism their parents had and come to share the widespread attitude among their inner-city peers that survival depends on brandishing an oppositional stance toward school authorities and, more broadly, a culture that looks down on them. "The learning of new cultural patterns and entry into American social circles does not lead in these cases to upward mobility but to exactly the opposite," Portes and Rumbaut contend, a process of "downward assimilation" that has created a new "rainbow underclass." Astoundingly, in a recent paper, Rumbaut and several doctoral students found that the incarceration rate among second-generation Mexicans was eight times higher than for the first generation; among Vietnamese, it was more than 10 times higher. Where the first-generation immigrants in their data were less likely to wind up in prison than native-born whites, the second (with the exception of Filipinos and Chinese) were more likely.

Such findings suggest the class and race divisions that cleave America's social landscape may prove decisive after all. In Sweden, a country with markedly less inequality and more generous social welfare policies—and far less violent crime—studies have shown the rate of offending tends to be lower for the second generation of immigrants than for the first. Of course, America has historically done an admirable job of assimilating newcomers, and the theory of "downward assimilation" has not gone unchallenged. Recently, a team of researchers completed a study in New York of more than 2,200 second-generation immigrants and 1,200 native-born Americans that allowed them to compare the rate of offending among various groups, West Indians versus African-Americans, for instance, or Russians versus American-born whites. According to John Mollenkopf, a political scientist at the CUNY Graduate Center, the arrest rates among the children of immigrants were the same or lower in every case. "The second-generation immigrants are doing better, on the whole, than the native-born," he said.

Clearly, the debate over assimilation will continue, as Sampson acknowledges. When I asked him why he thought the positive trends he and his colleagues had discovered in Chicago seemed to become diluted by the second and third generations, he paused.

"That's another $64,000 question," he said, chuckling softly. Part of the explanation, he went on to speculate, may rest in the exposure subsequent generations have to the things that often lure young people in America's cities to engage in illicit activities: drugs, cash, cars, contraband. Part of it, as well, might be the adoption of streetwise attitudes that lead people to react quickly to insults in the United States. One thing it is difficult for Americans to realize, he said, is how unusually violent their country is, particularly in light of its inordinate wealth. Recently, scholars have become increasingly interested in the historical origins of American violence. Richard Nisbett of the University of Michigan and others have traced our "culture of violence" back to the valorization of retribution and dueling among Scotch-Irish immigrants in the American South, suggesting that antique folkways have become encoded into the nation's DNA.

It is a dark view, perhaps, but Sampson is hopeful that the good news about crime in recent years can continue, albeit under certain conditions, among them less alarmism about the supposedly dangerous foreigners in our midst. Sampson shook his head when describing some of the correspondence he has received from people absolutely certain that immigrants are sowing mayhem in our streets. In the last few years, he noted, such people have had somewhat less cause for worry, since the numbers show the flow of newcomers has subsided a bit. Meanwhile, the crime rate in some cities has begun to creep back up. Sampson, for one, does not think this is a mere coincidence. Those clamoring for America to close its borders in order to prevent violence-prone strangers from flooding our shores may well get their way, he acknowledged, but they ought to be careful what they wish for.

Discussion Questions

1. Discuss why some believe immigrants make society much safer with regard to crime.

2. Discuss the results of the multiyear longitudinal study of immigrant children in Miami and San Diego conducted by sociologists Portes and Rumbaut. What implications do the results offer with regard to the relationship between immigration and crime?

3. Why do you believe the public generally feels that greater immigration rates result in more crime? After reading this article, are you convinced that immigration may reduce the crime rate?

40

The CSI Effect

By Kit R. Roane

EDITOR'S COMMENT

Criminologists often critique the media for various reasons. For instance, the media are accused of sensationalizing crime, distorting public fear of crime, and perpetuating unsubstantiated crime waves. However, criminologists also recognize the contributions of the media. Anticrime programs and crime prevention efforts designed to deter criminal behavior and help potential victims protect themselves have helped society in several ways. Criminologists also recognize the benefits of fictional TV dramas that have notably encouraged students to study both criminology and criminal justice.

On a personal note, my career was influenced by a TV drama. While a freshman undergraduate business major I regularly watched the popular TV show LA Law. After realizing I wasn't business school material, I decided I wanted to study law, just like the characters on the show. So I switched majors from business to criminal justice. I was going to law school—in theory at least. To make a long story short, I ended up being influenced by a criminal justice professor and chose to go into academia. Why am I sharing this account? Years after assuming a career in academia, I did a bit of self-reflection and was somewhat discouraged that a TV show shaped my career. However, I would soon find out that I'm not alone.

I've noticed over the years that many others have had career choices influenced by TV shows. Those in academia who teach criminology and justice studies can attest to the notable number of students hoping to become profilers after watching the popular TV show Profiler. Most recently, CSI and its derivatives (e.g., CSI: New York) have led more than a few students to major in criminal justice. While these and related shows may distort reality primarily through sensationalizing and/or distorting crime, there's no doubt that they have encouraged students to study criminal justice. Whether or not criminal justice or criminology as disciplines can prepare students for positions as profilers or crime scene investigators is another story. Many academics in criminal justice will agree that the change in student interest from profiling to crime scene investigation was welcomed, as it's much easier for students to become crime scene investigators than to become profilers.

Crime dramas have also shaped courtroom practices, as jurors who watch shows such as CSI come into the courtroom with certain expectations regarding how cases transpire. For instance, jurors may expect that anything short of DNA analyses suggests a lack of effort on behalf of the prosecutor. In reality, our crime labs are expensive to operate and are overburdened with requests for analyses. At some point, jurors must realize that not every criminal case receives the same level of attention as depicted on TV, or perhaps the influences of the show will prompt the construction of additional crime labs.

It's possible that the added pressure to provide more concrete scientific evidence will raise the stakes in our courtrooms. Maybe increased public demand for sophisticated analyses of evidence will reduce the number of wrongful convictions. On the other hand, increased juror expectations for scientific analyses could result in some guilty offenders going free, assuming the prosecution cannot provide the level of evidence television-influenced jurors need. It seems that increased juror expectations regarding scientific evidence in the courtroom shift criminal justice practices toward what Herbert Packer years ago referred to as the "due process model" of criminal justice, and away from the "crime control" model. Only time will tell what crime drama will next influence student, juror, and societal opinions of crime and justice.

On TV, it's all slam-dunk evidence and quick convictions. Now juries expect the same thing—and that's a big problem.

Picture this: A middle-aged woman from out of town digs into a bowl of chili at a fast-food restaurant in California. Each bite is more delicious than the last. She chews. She savors. Then something goes terribly wrong. She spits. She screams. She vomits. All eyes focus on the table, where a well-manicured fingertip peeks out from a mound of masticated chili. Lights and sirens. Forensic experts troll for evidence. Pimple-faced fry cooks are lined up. Fingers are pointed, and fingers are counted. The nub is popped into an evidence bag to make the forensic rounds. A fingerprint is taken to run through a national database. DNA tests are done. Detectives search for clues.

If this were an episode of *CSI: Crime Scene Investigation*—and it might well become one—the well-coiffed technicians who star in the show would solve the mystery lickety-split. Fingerprints or DNA evidence would identify the victim, a leggy blond, within 45 minutes. Then, in a twist, a smudge of blood still under the nail would lead to her killer, a jealous fashion photographer, unwilling to let go of his star.

But this is real life. Anna Ayala reported her disturbing find at a Wendy's restaurant late last month. And as of last week, investigators were still stumped. Ayala hasn't confessed to any fraud. The fry cooks all had their fingers. The print wasn't a match. And the DNA test still hadn't come back from the lab. On CBS's *CSI*, the forensic science is sexy, fast, and remarkably certain, a combination that has propelled the three-show franchise to top ratings, attracting nearly 60 million viewers a week. The whole investigation genre is hot, from NBC's *Law & Order* series on down to the documentary-like re-creations of A&E's *Forensic Files*. America is in love with forensics, from the blood spatter and bone fragments of TV's fictional crime scenes to the latest thrust and parry at the Michael Jackson trial.

That's good, right? Jurors are smarter, and understaffed government crime labs are using the trend to seek more funding. But not so fast. Stoked by the technical wizardry they see on the tube, many Americans find themselves disappointed when they encounter the real world of law and order. Jurors increasingly expect forensic evidence in every case, and they expect it to be conclusive.

"YOUR CSI MOMENT"

Real life and real death are never as clean as CSI's lead investigator, Gil Grissom, would have us believe. And real forensics is seldom as fast, or as certain, as TV tells us. Too often, authorities say, the science is unproven, the analyses unsound, and the experts unreliable. At a time when the public is demanding CSI-style investigations of even common crimes, many of the nation's crime labs—underfunded, undercertified, and under attack—simply can't produce. When a case comes to court, "jurors expect it to be a lot more interesting and a lot more dynamic," says Barbara LaWall, the county prosecutor in Tucson, Ariz. "It puzzles the heck out of them when it's not."

A disappointed jury can be a dangerous thing. Just ask Jodi Hoos. Prosecuting a gang member in Peoria, Ill., for raping a teenager in a local park last year, Hoos told the jury, "You've all seen CSI. Well, this is your CSI moment. We have DNA." Specifically, investigators had matched saliva on the victim's breast to the defendant, who had denied touching her. The jury also had gripping testimony from the victim, an emergency-room nurse, and the responding officers. When the jury came back, however, the verdict was not guilty. Why? Unmoved by the DNA evidence, jurors felt police should have tested "debris" found in the victim to see if it matched soil from the park. "They said they knew from *CSI* that police could test for that sort of thing," Hoos said. "We had his DNA. We had his denial. It's ridiculous."

Television's diet of forensic fantasy "projects the image that all cases are solvable by highly technical science, and if you offer less than that, it is viewed as reasonable doubt," says Hoos's boss, Peoria State's Attorney Kevin Lyons. "The burden it places on us is overwhelming." Prosecutors have a name for the phenomenon: "the CSI effect."

Some of the "evidence" the *CSI* shows tout—using a wound to make a mold of a knife, or predicting time of death by looking at the rate at which a piece of metal might rust—is blatant hokum, experts say. But more and more, police and prosecutors are waking up to the need to cater to a jury's heightened expectations. That means more visual cues, with PowerPoint and video presentations, and a new emphasis during testimony on why certain types of evidence haven't been presented. If there are no fingerprints in evidence, more prosecutors are asking investigators to explain why, lest jurors take their absence as cause for doubt.

The same goes for DNA or gunshot residue. Joseph Peterson, acting director of the Department of Criminal Justice at the University of Illinois–Chicago, says DNA is rarely culled from crime scenes and analyzed. Crime scenes today are much like they were in the 1970s, Peterson says, when his studies found that fingerprints and tool marks were the most common types of evidence left at crime scenes. Blood was found only 5 percent of the time, usually at murder scenes.

Like crime scenes, many crime labs also haven't changed that much—at least in one respect. Many are still understaffed, and they often don't receive all of the relevant physical evidence from the crime scene, either because police investigators don't know what they're looking for or because they figure—possibly wrongly—that the case is strong enough without it. A crime lab's bread and butter is testing drugs found at crime scenes, doing toxicology screens, and comparing fingerprints. DNA matches are way down the list, mainly because they're time consuming and expensive. How much time? A Cape Cod trash hauler gave police a DNA sample in March 2004. The lab was backlogged. Last week, after it was finally analyzed, he was arrested for the 2002 murder of fashion writer Crista Worthington.

Defense attorneys, predictably, are capitalizing on the popularity of shows like *CSI*, seizing on an absence of forensic evidence, even in cases where there's no apparent reason for its use. In another Peoria case, jurors acquitted a man accused of stabbing his estranged girlfriend because police didn't test her bloody bedsheets for DNA. The man went back to prison on a parole violation and stabbed his ex again when he got out—this time fatally.

The CSI effect was raised in the acquittal last month of actor Robert Blake in the murder of his wife. The L.A. district attorney called the jurors "incredibly stupid," but jurors noted that the former Baretta star was accused of shooting his wife with an old Nazi-era pistol that spewed gunshot residue. Blake's skin and clothes, a juror told U.S. News, had "not one particle."

"ON THIN ICE"

Still, forensic evidence and expert testimony can add a lot of weight. Confronted with a possible fingerprint or DNA match, many defendants will plead guilty instead of risking a trial and the possibility of a heavier penalty.

At trial, many juries tend to believe forensic experts and the evidence they provide—even when they shouldn't. Sandra Anderson and her specially trained forensic dog, Eagle, are a case in point. Dubbed a canine Sherlock Holmes, Eagle and his trainer were the darlings of prosecutors and police across the country. They appeared on TV's *Unsolved Mysteries* and headlined forensic science seminars. The dog seemed to have a bionic nose, finding hidden traces of blood evidence, which Anderson duly corroborated in court. In one case, Eagle's million-dollar nose gave police enough for a search warrant after he found damning evidence in the house of a biochemist suspected of murdering his wife. Plymouth, Mich., Police Lt. Wayne Carroll declared at the time: "Before we brought that dog down there, we were on thin ice." Anderson and Eagle, however, were frauds. After she admitted planting blood on a hacksaw blade during the investigation of the suspect, Azizul Islam, he was granted a new trial last year. It was one of several cases in which Anderson faked evidence. She is now serving a 21-month prison term after pleading guilty to obstruction of justice and making false statements. Lawyers and forensic experts say Anderson is just one of the more bizarre cases of forensic specialists lying under oath, misreading test results, or overstating evidence.

In recent years, the integrity of crime labs across the country, including the vaunted FBI crime lab, have come under attack for lax standards and generating bogus evidence. One problem is that crime labs don't have to be accredited. All DNA labs seeking federal funding will have to be accredited by next year, but roughly 30 percent of the publicly funded crime labs operating in the United States today have no certification, a recent Justice Department study found. The FBI's lab gained accreditation in 1998, after it was embarrassed by a series of foul-ups. A Houston lab sought accreditation this year, following a scandal that has so far resulted in the release of two men from prison and cast doubt on the lab's other work.

Dozens of coroners, crime lab technicians, police chemists, forensic anthropologists, crime-reconstruction experts, and other forensic specialists, meanwhile, have been fined, fired, or prosecuted for lying under oath, forging credentials, or fabricating evidence. It's hard to find anyone in law enforcement who can't recite a story of quackery on the stand or in the lab. Forensic practitioners say the popularity of the field may make things even worse, noting that new forensics-degree programs are cropping up all over the place, some turning out questionable candidates. "For some reason, the forensic sciences have always had their fair share of charlatans," says Max Houck, director of the Forensic Science Initiative at West Virginia University. "Because of the weight the analysis is now given, professional ethics and certification of labs has never been more important."

"DEAD-BANG EVIDENCE"

One of the most infamous charlatans worked his magic just down the road from Houck at the West Virginia State Police lab. Fred Zain, who died in 2002, was a forensics star, a lab chemist who testified for prosecutors in hundreds of cases in West Virginia and Texas, sending some men to death row. No one ever bothered to look at his credentials—including the fact that he had failed organic chemistry—or review his test results. When two lab workers complained that they had seen Zain record results from a blank test plate, they were ignored. Zain was undone when DNA test results performed on Glen Woodall—serving a prison term of 203 to 335 years—proved that he could not have committed two sexual assaults for which he'd been convicted. Zain had told the jury that the assailant's blood types "were identical to Mr. Woodall's." After Woodall's conviction was overturned, in 1992, the West Virginia Supreme Court of Appeals ordered a full review of Zain's work. Its conclusion? The convictions of more than 100 people were in doubt because of Zain's "long history of falsifying evidence in criminal prosecutions." Nine more men have since had their convictions overturned.

Forensic science experts say the solution is to tighten standards for experts and increase funding for crime labs. A consortium of forensic organizations is lobbying Congress now to do both. "In many places, crime labs are the bastard stepchildren of public safety," says Barry Fisher, a member of the Forensic Science Consortium and director of the L.A. County Sheriff's Department crime lab. Asked about the importance of mandatory certification, he adds: "I don't know if I would go to a hospital that wasn't accredited. The same goes with labs."

Some forensic experts, however, question the value of certification. Psychologist Steve Eichel, a longtime critic of what he calls "checkbook credentials," secured credentials for his cat—"Dr. Zoe D. Katze"—from four major hypnotherapy and psychotherapy associations. Critics have questioned the rigor of the American College of Forensic Examiners International, the largest forensic certifier in the country. Its founder, Robert O'Block, who was charged with plagiarism and fired from the criminal justice department at Appalachian State University shortly before starting the organization, strongly denies assertions that he runs a certification mill, blaming those accusations on disgruntled competitors; the Appalachian incident, he says, was retaliation for reporting improper academic practices.

Even accredited crime labs, however, can make mistakes. Most publicly accredited labs gauge their proficiency through declarative tests, where lab workers know they're being tested. Although most labs do well on such tests, some experts question their ability to judge labs' day-to-day performance. And even in declarative tests, deficiencies can be glaring. According to 2004 proficiency results from one private testing service reviewed by U.S. News, a few labs failed to properly match samples on simple DNA tests, mysteriously came to the right result after making the wrong interpretation of the data, or accidentally transposed the information from one sample onto another. In a ballistics test, one lab matched a slug with the wrong test gun.

Such errors can have real-world consequences in court. In 1999, a Philadelphia crime lab accidentally switched the reference samples of a rape suspect and the alleged victim, then issued a report pointing to the defendant's guilt. Last year, a false fingerprint match led the FBI to wrongfully accuse an Oregon lawyer—and converted Muslim—of complicity in the al Qaeda-linked Madrid train bombings. The FBI later blamed the foul-up on the poor quality of the fingerprint image. "There are a number of cases that deal with what on the surface ought to be dead-bang evidence," says Fisher. "But it turns out it was the wrong result. Improper testing or improper interpretation of data left the innocent convicted."

For all the setbacks and scandals, science has made considerable progress in the courts since the advent of forensic investigation. In the 1600s, the evidence against two London "witches" accused of causing children to vomit bent pins and a twopenny nail was . . . a bunch of bent pins and a twopenny nail. So it must have seemed fairly revolutionary in the 1800s when a Brussels chemist named Jean Servais Stas devised a way to separate a vegetable poison from the stomach of a countess's brother to prove how he had been killed. Or when an English investigator around the same time solved the case of a murdered maid by matching a corduroy patch left in the mud at the crime scene to the pants of a laborer working some nearby fields.

"OBVIOUS" PROBLEMS

That doesn't mean forensics can always be believed, however, even when the data are accurate. As Sherlock Holmes said, "There is nothing more deceptive than an obvious fact." DNA is a case in point. While DNA testing is the most accurate of the forensic sciences, experts can make vastly different interpretations of the same DNA sample. Criminal justice experts say most lawyers and judges don't know enough about any of the forensic sciences to make an honest judgment of the veracity of what they are told. Prosecutor Mike Parrish in Tarrant County, Texas, decided to get a second opinion on his DNA evidence in a capital murder case three years ago after the local police lab amended its result to more strongly link his suspect to the crime. Suspicious, Parrish had the sample reanalyzed by the county medical examiner, whose results were much less definitive. In the end, Parrish said, because of the conflicting DNA reports, he chose not to seek the death penalty.

Other forensic tests are even more open to interpretation. Everything from fingerprint identification to fiber analysis is now coming under fire. And rightly so. The science is inexact, the experts are of no uniform opinion, and defense lawyers are increasingly skeptical. Fingerprint examiners, for instance, still peer through magnifying glasses to read faint ridges.

Many of these techniques and theories have never been empirically tested to ensure they are valid. During much of the past decade, coroners have certified the deaths of children who might have fallen down steps or been accidentally dropped as "shaken baby" homicides because of the presence of retinal hemorrhages—blood spots—in their eyes. Juries bought it. Noting that new research casts grave doubt on the theory, Joseph Davis, the retired director of Florida's Miami-Dade County Medical Examiner's Office and one of the nation's leading forensics experts, compares proponents of shaken-baby syndrome to "flat Earthers" and says its use as a prosecution tool conjures up "shades of Salem witchcraft" trials.

The list goes on. Ear prints, left behind when a suspect presses his ear to a window, have been allowed as evidence in court, despite the fact that there have been no studies to verify that all ears are different or to certify the way ear prints are taken. The fingerprint match, once considered unimpeachable evidence, is only now being closely scrutinized. The National Institute of Justice offered grants to kick-start the process this year. Other "experts" have pushed lip-print analysis, bite-mark analysis, and handwriting analysis with degrees of certainty that just don't exist, critics say.

Microscopic hair analysis was a staple of prosecutions until just a few years ago and was accorded an unhealthy degree of certitude. "Hair comparisons have been discredited almost uniformly in court," says Peterson of the University of Illinois–Chicago. "There are many instances where science has not come up to the legal needs," adds James Starrs, professor of forensic sciences and law at George Washington University. Everyone, including the jury, wants certainty. But it seldom exists in forensics. So the expert, says Starrs, "always needs to leave the possibility of error."

Discussion Questions

1. How have TV shows such as *CSI* impacted the criminal justice system?
2. Discuss how the practices portrayed on *CSI* differ from criminal justice practices in the real world.

3. Do you believe it is in the best interest of governments to spend significantly more resources on crime labs given that jurors expect more scientific-based evidence in the courtroom?